73321A

Freedom and Tolerance

This volume was prepared and published under the auspices of

THE COUNCIL FOR THE STUDY OF ETHICS AND PUBLIC POLICY

QUEENS COLLEGE
CITY UNIVERSITY OF NEW YORK

List of the Author's Previous Books

JURIDICAL POSITIVISM AND HUMAN RIGHTS (1981)
WAR OF THE VANQUISHED (1971)
HISTORY OF POLITICAL AND JURIDICAL IDEAS,
    5 vols. (1963-1968)
FOUNDATIONS OF POLITICAL SCIENCE, 3 vols. (1967-1968)
MACHIAVELLI: A MONOGRAPH (1968)
ART OF POLITICS (1967)
THE FUNCTIONS OF THE STATE (1963)
THE ACTIVITY OF A SOCIALIST STATE (1957)

FREEDOM
and
TOLERANCE

Mieczyslaw Maneli

OCTAGON BOOKS

A Division of Hippocrene Books, Inc.
New York

Second printing 1987

Copyright © 1984 by Mieczyslaw Maneli

For information, address: Hippocrene Books, Inc.,
171 Madison Avenue, New York, New York 10016.

Manufactured in the United States of America.

Library of Congress Cataloging in Publication Data

Maneli, Mieczyslaw.
  Freedom and tolerance.

  Includes bibliographical references and index.
  1. Liberty—History.   2. Toleration—History.
I. Title.
JC585.M5257   1984   323.44   84-5215
ISBN 0-88254-630-9
ISBN 0-88254-635-X (pbk.)

FOR MY CHILDREN
Elizabeth and John, Les and Janis

Contents

CHAPTER III
THE EVOLUTION OF TOLERANCE

CHAPTER IV
TOLERANCE

Acknowledgments

This book was written within the framework of the Council for the Study of Ethics and Public Policy, Queens College, City University of New York.

The chief philosophical position elaborated on these pages coincides with the spirit of the Council's activity. It was the creative and tolerant atmosphere prevailing within the Council which inspired and influenced my attitudes and thinking.

Special thanks go to my close friends and collaborators, Professors Thomas E. Bird and Ben-Zion Bokser, who alerted me to pertinent questions raised within Christian theology and Judaism.

I held numerous conversations with Professor Chaim Perelman of the Université Libre, Brussels. The influence of the philosophy and methodology propounded by him, his new system of argumentation and revised Aristotelian approach, will be found throughout this work.

Stimulating discussions with Professor John Hazard of Columbia University greatly aided me in my evaluations and reinterpretations of various aspects of the East-European and Western traditions.

I gratefully acknowledge having had the privilege of exchanging ideas with my learned colleagues, Professors Elżbieta Chodakowska of the Massachusetts Institute of Technology, and Seweryn Bialer and Alexander Rudzinski of Columbia University.

This work has been put into its final editorial and stylistic form by Dr. Richard A. Kramer. I consider myself fortunate to have been able to draw upon his philosophical and juridical knowledge.

I wish to express special appreciation to my long-time collaborator and researcher, Ilse E. Previti. Without her loyal and patient industry and effective assistance, many of the projects I have undertaken since my arrival in the United States would not have been completed.

The assistance given me by the Department of Political Science, and in particular by its Chairman, Professor Henry Morton, is deeply appreciated. The rescheduling of my lectures and seminars afforded me valuable time to devote to research and writing, as did a grant from the Mellon Foundation.

The help extended to me by the editor of Hippocrene Books, Mr. Robert Pigeon, went beyond the usual limits of author-editor cooperation, and I gladly acknowledge it.

Foreword

Professor Mieczyslaw Maneli's study of the evolution of dogmatically governed societies toward freedom and tolerance is masterful.

This volume continues the attack on the arbitrary use of power begun in his *Juridical Positivism and Human Rights* and strikes a blow for pluralism, which he sees as a means of undermining ideological monopolies.

His analysis of history focused on the evolution of liberal views within many political systems and societies leads him to conclude that each society has within it forces leading to the ultimate destruction of dogmatism.

He notes that there are always within each society persons of broader vision than those with orthodox views. Their views come to be adopted as societies make their demands for freedom so effectively that they cannot be resisted. Maneli has faith in these masses. He expects them to innovate new pluralistic systems strong enough to overcome leaders attempting to preserve personal power.

Having lived under many dictatorships, he has been stimulated to study the forces within large ideological systems capable of undermining them. He refuses to accept the claims that these monopolies are impregnable as governing powers. Using the expression made famous by Karl Marx, he concludes that every ideological monopoly has within its ranks its own "gravediggers." Eventually, and of this he is confident, there will emerge a new current of thought powerful enough to bring the society in which the monopoly flourishes to a new age—the age of freedom and tolerance.

The road to freedom and tolerance has been long, stretching over centuries, and there is still great distance to be traveled in Maneli's view. Not all resistance to change comes from the dictators themselves, regrettably, for Maneli agrees with Erich Fromm that there are many people who do not cherish freedom—indeed, they are afraid of it. They seek security in espousal of an ideology; in a life subjected to institutions of authority. People of this persuasion are hard to move, but in Maneli's view there have been historical moments when they have been moved to strike out for freedom. Poland provides him with such an example.

In the last decade, life in Poland became intolerable, not only for great numbers of intellectuals, but for the masses themselves in whose name the Communists ruled. Maneli finds that the people themselves became sufficiently conditioned by the sloganeering of the leaders professing to be Marxists to demand restitution of structures of government responsible to the society. Disillusioned with the Communist government they turned against it and forced its leaders to listen. Only when the leaders concluded that pressures were too strong to permit them to maintain their power was a deaf ear turned to the demands of the people. The leaders feared a popular rising, and their fears were reinforced by Soviet leadership, which saw danger not only to the Polish Communists but to themselves. At this point, Polish military forces were necessary.

Maneli concludes from this example that naked force can keep order, at least in the short run. Still, he expects that the quiet imposed by force must eventually give way to the demands of the people. Out of the collapse of the system will emerge an alternative to what Maneli calls "bureaucratic despotism." Maneli cannot now perceive the right structure of the alternative, but he expects it to be some kind of pluralism which will rest upon a variety of new forces and forms.

Maneli is encouraged to make his predictions by findings in what he calls his "long philosophical journey through the ages."

Maneli begins this journey in the fifteenth century and includes flash-backs to even earlier times. He is searching for the "grave-diggers." He finds early examples of philosophers within the Catholic Church, who became, in his words, more skillful than the orthodox masters in manipulating quotations to support their arresting new ideas. This is a theme that runs throughout Maneli's account. Some documents that reveal change include even the great Papal Encyclicals, and Maneli studies them in detail. He demonstrates the gradual process in which liberalizing ideas are formulated in repudiation of almost impregnable orthodox positions. He discloses the terminology that Popes used to mask subtle repudiation of what had been regarded as eternal dogma. Even after the doctrine of infallibility was pronounced in the nineteenth century, Encyclicals of succeeding Popes disclosed that their authors were not content to follow the thinking of predecessors. Leo XIII and John XXIII are two such examples. To Maneli the Church can never be the same after Vatican II and the initiative of John XXIII. Ecumenism became an established policy as did collegiality, the practice of consultation with all levels of the hierarchy and the laity.

Maneli does not expect the advances made by John XXIII necessarily to be continued. Indeed, he warns that advances toward freedom and tolerance are sometimes followed in all societies by retrogressive periods. Although freedom and tolerance may be stalled, Maneli expects the forward movement to be renewed. How? one may ask. Maneli's answer is simple: through "work" and "participation in social endeavors" societies will realize their intellectual, emotional and physical potential. The therapeutic nature of work is a philosophy still presented by Communist leaders in the states in which they have power. Yet, Maneli points out, these Communists have crushed the attainment of free expression through work by imposing the conflicting theory that man needs to be led. The result is that Communist leaders place a damper over the ingenuity of those who work, for they ask not what the masses want but what will enhance leadership power. Because of this, freedom, which could otherwise be expected to emerge, is held in check.

Maneli, however, proves himself still to be philosophically an optimist of the future. He places his faith in the masses, in those who work with mind and muscle. He believes that if people are given freedom to think and experiment, they will come closer than their predecessors to a social structure satisfying to all.

Maneli places his hope in the defectors from monopoly ideologies, whether they come from Communist, capitalist, Catholic or Protestant camps. These defectors are the heretics who know the evils of the *status quo* within their respective domains, for they have discovered them through personal experiences. It is these heretics who challenge the various establishments. It is they who are recognized by those in power as the real danger, not the classical opponents of other camps. The heretics "strike at the vital nerve centers of ossification." Maneli sees these centers to be the bureaucracy of each establishment, the force that Maneli calls "the cancer of our century." Bureaucracies must, therefore, be combatted, for they create the danger of totalitarianism and, in our age, nuclear annihilation.

In the last analysis it is social reorganization that is needed to achieve freedom and tolerance. Without social change Maneli sees no likelihood of creating an environment conducive to living according to the principles of morality. The reader may ask whether there exists a core of persons around which those who look to such a future can rally.

Maneli turns at the end of his stimulating study to an analysis of the Judeo-Christian tradition in his search for the forces capable of opposing new forms of oppression, totalitarianism, and the imminent danger of nuclear destruction. In this tradition, combined with humanism, rationalism and liberalism, he finds evidence of growth toward freedom and tolerance.

Maneli does not expect the new pluralism to be based upon the present economic and political systems. It will be a novel social organization in as yet undetermined forms. He is not discouraged with the setbacks. He has hope for a resurgence of liberating forces.

In sum, a new dawn may be anticipated, as humanity, imbued with a religious and secular sense of responsibility, makes itself heard. Dogmatically governed societies cannot stand against such a development. Maneli does not expect to be disappointed.

JOHN N. HAZARD
Columbia University

INTRODUCTION: THE POPULAR YET DETESTED THEME

Classic scholarly tradition requires an author to present his own definitions of the topics which he intends to treat. There are few reasons for defying this well established custom. But there are, as usual, exceptional themes which can be presented more fully and clearly when they are not delineated by definitions. Tolerance and freedom are among those historical, philosophical, and political notions which are so broad and have so many aspects that any attempt to define them concisely, instead of clarifying, would only limit and impoverish them. One ought of course to remember Descartes' recommendation that in order to understand a subject and to attain truth, one should see clearly and distinctly. But general definitions of tolerance and freedom can hardly present distinct shapes, forms, contents, and boundaries. Can one express distinctly what in life is not, cannot be, and possibly should not be, fixed definitely?

Were not Dupreel and Perelman right when they argued that sometimes less strictly defined notions have helped mankind to progress and to preserve its freedom, whereas supposedly absolutely precise ideas have often led to dogmatism and political despotism?

Spinoza used to say: *omnis definitio perniciosa est* (every definition is pernicious), but he himself engaged in a search for explanations and definitions in which he tried to reach mathematical precision. His greatness comes not so much from his geometrical reasoning and presentations as from the corollaries and addenda which simultaneously limit, broaden, and enrich the scope of his every assertion, observation, and explanation.

The questions of freedom and tolerance have so many aspects, historical and topical, individual and social, humanistic and political, that instead of trying to narrow the subject to a definition, one should rather proceed with an analysis step by step gradually encompassing various notions, meanings, forms, appearances, and aspects of these inexhaustible ideas.

We will concentrate our attention on the social and political aspects of freedom and tolerance. The other aspects will be treated as far as necessary for a logical presentation of our views on these chief problems. This limitation of the subject of our interest still leaves it extremely broad.

The ways to restrict political freedom are unlimited; the enemies of political liberty and tolerance never lack invention. Every new attack against freedom and tolerance both enriches and impoverishes the content, form, and meaning of freedom. The forms of slavery, oppression, injustice, and persecution are as endless and inexhaustible as the forms and meanings of freedom and tolerance. In modern times the traditional forms of oppression have also been modernized. The notions of freedom and tolerance must therefore be expanded beyond these traditional limits which may be procrustean. Since 1950 the dangers menacing traditional Western freedom and tolerance have been increasing worldwide. We have long been cured of the Enlightenment's illusion that the quest for freedom is a natural, ingrained, obvious, typical activity of all human beings. We know well from recent history as well as from philosophical and sociological research that freedom is not generally desired, that for many people it may even be frightening. Freedom may be regarded not only as a blessing but also as a misfortune to which we are condemned, as Jean-Paul Sartre has declared.

How could it happen that four centuries after the Renaissance, two—three centuries after the victories of the great revolutions in Holland, England, America, and France, a century after the rise of governments based on constitutional liberties, parliamentary elections, due process of law, liberalism, and individualism, we see ominous new signs of a rising wave of autocracy, of intolerance, and of hatred of freedom?

It is not the purpose of this book to give a complete answer to these important questions, but to draw attention to certain social and political facts which, however well known, are not widely understood in their most significant bearings. It is also the purpose of this treatise to re-analyze and re-evaluate the historically developed notions of freedom and tolerance, their forgotten qualities and their new ones, their good and bad sides.

The ideals of freedom and tolerance are a result of the historical evolution of human society and the development of human thought, especially in the fields of legal, social, religious, and political philosophy. At every stage of social evolution, freedom and tolerance have found new adherents and new adversaries; they are welcomed by certain social forces and shunned by others. The more powerful the appeal of the ideals of freedom and tolerance, and the more numerous and forceful their supporters, the more ruthless are their opponents.

One way to defend freedom and tolerance is to explore their meaning in the past and at present. Many of these notions have become richer in every succeeding period, while at the same time becoming more specific. However, other understandings of freedom and tolerance have become oversimplified and impoverished, whether that is the work of their adherents or their enemies. Possibly one of the most effective ways of fighting freedom and tolerance is to reduce those concepts to such a primitive level that, in their one-sided simplicity, they are inadequate for dealing with the complexities of real life. In that way they become meaningless platitudes and therefore easy prey.

Today there is almost no politician who has failed to declare himself a friend of freedom, peace, and human rights—even dictators do so. It is not difficult to unmask the authoritarians, totalitarians, racists, obviously illogical preachers, and self-proclaimed prophets. But it is quite difficult to expose the true nature of those thinkers or politicians who may be convinced that they favor a certain kind of freedom and certain forms of tolerance, but attribute to these ideas a primitive content, which is so distorted and so deprived of articulation, that they are a burlesque of the concepts in whose defense they are raised. This is an additional reason why we decided to present a brief historical review of the ideas of freedom and tolerance. It is our belief that today the presentation of those ideas in their full human complexity may itself serve to defend and promote them.

More than ever before, people are asking the basic question that was posed by Léon Blum in the following manner:

> The human race had the wisdom to create science and art; why should it not be capable of creating a world of justice, brotherhood and peace? The human race has produced Plato, Homer, Shakespeare, Hugo, Michelangelo, Beethoven, Pascal and Newton—all of them human heroes whose genius lay in their contact with the fundamental truths, with the innermost essence of the universe. Why then should the same race not produce leaders capable of leading it to those forms of communal life which are closest to the life and harmony of the universe?[1]

It seems that humanity is so torn by antagonistic economic and political interests, by religious and national ideals, that it is unable to overcome its differences even when faced with annihilation. The existing contradictions seem to be so strong, objectively and subjectively, that even the fundamental conditions necessary to preserve the reasonable existence of societies, of nations, and of mankind, have become controversial, even including the pursuit of "justice, brotherhood and peace." For we have indeed reached a stage in the development of our civilization at which such ideals must be more or less universally accepted in order to preserve that civilization and even our very existence. If we are to achieve this minimum mutual understanding an uninterrupted flow of discussion and argument is indispensable. Today more than ever in the past, dialogue and persuasion are the essential forms not only of tolerance, but of self-preservation.

It is one of our contentions—we repeat this point—that in the last quarter of our century, freedom and tolerance are essential for the mere survival of our civilization and of humanity.

Tolerance has always been an instrument for advancing progress, creativity, a more comfortable life, and personal happiness. It has been an attribute of personal and political freedom and of democracy. In our times tolerance has all those functions with one important addition: it has become a method and a means, a very special device to secure the existence of our civilization.

This book is intended as an analysis of the controversial problems of freedom and tolerance at the end of our century; it is not a new general philosophical treatise presenting ideas believed to be valid eternally and universally. General doctrines that have been elaborated throughout the centuries will be used as a springboard to develop the ideas that are crucial for the future years: What in our times is the meaning of freedom and tolerance? What endangers their existence? What should be done to preserve and expand individual freedom? Historical antecedents are discussed in this book simply to clarify theses concerning the times we live in; history provides lessons and useful illustrations of general theses, but proves nothing.

The concept of tolerance has traditionally been linked with human dignity. Both are philosophically and historically variable and socially determined. The concept of human dignity has undergone many basic changes and been substantially broadened since the days of Mirandola's address, *"De dignitate hominis." (Of Human Dignity)*. The notions of what is tolerable or intolerable, free or unfree, have been widened and concretized as well.

Today, it is obvious and incontestable that genocide and torture by their very nature deny the dignity of torturers and the tortured alike, and cannot be tolerated under any circumstances. Yet there are countries in which oppression and torture are practiced daily by the police as part of the regular course of governmental business. Nevertheless, the condemnation of this practice is so widespread that it cannot lead us very far in our consideration of freedom and tolerance. In order to explain these notions, one must explore their content and forms.

II.
EVOLUTION OF THE
PHILOSOPHY OF FREEDOM

1. The Philosophical Foundations of Freedom

a. Pico Della Mirandola—A Saga on Creative Man

1487 was a turning point in the philosophy of freedom: Giovanni Pico, younger son of the Count Della Mirandola and Concordia, wrote nine hundred theses, *Conclusiones,* which he proposed for a public disputation.

They had an introduction titled: *Oration on the Dignity of Man.* In this address the foundations of the modern concept of freedom were laid down.

Catholic Church authorities found that several of the *Conclusiones* were heretical and several were suspect, the public disputation was suspended by Pope Innocent III. Although the ideas of the *Oration* were not publicly discussed, they could not have been extirpated. Once formulated and published, they became an inexhaustible source of inspiration. Combining *dignity* with *freedom* became a watershed in the philosophy of society, politics, and morality.

For the first time in history the concept of freedom was bound in one entity with human intellectual and physical power, with creative thought and practical activity, with overcoming inner inertia and external resistance, with self-development of one's personality and deliberate changes in nature and society.

Giovanni Pico studied canon law and theology and was exposed to the great ideas of the Renaissance; it cannot be surprising that his secular arguments were based both on Holy Scriptures and the ancient philosophers. He knew Latin, Greek, and Hebrew. He continued the great tradition of the secularization of theology and he made his own imprint on both theological and philosophical thought. His heresy flared up when his knowledge surpassed the scholarship of the orthodox masters, when he became more skillful than they in manipulating quotations to support his own original thoughts. He added a flair of a dogmatic faith to his undogmatic and original ideas.

His basic ideas on freedom were put into the mouth of God himself.

On the sixth day of Creation, the Great Maker found that something important and very personal was lacking in his accomplishment, an element truly divine: "a work of indeterminate form."[1] Therefore, God took up man, placed him at the midpoint of the world and delivered a speech defining man's spectacular role in the universe:

> We have given to thee, Adam, no fixed seat, no form of thy very own, no gift peculiarly thine, that thou mayest feel as thine own, have as thine own, possess as thine own the seat, the form, the gifts which thou thyself shalt desire. A limited nature in other creatures is confined within the laws written down by Us. In conformity with thy free judgment, in whose hands I have placed thee, thou art confined by no bounds; and thou wilt fix limits of nature for thyself. I have placed thee at the center of the world, that from there thou mayest more conveniently look around and see whatsoever is in the world. Neither heavenly nor earthly, neither mortal nor immortal have We made thee. Thou, like a judge appointed for being honorable, art the molder and maker of thyself; thou mayest sculpt thyself into whatever shape thou dost prefer. Thou canst grow downward into the lower natures which are brutes. Thou canst again grow upward from thy soul's reason into the higher natures which are divine.[2]

As if this account of human freedom were not clear enough, Pico added: Man has been supplied by the Heavenly Father with every sort of seeds and sprouts, of every kind of life. He can grow into a brute; he can come out a "heavenly animal" if he will be rational; if intellectual—he can become an angel and "a son of God."[3]

And even more.

God created man in his own image—he has given him the seeds to go so high and to become so powerful that he can create himself, therefore "he will stand at the head of all things." Briefly: man was given the seeds to function as if he were . . . a God.

This is the essence of man's freedom and power, this is the potential which he can realize if he wants to.

The sky is the limit—a human being can even remake his own nature and reproduce his own "angelic" seeds.

The human creature was not created in order to be meek and humble; "holy ambition"[4] should invade his mind, he should never be content with "mean things." He should aspire to the highest heights, strive with all his forces to attain them and he will accomplish what he will: ". . . for if we will to, we can."[5]

This is the gist of Pico's philosophy: the human being is equipped with everything that is necessary to achieve his most ambitious aims. This is the way God has preconceived him and having been created, he should act according to the original plan, he ought to reach for the unknown and rely on his own forces.

Man should be dedicated to an active life. Two natures are planted in his soul: by one he can rise to heaven; by the other, fall downward to "the lower world."[6] The choice belongs to him.

One nature of human beings leads to peace; but Pico also agreed with Heraclitus according to whom "our nature is born of war."[7] Peace can be achieved through effort, through struggle because—here one can detect another impact of Heraclitus—controversy is everywhere, it molds human beings.

The happiness of every individual can be achieved through everlasting struggle and it depends on one's knowledge and studies. Pico despised "brutes," "barbarians," "ignoramuses" who did not want to look for wisdom even in the works of the ancient philosophers—Greek, Roman, Oriental, and Hebrew. In order to be free—one must seek the truth and know it. Truth cannot simply be given or revealed, it emerges from struggle and controversy. Truth has its enemies; it always will be attacked, but these attacks should not cause anxiety; truth will prevail and will be reinforced by its critics:

> ... If there is a school which attacks truer doctrines and ridicules with calumny the good causes of thought, it strengthens rather than weakens truth, and as by motion it excites the flame rather than extinguishing it.[8]

Truth can be derived not only from correct doctrine, but from "every sort of doctrine." From many sects' writings, and discussions we can reach the stage when the "radiance of the truth . . . might shine more clearly upon our minds, like the sun rising from the deep"[9]

This may be the deepest, often overlooked, comparison used by Pico: truth rises from the unknown, from the darkness, from the depths. Truth cannot be revealed full blown, by a single discovery, it results from a long process of search. Our wisdom "flowed from the barbarians to the Greeks, and from the Greeks to us."[10] The Greeks continued to develop what they inherited and transmitted their knowledge from generation to generation. In order to understand the philosophy of the Peripatetics it is not sufficient to study their writings, one must also return to the Platonic Academy, because they influenced their successors (including St. Augustine). In order to possess a deeper knowledge of Christianity one must also study the doctrines of the Chaldeans and the Jews.[11]

Pico Della Mirandola challenged the official ecclesiastical approach according to which the Church is the depository of truth. When he argued that truth had a thousand sources and tracks of evolution, he asked for *tolerance* of various views, because otherwise human beings would not be able to create anything *new*, and this is the *human* way to act.

Every school of thought has something unique and valuable; one should know it—but not for the sake of knowledge or understanding only, but for the sake of further creative development. Pico wrote:

> What good was it to have dealt with the opinions of others in any number, if, as though coming to a banquet of the wise

without contributing anything, we brought nothing which would be our own, given birth and perfected by our mind. Indeed it is ignoble, as Seneca says, to know only by way of commentary, and, as if the discoveries of the ancients had closed the road for our industry, as if the force of nature in us were exhausted, to give birth to nothing from ourselves, which, if it does not demonstrate truth, at least points to it as from a distance. But if a farmer hates sterility in a field, and a husband in a wife, certainly a barren soul is hated by the divine mind woven into it and allied with it, the more a far nobler offspring is desired from it.[12]

A mind which does not produce anything new is sterile, therefore he, Pico Della Mirandola, has chosen "to bring forward a new philosophy."[13]

Whoever disagrees—let him refute it; only after that can it be condemned; if the new philosophy is successfully defended—it should be praised. It should be judged on its own merits, one "should reckon up not the years of the author, but rather the merits or demerits of these things."[14]

—Truth is truth, no matter who expresses it—no one should claim to be an oracle.

No one should claim a monopoly on wisdom, prudence, morality, or knowledge. In our world of controversies and struggles, a human being can become truly humane by creating new ideas and a new intellectual environment, transforming himself from an "indeterminate form" into a higher and a better one. Human freedom and creative power can prosper in battles in which people should not destroy each other, but "engage hands in combat."[15] Controversies and cooperation, tolerance and dialogue—this is the way of truth and progress, of human creativity and freedom.

b. Niccolo Machiavelli: An Appeal to Self-Made Man

In 1469 a humanist, philosopher, and politician was born in Florence whose name became a symbol of a certain style of politics, of diplomacy, and of exercising power. Niccolo Machiavelli has been attacked and praised by writers, thinkers, and politicians of all kinds. There were those who regarded him as depraved, others considered him a realist describing the actual course of events, not interested in values or moralizing. There is no epithet, negative or positive, which has not been aimed at him. His most vehement critics were usually those who either did not know his writings, did not understand them, or who were using the methods known as Machiavellian, but did not want to admit it and preferred to pretend to be critics of the great Florentine.

Machiavelli assumed that humanity is a huge field of energy in which various antagonistic forces are in a constant and perpetual struggle. A superficial observer might believe that he is surrounded by chaos, but a careful examination would show various regularities, connections, and dependencies. There are causes and effects. There are certain events and activities which are a source of inevitable and foreseeable consequences. Any reasonable man, especially a statesman, should know the mutual interdependencies, should be able to foresee trends of development, and should be able to adjust to the course of events.

In the interplay between causes and effects there is nothing to be evaluated from the moral point of view, wrote Machiavelli.

History doesn't care about what ought to be, he stressed, because it is only a compilation of facts. A historian should examine what really happened and look for the effects of the previous events and activities. From these considerations, Machiavelli concluded that any reasonable individual who wants to take an active part in social or political activities should not fall victim to his illusions or wishful thinking, but should take into account the facts only, the real course of events, and their requirements.

Machiavelli continued the dialectical way of reasoning of the great masters of ancient thought—especially Heraclitus, the Sophists, Aristotle, Epicurus, and the skeptics according to whom the whole universe, and of course humanity as a part of it, is in permanent motion and transformation. *Panta rei*, this observation should be referred to every society, to every political form, to every state and governmental institution, to all kinds of fashions and ambitions. Although everything changes, there are certain elements which are stable, according to Machiavelli. One such unchangeable element is human character; it is always the same. People are incessantly under the influence of passions and ambitions; they desire power, honor, and wealth.

It is a paradox that human nature is constant in a world in which everything else changes. The generators of emotions and struggles, human ambitions, are always the same, but the circumstances in which people act are in flux. Every moment, argued Machiavelli, creates new events and new conditons. In new situations we face new combinations of facts. Therefore an individual cannot foresee anything with an absolute certainty. On the other hand, wrote Machiavelli, if a statesman knows history, if he is able to analyze human experience, he will be better equipped to elaborate his own ends and means, the correct modes of behavior, activity, and policy.

On the basis of this general approach, Machiavelli discussed the fundamental problem posed by philosophers: What kind of creature is a human being? How may he be defined? He answered that the very question presupposes that there is a human essence which can be found. Such an approach, according to Machiavelli, is unreasonable in itself. Such research should be left to theologians. An unreasonable question cannot be reasonably answered. It would be as useless, he wrote, to ask what is the nature of a lion? or of the universe? One could get engaged in endless discussions without any satisfactory conclusions useful for practical human activity. If one wants to know what kind of creature man is, one should examine what he does, how he functions. Instead of asking for an abstract philosophical or theological essence, one should take into account how people act in given circumstances. What are their attitudes and their behavior?

A human being, according to Machiavelli, is only a part of nature, a small particle of the universe. He has no higher purposes, his life has no innate, autonomous, imminent goals. The end of human life is life itself. The sense of human life is being constructed by constant, endless changes. One should bear in mind all these facts in discussing evil and good, morality and immorality.

The history of philosophy and theology is a history of effete speculations about the ends and purposes of man, not about how to live a good life. Philosophers and theologians said what man was instead of analyzing how he acted. Machiavelli had one common feature with his great contemporary, the astronomer Nicolaus Copernicus. The great scientist discontinued speculation concerning the essence of the earth and the planets, he started to look for the laws of their motions. Machiavelli adopted a similar pattern. He tried to find out what the principles are behind human decisions, he wanted to discover the hidden sources and motives which determine human thoughts, decisions, and deeds. He believed that once these secret wellsprings were exposed and understood, it would be possible to foresee the typical, usual, and normal patterns of behavior. If the source of all human passions is selfish interest, one should expect the people to act accordingly—this is the basic conclusion which Machiavelli drew from the observation of life and from available literature.

Self interest, Machiavelli further elaborated, is caused by the existence of private property.

Machiavelli did not analyze what property was or how it originated. He was not interested, as Plato was, in whether human passions were the source of private property or vice versa, whether private property shapes human nature. Machiavelli only stated that there is an interdependence between property and human behavior. There is a relationship of causes and effects between human ways of thinking and acting and of becoming rich. Is it bad or good? This question was irrelevant for Machiavelli because the objects of his interest were facts which should not and could not be evaluated from the moral point of view.

Machiavelli was one of the first to apply general philosophical observations concerning private property in the formation of human character and passions to an analysis of historical events. In his *History of Florence* he presented the course of events as a continuous struggle between rich and poor, between the powerful *"grandi"* and the rich *"popolo grasso"* on the one hand, and the poor *"popolo minuto"* on the other hand. The struggle between these social strata continued throughout the whole history of Florence. One cannot understand the past, wrote Machiavelli, without taking into account that the underlying reasons for the endless struggles are pecuniary interests, the competition for honor, privilege, power, and office.

After such a presentation Machiavelli approached the problem most important for our further considerations on the nature of freedom: Can an individual have any substantial importance in society? Can a human being be regarded as free? and in what sense? Doesn't Machiavelli's general philosophy logically lead to the conclusion that an individual is like a straw tossed about by powerful and blind historical forces?

Machiavelli saw that every individual is part of a chain of causes and effects; he did not consider that individuals are mere links, balls in the arena pushed by anonymous players. Machiavelli believed that an individual can influence his own fate— regardless of circumstances; his success depends on his own physical, moral, and intellectual forces.

Human beings are neither absolutely free nor absolutely chained, according to Machiavelli. People are not independent of the circumstances and conditions in which they live nor are they mere snowflakes in an avalanche either. The fate of every individual is only to a certain extent determined by the correlates of time and space. They influence his way of thinking and behaving but do not determine them entirely. Machiavelli was not a traditional philosophical or theological fatalist. There is room for individual initiative, invention, concentrated will, and activism enabling any individual to achieve his self-determined goals in his particular circumstances. An individual's fate is not only determined by objective circumstances and not only by the capricious goddess *Fortuna.* Every individual also has his own brain, will, energy. The totality of these subjective elements Machiavelli calls *virtù.*

Virtù in the writings of Machiavelli has little in common with the well known Latin word, *virtus,* usually translated into English as *virtue.* Machiavelli's concept of *virtù* is neither a moral nor even a Christian idea. He continued rather the Greek and Roman tradition of *virtus* interpreted as a characteristic of a citizen who is conscientious, self-assertive, consciously working for the benefit of his state and society. According to Machiavelli, an individual can cope with the adverse conditions created by *Fortuna*. For a person to achieve his goals and ambitions and fulfill his passions, he must use all available physical and spiritual forces. He must stand ready to analyze, foresee, and connect the experience of the past with current events. He should be able to adjust to the requirements of new situations, fight whenever necessary, retreat when advisable, and enter into compromises whenever profitable. When Machiavelli described *virtù* as concentration, as the totality of physical and spiritual forces of an individual, he did not mean the brutal physical force of a barbarian, he meant an enlightened power, the civilized strength of an intelligent man.

The fate of a person is determined by the relationship between *Virtù* and *Fortuna*; the course of a person's life depends only partially on his own will, mind, and activity. The combination of these factors is not given once and for all and no determination can apply to all people to the same degree. The *virtù* of every individual must adjust to the external circumstances in which he is living. *Fortuna* reminds us of the capricious Greek Goddess, nobody could foresee her winding paths. Whoever understands the spirit of his times and is able to adjust his goals and modes of activity to the existing forces and prevailing circumstances in addition to being reasonable and willing to use all his physical forces, strain every nerve, take advantage of the power of his brain—such a person can expect success. The wisdom and prudence of a man, wrote Machiavelli, consists in the ability to understand new situations and in the art of speedy adjustments to the requirements of the circumstances.

The Goddess *Fortuna* was presented by the Greeks as a woman spinning a thread. A man, continued Machiavelli, can be successful when he is able to continue spinning *Fortuna's* thread. Anyone who opposes the wishes of *Fortuna* will be crushed by history. Anyone who catches the thread and spins it in the direction indicated by *Fortuna* will be promoted by the same Goddess and will reach the highest peaks of success.

There is a relationship between *Virtù* and *Fortuna*. If a man is weak, if his physical and mental resources are limited, if his *Virtù* is restricted, then *Fortuna* will trick him mercilessly. The weaker he is, the more adverse will be *Fortuna*.

And vice versa; the more active an individual is, the more prudent, the stronger physically and mentally, the stronger his will, the greater his chances to become a beloved hero of *Fortuna*. She will assist him to overcome difficulties, obstacles, and antagonists.

Theoretically, the initial proportions between the influence of *Virtù* and *Fortuna* are, according to Machiavelli, equal. But everyone should keep in mind that this proportion, as already stated, is ephemeral and can change any time to a person's advantage or disadvantage. Changes in these proportions are inevitable because everything is in motion, in a state of development or decline, therefore the tactics used to achieve success must also be capable of change.

One of the preliminary questions which people ask is: How to react in new circumstances? Should one be careful or impetuous, should one decide quickly or act only after long meditation and hesitation? Is it better to wait and see or is it more advantageous to make quick decisions and use force to achieve the goals desired? Machiavelli asserted that the answer to these questions cannot be unequivocal. The success of every tactic depends on its circumstances. Sometimes one has to be audacious. Sometimes it is better to delay. Sometimes one has to catch the moment, because very often *Fortuna* creates an occasion only for a very short time and once one has missed it, it may be lost forever.

People should also remember that a tactic which was once a tremendous success could be harmful under new conditions and circumstances.

People are usually conservative—this is one of the most important premises in Machiavelli's philosophy—and too often they fall victims to the illusions that once they were successful using certain methods those methods will always succeed. Dogmatic attachment to any goals, methods, institutions, parties, or political alliances, must sooner or later prove ruinous. The drive for success requires constant change, adjustment, and innovation.

These considerations should by no means be frightening. One should draw optimistic conclusions from them: those who have been defeated should never quit! They should remember that the same *Fortuna* which punished them for acting against the spirit of the time may help them when times change, when new circumstances arise and they are able and willing to take advantage of them. The same tactic which was disastrous on one occasion might be most advantageous and brilliant under new conditions. One should never give up, remembering not only the successes of great people, but also the occasions when they were defeated, humiliated, imprisoned, and yet after some time, triumphantly returned to power, glory, and the highest esteem.

But there is still a question posed by Machiavelli and mentioned already: is it more advantageous to be cautious and slow or brave, audacious, and fast? Although Machiavelli wrote that the answer cannot be dogmatic and unequivocal, he indicated very often, especially in *The Prince*, that *Fortuna* is like a woman: Whoever wants to possess her should incline to use force rather than persuasion, should be resolute, audacious, and even violent, rather than modest. *Fortuna* is like a woman who prefers those who are younger and are determined to command and demand.

This is one of the most famous comparisons of Machiavelli in which he wanted to express his deep conviction that life is too short and too complicated to tolerate those who reflect and hesitate. Most important is the ability to catch the unique opportunity, the moment which might never come again. A human being can be free provided that he wants to use his freedom and fight for it.

This is the key to Machiavelli's philosophy of freedom. The freedom of every individual is connected with his moral and physical powers, with his will and ability to act. The presence or absence of favorable circumstances limit the spheres of a person's activity, they may not exist for a majority of people, but the potential is always there. One is not born free and one will not be in chains forever. Free men are self-made men. Machiavelli analyzed hundreds of examples of people who came from the most modest backgrounds, the lowest classes of society, had no education, but were able to perceive opportunities which stood before them and were able to rearrange them to their advantage without hesitation or scruples. *Fortuna* blessed them and placed them at the pinnacle of their societies.

In Machiavelli's writing are also warnings addressed to all future politicians. They should never forget that politics is a demonic force. Anyone who decides to make a political career should remember that his soul is at stake. One who is not prepared to lose it should not enter the political arena. But once you have made up your mind and have entered the political game, you should act according to the rules of politics. You should always behave *politicante*. One's freedom is restricted by many factors, including the rules of the art of politics. The requirements of this art are neither moral nor immoral; they are *amoral*.

There is a basic difference between politics and morality, Machiavelli asserted. In the sphere of morality, the decisive factors are intentions, whereas in the sphere of politics, intentions are irrelevant. What counts in politics is success. Politicians can be either successful or unsuccessful, which does not mean— Machiavelli stressed—that a moralist or theologian should not describe them as moral or immoral, but for one's private use only. These epithets are irrelevant from the political point of view because the spheres of morality and politics do not overlap.

People often have the illusion that it would be better to have a moral, decent ruler than an immoral, indecent one without fear of God. These feelings are naive. The purpose of government is the preservation of the state, and the ruler must act in the arena of politics, which is a jungle. One is surrounded by lions, tigers, and foxes. One cannot win or even preserve one's life if one doesn't use the methods which are necessary to defeat the predators. Anyone who would like to use less effective methods, will become a victim, will lose himself and his state. The citizens of the defeated country will also be losers. Therefore, in the final analysis, rulers who are able to combine the strength of the lion and the shrewdness of the fox are more useful for the state; they contribute more to the freedom of their citizens than those who preach and follow the precepts of morality.

According to Machiavelli, the defense of freedom requires the use of all available and necessary political means.

Machiavelli continued the basic trend represented by Pico. Human freedom is closely connected with human activity. It is not an internal feeling; it exists because human beings act and live in communities, they are not abstract, contemplative, isolated, creatures. What Pico said about freedom in general, Machiavelli adjusted to the sphere of political activity and elaborated the idea of freedom as related to the sphere of political struggles. But in every sphere of life a free man can only be one who is able to make and keep himself free.

c. Thomas Hobbes—The Prince becomes a Leviathan. Freedom as Power

During his third continental trip (1634-7) Thomas Hobbes—while enjoying scholarly company around Mersenne—left Paris for Florence and, full of veneration, paid homage to Galileo Galilei. He deeply admired Galileo's creative mind, his scholarly discoveries, his philosophy of science and his moral attitude. He was influenced by Galileo's vision of the world as an arena in which everything is in motion, being a result and a cause of it. But Florence, known as the pearl of the Italian Renaissance, was also a city in which Niccolo Machiavelli worked and lived. There is no doubt that Hobbes who studied every writing of Bacon, knew that Bacon regarded Machiavelli as a political realist who was not immoral but amoral. He himself was deeply impressed by the writings of Machiavelli; his stay in Italy enabled him to understand better the doctrine of the most modern student of politics. Similarities and analogies between *The Prince* and *Leviathan* are striking and far reaching.

Hobbes took over the basic Machiavellian philosophical principles concerning the eternal changes, contradictions, passions, and ambitions of human creatures. Hobbes incorporated in his writings the Machiavellian concept of *Virtu,* without using this expression. He also adopted Machiavelli's point of departure that politics is a jungle, that political struggles are perennial and that people are compelled by events to do what they must to avoid extermination by "lions" and "wolves."

Based on these premises, Hobbes took further decisive steps in the development of Machiavellian realism; he expanded the question which was inherent, although unanswered, in Machiavelli's writings: what concrete legal and administrative measures should be taken in order to preserve not only an individual's life, but also his freedom and happiness?

Machiavelli wrote in a period when Italy was divided and torn by internal wars and struggles against foreign invaders.

Machiavelli wanted to elaborate practical recommendations on how Italy could be united. His chief answer was that Italy needed a powerful Prince, a Sovereign Ruler, who would be mighty and fearless, being at the same time reasonable and benevolent.

Hobbes was influenced by the decline of the old society and regime and by an approaching civil war; he witnessed the total disintegration of the government, domestic struggles, and finally the execution of Charles I, the victory of the Revolution and the Restoration.

Machiavelli and Hobbes were deeply influenced by the same book—Thucydides: *The Peloponnesian War*—they both regarded it as topical and instructive. Both learned from Thucydides about the nature and the character of human beings, about the art of politics and war. Both tried to adjust the ancient wisdom and experience to the new circumstances, both wrote historical and philosophico-political treatises in a similarly realistic vein. Machiavelli elaborated his vision of a Prince, a liberator and lawgiver. Hobbes transformed the idea of a *Prince* into a *Leviathan,* an artificial man, of "greater stature and strength than the Natural,[1]" the "Mortal God" to whom we owe "our peace and defence."[2] Machiavelli's Prince-Liberator was surrounded by some romantic aura; the Hobbesian Sovereign is a down-to-earth, efficient, super-policeman, judge, and administrator.

i. . Eternal Motion. The State of Nature

We know that Hobbes was familiar with the ancient philosophy of motion and contradictions first outlined by Heraclitus. Personal contact with Galileo in Florence had, however, a special impact on Hobbes' reasoning in this respect. It was under his direct influence that Hobbes introduced into his politico—philosophical theory and methodology the basic dialectial premise of motion.[3]

Afterwards he tried to apply this notion to his analysis of every political phenomenon. He regarded motion as an internal, inherent, omnipresent quality of everything, including human nature, life, freedom, and power. The human desire for power is perpetual and restless, it ceases only in death. It is possible that an individual may become satiated, does not want more pleasures, and is content with moderate power—but "he cannot assure the power and means to live well, which he hath present, without the acquisition of more."[4] The nature of social relations pushes everyone into a competition for more power than necessary to survive and to preserve what has already been achieved. The nature of social relations drives everyone into competition for more power than necessary for survival.

Hobbes' own methodology led him to a problem which he tried to examine; he correctly perceived it, but was unable to solve it: how could we achieve and protect our security and stability when everything is in motion, when antagonisms, contradictory interests, and unsatisfied ambitions, prevail on the social and political scene?

His partial answer was: there must be a Leviathan, a mighty rock on which social order and political security are established to withstand all storms.

The idea of struggle and motion was also used as a point of departure for his theory of "the natural condition of mankind" and consequently, of the philosophy of the state and freedom.[5]

Nature has made men equal "in the faculties of body, and mind."[6] There are abilities which certain individuals possess in a higher or a lower degree, but that does not matter from the viewpoint of equality. People can, in many ways, make up their partial deficiencies. For instance, a group of weaker can band together in order to defeat the stronger.

The best proof that wisdom and wit are equally distributed, argued Hobbes, is the fact "that every man is contented with his share."[7]

From the equality of ability arise, continued Hobbes, equal hopes to achieve one's ends and to fulfill one's ambitions. The resources of mankind are restricted, therefore people must compete for them.

There are various kinds of competition. The extreme ones take the forms of violence and invasion. People endlessly fight for Gain, Safety, Reputation.[8] Without a common power keeping them all in awe, they would be in a condition of a war of "every man, against every man."[9] It is a war which does not consist in one or few battles only, but in a "tract of time," combined with a disposition to fight.

In the state of nature, good will, mutual understanding, assistance, gratitude, justice, and equity do not exist; even if they were known, their exercise would be harmful. Possibly people never killed each other in a cold-blooded (with exception of "official" wars) manner, but they could have acted in such a way *in extremis*. Therefore people have to protect themselves by organizing a powerful institution for mutual protection and assurance. The ruler must be stronger, of course, than any of the contestants.

In such a society must an individual live; this is the only available environment in which he can be free.

The state of nature should not be regarded as a pure, abstract fantasy which never existed. Indeed, the presentation of this state is an ideological reflection of the real relations in the world of economic and political competition; of the first primitive accumulation of capital and decomposition of the obsolete social hierarchy which was not prepared to leave the scene without resistance.

Hobbes was not a neutral spectator only, he was a participating actor. When he was describing this "state of nature" he was relaying to his contemporaries on both sides of the barricades: *de te fabula narratur.* (THIS TALE IS ABOUT YOURSELF).

This truth was unpleasant for everybody, therefore he had enemies on both sides. His fate became similar to Machiavelli's own: the republicans regarded him a monarchist; the royalists—a disguised republican and an obvious freethinker; the Catholics could not forgive his criticism of the Pope and denial of his prerogatives.

All parties were in turn criticized by Hobbes, nobody's claims to power were fully accepted by him, he was too rationalistic.

For many years Hobbes felt personally endangered. The fears prevailing in the state of nature were his own. Possibly the other features of this image are caricatured—but they are still a reflection of reality, although exaggerated.

Writing about the state of nature, Hobbes was conveying a message that people are not and cannot be friendly, and when it comes to basics—their power, their real interests, their social positions, and prestige—they will and they must fight relentlessly.

ii. . Sovereign Power

The "natural condition of mankind" is truly miserable: every man is an enemy to every man; there is no security, one must think about self defense only; there is no place for industry, culture, art, navigation, transportation, trade, export and import, no common buildings. Envy and hatred prevail.

... and which is worst of all, continuall feare, and danger of violent death; And the life of man, solitary, poore, nasty, brutish, and short.[10]

The only way to get away from these conditions is to erect a Common Power, who keeps all the competitors in fear, directs them to the common benefit, secures their lives, preserves internal peace, and fights against foreign invaders. This Power, known as Common Wealth, is organized by a covenant of every man with every man in such a way as if every man has said:

> *I Authorise and give up my Right of Governing my selfe, to this Man, or to this Assembly of men, on this condition, that thou give up thy Right to him, and Authorise all his Actions in like manner.*[11]

The consequences of the covenant are the following:

—The subjects cannot change the form of government; its form is unimportant anyway; every government, whatever its name, must be sovereign and absolute;

—The sovereign determines what is necessary for peace, the subjects may not protest against his decisions or actions, they cannot accuse him of being unjust, because he sets the standards of justice;

—The sovereign appoints his collaborators;

—The sovereign decides which opinions should be allowed, taught, or prohibited.

One may argue that such a state will not only be sovereign and absolutistic, but outright despotic. Hobbes answered that every government either is sovereign, indivisible, supreme, efficient, and absolute or it is subject to some other power possessing these qualities. Since every true power must have these attributes, it does not matter whether it is a monarchy, aristocracy, or democracy. If one calls one of these forms of government a tyranny or oligarchy, one uses different names for reasons of political competition.

The real problem which arises and should be solved concerns freedom and tolerance. Are they compatible with such absolutism? This crucial matter will be considered.

iii. . Freedom

Hobbes took into account that there is—as we would call it today—a stratification within society. From this fact he derived the recommendation that the Sovereign must keep in awe not only individuals, but—which is even more complicated and important—entire social strata or classes. His call for justice does not refer simply to equal justice which should be administered in regard to individuals, he also *expressis verbis* recommended the same attitude towards the poorest and weakest groups of society.

> The safety of the People, requireth further, from . . . the Sovereign Power, that Justice be equally administered to all degrees of People; that is, that as well the rich, and mighty, as poor and obscure persons, may be righted of the injuries done them; so as the great, may have no greater hope of impunity, when they doe violence, dishonour, or any Injury to the meaner sort, than when one of these, does the like to one of them: For in this consisteth Equity . . .[12]

The sovereign must rule over a society divided into poor and rich, where "the rich, and mighty" try to use their position in order to get special privileges. The authorities cannot change existing social divisions, but they should administer justice equally in order to preserve peace, life and freedom.

> Liberty, or Freedome, signifieth (properly) the absence of Opposition; (by Opposition, I mean external Impediments of Motion;) . . .[13]
>
> By LIBERTY, is understood . . . the absence of external Impediments: which . . may oft take away part of a mans power to do what he would; but cannot hinder him from using the power left him, according as his judgement, and reason shall dictate to him.[14]

These famous sentences express one of the most popular notions of freedom and they are, at the same time, a source of many oversimplifications. Hobbes himself was responsible for certain misunderstandings when he pointed out that his description of liberty may be applied to rational, irrational, or even inanimate creatures. In his further considerations he tried, of course, to clarify his position and he continued, with the usual power of his mind, the fight against misconceptions caused by "learned" professors and theologians.

> But it is an easy thing, for men to be deceived, by the specious name of Libertie . . . And when the same errour is confirmed by the authority of men in reputation for their writings in this subject, it is no wonder if it produce sedition, and change of Government.[15]

Hobbes endeavored to explain that there was nothing mysterious about the meaning of freedom, that this concept is bound up with the very existence of every human being and his activity. As usual, instead of the word "activity" he used the word "motion," as if he wanted to stress once more that the world of physics and politics were not two completely different spheres, both could be explored rationally.

The above quoted definition of freedom is the most general, therefore Hobbes tried to make it more concrete in his further considerations. A free man, he continued, is a person who "in those things, which by his strength and wit he is able to do, is not hindred to doe what he has a will to."[16]

He also tried to dispel the mystery in the concept of free will, a notion so often misused by theologians. He wrote that from free will no liberty can be inferred to the real will, desire, or inclination, because only such a man is free who is not stopped in doing what he desires or has an inclination to do.

The freedom of a person to overcome obstacles and impediments depends on his own power:

"The *Power of a Man,* (to take it universally), is his present means, to obtain some future apparent Good."[17]

Powers which could be at an individual's disposal can be divided into two categories: original and instrumental.

Natural power is "the eminence of the Faculties of Body, or Mind," as for instance: strength, form, prudence, art, eloquence, liberality, nobility.

Instrumental powers are acquired either with the help of natural power or by fortune. To them belong: riches, reputation, friends, and "the secret working of God, which men call Good Luck."[18]

Power has a strange nature, wrote Hobbes: it increases with its proceedings and mere existence. It is like the motion of heavy bodies: the further they go, "make still the more hast."[19] Power tends to be compounded. For instance:

—Riches joined with liberality procure friends and servants, and they constitute Power;

—The reputation of power is Power in itself, because it draws adherence of those who need protection;

—The reputation of Prudence in the affairs of Peace and War, is Power because prudent people prefer a government of the prudent rather than the incompetent;

—Eloquence is Power, because it is regarded a sign of Prudence.

—The affability of men already in Power increases Power, because it gains love and friends.

When an individual is more powerful, he is more free, because he has more means—as is stated in the definition—"to obtain some future apparent Good."[20]

Whoever has more means available is more valuable in the eyes of society. Thus we approach a new fundamental question: how much is a man worth?

"The *Value*, or WORTH of a man, is as of all other things, his Price; that is to say, so much as would be given for the use of his Power."[21] This value is "relative" only, it depends—as the price of any commodity—on the "need" and "judgement" of other people.[22] When the "market" changes, the "values" of certain individuals rise or fall. For instance, the price of an able officer is greater during hostilities; an uncorrupt judge is worth more in time of peace than in war.

Hobbes, as if elaborating on Machiavelli's *Virtu*, recommended that every individual should observe the changes on the market and act accordingly in order to expand his sphere of freedom, his Power.

When people "honour" a given person—they honor not his absolute qualities, but his value; they can flatter him, show signs of love or fear, praise or "magnifie"[23] his opinion.

When the people esteem the "value" ("worth") of a man low, they dissent with him, disobey, refuse his wishes, they speak to him rashly, behave before him "obscenely, slovenly, impudently"—they "dishonour" him.[24]

The value of a man also depends on many qualities which one could call subjective. For instance:

> Timely Resolution, or determination of what a man is to do, Honourable... And Irresolution, Dishonourable... For when a man has weighed things as long as the time permits, and resolves not ... he overvalues little things, which is Pusillanimity.
>
> All Actions, and Speeches, that proceed, or seem to proceed from much Experience, Science, Discretion, or Wit, are Honourable; For all these are Powers. Actions, or Words that proceed from Errour, Ignorance, or Folly, Dishonourable."[25]

These qualities must be externalized in order to add to the power and value of an individual.

One could argue that Hobbes made no advances in exploring the problem of the relationship of individual freedom and the "free will," that he only shifted the problem from one terminology into another. But he achieved one main purpose at least, he presented one more argument that freedom should not be interpreted in a contemplative way, that it is an attribute which must be used. In this way he continued the Renaissance tradition of trying to overcome the vestiges of human passivity.

Another great contribution of Hobbes to the philosophy of freedom was his statement that liberty and necessity are consistent with one another. Whatever men do voluntarily, they do because of some causes—he argued; the immediate causes determining one's will proceed from another cause; the continual chain of causes

> proceeds from necessity. So that to him that could see the connection of those causes, the *necessity of all men's voluntary actions, would appear manifest. And therefore... the liberty* of man in doing what he will, is accompanied with the necessity of doing which God will ... no more nor lesse.[26]

Man's freedom to do what is necessary—is his *natural* freedom, "which only is properly called *liberty.*"[27]

Hobbes' philosophy of freedom and necessity constitutes a milestone on the road to the understanding that freedom is necessity understood, as Hegel stated. In Hobbes' writings the connection between freedom and necessity is rather the guess of a genius than a fully developed theory. He paved the road for further research.

He was able to make a good case for the concept that one can discuss the problem of human liberty only in conjunction with real people who are always inextricably involved in an endless chain of causes and effects. Men can be free within the framework of necessity, not beyond or above it, as is suggested by misleading theories of free will.

This approach, inspired by the natural sciences, helped Hobbes to clarify in his own philosophy the relationship between individual freedom on the one hand, and political structure and laws on the other.

In this connection Hobbes substantiated Machiavelli's demand that church and religion should be subject to the state. For Machiavelli, this demand was a part of the art of politics, connected with the idea of national liberation and the preservation of the state and its sovereignty; for Hobbes it was a broad question of principle, important not only for the defense of the state, preservation of the internal peace, and the execution of the laws, but also for the protection of the liberty of the subjects.

Hobbes decided that one should officially and publicly acknowledge the supremacy of the secular state in its not-so-holy war against Theology, Dogmas, and the Kingdom of Darkness. The constant struggle between the "two swords," between the civil and spiritual domains, must be dangerous to every individual. It undermines the Power, i.e. the freedom of the citizens, because they can be free only within the framework of the civil laws. This idea of freedom is completely different from the religious concept according to which a free man is one who has liberated himself from passions and sins.

According to Hobbes' own proclamation, a true ruler must be an absolute sovereign. This absolutism, as one can easily deduce, is to a great extent limited by the requirements of the natural law and especially by the basic provisions of the social contract, guaranteeing the right to life and to property. But there are other provisions of natural law, enumerated in Chapter 15 of the *Leviathan,* which bind the ruler if not legally, then morally, by force of reason itself. Therefore, the abolutism of the Hobbesian ruler is limited by a net of laws within which a citizen can act according to his own wishes.

Even more important is the idea that citizens have a duty only externally to observe the law. Authorities can take into account only behavior, not mental or moral attitudes. In this way, Hobbes excluded any idea of governmental interference in the spiritual life, in "the soul" of the subjects. This is one of the basic differences between the attitude of the Inquisition (and let us add: the modern totalitarian state) and the philosophy of Thomas Hobbes.

The authorities should not intrude into the depth of one's mind!—this is historically one of the first victories of the Western concept of personal freedom. At this stage of the evolution of the idea of freedom, an individual is not attributed a right publicly to express his opinions and openly fight for them politically; but one is free from persecution for deeply held beliefs. One should by no means be tortured in order to confess what one really thinks in the bottom of one's heart. It is just sufficient that one acts according to the law. If the law requires certain statements, even a "profession of faith," one should make it—and utter the required words without any obligation to believe in one's declaration.

iv. . Tolerance

Hobbes drew two kinds of conclusions from his main premise that the right to defend one's life is a basic law of nature.

One trend leads to an absolutistic concept of power; the second trend, to some kind of tolerance which should prevail among the people and—which is even more important—between the power-holders and the people.

The essential problem caused by these two trends, seemingly irreconcilable, could be narrowed down to the following: can an absolute government allow tolerance?

Reasonable, well educated people know that there is no point to compete for unimportant things,[28] that one should be tolerant—Hobbes does not use this term, but this is precisely what he meant as one can deduce from his reasoning. Unfortunately, people are so stubborn and passionate that they would be prepared—this is one of the greatest comparisons of Hobbes—to destroy all the books of geometry if the geometrical axioms were perceived as harmful to their political interests.

Hobbes drew his determinations concerning tolerance unexpectedly but logically from his dogmatic axiom that all people seek peace.

Reason itself concludes from this maxim that for the sake of peace and life one should give up one's unrestricted (in the state of nature) right to all things and should "be contented with so much liberty against other men, as he would allow other men against himselfe"—this is the second law of nature.[29]

In other words: people should divest themselves from a portion of their liberty in order freely to enjoy the rest.

There are, however, some rights which cannot be transferred, they are "not alienable" (Hobbes' expression). Especially: the right to resist an assault by force; the same can be said "of Wounds, and Chayns, and Imprisonment."[30] No man can be obliged to accuse himself, or his parents, wife, or benefactor—such an accusation would be a "corruption of Nature."[31] No man is obliged to tell the truth under torture; whatever he says in order to save his life or health should not be regarded as testimony because it cannot be credited.

These conclusions from the right to life expand in a substantial way the concept of personal freedom. Hobbes tried to protect not life in itself, not "naked life," but life with certain human, civilized qualities, which should be secured in a "tolerant" manner.

The laws of nature enumerated by Hobbes impose on people such obligations which clearly direct them toward tolerance:

—They should be just, and perform the requirements of their

covenants and have the constant will to give to every man his own;[32]

—They should be grateful; when they receive benefit from another's grace, they should endeavour that one should not repent of his good will;[33]

—Every man should "strive to accommodate himselfe to the rest."[34] The observers of this law can be called sociable (in Latin: *commodi*); the contrary: stubborn, forward, intractable, unsociable;

—One ought to "pardon the offences. . . of them that repenting, desire it".[35] Pardon—is nothing more than granting peace; one should not look for revenge for the sake of punishment only. In revenge one should not think about the past, but about the future good, one should look for correction and not for cruelty. Cruel is a person who does not forgive under any circumstances. Cruelty endangers peace;

—No man should declare *hatred* or *contempt* of another by deed, word, countenance, or gesture. The breach of this law is *contumely*;

—Every man should acknowledge others as *equal*. The violators of this precept are *pride,* they think others are less worthy, reasonable, or "witty." Pride is against nature and experience;

—People should be *modest*, they should not require more rights than they are prepared to grant to others; the violators of this maxim are *arrogant*;

—People should equally use common things; when trusted to judge, one should deal equally between parties—this principle is called *equity*; in case of controversies, the law of nature requires submission to an arbitrator; mediators should be guaranteed "safe conduct"; no man should be a judge either in his own case, or in a case where he has a cause of partiality.

All these "laws of nature" oblige always, "eternally," *in foro interno*, in conscience. These laws are "dictates of reason," "conclusions", "theorems"[36] indicating how one should behave in order to preserve peace.

A close examination of these "precepts" leads to the conclusion that the citizens in a well organized, secure, state should act and behave in a way which could be briefly described as tolerant.

Although Hobbes did not use this expression, all his practical "commandments of reason" dictate that one should treat his neighbor in a polite, dignified, and respectful manner; one should be grateful, should not keep grudges, one should avoid arrogance and superiority; one ought to listen to the opinions of other people respectfully and without prejudice, with an open mind, because one's neighbor is no less "witty" or "worthy." One should also realize this basic philosophical determination, that

> . . . there is no conception in a man's mind, which hath not at first, totally, or by parts, been begotten upon the organs of sense . . . The rest are derived from that originall[37]

We are equal because we read from the same book: nature. We are different, because one can have more or less experience, but in the final analysis we all have the same potential and it is easy to make up for lack of experience in a given domain. The theory that our perceptions are nothing more than reflections of reality—was consciously used for the purposes of advocating tolerant cooperation as a way to preserve social peace, order, equality, and mutual respect.

And what about dogmas which eventually can be imposed for political reasons? They should be swallowed—Hobbes recommended—like a medication: quickly and without chewing. Authorities should only be interested in external compliance in any event.

In such an atmosphere of tolerance, under the vigilant eye of *Leviathan*, the people can use their Power and Freedom.

v. . Freedom—Tolerance—Happiness

Everybody's aim is to achieve happiness (Hobbes used the term Felicity). Human felicity, like all phenomena in the world, is not static but an emotional state in constant flux,

> . . . the Felicity of this life, consisteth not in the repose of a
> mind satisfied. . . Felicity is a continuall progresse of the desire,
> from one object to another; the attaining of the former, being still
> but the way to the later.[38]

There is no such thing, stressed Hobbes, as a *finis ultimus*
(ultimate aim) or a *summum bonum* (supreme good) recommended by "moral philosophers."[39] They neither understand
nor remember that human desires never end, human senses and
imagination can never rest. Therefore, the object of human
desires, whose fulfillment leads to happiness, "is not to enjoy
once only and for one instant of time, but to assure forever."[40]

In a world of constant motion, there is no possibility of assuring anything "forever." The human inclination to seek happiness is one more reason for constant struggle, for incessant use
of one's power for one's own benefit and . . . freedom.

Men can freely enjoy their power when they are secure; they
want to be free from unexpected attacks carried out either by
their countrymen or by the governmental authorities; they want
to live in a situation of predictability, where they know that given
causes will result in predictable effects. These philosophical
political premises undoubtedly contributed to Hobbes' geometrical orientation, leading him, under the influence of Euclid's
Elements, to apply the Euclidian method to his political philosophy.[41]

Hobbes' view of politics, law, and freedom was more bourgeois than any theory of his predecessors or most of his successors. He is open, classically clear, amazingly farsighted,
astute, and penetrating. Every important question and every
conclusion starts and ends with the experience of the "market."
Let us compile all the basic bourgeois premises in his works:

—The value of a person is determined in the market according to his Power, made up of wealthy connections, and appearances which are regarded important;

—Labor is a "commodity, exchangeable for benefit, as well
as any other thing. . . ." Affluence depends only "on the labour

and industry of man."[42] Needless to point out, it was more than one hundred years later that these theses became the pillars of the classic bourgeois political economy of Smith and Ricardo.[43]

—The state should be strong and efficient in order to protect life, property, and a smooth exchange of commodities. Capitalists can safely compete, but—as C. B. MacPherson observed—they must pay an appropriate price for this safety: "an obligation to obey the laws of the sovereign so long as the sovereign was able to protect them." This is the price, but it did not seem too high to Hobbes: "It was the sort of long term contract a businessman could be expected to understand and to enter into with a view to his own advantage."[44]

—Human freedom is the capacity to use one's power, determined chiefly by capital and social position.

A human being is a creature with passions, desires, emotions, and ambitions. In order to satisfy the natural inclinations (which are neither good nor bad, they are just natural) a person must overcome many social and natural impediments. He must fight for everything, against everybody. It is quite natural that human society is an arena of war of all against all.

Every human being is endowed with natural and instrumental powers which enable people to achieve their ends.

A person who gets what he wants will be happy for a short while only. One must fight for every moment of happiness and use all the power available in order to prolong happiness or achieve a new state of felicity.

The government, Leviathan, should guarantee life and property, should create and enforce a system of law within which the people can compete, struggle, use their power, achieve felicity, without killing each other or violating the laws and rights promulgated by the government. In order to preserve peace, they should be tolerant.

The state, in this philosophy, is an external framework within which an individual is as free as his physical and mental forces allow him to be.

The problem—whether sovereign secular power can become a

source of oppression and danger to life and what should be done to prevent abuses of absolute power—Hobbes dismissed as illogical. But questions remain. Partial answers to them were given by, among others, John Locke in England, Montesquieu and Rousseau in France, Staszic and Kollataj in Poland, Kant in Germany, and the Founding Fathers in the United States.

2. The Essence of Freedom

Kant, Hegel, Marx, and Dewey represent four stages in the evolution of the idea of freedom. They are qualitatively different from one another, yet at the same time they are related. In most writings of these authors the Hegelian *Aufhebung* is in evidence. Their ideas complement one another, they deny one another, they are at the same time precursors and continuators of one another, because the sequence of time becomes unimportant in the case of dialectical interdependence. Kant, Hegel, Marx, and Dewey try to answer the eternally recurring, fundamental questions of the philosophy of freedom. The problems did not originate with them; their answers are not conclusive, they pose the questions in a new way and add new queries to the old list. They arrive at the theoretical limitations previously established, but as Hegel observed, one who approaches the frontier has in fact already passed beyond it.

These authors are among the world's most controversial. In fact, Kant's theory of politics, morality, and freedom, generally is dismissed as unrealistic and of no practical significance. Hegel and Marx on the other hand are among the most unpopular philosophers in Western academic centers; whereas in Communist countries they are acclaimed officially while being flagrantly misinterpreted. They are branded as adversaries of freedom in the West, as partisans of dictatorship, violence and bureaucracy. They are accused of every vice inimical to the very foundations of freedom.

Dewey's philosophy of freedom is unknown in Europe and underestimated in his own country.

These thinkers have made a truly historic contribution to the philosophy of freedom. Without it, the modern, rationalistic concept of freedom would not have developed as it has and the mere notion of freedom would have been poorer. Many contemporary philosophers will not admit that Kant, Hegel, and Marx have been sources of their intellectual endeavors, because such an intellectual heritage is looked upon with disfavor by so many. It is the more urgent, therefore, to vindicate the historical truth, to a certain extent at least.

a. Kant: Freedom as Autonomy

Kant's concept of freedom is central to his theories of politics, law, and morality. Many of his ideas are open to various interpretations, leading to ever increasing philosophical and political literature on the subject. One thing seems to be indisputable: An analysis of Kant's concept of freedom should start with his distinction concerning the dual nature of the human being, namely that man is a *phenomenon* and a *noumenon* at the same time.

The phenomenal human being is part of the physical world and in this world man is subject to the laws of nature. He is part of the chain of causes and effects. As a physical being man cannot rightly be regarded as free.

But man is also a "thing-in-itself." He is a *noumenon* and as such he has freedom of choice. This freedom is the most important and the most characteristic feature of his humanity. The concept of freedom is connected with the existence of reason. Kant went so far as to say that freedom is man's only birthright. All other rights are acquired.

For a human being freedom means that he is not dependent upon the will of any other human being:

> Freedom is independence of the compulsory will of another; and in so far as it tends to exist with the freedom of all according to a universal law, it is the one sole original inborn right belonging to every man in virtue of his humanity.[1]

Because man is born free, it follows that there exists an "innate equality belonging to every man," which consists of his right "to be independent of being bound by others to anything more than that to which he may also reciprocally bind them. It is consequently the inborn quality of every man in virtue of which he ought to be his own master by right (*sui juris*). "[2]

Because freedom is a "birthright," Kant wrote, one must assume that man also has "the natural quality of justness" attributable to a man as an unimpeachable natural right, because he has done no wrong to any one prior to his own juridical actions. In this complicated manner a well-known juridical idea was rediscovered and defended, the presumption of innocence.

Kant also drew the concept of freedom of contract from the idea of freedom as a birthright: "there is also the innate right of common action on the part of every man, so that he may do towards others what does not infringe their rights or take away anything that is theirs unless they are willing to appropriate it . . ."[3]

We observe one of those marvelous coincidences which are so characteristic of Kant's philosophy: He drew conclusions corresponding to practical, social, political, and juridical experience from pure reason, allegedly not influenced in any way by the external world of phenomena. The ancient Greeks and Romans already knew that in order rationally to enter into a civil contract the equality and free will of each partner are presumed. They also knew that an organized society could not function well without a presumption of innocence. In criminal procedures under absolutistic and terroristic regimes of course, this presumption is not consistently followed, but it is never wholly denied to society as a whole nor indiscriminately to all its members.

Kant was right when he combined freedom with the presumption of individual innocence. In practice, in political life and juridical procedure, however, these two ideas do not always appear together. History knows many examples of regimes which officially proclaimed their adherence to the presumption of innocence, but at the same time democratic liberties were almost reduced to a nullity.

On the other hand, Kant wrote, human freedom should also be limited because it is subject to reason. As controlled by reason, freedom cannot be identified with license or unbridled desire. According to Kant, freedom can be conceived only as *rational* freedom, that is, subject to the "laws," and "requirements," of reason; it is the freedom to use one's reason at all times.

Kant called man free by the mere fact that he has the power of reason. Nathan Rotenstreich calls this aspect of freedom the "cosmological aspect of the concept of freedom."[4] Freedom in the cosmological sense is independent of time and of all sensible factors. In the Preface to the *Critique of Practical Reason,* Kant wrote that the mere existence of the pure practical faculty of reason establishes the existence of a transcendental freedom, which he also calls freedom in the absolute sense. Freedom proved by the apodictic law of practical reason is the keystone of the whole system of pure reason and even of speculative reason. There are three basic elements of pure reason: God, immortality, and freedom. But freedom is the only idea of speculative reason whose possibility we know *a priori,* for this idea is revealed in the moral law.

Kant's explanation of this complicated problem is:

> To avoid having anyone imagine that there is an inconsistency when I say that freedom is the condition of the moral law and later assert that the moral law is the only condition under which freedom can be known, I will only remind the reader that, though freedom is certainly the *ratio essendi* of the moral law, the latter is the *ratio cognoscendi* of freedom. For had not the moral law already been distinctly thought in our reason, we would never have been justified in assuming anything like freedom, even though it is not self-contradictory. But if there were no freedom, the moral law would never have been encountered in us.[5]

The most important conclusion to be drawn from these thoughts is that freedom, an indispensable and inalienable attribute of mankind, also is the foundation and source of moral and legal responsibility. Without freedom neither the categorical nor the practical imperatives, neither legal obligations nor rights would make any sense.

A reasonable man knows what he *should* do and once he knows it, he *can* do it. This Kantian conclusion has spawned many misunderstandings. Very often it is expressed in the sentence "ought implies can." Kant wanted to express a very simple idea which is basic for his system: If you have a duty, you *can* carry it out. If someone has a right, others *can* observe it.

If, however, one is ordered by a legitimate superior to do an act contrary to one's consciousness of duty, based on the categorical imperative, one should reject such an order and act according to one's true duty instead. He who acts according to his duty (based on the categorical imperative) is free, even if he is persecuted by the author of immoral orders.

One explanation is necessary: For Kant, "can" means the capability of the free will; it does not mean that any tangible results will occur in the world of phenomena.

Kant's freedom, as something which belongs to the world of the *noumena,* is truly abstract. From the point of view of traditional empirical philosophy, it is also subjective. Kant regarded freedom as a potential existing in every individual rather than as a reality in social relations. His concept of freedom is independent of human activity but depends on subjective human thinking.

Freedom of the will is very far from the true freedom of the individual. According to the tradition of ancient philosophy, which was rejuvenated during the Renaissance and the Enlightenment, an individual is free when he can act according to his desires, will, and talents. True human freedom must be expressed in social activity and not limited to the process of thinking, even the most rational. This is the basic deficiency of Kant's philosophy of freedom. He did not bind freedom to free human activity. His concept of freedom is theoretical, whereas the chief problem of freedom is practical: how to free people to do good deeds and develop their talents. Nevertheless, Kant tried to draw political conclusions from his concept of freedom.

Kant wrote that even the most absolute ruler is interested in preserving freedom of thought and speech because he wants to know the real situation existing in his country and the opinions of his subjects. Therefore, pure reason requires the preservation of freedom of conscience, thought, speech, writing, and publication in every country and under every form of government. Kant deduced the need for and the right of these freedoms from reason itself.

This approach demonstrates how wholly impractical Kant's thinking was. History knows many rulers who were wholly indifferent to the true opinion of their people, even though they may thereby have remained ignorant of the existing situation. If despotic rulers wanted to know what was going on in their countries, they used other means to gather information, such as secret police and informers. Deception, camouflage, and lies are inherent in such regimes. They fear free speech and a free press more than they do being misinformed. It could be argued that Kant was right in saying that reason requires freedom of thought, speech, and press: but everybody knows that these requirements and rights can exist in reality only in a more or less democratic country. Rulers are not motivated by reason alone. In his time, democracy was even rarer than it became in the following centuries. His conclusions were logical, but have not proved practical.

Kant's belief that intellectual freedom can balance political terror is unrealistic. Despotic and terroristic governments must suppress intellectual freedom as an essential part of any comprehensive system of control. There can of course be brief periods when an oppressive government may tolerate free speech and a free press; such a regime might even tolerate free speech and press more than freedom of association. Every despotism has its own peculiarities and periodically may allow limited forms of criticism as a safety valve. But, as all experience shows, anti-democratic terroristic regimes will never be overthrown by intellectual freedom alone. The belief that they might is an illusion possibly nourished by Kant's admiration for the "enlightened" Prussian ruler, Frederick II. History shows that there have always been many more unenlightened despots than enlightened.

Notwithstanding his impracticality, however, Kant had an impact on the development of the theory of freedom and morality, and even on individual behavior and attitudes.

On July 23, 1943, Kurt Huber, Professor of Philosophy at the University of Munich, Germany, was executed. He was condemned for the crime of high treason against Hitler's regime.

In his final statement to the judges of the People's Court, he referred to Kant's philosophy as the inspiration for his opposition to the Nazis:

> . . . I deem it to be not only right, but also my moral duty to speak out against political misconduct . . . It had been my endeavor to awaken the student body to an awareness of existing conditions, to appeal to moral reflection, a return to clearcut ethical principles, to a politics of right, to a preservation of the dignity of man. . . . I have asked myself with a view to Kant's categorical imperative, what would happen if these subjective maxims of mine were to be made universal law . . . There is but one answer: There would be order, security, confidence in our government. Every morally responsible voice would be raised against the threat of rule of sheer might over right, of simple caprice over the will of the morally good, against the wanton trampling upon the rights of self-determination of principalities all over Europe, against the inhuman fostering of distrust of man against man so that the very foundation of human relationships has been undermined and neither father nor neighbor feels secure before his son.
>
> Every external legislation reaches its ultimate limitation through untruth and immorality, through overt transgressions of right, through the covert cowardice which prevents open criticism of such practices and smothers exhortations to a return to the moral order with accusations of treason. . . .
>
> I am jeopardizing my life with this defense of my inner convictions. I have acted through my convictions in accordance with the dictates of that inner voice . . . I am accepting the consequences of my actions, accepting the responsibility therefor . . . I demand that freedom be restored to our people, that they be

released from their chains of slavery . . . I am convinced that the
relentless course of history will vindicate my willing and
acting. . . [6]

This moving example shows how influential Kant's ideas
still are. At the same time, it indicates that Kant's influence
never extended beyond a narrow circle of intellectuals. It also
shows that a simplistic notion of natural law and rights is not a
necessary background for disobedience. The moral imperatives
are as good a justification.

Kurt Huber remained free in the Kantian sense till the last
moment of his life. He was murdered as a *free* human being; this
is the paradox of Kant's subjective, purely intellectual, view
of freedom.

It would seem that Kant was a follower of the tradition of
subjective freedom. It was St. Augustine who drew the most
amazing political conclusions from the concept of subjective
freedom: a slave can be freer than his master, provided that he
has been liberated from his passions. St. Augustine argued that
it is better to be a slave of one (human) master than of many
(passions). Such sophistry was used for immediate political purposes throughout the centuries: Slaves, serfs, servants, and the
poor who had no rights were told they had no reason to rebel
against their legitimate masters.

Kant's political and social ideas were different, he was a
philosopher of Enlightenment but more moderate than his contemporaries, his French, English, Dutch, and Polish counterparts.

According to Kant, the idea of freedom must be placed at the
foundation of the constitution of every state and of every law
issued by a government. The ideal should be: "A constitution
allowing *the greatest possible human freedom* in accordance
with laws by which *the freedom of each is made to be consistent
with that of all others*—I do not speak of the greatest happiness,
for this will follow itself—it is at any rate a necessary idea, which
must be taken as fundamental not only in first projecting a constitution but in all its laws."[7]

Kant understood that this ideal would not be reached

without obstacles. These obstacles do not necessarily arise out of human nature, but rather out of previous legislation. No true philosopher would argue that the ideal is unattainable because of adverse previous experience. If there has been such bad experience, then, Kant argued, we should be even more energetic in our endeavors to harmonize legislation and government with the ideal.

Kant wrote that he would be prepared to accept Plato's ideal as his own: a society in which punishment is unnecessary and therefore non-existent. He says that it would be impossible to achieve this ideal, but he insists that we should have an archetype, a standard against which to measure all existing laws and governments. It is possible to improve laws and governments. No one after all can say how wide the chasm should be between the ideal and reality. No one can say where the development of human nature and its perfectibility will stop. Because of these unknowns, we should agree "that it is in the power of freedom to pass beyond any and every specified limit."[8]

It is obvious that Kant distinguished between an ideal of political freedom and the reality of political freedom. The ideal should be an absolute harmony between the freedom of each and the freedom of all. But he knew that reality was far from the ideal. Kant distinguished various levels of perfection of actual freedom. The ideal of freedom is unchangeable; the reality of freedom however is always in a state of transformation.

In this way, Kant prepared the ground for the Hegelian dialectics of freedom. Kant's *a priori* idea of freedom was easily transformed into the absolute idea; the rest depends on logic and profound studies of historical realities. This historical task was performed by Hegel.

Even more important is Kant's contribution to the theory of law. He connected the general idea of freedom with human rights as an instrument of the limitation and realization of freedom. Kant is perhaps the first philosopher who was able to substantiate the idea that the philosophical notion of freedom is inseparable from the juridical and political concepts of the rights of man.

b. Freedom as Necessity Understood

There are fervent adversaries of Hegel's philosophy in the Western as well as in the Eastern world. Even now, a hundred and fifty years after his death, Hegel is still attacked as a living antagonist. Such animosity usually is founded on preconceived ideas and simple ignorance. One might say the same about Hegel that Jean-Paul Sartre wrote about the Jewish people: They have many passionate and powerful enemies and a few friends who defend them without enthusiasm.

Bertrand Russell was attuned to the temper of Anglo-Saxon prejudices when in one of his "unpopular essays" on Hegel he wrote:

> It follows from his metaphysics that true liberty consists in obedience to an arbitrary authority, that free speech is an evil, that absolute monarchy is good, that the Prussian state was the best existing at the time when he wrote, that war is good, and that an international organization for the peaceful settlement of disputes would be a misfortune ... What he admired were ... order, system, regulation and intensity of governmental control.[9]

Nearly every word of Russell's evaluation is incorrect.

Hegel's reputation was not much better in Eastern Europe. There was a short period during the 1920s when Hegel's philosophy gained an officially sponsored popularity. The Soviet philosophers associated with A. Deborin vigorously promoted Hegelian studies. Deborin and his friends often quoted Lenin's famous statement that without serious study and understanding of the Hegelian dialectic it would be impossible truly to understand *Das Kapital.*

Hegel became one of the first victims of Stalinism in the 1930s. Neither the right-wing, nor the left-wing dogmatists could endure Hegel's dialectic and his views about freedom.

It was Stalin himself who gave the official interpretation of Hegel's philosophy to the socialist world in the 1930s. He stated that Hegel expressed the spirit of the Prussian *Junkers,* the militarists, and expansionists. He considered Hegel's philosophy to be a reaction to the French Revolution. Every one of Stalin's views was wrong.

It would appear that both Russell and Stalin regarded Hegel as the propounder of all or very many social and political evils, including Nazism, against which they had been struggling.

The antipodes—Russell and Stalin—spoke about Hegel in almost the same manner. When two antagonists come to the same conclusion, usually both are mistaken.

There are many good reasons why so many politicians, in the East and in the West, in Communist and in non-Communist countries, wish to push Hegel, the controversial philosopher, into the closet of oblivion. Hegel's ideas are too offensive and controversial for the minds of present-day politicians and for many modern conservative philosophers and political scientists, both in the East and in the West.

Hegel wrote that most people equate freedom with arbitrariness. They think that they are free when they are able to act according to their impulses. The most frequently repeated definition of freedom, according to Hegel, is that freedom is the ability to do what we please. One who thinks in this way, Hegel argues, reveals "an utter immaturity of thought."[10] Why? Because those who identify freedom with the ability to do what they please disregard the nature of social life, of right, of morality, of law, as well as the needs of everyday life. Freedom must be connected with understanding, responsibility, and an awareness of moral obligation at all stages of development.

In this way Hegel approached one of his most important statements, namely, that freedom is necessity understood; hence there are two elements in freedom: the subjective and the objective. Man can be free not from the laws of nature, but thanks to the laws of nature. The more he understands, the less he is subject to the caprices of the external world. When man understands, he can control.

The history of mankind is the history of the acquisition of knowledge. Hegel, therefore, described the history of the world as the "progress of the consciousness of freedom."[11] He continued: "The idea of freedom . . . is the absolute goal of history."[12]

Whenever Hegel wrote about history, he meant the history of the people who struggle for survival, have their own interests, passions, and ambitions. Every individual tries to attain his own goals, but what he achieves usually is contrary to his intentions, particularly in political and social life. People build their future in the same way architects build houses. They use the forces of nature and the raw material provided by nature. The result is that the house stands against the forces of nature, against the violence of rains, floods, winds, and fire. The situation is similar in society: people develop law and order but ultimately these measures work against them. The history of mankind is: "the slaughter-bench at which the happiness of peoples, the wisdom of States, and the virtue of individuals have been victimized."[13]

Such is the history of mankind, according to Hegel. He means that the idea of freedom was a product of battles in the social jungles, where freedom was hardly a welcome guest. On the other hand, whenever happiness prevailed, history was uneventful. As a matter of fact, periods of happiness are blank pages; they are the periods of harmony. The contribution of these periods to the idea of freedom is minimal.

Whenever people feel satsified and happy, they give up struggling and their energy drops; their imagination decreases. Most energetic people are unhappy; their perception of the prevailing evil is the source of their new ideas and their attempts to broaden their possibilities to achieve, to augment, and realize their freedom.

We now have approached the problem of the dialectic of freedom which is part of Hegel's general dialectic.

The essence of any dialectic, including the Hegelian and Marxian dialectic, is the concept of the struggle of antagonistic forces. A thesis exists in unison with its antithesis. The forces are antagonistic, but the one cannot exist without the other. It would appear that there is an absolute difference between light and darkness, but in reality the existence of darkness would be impossible without light. One cannot see anything, either in absolute darkness or in absolute light. It is the same with good and evil. The existence of good presupposes the existence of evil, and *vice versa*. Without evil people the existence of the good would be senseless. Without the existence of sin the concept of reward would be unnecessary. A kingdom of heaven does not make sense without a purgatory and hell. And finally, the idea of freedom was elaborated because people were not free and did not feel free.

If the history of mankind is the history of the development of the idea of freedom, then one can say with the same justification that the history of mankind is the history of various kinds of slavery, of unfreedom. In every successive epoch forms of slavery, of unfreedom, have become more sophisticated and refined. The ideas of freedom therefore also became more developed and refined. Hegel believed that in his epoch people finally began to understand the idea of freedom and that in his philosophy of freedom the idea finally found itself. There are philosophers who argue that Hegel regarded his own system of philosophy as closed. They cannot be right. Hegel's dialectical method can never be regarded as finished. Although Hegel did not wish to predict the future, it would accord with the spirit of his dialectical method to state that in the future, gigantic struggles between the idea of freedom and the forces of unfreedom would still occur. This conflict will never be resolved. The history of the twentieth century is the best proof of how correct his dialectical approach was.

The realization of the idea of freedom, according to Hegel, as we already mentioned, is the substance of the history of mankind.

If one should wish to translate this statement into more comprehensible language, one would have to say that the highly acclaimed individual freedom is not a state or a condition enjoyed by individuals, societies, and nations. Freedom is always a process of fighting for freedom, of the struggle for its own expansion in the face of forces, which, consciously or unconsciously, oppose it vigorously. Freedom is a way of life and of struggle; it is the expansion of human possibilities and powers. It is a way of operating in order to make maximum use of an individual's talents and skills.

A man cannot find freedom, Hegel argued, in a non-societal state of nature. It would be nonsense to think that savages could be free. Hegel wrote: "The savage is lazy and is distinguished from the educated man by his brooding stupidity."[14]

When Hegel writes about savages, the word "savage" should not be interpreted in the narrow sense of the savage who lived in primitive society thousands of years ago. A savage is any person who is not educated up to the level of our civilization. In other words, a savage is any person who mixes his subjectivity with objective possibilities, his unreasonable wishful thinking with reality. This species of brooding stupidity has not yet disappeared by any means and never will.

"Slavery is in and of itself injustice, for the essence of humanity is freedom; but for this man must be mature."[15] When will man mature? According to Hegel, that will happen in a very distant future. He will mature and the forms of freedom will mature with him in an endless historical process.

Will he become happier when he becomes more educated, civilized, and mature?

One could argue that there are misfortunes and sorrows which are well known to our civilized society which were unknown to savages. Consequently it would be better for man to remain ignorant. This alleged advantage is merely negative, Hegel wrote: "While freedom is essentially positive, it is only the blessings conferred by affirmative freedom that are regarded as such in the highest grade of consciousness."[16]

This is one of the most important contributions of Hegel's philosophy of freedom, that freedom is essentially positive, that its blessings consist of affirmative activity not in isolation from society. Freedom does not consist of erecting walls around spheres of influence separating one person's sphere from that of his neighbor, as is argued in the Kantian philosophy of freedom. This is the basic difference between Kant and Hegel: Hegel insisted that one should approach the problems of freedom from the positive, affirmative point of view, not the negative.

The extent of freedom, at any stage of the historical development of society, is determined by the totality of the objective and subjective conditions, by the totality of economic and social relations, and by the consciousness of the people, their understanding, beliefs, and prejudices.

> External superiority in power can achieve no enduring results: Napoleon could not coerce Spain into freedom any more than Philip II could force Holland into slavery.[17]

This observation of Hegel either has been underestimated or forgotten; it is a key to understanding many puzzles of the political life of our day.

Let us try to penetrate this observation: The reality which determines the historical content and limits of freedom is a totality of objective and subjective elements, that is, of the economic, political, and social conditions plus the way of thinking of the people, their inclinations, their obsessions, their emotions, prejudices, their experience, and their ability to think critically, their fears and their civil courage. Economic welfare and poverty also influence popular thinking, but in various directions, for and against freedom, for progress and for conservatism, if not reaction. One could put it even more bluntly: If the people who are given a free choice in a universal election do not use common sense they will end up with a government that will not help to create the conditions required to extend the scope of freedom. If people do not use their powers of judgement to evaluate the changing material possibilities, the reality of freedom, its contents and frontiers, must be delimited and they must wait a long time for the next step in the historical process that might again foster the dialectical evolution of freedom.

Why does Hegel assert that Catholic Spain could not have been forced to be free? The reason is that the people of Spain did not understand and did not want to understand the reality of their own condition; they did not think freely and creatively because they had become accustomed to autocratic dogmas and did not feel the need for change. Every attempt to impose reform and liberty on them was doomed. At the beginning of the 19th century the people of Spain had not been enlightened, they were intellectually and morally primitive. They were not prepared to accept new ideas and institutions. The French words "liberty, equality, and fraternity" were unknown to them; the notions were unfamiliar, therefore empty and, what is worse, perhaps inimical to them. People cannot be compelled to use their minds when they refrain from thinking, or fail to do so; they will have difficulty understanding necessity, i.e., the objective conditions in which they live; they will face obstacles in attempting to accept freedom.

It was not possible to impose slavery on the Netherlands, Hegel continued. Why? Because a reformation of minds had taken place in the Netherlands; because people had come to reject the old dogmas and had started to think creatively and critically; they refused to accept what others regarded as unshakable, absolute truths.

The same observation which Hegel made might be applied to Communist countries today. All Communist countries today have authoritarian governments; the rule of the centralized party apparatus is absolute; the will of the party bosses has the force of law; the security police is omnipotent; censorship is unlimited. And yet there are differences and degrees of slavery, servility, and freedom in each of those countries. There is an obvious difference in the atmosphere of Poland from that which exists in the Soviet Union and East Germany. Polish literature, art and the press are conspicuously more creative and interesting than they are in any other Communist country. Why? *Because the social pressures, the intellectual and moral standards of the nation* do not allow authors and artists to be as dull, faceless, and corrupted as are those of their counterparts in the Soviet Union and other Communist countries. Polish intellectuals feel traditionally connected with the Enlightened West, whereas the Russians traditionally regarded the West as a hotbed of moral corruption and spiritual decline. The Poles never viewed their government as a source of inspiration. Up to the end of the 18th century when they had been free, they had favored a weak, limited government. Afterwards, when they were under Russian, German, or Austrian rule, they considered it their duty to fight the foreign occupier. This national tradition, this way of thinking, this rejection of political supremacy bordering on anarchy, the traditional abhorrence at having to collaborate, all these are reasons why Polish reality, although juridically and formally the same, is yet so different from the Russian, German, Rumanian, or Bulgarian realities.

And what is real can also be an objective necessity. When a person with the ability to choose votes for stupidity, he is not free but a brooding savage even if he be dressed in silk clothing.

It is well known that Hegel is accused of being a philosopher who extolled and praised the state. His sentence that the state is the *"Gang des Gottes in der Welt,"* incorrectly translated as the march of God in the world, is often quoted.[18] Hegel wanted to express the very simple idea with this sentence that, without the state and its law, it would not be possible to put limits to the brutal passions and deeds of violence of the people. There must be a ruler whom the people fear. Hegel did not deify the Prussian state. Every form of the state, according to Hegel, is limited in its efficiency and cannot be eternally reasonable. The best form of the state is the one which coincides with the social relations. When these relations change, and such a process is inevitable, the form of the state must change. The state which once was reasonable, becomes unreasonable and must necessarily be *"aufgehoben,"* which means that some elements will be rejected and forgotten and some elements will remain under the new relations. Every form of state, according to Hegel, is only a moment in the history of mankind. The state is necessary for the realization of freedom, but when some of its forms become hostile to freedom, then, sooner or later, they must be abolished. The state must exist, but the government in power has only relative and temporary importance.

Freedom, or necessity understood, differs in every country because the reality differs in each and therefore the process of understanding and transformation must differ as well. With every change the process of freedom gains new friends and creates new adversaries; the eternal struggle to preserve freedom continues.

Hegel's historic contribution to the theory of freedom, law, and the state can be narrowed down to the following theses: there exists an intrinsic interdependence between every stage of human civilization and the forms of freedom, law, and the state. Legal forms are necessary for the assurance and realization of freedom. They may not, however, be capriciously or arbitrarily imposed on society. When juridical norms are either too conservative or too "progressive," too far ahead in any given stage of evolution, when the law is incompatible with prevailing social conceptions of what should be done and what should be prohibited, then these laws will simply be "unreal;" they will be "ghosts," "appearances," empty pronouncements in books, but they will not be "laws in life." Hegel's dialectic can be regarded as one of those philosophies which could lead to the famous American distinction between "law in books," and "law in life."

Hegel criticized all the theories of natural rights because they proclaim certain rights in an unhistorical way. He sympathized, however, with those concepts of natural law which have a concrete content, which may be reasonable and necessary, for example, in order to counteract the "unreasonable" absolute monarchy of Louis XVI.

Once Hegel interpreted the development of the idea of freedom as being in constant evolution from more restricted to more universal forms, then the legal and political systems, which for him were concrete and historically determined reincarnations of the idea of freedom, tended to become more universalistic, more comprehensive, versatile, and many-sided.

It is true in some of his writings Hegel extolled the merits of the Prussian monarchy. He lived in that historical period. One should not, however, interpret his philosophy on the basis of selected, opportunistic utterances, but in connection with the *Weltgeist,* with the inevitable negation of everything, and with the joy which was evoked in his "old heart" (his own words), by the advent of the French July revolution, which obviously did not represent the parochialism of German nationalism, nor did it appeal to it.

Hegel's concept of the development of the idea of freedom as transcending more and more its boundaries and localisms, his concept that the new content of freedom must sooner or later be accompanied by appropriate legal norms and political institutions—all these Hegelian dialectical concepts lead towards the possibility which ultimately becomes "real," "necessary," and "reasonable"; they lead to notions of "democracy" and "rights" more universal than before. These ideas were premature some hundred and fifty years ago, although they could have played a progressive part in the political struggles of that time. In the new epoch, with its new universalistic developments—the new concepts of freedom expressed in various documents, constitutions, and declarations on human rights—these general notions of rights and liberties are in accordance with the "spirit of history," they reflect the wishes of the newly enlightened people, they are instruments which undermine the old nationalistic barriers and despotisms as well as the "unreasonable" interpretations of state sovereignty.

The above interpretation of freedom and human rights represents the new application of traditional, and Hegelian, dialectics.

Such a shift in philosophy was not foreseen, although it might have been foreseen by the founders and masters of the dialectical method. This application of the Hegelian dialectic to the new concept of human rights is a dialectical negation of the traditional concept of natural rights, albeit in accordance with the spirit of the dialectical method. It does not represent the previous "letter" or temporary "contentions" of dialectic, but its own internal logic.

The fact that Hegel's dialectical philosophy of law and politics can lead toward the concept of universal human rights, as understood at the end of this century, is proof that in this century "all roads lead to Rome," and "Rome" in our century are the historically determined notions of freedom, tolerance and their juridical expression, human rights.

c. Marx: Freedom and the Social Structure

What Marx wrote about freedom might be termed an *Auf-*

hebung of Hegel's philosophy. He affirmed, continued, and negated Hegel's philosophy. Marx was particularly impressed by Hegel's view that freedom has a concrete content and form at every stage of history. Marx understood, as Hegel did, that limitations on freedom were necessary in all previous societies. The most important stages in human development, primitive society, feudalism, and capitalism, he regarded as stages in the development of exploitation, oppression, and of free human activity within society. These were not, however, as Hegel implies, different stages in the development of the idea of freedom, because Marx absolutely rejected absolute ideas. For Marx the ideas of freedom developed according to the evolution of civilization, of the economic bases and political institutions which constitute the essential parts of superstructures of all societies.

All this notwithstanding, Marx and Engels still wrote that it was Hegel who made the greatest contribution to the philosophy of freedom because he had established that freedom was necessity understood. They firmly believed that anyone who disregarded Hegel's philosophy of freedom would fall into the errors of previous times and then would be obliged to start from the beginning. They reiterated that neither scientific socialism nor modern times could be grasped without a knowledge of Hegel.

In undertaking an analysis of Marx's theory of freedom, we must define his particular contributions which went beyond Hegel's philosophy. It is also well to distinguish between Marx's philosophy of freedom and the primitive theories now being promulgated by "Marxists" who unceremoniously falsify Marx's theory for their own advantage.

Marx claimed that philosophy, political theory, and practice should be closely interconnected; he proclaimed that it is not enough for a philosopher to explain the world but that he should truly seek to change it. There is an obvious gulf between Marx's predictions concerning the future Communist state and the practical application of his theories in the 20th century.

It is significant that the first signed political and philosophical article published by Marx concerned the problem of censorship. He never disowned the points he raised in it. They cannot be regarded as products of youthful romanticism as Stalinists and neo-Stalinists usually declare, for they were many times repeated by the "adult" Marx.

According to Marx, no government should ever impose restrictions on freedom of thought and publication. The democratic freedoms of conscience, speech, and publication should not be restricted under any circumstances. Every restriction, every censorship, is the cry of a "dirty conscience," according to Marx. Needless to say, these words have never been quoted in Communist countries and several attempts to remind people of them in the Communist bloc were requited with reprisals against such rash "heretics."

In a speech in his own defense, when he was tried for publishing articles in the *Neue Rheinische Zeitung,* Marx said: "It is the function of the press to be the public watchdog, the tireless denouncer of the rulers, the omnipresent eye, the omnipresent mouth of the spirit of the people that jealously guards its freedom."[19]

He concluded his speech with these words: ". . . once and for all it is the duty of the press to speak up for those oppressed in its immediate vicinity . . . It does not suffice to fight general conditions and the higher authorities. The press must decide to enter the lists against *this* particular gendarme, *this* procurator, *this* district administrator."[20]

Marx expressed these ideas in March 1849, one year after publication of the *Communist Manifesto.* Here the "mature" Marx speaks, not a "young" Marx. He regarded freedom of the press as the guarantor and defender of freedom in general. The press should be the "public watchdog" and the "tireless denouncer" of rulers. The press should defend the weak against the oppression of higher authorities and should protect those within its purview.

Could Marx have foreseen that freedom of the press would be so drastically curtailed after the socialist revolution? He characterized socialist society, that is, society in the first stage of Communism, as a society which would bear all the afflictions, all the "dirt" of the past. In order to clean out this "dirt," and in order to assure the growth of freedom, civil liberties, free press and freedom of assembly must be expanded, he insisted.

Whatever Marx's vision of the dictatorship of the proletariat might have been, one thing seems certain: He never anticipated that such a system would be accompanied by the triumph of censorship and the abolition of the civil liberties enjoyed under parliamentary democracies. There is nothing to indicate that Marx and Engels believed that the future state would be a centralized, despotic bureaucracy. On the contrary, in analyzing the Paris Commune of 1871, Marx stressed that under that system every official had been freely elected by the people and could have been recalled at any time:

> The commune ... must ... safeguard itself against its own deputies and officials, by declaring them all, without exception, subject to recall at any moment.[21]

Marx wrote that the Commune had to protect itself against its own servants; the newly acquired freedoms had to be defended against their own defenders and the Commune therefore made use of two "infallible" means:

> In the first place, it filled all posts—administrative, judicial and educational—by election on the basis of universal suffrage of all concerned, subject to the right of recall at any time by the same electors. And, in the second place, all officials, high or low, were paid only wages received by other workers... In this way an effective barrier to place-hunting and careerism was set up ...[22]

Unfortunately, the two devices which Marx and Engels regarded as "infallible" were of doubtful value. Neither has ever been employed in any Communist country for long. Although we have no direct evidence to judge their efficacy, we have every reason to believe that had these devices ever been consistently tried in Communist countries, they would not have effectively protected the people against the cancer of a centralized bureaucracy.

It is impossible in any modern state with millions of inhabitants to fill the thousands of administrative, judicial, legislative, economic, and even educational posts by election. Such an election would be a farce because no one could conceivably be familiar with so many candidates. Instant recall is even more likely to lead to the same dead end as recall which is now part of the constitutions of many western states. Lenin did impose the "Party-maximum" pay for officials at the central level and built up his dictatorship upon the power-seeking officials who served him at modest salaries. Pay is not the only value that is sought by place-hunters and careerists, for "not by bread alone . . ."

The socialist revolution did not take place in any highly developed European industrial countries, as Marx and Engels predicted; it did not take place in Germany where the workers had a better understanding of social theory; instead, it succeeded in a country whose majority was illiterate and did not even understand the word theory. Hegelian freedom for them was meaningless.

The predictions of Marx and Engels concerning freedom could therefore not become a reality in Eastern Europe and in Asia, even had their theory been otherwise appropriate.

The real attitude of Marx and Engels toward political freedom is expressed in their prediction that the Communist state would wither away, and not, as Stalin and his successors declared, many generations after the Communist revolution i.e. after the complete Communist victory all over the world. According to Marx and Engels this process was to start immediately after the socialist revolution. The first day of the dictatorship of the proletariat was to be the first day of the withering away of the state. Each day, more and more of the functions of the state would be eliminated, and day by day the interference by the state authorities would narrow. Ultimately all state's functions and institutions would be sent, as Engels wrote, to the museum of prehistoric mankind.

The state exists, Marx wrote, solely to limit the freedom of individuals; that is its purpose. When it withers away, individual freedom is won. It is one of the greatest ironies of history that the most despotic totalitarian states were built in the name of Marx, who so carefully developed a theory of the withering away of the state.

There is no question that Marx regarded all the democratic liberties proclaimed in Western constitutions and enjoyed by the nations under parliamentary regimes to be beyond any need of justification. The withering away of the state, for Marx, contains no restrictions upon individual liberties, but rather their maximum expansion. With the withering away of the state, the areas free of state interference must inevitably increase. In these political circumstances, truly human freedom would be realized.

An analysis of political freedom is not the same as an analysis of the philosophical notion of freedom. Let us therefore go deeper into the philosophical notion of freedom. In *Anti-Duehring*, which was written by Engels but corrected by Marx, the following elaboration of Hegel's concept of freedom, and especially the appreciation of necessity, was developed:

> Freedom does not consist in the dream of independence of natural laws, but in the knowledge of these laws, and in the possibility this gives of systematically making them work towards a definite end ... Freedom of the will therefore means nothing but the capacity to make decisions with the real knowledge of the subject. Therefore the freer a man's judgment is in relation to a definite question, with so much the greater necessity is the content of his judgment determined ... Freedom therefore consists in the control over ourselves and over external nature which is founded on knowledge of natural necessity ... The first men who separated themselves from the animal kingdom were in all essentials as unfree as the animals themselves, but each step forward in civilization was a step toward freedom.[23]

This is a clear continuation of Hegel's dialectic of freedom, of freedom's being a result of the interdependence of objective and subjective elements. An ignorant person cannot be free because judgment and choice based on ignorance are not free. Ignoramuses usually are self-confident, make their own decisions quickly and freely; they live in a world of their own illusions, but they are not free. In order truly to be free one must know reality and by knowledge exercise control over it. To be free, a person must live in a society in which the results of activity conform with reasonable expectations. To be free, a person must live under circumstances which allow personal effort to bring forth desired effects.

Marx and Engels believed that the ideal of individual freedom would only be attained in a society without a state and without a government, without private property, and without wars. Such is the Marxian vision of the kingdom of freedom, described by his adversaries as utopian, and by Marx himself as a scientific prediction of the future.

> Men's own social organization which has hitherto stood in opposition to them . . . will then become the voluntary act of men themselves. The objective, external forces which have hitherto dominated history, will then pass under the control of men themselves. It is only from this point that men, with full consciousness, will fashion their own history; it is only from this point that the social causes set in motion by man will have, predominantly and in constantly increasing measure, the effects willed by man. It is humanity's leap from the realm of necessity into the realm of freedom.[24]

As we see, for Hegel and Marx freedom is not static. A free man is not passive; he is a social being continually overcoming objective and subjective difficulties along the path of his development. Man is not born free; he may become free. Freedom does not lie in a separation from society; man is not a monad living in a cell separate from all others; he can realize and extend his power over external circumstances only in cooperation with other free people. Freedom is not a subjective feeling, as St. Augustine would have it; freedom is a result of the combination of subjective and objective elements. Man cannot be liberated by a mechanical transfer from the country of bondage to the kingdom of freedom. Mere institutional, social, and economic changes by themselves cannot truly liberate people. Prior to and during liberation, the minds of the people must be reformed and adjusted to the new circumstances in which they can make their own decisions and choices with maximum consciousness.

Hegel wrote that man used the forces of nature (water, fire, gravity) in order to build shelters against the ravages of the forces of nature. Marx and Engels wrote that man must use the social forces and evolutionary tendencies to serve as the material with which to build a society in which an individual can be the master of his own destiny instead of being like a dice thrown about by blind, inscrutable forces.

The man of the future, the free man, will be educated, civilized, and disciplined. He will voluntarily observe the moral norms and accepted rules of social behavior. He will not regard them as a burden, they will be self evident for him. They will not restrict freedom but be its precondition. In this society, man will be able to develop all his natural talents and reasonable inclinations. Not everyone will have the talent of a Raphael or a Leonardo da Vinci, Marx observed, but everyone possessing such a genius will be given the opportunity to develop it for his own and the public's benefit.

The gist of Marx's considerations on freedom is:

> In Communist society, where no one has any exclusive sphere of activity, but each can be accomplished in any branch he wishes, production as a whole is regulated by society, thus making it possible for me to do one thing today and another tomorrow, to hunt in the morning, fish in the afternoon, rear cattle in the evening, criticize after dinner, in accordance with my inclination, without ever becoming hunter, fisherman, shepherd or critic.[25]

Marx's prediction that division of labor will disappear in the future society is one of the weakest elements of his theory; it is an obvious utopian wish.

On the other hand, one aspect of this theory should not be overlooked: in order to develop his personality a truly free human being should be given more opportunities to use fully *all* his latent talents and dormant interests. Marx interpreted social freedom as a liberation of the individual. That individual will be conscious of social needs, he will understand that he must work for society, but not in the sense of self-deprivation or asceticism. The liberated individual will nevertheless remain an individualist and a hedonist.

An individual in the future Communist society will on the one hand be disciplined; on the other, however, he will resemble the "anarchistic" intellectual. His way of life will constantly change, together with his profession and his artistic tastes. He will lose private property, but he will have the right to satisfy his reasonable personal drives and desires.

* * *

Hegel ridiculed Kant's philosophy of pure reason. He compared this kind of knowledge with that of persons who wish to learn how to swim without entering the water. Hegel wrote that if no one can know the thing-in-itself, as Kant argued, then one cannot even be sure that the thing-in-itself exists. He referred with contempt to those who admire Kant for having taught the art of philosophizing, but not philosophy. For Hegel, that is tantamount to teaching carpentry without teaching how to make a table, or a chair, or a door.

And still, Hegel is a direct continuator of Kant's grand notion of freedom. Hegel's point of departure is a strange amalgam of Kant's *a priori* ideas: freedom, infinity, and God. Hegel's Idea of Eternal Freedom is abstract, and it is a God-creator. Man becomes more and more enlightened according to Kant; he becomes more and more critical, outgrowing the age of nonentity, of tutelage, and eventually reaches a clearer understanding of what freedom means. The horizons of understanding incessantly broaden, Kant wrote.

How similar, and yet how different, Hegel sounds when he speaks of the history of the Idea of Freedom (which he identified with the Absolute Idea). It is the authentic history of mankind and conversely, the history of mankind is the history of the transformation of the Idea of Freedom. This is so because the Absolute Idea is the demiurge of history.

It was Kant who prepared the way for the Pure Idea of Freedom in Hegel's philosophy.

The supersensuous world being the fountainhead of the idea of freedom is one of Kant's philosophical foundation stones. This notion was incorporated in Hegel's writings and connected with his ideas on dialectical contradictions. The abstract idea of freedom thus became alive and concrete. Hegel ultimately forgot that his idea of freedom once was an abstract notion, and whenever he analyzed it, he did what a true historian should do: he analyzed the whole economic, political, and cultural situation of a given society. The enlightened reader should simply ignore Hegel's assumptive use of the idea of freedom and concentrate on his superb analysis of how societies struggle each in their own circumstances and the manner in which he affirms or denies the concrete freedom of historically real individuals.

In this way Hegel prepared the ground for Marx's sociological notion of freedom and simultaneously became a contributor to Marx's return to Kant.

Marx began his considerations on freedom with an analysis developed by Hegel: The notion of freedom has a different meaning in every different social epoch. Hegel asserted that the evolution of the idea of freedom was the cause of changing social and political relations; according to Marx the ideas of freedom are determined by those relations, by the "real," "material" basis of those relations.

As Marx himself declared, he turned Hegel's idealistic dialectic upside down and thereby made the idea of freedom come up feet first.

According to Hegel the idea of freedom went through four basic periods: oriental despotism, the Greek and Roman states, Christianity, and the German societies. According to Marx the ideas of freedom were different under each of these socio-economic systems: primitive communism, slavery, feudalism, capitalism, and once again the future communist society. According to Marx there were two basic philosophies of freedom under every society based on exploitation: that of the oppressed exploited masses and that of the exploiters. In the future communist society, lacking class antagonisms and political oppression, when the state and law will wither away, the freedom of each individual will be compatible with the freedom of all—and this is the Kantian "powerless" (Engels) ideal. There will be no law, Marx continued, meaning that there will be no external restrictions or commands; they will be replaced by the conscious discipline of highly educated, enlightened, self-disciplined, and unselfish members of the communist society. These members will govern themselves, ultimately expressing the Kantian ideal of self-legislation (not Hegel's *boese Wirklichkeit*).

Communist society will realize the Kantian ideals as forecast by "scientific communism." Kant, however, doubted that his optimum state of self-legislation could be attained. Marx and Engels had no doubts. For them such a future was not a speculative ideal of pure reason, but the inevitable stage which society must reach in accordance with the "iron" laws of its development. Marx and Engels were more Kantian than Kant himself.

What about the Hegelian dialectical contradictions which are the soul of the social sciences and social development? They will become non-political, Marx asserted; they will cease to be poisonous and vicious because the free non-antagonistic society can easily overcome them. It would appear that the Hegelian concept that freedom is a process of self-realization and always is a state of strife for self-preservation and expansion will also find its place in the "museum of antiquity" next to the state, law, and religion.

Hegel's theory of freedom acted as an intermediary between Kant and Marx, and between Marx and Kant.

d. Dewey's Pragmatic View of Freedom

In his essay, "Philosophies of Freedom," Dewey criticized the notion of freedom which, he thought, prevailed in the West.

According to this theory, Dewey wrote, freedom consists in having the opportunity of choice. Without freedom of choice there would be no basis for praise or blame, no reward or punishment, no responsibility or liability. This assertion is often regarded as the crux of freedom although it is only the beginning of the problem, Dewey pointed out.

A man nevertheless, Dewey argued—and here appears a fundamental link with Hegel's philosophy—is always a human being in the concrete and his so-called free will is not an unmotivated force. On the contrary. The will is an amalgam of habits, desires, and purposes determined by society and by historical development.

Man, Dewey wrote, is susceptible and sensitive; he undergoes varied and opposing experiences. Innumerable factors influence his preferences, diversify his behavior, and are involved in choice as a mode of freedom. When the author of a decision comprehends more of the factors involved, he also becomes more hesitant.[26]

"Alternative choice," Dewey wrote, "in the human and generic sense, presents itself as one preference among and out of preferences;" choice is "the formation of a new preference out of a conflict of preferences."[27] Choice, Dewey concluded, is the selectivity of behavior.

An intelligent choice on the part of an individual reflects his forecast of the consequences of acting upon the various competing preferences; it reflects the anticipation of the results of acting one way or another.

Once Dewey connected the problem of choice with the question of future activity and participation, he shifted his attention from thought to practicality, from subjectivity to objectivity, from ideas to effects, from thinking to acting.

He wrote: "Freedom is the power to act in accordance with choice. It is actual ability to carry desire and purpose into operation, to execute choices when they are made."[28]

It might seem that in his way Dewey reached the Hobbesian conclusion that freedom is a lack of obstacles, of impediments. But that is misleading.

Institutions and laws, Dewey argued, can constitute obstructions preventing the free execution of one's choices. These obstacles are called oppression. The struggles for freedom, the endless battles for it, have never been battles for freedom of choice, but for freedom of *operation* and *execution* of choice. A freedom which is worth fighting for can be attained by the abolition of impediments which traditionally were the oppressive measures of government, its laws.

The process of the abolition of oppression is a process of liberation, of achieving "rights."

The desire for this type of freedom—the freedom to act according to one's choice—caused revolutions and social upheavals, the overthrowing of dynasties and regimes. This is the freedom which "supplies the measure of human progress in freedom."[29]

Let us once more observe the influence of Hegel's philosophy in the above: freedom is interpreted as a process. History for Hegel is the evolution of the idea of freedom; for Dewey it is "human progress in freedom." For both philosophers freedom takes on various forms; it embraces multiple contents; it must overcome endless obstructions that arise.

In the eighteenth and nineteenth centuries the concept of freedom, as initiated by John Locke, converged in the ideas of liberalism, Dewey wrote. According to the economic and political ideas of *laissez-faire,* every positive action of the government must be oppressive; "hands off," therefore was the main slogan of the liberals. Freedom, by its very existence, they believed, would solve all economic and social problems.

Dewey thoroughly knew the historical contribution of liberalism to human progress in every sphere of life, but he also understood its political, social, and philosophical limitations.

Only some of the social strata were liberated, not all of humanity. Liberal ideas helped the new industrial class which "actually imposed new burdens and subjected to new modes of oppression the mass of individuals who did not have a privileged social status,"[30] according to Dewey. This assessment of liberalism led Dewey to his own concept of individualism.

"The common criticism (from the left and right[31]—M.M.) is that the liberal school was too 'individualistic'; it would be equally pertinent to say that it was not 'individualistic' enough. Its philosophy was such that it assisted the emancipation of individuals having a privileged antecedent status, but promoted no general liberation of all individuals."[32]

It is absurd to suppose, as liberals do, that everyone has the same opportunities irrespective of differences in education, social environment and property status. Social and economic choice "depends upon positive and constructive changes in social arrangements."[33]

Dewey never elaborated on the specific set of social arrangements which may be necessary to secure freedom as power in action. He stressed, however, that it was the government that should take the initiative to remove all kinds of obstacles, especially economic, where self-expression "of a few may impede, although manifested in strict accordance with law, self-expression of others."[34] Dewey many times expressed that unrestricted economic freedom for a few becomes an impediment to the freedom of others. Therefore, in the 20th century, inactivity of the state is harmful for freedom. What is needed is a positive, affirmative action by the government to create the necessary social conditions in which an individual can operate according to his free choice.

The problem of choice arises here once more. Should every choice be socially accepted as a precondition for freedom in action?

The intrinsic connection, Dewey wrote, which exists between freedom of choice and freedom of action, depends on an *intelligent* choice. It must be a choice which is able to generate actions and powers which are desired by us, which affect or create the causes of expected and desired effects.

And here Dewey drew from the "Hegelian deposit" all the conclusions which fit his philosophy:

A choice which intelligently manifests individuality enlarges the range of action, and this enlargement in turn confers upon our desires greater insight and foresight, and makes choice more intelligent. There is a circle, but an enlarging circle, or if you please, a widening spiral.[35]

Hegel wrote that freedom is "comprehended necessity"; Dewey wrote that freedom depends on intelligent choice.

Hegel wrote that history, being the evolution of the idea of freedom, develops as a spiral; Dewey asserted the same: an intelligent choice enlarges our sphere of action, and then the new, greater experience opens wider possibilities of an even more intelligent choice and therewith the *spiral* of freedom widens.

Freedom is in something which "comes to be"; it is "in consequences, rather than in antecedents;" we are free not in a static but in a dynamic sense; we are free "as far as we are becoming different from what we have been."[36]

Let us now summarize the main theses of this section.

Both Marx and Dewey rejected the Hegelian notion of freedom as an absolute idea. But they adopted Hegel's view that freedom always has concrete content and form determined by the given state of human development.

Both Marx and Dewey interpreted freedom as a dynamic interplay of epistemological and ontological conditions. Both agreed with Hegel that freedom is understood necessity, but their conclusions went in different directions. Marx tried to find what is necessary and concluded that a communist society is a historical necessity which should be understood accordingly. Dewey did not search for predictions of the future along these lines; he favored intelligent choice in order to enable individuals to achieve pragmatic, operational, successes.

Hegel wanted to use the centralized state power against feudal stratification, which he regarded the main impediment to freedom. In this way he reached his famous conclusion that the state is a "kingdom of freedom," a conclusion which has often been misinterpreted. Marx radically rejected any defense of the state, writing that states exist in order to restrict freedom. State power, therefore, should be limited and diminished to the point of eliminating it altogether. This sounds like a paradox; in fact, however, Marx moved from Hegel towards liberalism. Dewey, in contrast, accepted Hegel's idea that the state should combat all impediments on the road to freedom. Such obstacles in the twentieth century are created by the powerful business corporations. The paradox here is that Dewey was more Hegelian and more anti-liberal than Marx. The state is a realm of freedom for Hegel, but for Dewey it is an instrument to gain freedom.

It is Hegel, nevertheless, who is the wellspring from which both Marx and Dewey began their separate roads in modern times. After initially parting company, they again met in the sense that they both fostered the so-called new individualism (Dewey) and opposed traditional liberal individualism, this time in the Kantian and Hegelian spirit. After this new confluence on the higher level of the Hegelian spiral, their ways parted once more, still drawing from the font of the master.

What Dewey wrote about the state should be applied to law and to the questions of juridical rights.

In 1929, John Dewey wrote in his *Individualism, Old and New:*

> We may then say that the United States has steadily moved from earlier pioneer individualism to a condition of dominant corporateness . . . Associations tightly or loosely organized more and more define the opportunities, the choices and the actions of individuals[37] . . . It was stated at a recent convention of bankers that eighty percent of the capitalization of all the banks of the country is now in the hands of twelve financial concerns.[38]

The remedy against this specific threat to freedom according to him is an active government. Provisions of law alone are not sufficient because the movement toward mergers is too vast, complex, and powerful. The Sherman Anti-Trust Act, Dewey wrote, is no barrier against trusts: "Aside from direct evasions of laws, there are many legal methods of carrying the movement forward."[39]

What is required to change this situation? "The political control of the future to be effective must take a positive instead of a negative form,"[40] Dewey wrote.

This is Dewey's main concept in the sphere of the theory of law and the state: laws are necessary but insufficient to save and to foster freedom; they should not only "protect," but also actively promote desired results.

Law, according to Dewey, can serve as a means to an end.[41] That end should be freedom. As political, economic, and social conditions change, laws must also change. Our civilization, culture, and mutual interdependence are becoming more and more universal. That is one of Dewey's most important observations, originally made in the 1920s and reaffirmed many times. It is therefore necessary that reasonable laws and rights also must become more and more universal and more humane in order to achieve the ends which more and more become universal, embracing all humanity.[42] The democratic rights of individuals guaranteed by republican systems all over the world are the necessary, although ponderous and difficult,[43] means which promote progress on the road to humanism. Progress must take place on the national and on the international scale.

THE EVOLUTION OF TOLERANCE

1. The First Battles: Religious Tolerance

The Roman Emperor Constantine granted official toleration of Christianity in 313. During the next century the new
religion became the official religion of the Roman Empire and
religious persecutions against rivals began. Arians and Dona-
tists were the first victims of the persecutions instituted by the
secular authorities, at the urging and with the blessing of the
Church.

In matters of conscience and religion the ancient Romans
were basically tolerant. They were prepared to allow any god
and religion provided that the believers respected the laws of the
empire. The Christians started to change this pattern. No wonder the senator, Symmachus, criticized the decision to give a
monopoly of truth and faith to the Christians with the famous
words reflecting the old civilization: *One cannot attain truth
using merely one path.*

Since the day these words were pronounced in the Roman
senate, in 384, discussions concerning tolerance symbolically
focused on the problem of whether more than one path can lead
to truth.

*** *** ***

The problem of the separation of State and Church became
historically the first, most important topic to give an impetus to
the campaign for tolerance in the Western world. In the West,
religious tolerance became the initial focus around which arguments for and against tolerance evolved.

Religious intolerance and persecution always come from
social and political causes. The hierarchical feudal system was

so oppressive that the lower classes—especially the peasants and the plebeians in the towns—had many good causes to rebel against their masters. But the specific reason for intolerance which aggravated the situation was a symbiosis between the Church and State. The merger between these two institutions transformed religion into the official ideology of the feudal system. Therefore, any opposition against the existing economic and social relations took on the form of religious heresy. Certain social and political postulates were expressed in religious formulas.

In the first thousand years after the emergence of Christianity and its transformation into the dominant religion in Europe substantial changes took place in the organization of the Catholic church. A loose network of small Christian communities became a universal organization with a central government. This organization was built on the principles of hierarchy and finally the Bishop of Rome became its undisputed chief.

Pope Gregory VII was for a long time credited with a short treatise under the title, *Dictatus Papae.* Although it is not his original work, nevertheless it reflected the prevailing mood in Rome and in the Church. *Dictatus Papae* is an expression of the dominance of the Pope in the Church and his claims that the ecclesiastical power is superior to the secular. *Dictatus Papae* drew political conclusions from the thesis that the Roman Catholic Church was founded by God himself and the Bishop of Rome, or Pope, was the successor of Jesus Christ and St. Peter. As successor and deputy of Christ, the Pope may depose and reinstate bishops; his legates take precedence in any council, before all other members. The Pope may depose emperors and he has the right to absolve the subjects of unjust rulers from their oath of allegiance. He cannot be judged by anybody, but he can proclaim as non-Catholic those who disagree with the Roman Church. And finally, he stated that the Roman Church had never, nor ever would err to all eternity.

The last statement is a precursor to the decision of the first Vatican Council, 1870, that the Pope is infallible in questions of faith. In the *Dictatus Papae* this privilege was reserved generally for the Roman Church. But taking into account the special position reserved for the Pope, one could assume that the road from *Dictatus Papae* to the decision of the first Vatican Council was not too long, although it took almost nine centuries to cover it.

In a letter to Henry IV, Pope Gregory VII presented a more detailed theological justification for his claim to supreme power. He especially referred to the words of Jesus Christ who ordered Peter, "Feed my sheep." (*John* 21, 15-17). He also referred to the words that Peter was given the keys to the Kingdom of Heaven and the assurance that whatsoever Peter shall bind or lose upon Earth shall be bound or lost also in Heaven. And finally, he pointed out the words of Christ that whoever would hear the Apostles would hear the Lord himself, and whoever would scorn them, scorns God. Whoever enters through the door kept by Peter, will be saved and "shall find pasture."

From all these quotations the conclusion was drawn that the Roman Bishop had a superior power given to him directly by Jesus. In this way the theological foundations for the Papal demands for acceptance of the Pope's supreme power not only in spiritual but also in political matters were laid down.

Pope Innocent III compared Papal authority to the sun and the authority of the Emperor to the moon. God created both lights, but of course the rule of the day is more important than rule of the night; the rule over souls is more important than rule over bodies. The moon gets its light from the sun, just as the soul should control the mortal body.

In this way not only the foundations of the papal superiority over secular government were laid but the basic principles of intolerance in religious and political matters also were expressed: the Church usurped the right to interfere in all political, civil, and private affairs under the pretext of guarding religion, truth, and morality.

* * *

St. Augustine started to develop arguments against religious tolerance long before the Middle Ages. In his writings one can detect the most important reasoning used against intellectual freedom in the following centuries. St. Augustine presented a melange of arguments mixing the interpretation of Holy Scripture with logical secular reasoning. It is impossible to untangle theology from philosophy in his writings.

St. Augustine's main thesis is based on a peculiar interpretation of a story told by Luke (XI, 15-23):

> A master ordered his servants to go to bring his invited guests to supper. The servants did what they were ordered, but because some of those invited refused to come, there was still room for more guests. "And the Lord said unto the servant, go out into the highways and hedges, and compel *them* to come in, that my house may be filled." (*Luke,* XIV 23)

This phrase, *compelle intrare*—compel them to come in—became ominous in the history of the struggles between ideas of freedom and tolerance against intolerance and persecution. St. Augustine argued that heresy, being a deviation from the officially promulgated dogma or doctrine, is a dangerous corruption for a soul and it is the duty of the state and church to save an individual from eternal damnation. If heretics do not want to come in—they should be compelled. Error should not be tolerated because nothing, including death, can be worse for the soul. Souls should not enjoy *libertas erroris* (freedom to err).

There should be no doubt that the state should use the sword in order to convert sinners. "For they bear not the sword in vain; they are the ministers of God to execute wrath upon those that do evil."[1]

Sinners indeed persecute the Catholic church, argued St. Augustine, therefore the Church has a right to defend itself by correcting their errors.

Using traditional Greek and Jewish philosophy concerning the motives (or intentions) of actions, St. Augustine tried to prove that persecution and oppression are not objectionable in themselves since everything depends on the motives of the persecutor. When Pharaoh oppressed the Jews, that was bad; when Moses punished the same people, that was good because they were guilty of impiety. Moses did it for the welfare of the people; his motive was love. Oppression which is caused by hatred which seeks to harm, should be condemned, but oppression caused by love, which seeks to heal, should be praised. It is "the dissimilarity of the causes (that) makes the real difference."[2]

It is right, according to St. Augustine, to deliver a sinner to the government for punishment. It is better to destroy flesh in order to save a soul than let a man go to eternal hell for heresy.

> Let us learn, my brother, in actions which are similar to distinguish the intentions of the agents; and let us not, shutting our eyes, deal in groundless reproaches, and accuse those who seek men's welfare as if they did them wrong. In like manner, when the same apostle says that he had delivered certain persons unto Satan, that they might learn not to blaspheme, did he render to these men evil for evil, or did he not rather esteem it a good work to correct evil men by means of the evil one?[3]

It is notable that St. Augustine regarded persecution as a means which was evil in itself, but he thought that it was right to use such means in order to achieve a good end. In this way the famous principle, the end justifies the means, was introduced into Christian theology and therefore one should distinguish between *just* and *unjust persecution.*

St. Augustine introduced two more principles into his reasoning praising persecution of the wrong and "the administration of discipline."

He believed that it was advisable and lawful to denounce those who were heretics or apostates to the state. It seems that the person to whom he wrote had some doubts concerning the morality of such behavior. St. Augustine tried to persuade him that if he regarded it lawful to petition the Emperor in order to recover his property, he should not hesitate to ask the Emperor to punish a "more heinous crime."[4]

The next principle is even more extreme and objectionable from our point of view. St. Augustine recommended that the property of those convicted of schism and obstinacy should be confiscated. In the period of the Inquisition, his advice was followed thereby enriching both the treasury of the government and of the denouncer. All absolutistic, police, and totalitarian states use this bounty approach to encourage denunciations and keep people in fear.

The salvation of souls is so important, according to St. Augustine, that all means are justified to achieve this end. It is justified to drive people, by fear of punishment or pain, to worship God and accept his teaching. Of course it would be better, added St. Augustine, if a man could be induced to worship by persuasion; however if these methods do not work properly and quickly, it is better first, to be compelled by fear and pain, and afterwards to accept voluntarily what was imposed. After all, the scripture says that there should be one flock and one shepherd (*John* XI, 16). And it would be an act of love that "we should take the utmost pains we can to correct the erring ones themselves"[5]; it is right to use the rod to return a lost sheep back to the herd.

St. Augustine did not distinguish between a criminal action and a "deviation" from the official way of thinking in questions of faith. His comparison between "physical" and "intellectual" served to justify the conception that the government can and should prosecute those who were pronounced heretics or apostates by the Church.

St. Thomas Aquinas developed the comparison between papal and royal power and soul and body. He argued that God is the governor of the Universe whereas Princes and Kings rule over only limited territory and population. Every king must realize that as the soul rules over the body, so God governs the universe. In this capacity he should help to attain the object of every human life, which is virtue. This end can be achieved only in communion with God. The forms of this communion can be determined and supervised by the Roman pontiff. "For those who are concerned with the subordinate ends of life must be subject to him who is concerned with the supreme end and be directed by his command."[6]

St. Thomas introduced into political philosophy a principle which has been especially important for exploring the problem of freedom and tolerance. He declared that the end of life should not be the exclusive domain of an individual because it is a concern of the higher authorities as well: of the state and of the church.

In the following centuries, after the superiority of the church had been shaken and rejected in favor of the sovereign national state, this principle of St. Thomas Aquinas was transformed, but not rejected. The governments, especially in modern absolutistic, despotic, and totalitarian states, also claim the right to determine the final and supreme ends of each individual's life.

Indeed, every philosophy of tolerance and freedom must be based on the principle that determination of the purposes or ends of a person's life should be the exclusive right and domain of each individual. Everyone has the right to decide for himself what constitutes his own happiness. Happiness is strictly subjective, varying from time to time, from place to place, and from person to person. What makes a person happy cannot be dictated by outsiders. Once the State or the Church claims a right to impose certain rules which must be observed in order to attain individual happiness or any other "supreme end," the use of terroristic measures becomes inevitable.

Religious and political tolerance are indispensable means in order to secure individual happiness, but they are not means only. The relationship and interdependence between freedom, tolerance, and individual happiness are so intertwined that both freedom and tolerance must be regarded as ends in themselves.

The Pope's claim that his authority was superior to that of governments was rejected by the Protestant reformers, but they never questioned that there was a close interdependence between government and spiritual power. The ideal of Martin Luther was the biblical King David, who was at the same time the highest priest and the king. In his later dealings with the secular powers and in his writings, Luther was inclined to subordinate his ministers to the prince, provided that the latter continued to interpret Holy Scripture according to Luther's theological teaching. In this way, the principle *cuius regio ejus religio* was elaborated. Carrying this maxim out was even more bloody sometimes than that of the *Dictatus Papae*.

At any rate, the Protestant principle was basically intolerant because it justified the interference of rulers into the sphere of human conscience and beliefs.

Religious and political tolerance starts with the conviction which was expressed by Frederick I of Denmark that he wants to be a king over the lives and property of his subjects, not over their souls. The same idea was expressed in the 16th century by the Polish kings, Sigmund II and Stephan Batory. These opinions of the Polish kings were a reflection and a confirmation of the great traditions of Polish tolerance during Poland's Golden Age.

* * *

Starting with the writings of St. Augustine, the Catholic Church for a thousand years elaborated a philosophy of intolerance which represents a consistent, logical system of arguments against tolerance. Christian theologians constructed this system for ten centuries with various arguments emerging at various times and in various circumstances.

The point of departure of the system of intolerance as it finally developed was original sin. According to this doctrine human nature was depraved and even after the redemption it did not become perfect. Once human nature is tainted, it must be inclined to commit wrong. People were endowed by the Creator with free will. With free will any individual makes his own choices which can either be good or bad, according to God's will and teachings, or against them. Once human nature is considered even partially depraved (the question of the extent of depravity and redemption, and their consequences, are a subject of endless theological discussions with many participants losing their lives, being victims either of Catholic or Protestant persecution), there are good reasons to suppose that various individuals will choose evil and falsehood instead of good and truth. Such decisions can endanger not only their own happiness (theologically interpreted, of course) and salvation, but also can undermine social and political life and thwart the magisterial function of the Church. Therefore, it is not sufficient to teach and to admonish the people, they should also be prevented from endangering their personal well being and the social order. The only question is what measures and means should be used in order to prevent individuals from harming themselves. St. Augustine, as we have said, introduced the concept that one should literally apply the parable from the Holy Scripture and "compel them to enter." In this way, they would be protected from error and have a chance to fulfill their obligation to truth.

All theologians of intolerance and the Inquisition assumed that every human being has a special obligation to pursue truth. In this connection they also used another parable from the Holy Scripture concerning the tares and the wheat. According to St. Matthew (Ch. XIII, 24-30), a man sowed good seed in his field. While he was sleeping, an enemy came and sowed tares (weeds) among the wheat. When the servants noticed tares "when the blade was sprung up" they asked the owner of the field what they should do. The sower answered, ". . . lest while ye gather up the tares, ye root up also the wheat with them. Let both grow together until the harvest; and in the time of harvest I will say to the reapers, gather ye together first the tares, and bind them in bundles to burn them: but gather the wheat unto my barn." (*Matt.* XII, 29-30) The proponents of the Inquisition stressed the recommendation that tares should be bound in bundles and burned, which in practical effect meant that heretics should be separated from the "good seed" and die by burning at the stake.

Other interpretations are also possible and those presented by the opponents of the Inquisition for the sake of tolerance are an example (see below and the chapter on the Polish tradition of freedom and tolerance).

St. Thomas Aquinas added a specific argument in favor of persecution of erroneous interpreters of Holy Scripture. He argued that if we all agree that a counterfeiter of money should be punished and eventually executed, we should also hold that it is a more serious crime to pervert or forge the faith. Faith is more important because it insures the life of the soul, whereas the forgery of money is inconvenient only for our temporal needs. A more severe crime should be liable to more severe punishment. When the criminal endangers his own eternal life and that of other "sheep" in the flock, the punishment should be infinitely more severe.

The teaching authority of the Church was also interpreted in a peculiar way by the proponents of the Inquisition.

Access to the Holy Scripture was restricted to clergymen who had the special education and knowledge of how to read and interpret the Bible. For hundreds of years the Roman Catholic Church was opposed to the study of the Bible by people who did not have the special authority to do so from the Church hierarchy. Therefore, one of the early modern forms of heresy (e.g., Waldenses) was the translation of the Bible into the popular languages in order to make the Holy Scripture available to all who wanted to study it and truly live according to God's admonitions. The translators and the distributors of the Holy Scripture were severely punished for this offense.

In this way, the Inquisition became total. The people were taught the official ideology by official spokesmen; they were not given any opportunity to think for themselves because even the text of the Holy Scripture was not available. Therefore, the philosophy of the Inquisition could have been based on a one-sided interpretation of the text which conveniently was withheld from the people.

Protestantism put an end to this perversion of the teaching authority of the church. Martin Luther translated the Bible into German and in a short time it became a custom in Protestant families to read the Bible on their own and to interpret it privately. This never caused Protestantism to become tolerant in principle, although new foundations of tolerance were laid down.

Martin Luther fought against intolerance in general, and against that of the Catholic Church in particular, as long as he wanted freedom for his own teaching. After his leadership had been accepted in certain lands, principalities, and kingdoms, he took over many of the arguments in favor of intolerance and adjusted them to a Protestant spirit. Luther also stressed that every individual had an obligation to truth and, therefore, an *erroneous conscience* should not be tolerated. Although, as he admitted, every individual had his own conscience and freedom, still, a person's conscience is bound by "the Word of God."

Martin Luther didn't solve the problem of the conflict between individual conscience and the requirements of truth, but by his reflections *On the Unfree Will* (1525) he made this problem even more visible and acute.

From the viewpoint of intolerance the problem of the free will, individual responsibility, morality, and conscience cannot be solved. Once an "erroneous conscience" is declared incompatible with the social requirements elaborated by the self-professed prophets of truth, physical terror as a means to change minds becomes a certainty.

It seems that Martin Luther did understand that iron and fire could not be effective against heresy. There was even a short period when he thought that as a spiritual entity, heresy was inevitable and although there was a duty to speak out against heresy no compulsion or violence should be used. Later, when he started to fight not only against Rome but also against the peasants' rebellion, he decided that one should distinguish between "spiritual" heresy and "external abomination." He became a proponent of intolerance under the pretext that although the government should not compel belief, it should suppress "external abominations."

When Luther was justifying the cruel and bloody suppression of the rebels, he introduced an especially ominous simile. He wrote that, after all, the massacre of the peasants was a trifle compared to the destruction of Sodom and Gomorrah by God Himself.

The first medieval heretics were mostly simple and uneducated people. They were outraged that representatives of the Church did not live by the example set by Jesus. They argued that Jesus Christ and His disciples were modest men, lived simple lives, didn't have riches, didn't aspire to have high offices, but observed the rules of decency and charity. The heretics, especially the early ones, were peaceful people who interpreted literally the commandment that one should love neighbors and not wage war against them. They especially referred to the words of Jesus, that he didn't want to use Peter's sword nor ask his father to send legions of angels to crush his persecutors. There were many heretical sects that believed that a true Christian should rather suffer persecution than persecute others.

The first heretics opposed an uneven distribution of wealth and believed it to be against God's will. In order to substantiate this opinion, they interpreted the words of God when he created Adam in an egalitarian spirit ("When Adam delved and Eve span who was then the gentleman?"). God gave Adam "dominion over the fish of the sea and over the fowl of the air, and over the cattle, and over all the earth, and over every creeping thing that creepeth upon the earth." (*Genesis* I, 26). The heretics regarded Adam as the representative of all mankind; God's words giving him dominion over the earth should mean that the Creator instituted common property for all mankind; whoever acquired private property violated the first commandment issued after the creation. From the social point of view, heresies were a criticism of the existing economic and social order and sought to reintroduce the spirit of the earliest period of Christianity. Representatives of the Church also understood that an interpretation of the Holy Scripture different from their own (be it Catholic or Protestant) indeed pertained to questions of economics and politics. When Zwingli criticized the Anabaptists for their ideas concerning communal property and their understanding of baptism, he pronounced the famous words: "The issue is not Baptism, but revolt, faction, heresy."

As the arguments against tolerance were in essence political, the arguments in favor of tolerance had to the same degree a social meaning. Even if they were not a direct attack against the Church, they undermined official attitudes and theories of the ruling Catholic, Orthodox, and afterwards, of the Protestant, theological establishments.

The main argument in favor of tolerance, from the theological, social, and moral points of view, were the references to the commandments of the Old and New Testament that true love of God is inseparable from charity and love of neighbor. Those in favor of tolerance argued that any compulsion over conscience was a sign of disrespect for the neighbor and violated the principles of charity and love.

The proponents of tolerance accepted the Biblical concept that man consists of body and soul, relegating faith exclusively to the soul. One can influence the heart and conscience only with words, persuasion, goodness, sympathy, and charity. Force can be used only against "external" parts of human beings. It is illogical, immoral, and against the commandments of Holy Scripture to try to change any "internal" essence by use of the sword. There were heretical theologians who believed that the very idea of persecution based on different interpretations of the Holy Scripture is the "devil's work." Those are the persecutors, according to them, who should be punished and not the victims who were truly convinced that they believed in genuine principles of religion.

These assertions gave rise to endless discussions concerning the rights of the *erring conscience* and the notion of what constituted a Christian. The proponents of tolerance argued that the decisive criterion should be subjective belief, deep persuasion in one's conscience, and eventually a person's style of life. Montaigne argued that a Christian is a person who is decent and just, even though he does not understand certain dogmas and their theological consequences. He expressed the famous opinion that one can be a Christian without knowing it, provided that one spontaneously lives like a Christian, truly observing the recommendations of Holy Scripture.

A very similar opinion was expressed by Erasmus of Rotterdam and the Polish thinker, Andrzej Frycz Modrzewski (Andreas Friscus Modrevius); it is sufficient to live according to the requirements of conscience in order to be saved.

The proponents of tolerance taught that every person should interpret Holy Scripture according to his own personal understanding without being involved in complicated theological speculations. Erasmus expressed a maxim which was afterwards accepted by most theologians: the number of dogmas should not be multiplied (in Latin, they used to say that dogma—*non sunt multiplicanda*). He thought that the fewer the dogmas, the fewer the reasons for quarrels and persecution. All the proponents of tolerance held that it was very difficult to define what was true and untrue, that there were many matters which were unclear because of their nature and that the obscurity could not easily be eliminated. Therefore people should have the right to doubt and to develop their own opinions, provided of course that their way of life is decent and according to the principles of charity.

Here once more emerged the problem which was introduced into theological literature by the theologians of the Inquisition, the famous parable of the tares and wheat. Contrary to the ideas of the Inquisitors, they argued that Christ did not recommend eradication of the tares before the harvest. He ordered the servants to wait until the harvest and only then to bind the tares. When was that? Of course, the harvest refers to the end of the world and the salvation of mankind. Before it, however, tares and wheat should "peacefully coexist."

In this connection, Castello argued that since it is so difficult to determine what is true or untrue, we ought to agree that we will harm the wheat if we try to uproot the tares. Therefore it is quite possible that in persecuting heretics, a just man might be killed by mistake.

This reasoning prompted Hubmaier, one of the heretics, to preach that the Inquisitors, not the victims, were the genuine heretics: they kill the tares, the alleged heretics, before the time of the harvest has arrived. Jesus didn't come on this earth in order to "butcher and burn," but in order to teach the people how to live in peace, love, and harmony.

Among the theologians who were proponents of tolerance, there were also representatives of consistent rationalism who argued that since reason cannot be compelled to accept any argument without being persuaded, those who interpret Holy Scripture in a way different from the official exegesis, should not be held criminally responsible for it. *Ignorance is no sin,* wrote Abelard.

It is characteristic that in this first period of the struggle for tolerance, the majority of the proponents of tolerance usually opted for certain restrictions in exercising it, at least by certain people.

For instance, Jacob Sturm, the famous Mayor of Strassburg and one of the greatest political proponents of tolerance, opposed freedom for Anabaptists.

Even John Locke argued that tolerance should not be accorded to atheists and materialists. In this respect, he followed the example of Thomas More, who taught that atheists could not be given the same freedom as heretics who believed in God, because atheists do not know the moral principles and cannot abide by them.

This argument against atheists is still repeated and is also used against so-called secular humanists.

In general, it may be said that in the formative period of the evolution of tolerance as an idea, most thinkers did not fully realize that the denial of freedom and tolerance even to one category of people or beliefs can undermine the very existence of tolerance. The clear understanding of this truth came much later.

2. Spinoza's Classic Arguments for Tolerance, Freedom and Peace

In voluminous, ever increasing, scholarly literature Spinoza is portrayed as a thinker who belongs to all of mankind. He dealt with questions and trends which are unendingly discussed in the West.

The purpose of this section is to examine problems which, from the viewpoint of freedom and tolerance, are especially topical today:

— Spinoza's philosophy of politics and of democracy.
— Spinoza's concept of human nature, constituting a basis for his theory about the indivisibility of mankind, of peace, and of the equality of nations.

— Spinoza's understanding that the preservation of freedom and tolerance are a prerequisite for internal and external peace.

a. Freedom and Knowledge

Spinoza's philosophy of the relationship between freedom and understanding has been explored in many monographs and in nearly every handbook on the history of philosophy.[1] But the link between these ideas and his philosophy of peace is a relatively neglected area. Nevertheless, in these times, this part of Spinoza's heritage is especially important.

Spinoza's philosophy can be defined from the anthropological viewpoint as a philosophy of man's liberation and self-determination. Man is not and should not be regarded as a cog in the world created and managed by some force above nature; man should not be subjected to the purposes of the Eternal Wisdom; the requirements of immortality should not dominate man's earthly life. Being autonomous and a value in himself, man should be treated as the end of every social organization, every political institution and system. Indeed, the main philosophical problem for Spinoza is the eternal question: what is man's place in the universe, how can he achieve, preserve, and extend his freedom?

Spinoza endeavored to present human nature and social life as realistically as possible. His specific political recommendations were well founded on a sober assessment of the existing political situation and of the contradictions in society. From time to time, however, he returned to his "impossible dream," his utopian vision of society. It seems that his utopia "was nearer to him than one could have deduced from the general premises of his theory."[2] This ideal can be defined in one sentence: cooperation of the people obedient to reason, and association of free people who serve one another because they act according to reason and not according to accidental passionate impulse.

Spinoza's description of the state of nature is almost the same as that of Thomas Hobbes. It is unimportant philosophically whether Spinoza really believed that such a state ever existed, that man ever lived or enjoyed freedom in such a state. The mere point that such a period preceded the formation of the state we are familiar with is sufficiently significant from the theoretical, ideological, and philosophical viewpoints.

The state results from the antagonism between the requirements of security and of freedom which Spinoza interprets in a Hobbesian way (freedom to do whatever I want to do or whatever I am able to do, freedom egoistic, unpredictable, unreasonable),[3] and not in his own.[4]

More than any other thinker before him, Spinoza sought to understand the relationship between rationality and freedom, or to use modern terminology, between comprehended necessity and freedom. Only reasonable men (those living in obedience to reason) can agree and live in harmony with one another.[5] Even more, men who are assailed by emotions (passions) are unable to distinguish the good from the bad. But rationally thinking people strive to achieve the good and get rid of what they deem bad. It follows that these men do such things which are necessarily good for human nature "and consequently for each individual man . . . in other words, such things . . . are in harmony with each man's nature."[6]

Men who are guided by appetite and not by reason are not free because they yield to the license of appetite. "But human liberty is the greater, the more man can be guided by reason, and moderate his appetite,"[7] Spinoza wrote.

The above notion of freedom indicates that Spinoza may be regarded as a predecessor of the philosophy of freedom of Hegel, Marx, and Dewey.[8] Each of those thinkers inherited important ideas from Spinoza and elaborated them in his own way.

Spinoza is not merely a theorist as far as intellectual and political freedom is concerned. He understood that it is not sufficient merely to be reasonable in order really to be free: "Reasonableness" *in abstracto* does not exist. In order to be able to reason truly a citizen must be informed. When people are uninformed they more likely than not are misinformed; they cannot judge properly and hence peace is endangered at home and abroad. "Lastly, as for the populace being devoid of truth and judgment, that is nothing wonderful, since the chief business of the dominion is transacted behind its back, and it cannot but make conjectures from the little which cannot be hidden."[9]

The people observe what the government does and draw their conclusions on the basis of incomplete, partial data. It happens that their conclusions are wrong. Should the people or those who withhold full information be blamed? Spinoza's contention is:

> So it is supreme folly to wish to transact everything behind the backs of the citizens, and to expect that they will not judge ill of the same, and will not give everything an unfavorable interpretation. For if the populace could moderate itself, and suspend its judgment about the t ings with which it is imperfectly acquainted or judge rightly of things by the little it knows already, it would surely be more fit to govern, than to be governed.[10]

Democracy and peace depend on the degree to which the people are informed on current political affairs. Misinformed people, Spinoza suggested, usually interpret events unfavorably. The citizens who are "imperfectly acquainted" are a menace to progress and peace. In this way Spinoza reached and substantiated an idea often regarded as a recent invention: maintaining peace depends on freedom of information.

b. Squaring of the Circle in Politics

Spinoza developed his own theory of the rule of law which should prevail in any regime including that of an absolute monarchy. On the one hand he asserted that the sovereign has the right to change the laws according to his will, but on the other, the sovereign should be reasonable and act for their preservation according to the necessities existing in a society. Even the kings of Persia, Spinoza wrote, who were worshiped as gods, did not have real "authority to revoke laws once established."[11]

Once the foundations of a dominion are established, they should be considered as if they were "eternal decrees of the king," which should be observed without exception. Ministers should refuse to execute later commands of a reigning king which are contrary to the very foundations of the dominion. Therefore reasonable kings instruct the judges to administer justice without respect to persons including the kings themselves, because they too can be "held captive by Sirens' songs." The behavior of Ulysses should be regarded as the ideal. He feared that he might be misled by the Sirens and therefore told his companions to bind him to the mast and disobey all orders to the contrary when they passed the treacherous creatures. When the danger was behind them, Ulysses praised his companions for having obeyed his fundamental orders and disobeyed the orders issued by him under stress. Nothing would be fixed in society, according to Spinoza, if everything depended on the inconstant will of one man.

This way of reasoning leads one to doubt the first premise of Spinoza's theory of law that the sovereign's will has the force of law. Spinoza answered: ". . . that a monarchial dominion (and all other forms of dominion—M.M.) may be stable, but it must be ordered so that everything be done by the king's decree only, that is, so that every law be an explicit will of the king, but not every will of the king, a law."[12]

The problem of how to restrict the sovereign by his own provisions of law has long been compared in juridical and political literature to the squaring of the circle.

In this respect Spinoza was one of the forerunners of two important doctrines: constitutional monarchy and juridical positivism.

Spinoza often used the expression "natural law" but he actually repudiated this philosophy as it was known in the 17th and 18th centuries. His theory of law was inseparable from his general philosophical premises, including the concept *Deus sive natura*. Experience shows, Spinoza wrote, and this can be regarded as the point of departure of his theory of law, that "Every natural thing has by nature as much right, as it has power to exist and to operate."[13]

By "natural right" Spinoza understood "the very laws and

rules of nature, in accordance with which everything takes place."[14] Montesquieu repeated this definition almost verbatim in *The Spirit of the Laws*. Spinoza applied these rules to all of nature, including man. Whatever man does he does by the highest natural right and "he has as much right over nature as he has power."[15]

Spinoza laid the foundation for his theory of law and the ultimate consequence of the concept of man's rights was drawn: "man's natural right extends as far as his power." The sphere of his power is also the sphere of his freedom, which he interpreted as comprehended necessity. Therefore, the next conclusion is, whoever wants to expand man's freedom should extend the boundaries of his power and discontinue the futile rhetoric concerning rights whether "inborn," "innate," or "given," because it is absurd to allege their existence.

Spinoza firmly entered the realm of juridical positivism: rights do not exist without positive laws, and positive laws can exist only in the state and they are created only by the state. Does this mean a state has unlimited arbitrary power in the promulgation of its laws? Spinoza's answer was, no, and this is one of the most complicated parts of his philosophy. Because the state is responsible for the preservation of the peace, it must therefore, argued Spinoza, act in a reasonable way. In this way he tried to square the circle. He did not endow the legislator with the capricious right of Creon. On the contrary, Creon, who was defeated and punished because he was not prudent, was not truly logical, although he pretended to be. Spinoza would have said that Creon was punished because he did not understand human feelings and affections.

The existence of laws is necessary because people do not act in accordance with reason alone. They also act according to their passions and desires. There are people ("divines") who believe that the ignorant disturb the course of nature when they follow their passion and not the dictates of reason. It is not an empirical point of view, Spinoza wrote; it is quite natural that people act according to their reason and passions. Nature itself puts an end to their too far reaching follies and blind passions

because everyone strives to preserve his or her own existence.
The instinct of self preservation is the source of the desire to be
under governmental rule. Although no one can use his reason all
the time, he can, thanks to the "supreme natural right," operate
more and more according to his reason. Mind, like body, is also
a link in the chain of causes and effects.[16] The mind of man is
more independent when it uses its reason aright.

> Nay, inasmuch as human power is to be reckoned less by physi-
> cal vigor than by mental strength, it follows that those men are
> more independent whose reason is strongest and who are most
> guided thereby. And therefore I am altogether for calling a man
> so far free as he is led by reason; . . . for liberty . . . does not take
> away the necessity of acting but supposes it.[17]

Thus we find in Spinoza's philosophy the following answer
concerning the problem of observing the provisions of law by the
sovereign himself. The more free and independent the sovereign
is, the better he will understand the necessity for observing his
own laws. The more reasonable he is, the more vigorously he
will strive to preserve peace at home and abroad.

The dominion of reason is necessary in order to preserve
peace, but it is not a sufficient condition. Reason itself can do
much to restrain and moderate the passions, Spinoza wrote. But
man "is necessarily always a prey to his passions . . . he follows
and obeys the general order of nature."[18] Whoever therefore
feels that the people distracted by politics can ever be induced to
live according to "the bare dictates of reason, must be dreaming
of the poetic golden age, of a stage play."[19]

Law is necessary to keep internal peace; could it play the
same role in international relations?

c. Reason and Democracy

Spinoza did not have a chance to elaborate his theory of
democracy fully. Chapter XI "Of Democracy," in *A Political
Treatise* ends in the middle of a sentence. But there are so many
remarks concerning democracy scattered throughout his writings that it is easy to follow his way of reasoning concerning this

form of government. We know reasonably well how he evaluated monarchy and aristocracy, their advantages and disadvantages, therefore one can deduce without any difficulty many of Spinoza's ideas on democracy with their strong and weak elements.

In *A Theologico-Political Treatise,* Spinoza made the following rather cautious statement:

> I think I have now shown sufficiently clearly a basis of democracy: I have especially desired to do so, for I believe it to be of all forms of government the most natural and the most consonant with individual liberty. In it no one transfers his natural right so absolutely that he has no further voice in affairs, he only hands it over to the majority of a society, whereof he is a unit. Thus all men remain, as they were in the state of nature, equals.[20]

Spinoza established two criteria of a good form of government: preservation of natural equality and consonance with individual liberty.

Spinoza did not idealize democracy, he regarded it as a better form of government than others because it is able to realize the criteria of a good government to a higher degree. He understood that democracy has its maladies, but all the ills of democracy he claimed, could be remedied only by more democracy itself. This is the only system that incorporates a capacity for self-healing.

Every government can issue laws and edicts which are unreasonable and the citizens are obliged to obey the commands of the sovereign, "however absurd these may be."[21] Spinoza nevertheless believed that governments will not try to impose "thoroughly irrational commands,"[22] because of their own interests and the desire for self-preservation. They should sooner or later begin to understand that *violenta imperia nemo continuit diu* (no one can reign long in a violent way—Seneca). There are good chances that in a democracy as a "society which yields all its power as a whole,"[23] irrational commands are still less to be feared for it is "almost impossible that the majority of a people, especially if it be a large one, should agree in an irrational design."[24]

Today we know that the experience of the three hundred years which have passed since Spinoza wrote those words has many times demonstrated that a majority is able to agree "in an irrational design." In Spinoza's philosophy, as in that of Bacon, Descartes, Locke, and Rousseau, there is a very strong belief that it is possible to distinguish rational from irrational means and that what is rational has a clear, firm and almost constant meaning. Although Spinoza went further and deeper in his philosophical and political analysis than did his contemporary Descartes, he was still unable to draw all the necessary conclusions from the facts (not unknown to him) that political passions and economic interest can completely blind a people. He knew, and wrote in his *Ethics* that avarice, ambition, and lust are species of madness, but he did not go so far as Hobbes when the latter observed that governments might be prepared to destroy all the books on geometry if the mathematical axioms were harmful to their interests.

Nevertheless, Spinoza's assertion that democracy, although imperfect, is less dangerous and less prone to error than any other form of government, is most important.

Democracy is a system more suitable for the preservation of peace than any other government. Spinoza wrote: " . . . the basis and aim of a democracy is to avoid desires as irrational, and to bring men as far as possible under the control of reason, so that they may live in peace and harmony: if this basis be removed the whole fabric falls to ruin."[25]

Democracy is presented as the system best able to preserve internal peace. Spinoza observed: " . . . everyone who judges things fairly will admit, that dominion is the most durable of all, which can content itself with preserving what it has got, without coveting what belongs to others, and strives, therefore, most eagerly by every means to avoid war and preserve peace."[26]

According to Spinoza there is an obvious link and an interdependence between rationality, democracy, and peace. Reason itself dictates that not only individuals, but also states should strive for peace and avoid war.[27] The meaning of the word peace is very broad for Spinoza and is directly connected with reason and freedom. Peace, Spinoza argued, does not consist in mere absence of war, but "in a union of agreement of minds."[28] This peaceful union can result only from the cooperation of reasonable, enlightened, well informed citizens, living under democratic governments.

d. International Law and Freedom

We have reached the point where we must analyze two questions: What did Spinoza think of international treaties and obligations? To what extent is a state bound by contracts to which it is a party? Spinoza's ideas changed in this respect. In his *Theologico-Political Treatise* Spinoza wrote that two states become allies when they sign a covenant for the sake of avoiding war or for some other advantage. Both states have an interest in mutual assistance in order to retain their independence. Such a covenant is valid only so long as its basis exists: that is, the existence of danger or the hope of gaining common advantages, Spinoza stressed. If this basis disappears, the contract becomes void. Why? Spinoza answered in a very simple way: "This has been abundantly shown by experience."[29]

Spinoza here followed the line of reasoning which, among others, is presented by Machiavelli: in politics one should take into account reality and political experience rather than abstract morality or religious commandments. But Spinoza, in this respect, expressed one idea which is not alien to Machiavelli but which he himself did not express in such a clear fashion, nor in so clear a context. Machiavelli simply wrote that the end should justify the means and that one should do everything that is necessary to preserve the state. Justification for the violation of contracts was for Machiavelli a purely political matter and he did not even pretend that one should look for moral justification, because these two spheres, politics and morality, are according to him completely separate.

Spinoza tried to move the problems of *pacta sunt servanda* and *rebus sic stantibus*, into the sphere of morality as well. Every state, he wrote, that enters into a treaty not to harm another must take every possible precaution against such treaties being broken by the stronger party. No one, Spinoza stressed, should rely on a contract unless there is sufficient proof that the other party will find it advantageous to keep his word. But if one has political experience and knows history and knows the right of sovereign power, then he would have to be out of his senses to rely on the word and promises of an ally who has the will and the power to do what he wants and who seeks above all the safety and advantage of his own dominion. Even if we consult loyalty and religion, Spinoza wrote, "we shall see that no one in possession of power ought to abide by his promises without breaking the engagement he made with his subjects, by which both he and they are most solemnly bound."[30]

The right to break a contract was not a question of mere political expediency for Spinoza. It was for him a problem of loyalty and the most sacred obligation toward one's own people. The purpose of the state is the protection of the interests of the people. This is the first and basic obligation of the ruler. His international obligations, promises, and words should be viewed and interpreted from the viewpoint of his basic duty towards his own people. Spinoza did not divorce politics from morality entirely. He just felt that international politics belonged to the sphere of efforts to preserve the freedom and independence of one's own nation.

A sovereign's duty towards his own nation is not only a political, but also a moral one, if not a religious one as well.

Spinoza's justification of the *clausula rebus sic stantibus* is the old Roman maxim: *Salus rei publicae summa lex debet esse.*

Before proceeding further, let us observe that all these recommendations were referred by Spinoza to the covenants between two states only. The situation changes when the partners of the contract are more numerous.

The ideas of the *Theologico-Political Treatise* which we analyzed were expanded in the *Political Treatise*. Spinoza once more stressed that states are in the same position to one another as men are in the state of nature: enemies. If they wish to make war on one another they may lawfully do so. But concerning peace, nothing can be decided without the concurrence of another state. It is indeed the law of peace that requires the existence of at least two contracting powers. If one power breaks the contract, as soon as the motive of hope or fear is removed, then the second commonwealth cannot complain that it has been deceived because it is folly to entrust one's welfare to an independent party whose highest law is the welfare of its own dominion. But if there are several commonwealths that contracted a joint treaty of peace, then, Spinoza wrote, the less each of them by itself is an object of fear to the remainder and, "the less it has the authority to make war. But it is so much the more bound to observe the conditions of peace; that is, . . . the less independent, and the more bound to accommodate itself to the general will of the contracting parties."[31]

This concept of Spinoza can be interpreted to mean that the international obligations come into existence not between two states but within a community of nations only. One can interpret Spinoza's ideas concerning the rights of a state within the community of nations similarly to the way one interprets the role of the individual within a society.[32] As long as man is isolated and in the state of nature, he is not bound by contracts. But when he becomes a subject of a state or a member of a community, he no longer depends on himself, but on the commonwealth whose commands he is obliged to execute, he does not have the right to vitiate the commands considered by him as just or unjust. The commonwealth expresses the will of all and therefore even the most iniquitous subject is bound to execute the commands. Once reason teaches us that one should seek peace, it teaches us also that a "commonwealth's general laws should be kept unbroken."[33]

When a union of states (Menzel and Verdross used the expressions *"Staatenbund"* und *"Voelkergemeinschaft"*) comes into existence and constitutes some kind of a *civitas maxima,* the states are no longer in a state of nature. In this new situation, international law and international obligations start to be binding and should be respected. One can therefore agree with Menzel-Verdross that "the teaching of Spinoza, followed to its conclusion, leads to the primacy of international law as soon as the real preconditions of a federation of nations last."[34]

What Menzel and Verdross consider as the precondition for creating binding international agreements by a union of nations should be interpreted in the spirit of Spinoza's philosophy as an effective working federation. This means that even a small state will be guaranteed its independent existence and the preservation of its vital interests to such a degree as they would be guaranteed to a citizen in a well-governed state under a reasonable government. International law and a union of states are necessary to protect both peace and individual freedom.

e. Freedom and Equality Among the Nations

Whatever the true reasons for Spinoza's excommunication may have been, social, political,[35] or theological, most indices seem to point to the fact that Spinoza's concepts of the Jewish people as the "chosen people" were questioned. Apart from the theological and emotional aspects of this problem, the political sense of Spinoza's reflections in this respect, during the period of his maturity at least, seems to be connected with his general philosophical vision: mankind should be treated as an indivisible totality.

Nations, according to Spinoza, do not differ from one another because of their specific stamina, characteristics, or intrinsic qualities, but they are:

> ... distinguished from one another in respect to the social organization and the laws under which they live and are governed; the Hebrew nation was not chosen by God in respect to its wisdom nor its tranquility of mind, but in respect to its social organization and the good fortune with which it obtained supremacy and kept it so many years.[36]

Spinoza maintained that no nation had the right to claim that it deserved special privileges in the family of nations; every nation has its own right to live and to survive. That is one of the points he made in his own peculiar, theologico-political way. And here one can find the deepest reasons why Spinoza was so adamant about denying the "chosen people" any features or rights which—in his opinion—might place this concept of the equality of men and nations in jeopardy.

The concept of equality and fraternity among nations and denominations was expressed by Spinoza in a letter to Isaac Orobio (1671) in an even more categorical way. Defending his *Theologico-Political Treatise* Spinoza elaborated his attitude toward the Moslem nations: "As regards the Turks and other non-Christian nations, if they worship God by the practice of justice and charity toward their neighbors, I believe that they have the spirit of Christ and are in a state of salvation, whatever they may ignorantly hold with regard to Mahomet and oracles."[37]

In the same letter Spinoza tried to be very clear that he did not deny that Mahomet was one of the prophets. He wrote about one of his critics: "Surely the burden lies with the prophets to prove that they are true. But if . . . Mahomet also taught the divine law, and gave certain signs of his mission, as the rest of the prophets did, there is surely no reason why he should deny that Mahomet also was a true prophet."[38]

That opinion has a deep theological and humanistic meaning and is, by the way, directly associated with the ideas of the Polish Unitarians: the Bible should be regarded as a Moral Code and whoever respects the norms of morality, irrespective of his correct or incorrect understanding of the theological dogmas, should be regarded as being a decent human being, and therefore "in a state of grace." Spinoza took one decisive step: members of every denomination (including Moslems) can be saved.

Spinoza's ardent defense of Mahomet as one of the true prophets (equal to Moses and Christ) constituted an additional element of his political ideology concerning mankind: it is indivisible, it is one totality and one unity. In this general frame the unity of the Jews, Christians, and Moslems is special because they are members of the monotheistic world. Because everyone in the world can be the holder of the key to truth and the exemplars, peace among the peoples is not only desirable but also possible.

f. Arguments for Tolerance and the Indivisibility of Freedom

The sovereign power of the state is limited by nature itself. Nature created people in a certain way and no state can change them. The state cannot force the people to think, feel, or believe in a manner prescribed by laws. This feature of human nature should be taken into account by every government and it would be ignorant for a government to attempt to prescribe ideas or feelings. To attempt to do so, according to Spinoza, would be a cause, if not a sign, of a government's weakness or incapacity to function properly. A government can compel the people through its agencies and laws to act or behave in a certain way; such laws can be enforced. The imposition of ideas, however, cannot.

One of the first conclusions to be drawn from Spinoza's reasoning is very simple: a government is obliged to tolerate and respect the ideas and feelings of the citizens. If a government is intolerant, it puts itself and its decrees in disrepute and contempt. People despise a ruler who does not know the limits of his own power. It is true that the people transferred their rights to the ruler in order to get protection. But they could not have transferred rights which are necessary to preserve human nature.

Spinoza tried to argue that a logical and inescapable consequence of the natural freedom of thought is freedom of speech. According to him one cannot separate freedom of thought from the freedom to communicate one's thoughts. A government attempting to dictate which opinions to express and which to withhold wants indeed to impose on the people its own understanding of what is true or false, good or evil. Even so authoritative and divinely inspired a man as Moses was incapable of gaining the adherence of all his subjects. According to Spinoza only a technical distinction can be made between freedom of thought and freedom of speech. He therefore rejected the argument that a dangerous thought locked in one's own mind is less harmful than the same thought expressed. Such a distinction may possibly be enforced for a short time only, with the result that a society becomes hypocritical, corrupt, and without true virtue. A state whose citizens are demoralized cannot be a strong one.

The real power of a state rests on the unity of its citizens. This unity must depend upon a community of interests and opinions. However, a community of opinions can be achieved only through a prolonged process of communication and persuasion. Freedom of speech is necessary for both domestic peace and the power of a state.

At any rate, the authorities should realize that if the people are restricted in their use of words (spoken or written) they will use other means to express their thoughts. No government can effectively control these modes of expression.

And finally, Spinoza reached his ultimate conclusion: freedom of thought and speech is inseparable from freedom of assembly. If the people are forbidden to assemble for social and political reasons, they will nevertheless do so surreptitiously. Any laws which interfere with this freedom will be abhorred and disregarded by the citizens; such laws will become ineffectual and the entire political structure will suffer from such alienation between citizens and their government.

Spinoza may have been the first thinker to have expressed the doctrine of the indivisibility of freedom in such a clear and astute manner. He regarded freedom of thought, speech, and assembly (freedom of religion is included) as links in a single chain of freedom. The rupture of one of the links would destroy the entire chain. He did not write that the government should grant these liberties to the citizens, but stressed that the government that curtails these liberties undermines its own existence.

A despotic government that interferes with the necessary liberties of its citizens is irresponsible and corrupt. Spinoza further observed (this was underestimated by his successor Lord Acton) that being powerless and deprived of freedom demoralizes the subjects as well. This is one of the conclusions of the *Political Treatise* (especially chapter VII, para. 27). A tyrannical, corrupt government, ruling over a corrupt people, endangers the welfare and peace of everyone.[39]

g. Peace Through Freedom and Enlightenment

Peace perpetuates peace, freedom reinforces freedom. One can easily find this idea in Spinoza's writings. "For men in time of peace lay aside fear, and gradually from being fierce savages become civilized or humane . . ."[40]

War is a source of savagery and cruelty; it is the source of returning primitivism. Peace makes people more humane and therefore more peaceful. But peace itself also begets new dangers, although of another kind. Men in peacetime "from being humane become soft and sluggish, and seek to excel one another, not in virtue but in ostentation and luxury. And hence, they begin to put off their naked manners and to put on foreign ones, that is, to become slaves."[41]

Spinoza did not elaborate in what sense people "become slaves." One of his ideas was that when the ruling group (aristocracy) thinks more about competition, ostentation, and luxury than about the good of their state, their continuing political dominion becomes endangered by internal corruption.[42] When the rulers become unreasonable peace must be endangered.

Peace perpetuates peace, but not in an absolute way; it is also charged with the seeds of self-destruction. In order to preserve peace, Spinoza observed, one should consciously work for its perpetuation by means of tolerance, freedom, democracy, law, education, and enlightened egoism.

3. Tolerance and Freedom—A Necessity for Human Nature

a. The Encyclopedists' Understanding of Tolerance

"Tolerance, in general terms, is the virtue of all feeble beings destined to live with creatures similar to themselves"—these opening words of the article on "Tolerance" in the Diderot-

D'Alembert *Encyclopedia* contain the main elements of this notion, according to the philosophers of the Enlightenment. We are condemned to live in mutual tolerance, they seem to say. Humanity must accept this verdict because otherwise nobody's life would be anything other than miserable and nasty.

"A man is great due to his intelligence;" he is also limited "by his own errors and passions." This is the reason that people are not open minded, that they cannot easily be inspired or persuaded. Human nature is the reason for many human troubles and dissension. In order to avoid disasters, tolerance must be practiced, the philosophers admonished. The lack of it is a source of misfortune, unhappiness, and calamity. Without tolerance peace and prosperity will never come.

M. Romilly, the author of the article quoted above, argued that there are many immediate sources of discord and disagreement. Mankind in this respect is truly fertile. The more reasons for disagreement, the more reasons we have to promote tolerance. An individual who despises tolerance acts against nature itself, and corrupts it. The adversaries of tolerance close their eyes to the obvious.

The most important and persuasive argument for tolerance, in Romilly's opinion, is also the simplest: the human mind is not a precise instrument; it is not perfect and therefore what is evident to one mind is obscure to another; a proof which is sufficient for one person is insufficient to persuade another. The quality of our receptivity and understanding depends on many factors including our education, experience, environment, prejudices and a thousand other unknown elements that may at any time endlessly modify our judgments.

The minds of people are even more diverse than physical objects. People may eventually agree on certain general rules, principles, or axioms, but they are so few and narrow that the specific, particular conclusions derived or deduced from them may be unlimited. Consequently, the sources of differences and antagonisms among people remain inexhaustible. Indeed, the further we proceed from these "generally accepted" first principles or axioms, the more doubts concerning the soundness of our judgments arise and become more and more divisive. In this way Romilly decided: "*. . . a million routes lead to an error, but only one to the truth; happy are those who find it!*"

This idea became one of the intellectual axioms of that period, doubtlessly under the influence of Descartes. The second part of the sentence however is dramatically incorrect: *there is not only one route leading to the truth, there are many.* If we agree that no one has a monopoly on truth and infallibility, then it is no less true that the means and tools for attaining reasonable political ends must also be manifold. If one agrees that every truth is limited, that it is not something static, but constitutes a process of acquiring knowledge, one has to admit also that the routes leading to the augmentation of our understanding are innumerable. It can easily happen that many scholars taking different roads will meet at the same point. A pluralism of minds requires both a pluralism of ideas and of methods. The virtue of tolerance is ingrained in pluralism.

Apart from this misunderstanding, the *Encyclopedia* correctly concluded: because everyone is proud on his own account and no one generally is able to persuade others of his own wisdom, let us at least adhere to one universal principle, *tolerance and humanity.* Our thoughts and sentiments divide us; let us therefore unanimously select one rallying point that unites us: *tolerance.* One should not reject one's neighbor because he is wrong. One should not hate one's brother because he is different. Whoever claims that he is the sole possessor of truth is arrogant; he is an enemy of public order and peace, he is a proponent of persecution. The claim to infallibility is an unforgivable error.

Lastly, the *Encyclopedia* makes a very important distinction which will be the subject of further reflection: Tolerance practical, and "speculative" (philosophical). Tolerance should be interpreted, according to the authors of the *Encyclopedia,* as an *attitude* and practical behavior. It should be differentiated from "culpable indifference."

The Encyclopedists argued that one should distinguish between a generous support for a humanity that claims tolerance for those who err, and the objectionable "speculative," "philosophical," tolerance of errors and unjust ideas, which should not be treated with indifference, magnanimity, or forgiveness. They should be criticized philosophically and intellectually in order to preserve freedom and tolerance and not to hurt their adherents. A tolerance of various religions consists in a charitable coexistence; the peaceful attitude does not by any means signify approval. When we tolerate something, it only means that we do not oppose it with force (even if this were possible), not that we agree with it. Tolerance should not be identified with a lack of values, with indifference toward evil, lies, and persecution.

Tolerance is a practical virtue and its practice is a difficult art.

That is the heritage which the age of the Encyclopedists has handed down to posterity.

b. Diderot: Tolerance and Happiness

"I wish to be happy: that is the first article of a code that takes precedence over all legislation, over any religious systems whatever"[1]—these words of Diderot constituted one of the intellectual pillars of the philosophy of tolerance and freedom in the age of the French Enlightenment.

It does not make sense to ask whether a human being has a right to be happy. It is natural for everyone to seek happiness and every legislator should remember that. Nature, wrote Diderot, has already made good laws in order to achieve this deeply rooted human goal; the legislator's task is to carry these rules out and never to contradict them. "Let your morality never forbid innocent pleasures."[2]

Diderot seemed to apply the well known medical maxim to problems of morality and politics: *primum non nocere* (first of all, do not harm). It is unreasonable and useless to compel people to act against their natural desire to be happy.[3] In order for people to approach happiness they must be left to themselves, to act according to their wishes, inclinations, likings, predilections, and whims, provided they do not hurt others. Do not interfere with their little and great pleasures!—admonished Diderot. Do not meddle, do not poke into anyone else's business. Do not intrude into your neighbor's soul! Be tolerant!

These rules and a few natural laws are all that are necessary to create conditions in which the people will have a chance to become happy; they should be observed by every society and government, otherwise the latter run the risk of self destruction. Intolerance, Diderot concluded, is to such a degree against human nature, that those who practice it act contrary to their own long-range interests.

"Before everything else, a society must be happy. It will be happy if freedom and property of individuals are secure . . . if virtue and talent are assured of a just reward."[4]

Man was not made only to plow and reap, Diderot continued. Being capable of feelings, he is destined to achieve happiness through thought and action.

A human being is also full of passions which are a source of pleasures, they alone can "elevate the soul to great things,"[5] deadened passions degrade man, annihilate his grandeur and nature.[6] Declamations against passions are directed against man's natural inclination to be happy. An individual without human passions becomes a monster.[7]

A person who tries to compel another to think according to his own prescription and silence his passions, seeks indeed to keep him in a state of brutishness, restricts his ambitions, dispossesses him of happiness, and acts contrary to human nature. It is also against nature to compel an individual to sacrifice his personal happiness "to the good of society."[8] One has no duty to devote oneself entirely to the community.

Happiness and tolerance require, first of all, that no government or any other political body, should be placed under the sanction of religion, asserted Diderot. Priests and preachers should not be given "a share in acts of sovereignty,"[9] because they teach that their god is superior to the sovereign. Theologians are able to put into their god's mouth whatever they wish.

It is worthwhile to observe that Diderot did not recommend

depriving those preachers of the right to express their opinions; he only sought to deprive them of the freedom to lie, to participate in government, or to influence political decisions.

He recommended the separation of state and church as a precondition of freedom and tolerance. He continued the Hobbesian line of reasoning: one who does not trust the priest does not insult God; one only questions the veracity of the person claiming to have credentials from the Almighty. The clergy use their position to promote their caste interests, they take advantage of those who trust them in order to deceive them. Therefore, Diderot held, the distance between altar and throne can be never too great, religion is a buttress which never fails to bring the whole edifice down in ruin.

The troubles with clergymen are caused by the fact, historically confirmed, that no government has ever been able to reduce them to the "pure and simple status" (Diderot's expression) of equality with others without the use of violence. After clergymen are compelled to be equal, the laws should protect and preserve their status in the interest of the whole community.

Theology is a "tissue of absurdities,"[10] which lives only because the people are kept in ignorance; the priests secretly and deliberately conspire to preserve this foundation of their privileges, fortune, and prestige. "Reason is the enemy of faith."[11]

Whenever intolerance is ingrained in the minds of young people it is a result, according to Diderot, of the deliberate policy of the Church and of the general ignorance which it tries by all means to preserve. The members of royal families are exposed to additional dangers because they are taught that the king is nothing in the sight of God, whereas the people are merely dust in the sight of the king who is their absolute master. Political absolutism, religious and social intolerance, arrogance and contempt toward the meek—these are the "tissue of absurdities" from which the whole edifice of oppression has been constructed.

Intolerance, according to Diderot's reasoning, does not

exist by itself as an autonomous phenomenon, it cannot be separated from the whole political fabric of the society. Intolerance is part and parcel of an intolerant political system which does not care for the people's happiness.

From among all the intolerant institutions, the Church is the worst. The Church is never satisfied with criticism or even condemnation of certain ideas or attitudes, it finally kills the people who hold them. Philosophers also criticize priests, but they did not kill even one of them. The Church cannot endure any variations from the accepted pattern; uniformity must reign even at the expense of lives.

The portrait of God as depicted by Christian theologians is inhumane; imagine, asked Diderot, those who suffer because they allegedly insulted God:

> What voices, what cries, what groans! Who has shut up in dungeons all these piteous wretches? What crimes have all these creatures committed? Some beat their breasts with stones, others lacerate their body with iron nails, all express in their eyes regret, pain and death. Who condemns them to such torments?[12]

The answer: the condemner and the judge is the "God full of goodness;" but is it possible, Diderot asked, that "goodness" loves to bathe in tears? Are not tears an insult to this kindness? Should we not apply the remark of Plutarch to such an image of God: I would prefer that the people thought that a Plutarch never existed, rather than consider Plutarch as "unjust, choleric, inconstant, jealous and vengeful."[13]

The prevailing image of the God is a result of superstitions which cast so many doubts that Diderot maintained that "superstition is more of an insult to God than atheism."[14]

Possibly this was the first time in the history of Western civilization that a defense of atheism was expressed so clearly and openly. The timidity and terror of centuries, if not millennia, were finally overcome. Atheists are not, Diderot dared to declare, the worst villains on earth; the religious bigots and imposters are worse!

The orthodox believers propagate fear, they depict the Supreme Being in such an ugly way that the most upright soul would be tempted to wish that such a Being did not exist. The vengeful God of the dogmatists evoked such awe that even Pascal was unable to overcome it so as to give himself entirely up to the search for truth without fear of offending God.[15]

Diderot himself was also unable to free himself from the prevailing fears; time after time, he denied being an atheist, he tried to present himself as a believer, but one using his reason. Even more; he asserted that it was only a deist who could effectively oppose an atheist. A superstitious man would be too weak mentally to answer an unbeliever.

Superstitious dogmatists can only insult atheists. They lack both knowledge and intelligence; when they run short of arguments they have to take refuge in invective. The insulting of atheists reminded Diderot of the answer of Menippus given to Jupiter: You thunder instead of answering, are you then wrong?

The persecution of atheists is an indication that the oppressors are not sure of the truthfulness of their case—this is Diderot's great argument in defense of free thinkers and against oppressors.

Nobody should be prevented from searching for truth. The search for it should be required of everyone, but not its attainment.[16] A fool, of course, can reach and profess completely wrong ideas; he should not be punished for that; after all, a fool is a fool, not a criminal!

The road to truth leads through questioning and doubts, argued Diderot. A philosopher who questions everything he is inclined to believe can be called a sceptic. Scepticism does not suit everybody, but scepticism which presupposes a profound and careful examination of every thesis "is the first step towards truth."[17] Scepticism is not identical with incredulity which is sometimes "the vice of a fool," whereas credulity is "a defect of intelligence."[18]

Scepticism may of course lead to atheism. Not always and

not necessarily, but such an eventuality should not restrain anybody from exploration.

"One day somebody asked a man if real atheists existed. Do you think, he responded, that real Christians exist?"[19]

Diderot never gave a straightforward answer to this double question, but he clearly indicated that the touchstone of every persuasion must be a critical examination of the given subject, including religion. A Christian is not released from the duty of critical thinking.

"If the religion that you announce to be true is true, its truth can be demonstrated by unanswerable arguments... Why pursue me with prodigies, when a syllogism serves to convince me?"[20]

His request: "Find arguments,"[21] was greeted by personal denunciations.

Intolerance is a source of many evils, wrote Diderot. One of the worst sicknesses caused by it is fanaticism. Fanaticism accompanies intolerance, according to Diderot, and it is its highest degree. But intolerance is not the only source of fanaticism. Some of its origins are unforeseen.

As a master of dialectical reasoning Diderot knew that it lies in the nature of every society that good elements can in a very short time easily be transformed into bad, and vice versa. Therefore, he warned against any attempt to transform a matter "for reason" or "rational conviction" into a matter for fanaticism or faith.

There are, from the viewpoint of rationalism, at least two types of fanatics: those who die for a false faith which they regard true, or for a true faith of whose truth they have not been convinced by proofs.[22]

A fanatic who dies for his convictions does not deserve to be called a true martyr; a genuine martyr dies for a *true* conviction whose *truth* has been clearly demonstrated to him.[23]

Fanatics, in church and in government, are afraid of every innovation, they usually exceed the limits of patience and moderation recommended to them even by their superiors or ideologues. Every dissent makes them nervous or fearful. The ideas in question might not even reach the foundations of the institutions, such as Christianity. Theologians, who always fear *rerum novarum* (new things), immediately attempt to silence and finally to destroy, at first, the writings and then, if possible, the authors as well.

Intolerance, religion, and fanaticism contribute to the laziness of human minds; they discourage the use of all the principal means of acquiring knowledge: observation, reflection, and experimentation,[24] Diderot wrote.

Especially harmful in this respect is the biblical story of creation. Diderot asked: if the Bible did not give such a theory that everything sprang from the hands of the Creator, if it were "permissible to entertain the slightest doubts" about the beginning and the end of nature and mankind, would not a philosopher suspect various natural patterns of transformations, decline, and evolution? Diderot used the term "evolution" and put it into the mouth of his beloved character, Dr. Nicholas Saunderson. He anticipated and even roughly described the evolutionary possibilities.

> Religion spares us many wonderings and much labor. If it had not enlightened us as to the origin of the world . . . think how many hypotheses we should have been tempted to accept as the secret of nature. And those hypotheses . . . would all have seemed to us more or less equally probable.[26]

Religion, in Diderot's opinion, is a simplistic explanation of complicated phenomena. People accustomed to intellectual pap look with suspicion at anybody who is searching for a deeper, scientific, non-stereotypic elucidation. They cannot truly be comfortable with the idea of tolerance.

c. Voltaire: Militant Tolerance—"Crush the Infamy"

I do not agree with a word you say, but I will defend to the death your right to say it—this maxim of Voltaire expresses in a concise way a great achievement of the human spirit struggling for tolerance. In order to achieve and preserve freedom and tolerance, an energetic campaign against fanaticism and bigotry should be fought. Therefore: *Ecrasez L'infame! Crush the Infamy!*—Those words, pronounced for the first time during the Calases affair, became Voltaire's battle cry till the end of his life. The passion for the defense of freedom and reason was so deeply rooted in his whole personality that it became a source for inexhaustible energy. France and the world were surprised at the output of a genius who was able day after day, year after year, to produce pamphlets, leaflets, letters, essays, stories, and books, dealing again and again with the same limitless and timeless topic: tolerance, dignity, freedom of the individual and of the whole society.

The cry: *Ecrasez l'infame!* added forever one more dimension to the notion of tolerance: militancy and fervor in attacking the adversaries of freedom and reason. Voltaire was the first great philosopher who criticized the fanatics not with scholarly treatises inaccessible to the broad public, but with short witty pamphlets, published almost every day. He kept the people in constant tension, relentlessly digging out new examples of terror and repeating his accusations against the Church and lay persecutors. Voltaire actively defended tolerance by exposing the intolerant villains and their villainy. He was the first "progressive propagandist" and he was the first to realize that "big books" do not appeal, they are "unfashionable." The fight for tolerance was transformed by him into a social and political campaign in which he and his companions did not kneel, but on the contrary: they attacked standing tall.

Voltaire was deadly serious in his fury against bigotry, prejudice, and fanaticism. Once he even reproached d'Alembert for not realizing that his was not a time to restrict oneself to mockery and satire. France is the country of the massacre of St. Bartholomew, Voltaire wrote. It is not a land of philosophy and pleasure. Sneering is not sufficient.

The struggle for tolerance was identified by Voltaire with the fight for reason. Fanaticism for him was composed of superstition and ignorance; it was a centuries-old hereditary sickness.

The question of fanaticism was of paramount importance for Voltaire, he discussed it in nearly every one of his many historical, philosophical, and political works. In *A Philosophical Dictionary,* Voltaire described fanaticism as "the effect of a false conscience which makes religion subservient to the caprices of the imagination and the excesses of the passions."[1] The madness of fanaticism, according to Voltaire, is "gloomy and cruel.[2] It is a spiritual pestilence."[3]

Voltaire did not confine the concept of fanaticism to religion alone. Quite the contrary. He saw traces of fanaticism in almost every sphere of beliefs, persuasions, and politics. Religion always occupied a special place in his angry eruptions against fanatics, because, as he stressed, all religions, including the Christian, have been polluted by fanaticism. Fanaticism is not, he admitted, inherent in Christianity but it has been invented and used by clever impostors to pursue their own ends; fanatics are not autonomous, independently thinking people, they are nearly always instruments in the hands of "knaves, who place the dagger in their hands."[4]

Fanatics are people who are possessed. Once this sickness has "gangrened the brain of any man, the disease may be regarded as nearly incurable."[5] The worst of all is the fact that every fanatic can become "a sincere and honest murderer for the good cause."[6]

Voltaire introduced a very important distinction here. Fanatics may be "sincere and honest," but their honesty is no consolation for mankind because fanatics are prepared to inflict murder and any other atrocity on anyone who disagrees with them. That is the essence of every kind of fanaticism and not only of that connected with religious beliefs. Voltaire was convinced that fanaticism was usually instigated by the ablest people who had power to make and guide fanatics to pursue their own interests.

A very instructive illustration in this respect is the discussion reported to have taken place between Cromwell and General Fairfax. Cromwell said: "How can you possibly expect a rabble of London porters and apprentices to resist a nobility urged on by the principle, or rather the phantom, of honor? Let us actuate them by a more powerful phantom—fanaticism! Our enemies are fighting only for the king; let us persuade our troops they are fighting for their God."[7]

Voltaire also observed that in order to inspire fanaticism one must be supported by the spirit of the times. The same can be said about the struggle against fanaticism. There are times, according to him, which are more or less conducive either to fanaticism or to the tranquility of individuals and societies. The very emergence of fanaticism was attributed by Voltaire to the deficiencies of mankind: "That our own holy religion has been so frequently polluted by this internal fury must be imputed to the folly and madness of mankind."[8] Only enlightenment can deliver mankind from fanaticism; for the time being, however, we should pray to God "that he would deliver us from fanatics . . . ."[9]

Voltaire did not attack the Holy Scripture directly. He rather tried to prove that the ecclesiastical hierarchy and theologians invented subtleties which could not be found in the Gospels. Not the Bible, but the theological glosses were the causes and pretexts for the bloody massacres which were so prevalent in Christian history. If the clergymen had lived up to their sermons on brotherly love—one could have forgiven them the absurdities, lying, and miserable sophistries they employed, but unfortunately, instead of charity they imposed their beliefs on others and threatened them: believe as we do, or God will damn you and you will be assassinated! In this connection, in his *Essay on the Customs,* Voltaire asked the perennial question: What right has a free-born person to compel another free creature to think like himself? And evoking the images of the poor and simple heretics he writes about his modest hero Zapata, who became a priest, rejected fanaticism, practiced virtue, and as a reward for decency, was burned at the stake.

Religion is so much abused for petty selfish reasons, that one might suspect, wrote Voltaire, that the first divine was the first rogue who met the first fool. Christianity, he added ironically, must be verily divine; the best proof is the fact that it lasted more than seventeen centuries in spite of all the villainy and nonsense. The Church instigated fear of God in order to make sure the people would be afraid of clergymen.

Voltaire did not reject religion entirely, he only wanted to free it from fanaticism, prejudices, and absurdities. A purified religion should be taught to the common, simple people. If they were philosophers, religion would not be necessary. But there are not many deep thinkers in the world, therefore for the sake of the morality of the "little man," it would have been necessary to invent God if he did not exist.

Thus Voltaire reached a point in which he contradicted himself.

If religion is truly founded on beliefs in absurdity, as Voltaire argued, that means that untruth and lying can be beneficial for morality. Such an admission clearly contradicts Voltaire's determination that tolerance and decency are inseparable.

Voltaire tried to resolve these contradictions by recommending freeing religion from superstition, which is a monster on the bosom of its mother, a serpent choking true beliefs. The head of the beast should be *crushed* without hurting the mother whom it devours.

God, presented in the religion recommended by Voltaire, is powerful, sensitive, and merciful. When he punishes, he does it without cruelty. He is reasonable and tolerant. One could say: *The Voltairian god is great because he is very humane.*

The religion which Voltaire worked out was without ostentation, without unintelligible metaphysics, and without dreadful terror.

Voltaire's god would have been inclined to approve the situation as described in the "Letters on the English:" a free Englishman goes to heaven the way he chooses. If in England there were one religion only, wrote Voltaire, one could be afraid of despotism; if two religions—the followers would have murdered each other; but since there are thirty religions in England—the Englishmen can live peacefully and happily (Letter No. VI—"On Presbyterians").

Thus Voltaire elaborated on one more social and political

dimension of tolerance: wherever there is a nation with one dominant ideology (religion) or with two ideologies (religions) only—the danger of tyranny, hatred, and persecutions exists. Pluralism creates the foundations for peace, tolerance, and freedom.

* * *

In his philosophy of freedom Voltaire concentrated on two questions which in the eighteenth century were the topic of heated discussions: the relationship between freedom and free will, and freedom and power.

Voltaire's arguments against identifying freedom with free will were directed against well-known theological assertions. He accused theologians of having rendered unintelligible the question of free will by their "absurd subtleties upon grace."[10]

Voltaire agreed with John Locke that liberty cannot belong to will any more than color and motion and that even the expression, to be free, signifies power. The concept of liberty as power should be interpreted as to the power to act. Freedom should be approached in the same way in which we approach the words "health" or "happiness." People are neither always healthy nor always happy. The words freedom and free will, also are abstractions which signify that people at times have the power to act according to their own will although they have to overcome too many obstructions. These may be objective (or material), but they may also be subjective. Even a great passion may deprive an individual of his power to act. One should never forget that when making decisions on what to do or not do, one should act reasonably, mindful of the laws of the universe. All is subject to the laws of nature and human beings should be aware of this fact.

In this way Voltaire approached the problem of freedom and necessity. He did not solve it but he indicated that there is a relationship between knowledge, reasoning, and the freedom to act.

In the story about Babouc (in: *The Way the World Goes*)

Voltaire described the adventures of this wise philosopher, Babouc, who was asked to advise his master, Ithuriel, whether Persepolis (i.e., Paris) should be destroyed for its sins. At the end of his mission he requested the best metal-worker in the country to cast a small image composed of metals, earth, dirt, and jewels so as to create a beautiful mixture of the most precious and worthless elements. He brought this piece of art to Ithuriel and asked: "Will you break this pretty image because it is not all of gold and diamonds?"

Ithuriel understood the meaning of the report and determined:

> . . . he would not think of punishing Persepolis, and would not interfere with *the way the world goes*; "for," said he, "if all is not well, still, it is passable." So Persepolis was allowed to remain unharmed.

The struggle for tolerance, Voltaire indicated, is a struggle for a world which is not perfect, but is *passable*. Those who wish to create a society without any reproach must become intolerant. It is not worthwhile to terrorize and exterminate people in order to achieve an unrealizable utopia. For the time being, one should be satisfied with conditions in which everyone might "cultivate his own garden" *(Candide).*

4. J.-J. Rousseau: Freedom and the General Will

There is no philosopher whose ringing words about freedom have become more famous than Rousseau's:
—Man was born free, and he is everywhere in chains.[1]
—To renounce freedom is to renounce one's humanity, one's rights as a man.[2]
—Man acquires with civil society, moral freedom, which alone makes man the master of himself.[3]

Apart from these slogan-sentences, Rousseau's contribution to political philosophy is that he posed questions which are crucial to every philosophy of law, democracy, and freedom: how can individual freedom be secured in a society in which inequality exists between the stronger and weaker, the richer and poorer? A corollary to this problem is: since individuals must live in society, how can their wills be harmonized with the will of the society? If a free man is one who is subject to his free will only, how can this freedom be reconciled with the will imposed by a community on its members?

Rousseau thought that he had solved these problems in his *Social Contract* when he introduced the distinction between the general will and the will of all. "The will of all," he wrote, "is simply the sum of individual wills which are influenced by private interests."

The general will, on the other hand, is the will of all, minus all excesses of private wills. The general will is the will of all from which all the "pluses and minuses" have been removed. They will cancel each other out at any rate. The result of this mathematical canceling will be the general will.

Rousseau also explained that the general will always tends to the public good whereas the will of all tends toward private interests and therefore takes into account various particular desires.

Rousseau's mathematical operation is fairly simple. Social life and politics however do not develop according to the axioms of arithmetic; they are much more complicated. Nothing in politics can be added, subtracted, or divided without a fierce fight. Even the notions of "pluses," "minuses," and "excesses" are colored by economic and political interests.

Jean-Jacques Rousseau consistently adhered to his notion of a general will and tried to build around it a logical system. Whenever he endeavored to define his fundamental distinction however, the more ethereal it became.

When Rousseau tried to prove that the general will did not need to be unanimous, the notion suddenly became mysterious. The mystery increased when in order to determine the general will all the votes must be taken into consideration and counted.

It seems that we are entering the realm of mysticism when Rousseau argued that the general will can never err, that the people, as sovereign, can never be mistaken. Rousseau nevertheless retreated from this position by his admission that after all, not all people are enlightened, that they do not always comprehend their own interests and at times even follow policies harmful to themselves. Rousseau understood that although the people always want what is advantageous for them, they do not always discern it (*The Social Contract.* Book II, ch. 3). Time after time however he returned to his thesis that the general will of the people is always right and that the sovereign is never wrong and tends toward the public good. The people is "never corrupted, but is misled; and only then does it seem to will what is bad."[4]

From the political viewpoint it makes little difference whether the bad result of the people's will is caused by corruption or ignorance. The result is bad for the people either way. This means, using Rousseau's terminology, that the sum of wills (which constitutes the will of all) is not correct. In such circumstances, how can the essence (the general will) of the erroneous sum, be right? No one, not even Jean-Jacques Rousseau himself has ever solved this problem, nor had anyone before him analyzed so many aspects and contradictions inherent in this question; no one was capable of raising the question fundamental to every democratic system in such a thought-provoking manner as Rousseau had done: there can, and there must be, a difference, if not an open contradiction or chasm, between the will expressed by the society as a whole or by its representatives on the one hand, and the individual wills and interests of those who constitute the community. The will of the state (be it legislative or an executive body) can never coincide completely with the individual wills of each of its citizens; to expect it is to expect the impossible. Rousseau understood this fact.

In his *Social Contract*, Rousseau concluded that man truly is free when he is in civil society and lives under his own individual will.

It took no longer than two years for Rousseau to retreat from his own dogmas. In his *Lettres Écrites de la Montagne,* he stressed another point: liberty consists not so much in doing one's own will, but rather in not being subject to another's will.

His previous presumption, which became a key to the construction of *The Social Contract* (freedom exists in exercising one's own will), was replaced with a near-Kantian view: In a state of liberty no one has the right to do what is harmful or forbidden by the requirements of the liberty of others. True liberty, Rousseau added in the elaboration of his observation, is never destructive of itself; the free man obeys the laws, but he is not a servant, he has no masters; he is ruled by laws and therefore he can remain himself.

Although Rousseau still lingered in the realm of generalities, it is evident that he was coming down closer to earth when his point of departure in philosophy was not abstract man, as one might judge from the tenor of his writings, but an individual who lives in society. Indeed, *The Social Contract* almost begins with a description of how civil society was established. All Rousseau's considerations revolved around an individual who is "by himself"[5] (not by nature!) "complete and solitary," but inevitably becomes "a part of a greater whole" from which he receives "his life and his being."[6] In other words, the problem is narrowed down to the miraculous transformation of man's physical and independent existence which he received from nature into a "moral and communal existence."[7]

> In a word each man must be stripped of his own powers and given powers which are external to him, and which he cannot use without the help of others. The nearer men's natural powers are to extinction or annihilation, and the stronger and more lasting their acquired powers, the stronger and more perfect is the social institution. So much so, that if each citizen can do nothing whatever except through cooperation with others, and if the acquired power of the whole is equal to, or greater than, the sum of the natural powers of each of the individuals, then we can say that law-making has reached the highest point of perfection.[8]

There is a paradox here. Rousseau's more general theses are often more concrete than his particular specifications.

Since a person could not continue to live in the state of nature and had to associate with others, he had to undergo a process of "total alienation" by which he gave himself "absolutely" with ''all his rights to the whole community.''[9] This sounds even more ominous than Hobbes' social contract. But Rousseau offered two consolations by stating that the alienation of man will not be so ''total'' or so ''onerous.''

In the first place, although every individual gives himself ''absolutely'' to the community, the conditions are the same for all and therefore ''it is in no one's interest to make the conditions onerous for others.''[10]

The second consolation is that since each person gives himself to all, '' he gives himself to no one.''[11]

How is this possible? Because everyone will be living under the supreme direction of the general will. This formula, of course, solves nothing, because the whole construction of the general will is flawed, as has been already pointed out. It does not help that Rousseau distinguished two sides in each person, man is a person and a citizen at the same time. As an individual he has a private will; as a citizen he is locked into the general will. The distinction is impressive theoretically. In practice, however, an individual remains the same person all the time and Rousseau acknowledged that a human being may speak with a very different voice as a person and as a citizen. A man might prefer to take rather than contribute; he may prefer to enjoy his rights over fulfilling his duties. In order to avoid ruin the political body must take decisive measures against such selfishness. Rousseau wrote:

> Hence, in order that the social pact shall not be an empty formula, it is tacitly implied in that commitment—which alone can give force to all others—that whoever refuses to obey the general will shall be constrained to do so by the whole body, which means nothing other than that he shall be forced to be free.[12]

Compelle intrare! Force them to be free! Change the word ''freedom'' into ''salvation'' and we arrive at the ominous recommendations of St. Augustine. Nevertheless, the analogy is superficial only.

Rousseau drew attention to the fact that not only is freedom always in danger in a society, but also that it can be achieved only if the people really want it. He brilliantly elaborated an idea which today has almost become a truism: there is a connection between freedom and violence, and the alienation of an individual is "natural" and "inevitable," but it can be controlled to a certain extent. Democracy is a system that is best for gods as well as angels[13] but there is some potential in the people and therefore it is worth striving for freedom and democracy.

When one disregards Rousseau's phraseology and his paradoxes and concentrates on their substance, one can see the simple truth that freedom and tolerance should be fought for in a society's development. On the road to freedom, the obstacles are endless; freedom in itself is contradictory, but Rousseau quoted the words which he attributed to a Polish statesman: *"Malo periculosam libertatem quam quietum servitium."*[14] Freedom with its dangers is better than peaceful servitude.

This quotation, in a few words, reflects a characteristic of Rousseau's philosophy: the road to freedom is not only difficult and troublesome, but one may get sidetracked in striving for it, as happened to Ulysses who was lulled by the voices of the sirens praising the attractions of peaceful servitude. Rousseau believed that a people's power and sovereignty would constitute the ultimate antidote to the attractions of slavery.

Republican and liberal writers did not entirely understand the depth of Rousseau's dialectic of freedom. They concentrated on the surface of his theory: the concept of the omnipotence of the people was identified with unlimited state interference.

The struggle against this possibility determined the strength and the weakness of their response to the questions posed by the citizen of Geneva.

5. Liberal Philosophy of Freedom and Tolerance

a. Adam Smith, Founder of Liberal Philosophy

The following maxims colorfully express the quintessence of the liberal theories, of state, law, politics, and freedom: Gournay's *laissez-faire, laissez-passer;* d'Argenson's *ne pas trop gouverner* (do not govern too much); Mercier de la Rivière's *proprieté sureté, liberté—voilà tout l'ordre social* (social order means property, security, freedom); and Galiani's *il mondo va da se* (the world moves by itself).

Jeremy Bentham wrote that whenever governments have a choice whether to do or not do something, it would be wiser for them to refrain, because everything they do is evil. Whenever the government considers its options it should remember that it is in a position akin to that of a physician: every option is bad because the patient is sick; every law is a restriction upon liberty; if a new law is needed, society, like the patients, already is in trouble.

Jules Simon wrote that the state which is most useful and desirable is one which endeavors to make itself useless; it should strive for its own demise.

Unfortunately, governments and states must exist. The liberals were sufficiently reasonable and realistic to understand that these institutions are required to secure obedience to law, social order, and external independence. The government should allow the people to do whatever they want, they argued, but it should restrain and punish anyone who endangers the life, health, and private property of others. The concept of a liberal state is an extension of the idea of free economic competition.

Adam Smith established the liberal theory of economics and politics. His historical contribution far exceeds the limits of political economy; he drew the necessary conclusions from the fact that an economic system is *political* as well, and elaborated the principles on which a well-organized liberal state should be based. He discussed problems from the historical point of view. He was one of the first thinkers to analyze the evolution of the institution of private property. He distinguished various phases in the development of social and political institutions and concluded that freedom has a variable content.

Smith was the first to demonstrate the close relationship between the value of a product and the quantity and quality of human labor invested in it. In his writings Smith verified what had been the guess of a genius, in Hobbes' *Leviathan.*

Smith's point of departure in economic, social, and political thinking was his thesis that human beings are basically egoistic, although no one is self-sufficient or an island unto himself. People must live in societies and need others for cooperation and mutual advantage. A reasonable egoist helps his neighbor because he accomplishes his own purposes by doing so; he serves himself.

Smith was a consistent individualist; he interpreted the public good of society as the sum of individual interests. He did not believe in an impersonal "common" or "general" good. The individual, not society, was basic. His was the typical, classic, liberal approach.

Political power, according to Smith, also results from social development. He argued that the government, based on hierarchy and subordination, had evolved from a society which had begun to divide into the poor and the rich, a division which might have occurred with the advancement of the division of labor and increased productivity. It was the beginning of the advancement in agriculture and craftsmanship. Economic evolution gave rise to the emergence of wealth. In a society where inequality and competition exist between rich and poor there will also be differing ambitions, ends, and manner of thinking. It is imperative that this be understood; Smith stressed that the affluence of a few rests on the poverty of many.

The wealth of a limited number is the cause of envy and discontent on the part of the disadvantaged. They incline to violate the property of their affluent neighbors. The rich are ever surrounded by enemies, Smith argued, and they are incapable of satisfying the envy of the poor.

Owners of wealth generally are denied the peace and serenity of quiet nights unless the powerful arm of a government secures it for them by punishing the violators of the existing social order. If the freedom of a people is to depend on private property, Smith concluded, this freedom must then be accompanied by a government with its hierarchy and chain of command. Increases in property and affluence require an increase in the development of government. Such a development is connected with a multiplication of government agencies and the adding of ranks to the hierarchical order. With increasing inequalities, new organs arise with appropriate levels and with new methods to carry out their activities. The *raison d'etre* of a government agency is to preserve private property, social inequality, and the governmental hierarchy. That is the essence of Smith's political philosophy.

The most affluent members of a society generally are more interested than anyone else in reinforcing the existing social and governmental structure. Those who are not so rich, yet still belong to the "haves," easily comprehend that their lesser privileges will be maintained only through the protection of the status quo as a whole; although they envy the rich, they must cooperate with them.

Smith presented the nature of hierarchy and subordination as follows: the rich exist thanks to the labor of the poor. Differentiation nevertheless must take place in the ranks of the upper classes. Manifold privileges are accompanied by minor privileges. The one cannot exist without the other. It is in the nature of events that small privileges must be subordinated to the higher ones.

Hierarchy and subordination in property relations must be accompanied by the same phenomena in politics and governmental organization.

Government has three basic functions:

—to protect the public against the attacks of foreign powers;

—to protect every individual against injustices and oppression that may be thrust upon him by other citizens;

—to maintain and promote such institutions and public projects as road, bridges, ports, channels, and certain educational and research institutions which individuals themselves cannot initiate or operate due to their unprofitability although they are necessary for the development of a nation.

A central government should perform such functions as cannot be carried out by local administrations. Every administration is evil, but a central one is worse than any other and should therefore be restricted to its bare essentials, Smith concluded.

Central and local governments must collect taxes in order to function. It should be borne in mind, Smith admonished, that every tax impoverishes society as a whole and its citizens in particular. Taxes represent an unproductive loss of national income; consequently, the best form of taxation is no taxation. Every tax inevitably contributes to an increase in the price of commodities and results in an increase of wages and salaries. Workers and farmers must earn as much as is necessary for them to be able to live above the level of poverty, Smith wrote. How can such a level be defined? Smith understood that it depends on historical and social conditions, that no general historical prescription can be laid down.

The concept that it is labor which, in the final analysis, is the source of the wealth of nations led Smith to an important, liberal, political conclusion: a government should be as inexpensive as possible. Once it is agreed that a government is unproductive, albeit necessary, it should waste as little as possible.

Smith was a proponent of unrestricted free economic competition. There were no doubts in his mind that the market is the best regulator of economic activity and the self-interests of the entrepreneurs, the source of great incentives, innovations, ambitious projects, and assumption of risk for business ventures. Free competition creates the foundation and environment in which an individual can be free, in which he can act according to his free will, personal perceptions, ambitions, inclinations, and aims. Government cannot make people happy or free; it can only protect the general economic and social conditions in which an individual's freedom can be realized and enjoyed.

A government exceeds its limits when it imposes detrimental restrictions on economic life and personal freedom. Government—and this is the quintessence of the liberal philosophy of politics and freedom—should provide a framework, in which competition and freedom can flourish, no more than that. The army and the police in this domain should act like referees, like impersonal observers of the actors on the stage. They should intervene only when they determine that the rules of the game have been violated, when the security of the property of the participants has been illegally endangered.

The stronger the armed forces, the firmer the guarantees of freedom, Smith asserted. The government that is secure in the knowledge that it can easily control any volatile situation, turmoil, or demonstration will not react hastily to such events because it knows there is sufficient time to reach prudent decisions.

The government of a liberal state should act according to the provisions of law. One should always remember, Smith argued in the spirit of the general principles of his philosophy, that every law is harmful in itself as is every act of the state. Nevertheless, a lawless government would be worse. Whenever legislators try to regulate the relations between the rich and the poor, between employees and workers, they seek the advice of wealthy employers.

The law cannot prevent owners from plotting against the workers, but it can effectively deny the workers' right to form their own associations. A nation as a whole, and those who are worse off in particular, are interested in fewer regulations, less legislative activity, fewer laws.

Smith concluded that there should be no laws to outlaw freedom of movement, the right to choose a profession or place of residence, or the right to set up one's own enterprise. Most obstacles created by institutions, laws, and customs are generally directed against the poor but usually protect the privileged.

Once all unreasonable laws and institutions are abolished, competition is liberated from all restrictions, and entrepreneurial freedom is restored, the wealth of nations and social mobility will increase, and the freedom of every individual will be expanded.

In this way, Smith laid the foundation for a new, expanded concept of freedom. His was the first mind to penetrate so deeply the relationships between economics, politics, and freedom. He was the author of the new ideas and the new illusions.

b. Benjamin Constant's Limitation of Government

The main political works of Benjamin Constant were written after the fall of the Jacobin dictatorship under the influence of Napoleon's rule and the restoration of the monarchy. Constant was deeply impressed by the new industrial development in Europe and the importance of the idea of legality, in particular, as embodied in the exemplary French Civil Code.

Constant was one of the first thinkers who identified the Jacobin dictatorship and terror as an incarnation of Rousseau's philosophy of the omnipotence and sovereignty of the people. The excesses of the revolutionary terror were dealt with in his writings as if their only source had been the ideas of Jean-Jacques Rousseau: that the people's power be unlimited and that the general will of the people could never err. His main criticism was directed against unlimited popular power. Constant argued that any unlimited power, no matter whether of one person or a group in a society, must necessarily lead to tyranny and terror.

It is not true, Constant argued, that freedom depends on those who exercise power. It does not even depend on the way they are selected. In the final analysis it is determined by the noninterference of the government in individual lives.

The main attributes of freedom are: freedom of profession, freedom of movement, freedom of conscience and religion, freedom of speech and the press. Citizens should live under law, be protected from arbitrary arrest, imprisonment, and torture. Citizens should be free to form their own organizations and parties, should enjoy freedom of assembly, demonstration, and to exercise freedom of will.

All these political and social liberties are inseparable from the right of property. The right of property should be unlimited;

the people should have the right of *utendi et abutendi* (use and abuse). Neither the state, nor any other social organization may interfere with the way ownership is exercised. According to Constant, economic freedom must lead to the development of personal wealth, thereby contributing to freedom.

Constant, more elaborately than any of his predecessors, maintained that there are two spheres of freedom: private and political. Every individual is a private person and a citizen of the state, according to Constant. Most important to an individual's life is his privacy. He regarded political or constitutional freedom a guarantee of the enhancement of private freedom. The government should be limited to these guarantees, he stated, and should not expand its activity.

Constant distinguished between the ancient and the modern concept of freedom. The ancient Greeks and Romans, in his opinion, believed that individuals might do everything permitted by law. According to the modern concept, the individual may do everything not prohibited by law. Constant pointed out that both Rousseau and Montesquieu failed to make this distinction clear. They were impressed that in certain periods of ancient Greece and Rome citizens participated in government in the legislative process, in the election of their rulers, and in the performance of judicial functions. This freedom, however, may not be identified with *la liberté civil* (civil liberty), Constant observed, because the individual was entirely subject to society. The Roman censors supervised even the style of life and intimate affairs of a family. The individual was more or less sovereign in political affairs but he was bound by the laws and customs of his region and permitted to do only what was explicitly authorized by law. In modern times, Constant wrote, freedom should be understood as freedom to do all that is not harmful to society or other individuals, meaning, everyone has the right to act according to his selfish desires and emotions. Even though harm should come to individuals through their own activities, that is not the government's affair. All such interference would be tantamount to limitation of free competition, free economic activity, and in the final analysis, personal freedom.

In this way Constant struck a nineteenth century note. Free-dom of economic activity is the basis of personal and political freedom, and vice versa, any restriction upon privacy and pol-itics could be detrimental to free competition.

Constant returned to the question of the sovereignty of government, and especially that of a people's government, from many viewpoints. In discussing this problem, the point of depar-ture, Constant wrote, should be the limitation of power and not the erroneous fiction advocated by both Hobbes and Rousseau (Constant recognized, however, that both thinkers proposed dif-ferent ends based on different presumptions). It is simply not true that sovereignty must be either unlimited or non-existent. Quite the contrary, Constant wrote, the needs and activity of every power are determined by the personal freedom of citizens. The laws should enhance this freedom and the government should desist from exceeding the laws. Any usurpation of power that goes beyond the law is dangerous for the entire system of legality and freedom even though transgressions have been minor. Constant concluded that the independence of individuals requires limiting government activity and social interference. There is no justification for a popular tyranny. In practice, Con-stant wrote, the people never exercise their power. It may have happened that people seized power for a short time after a revolution, but soon, very soon, they lost it to their leaders. The power of all is reduced to the power of the majority, afterwards to the power of the minority, ultimately to that of a selected group, and lastly to individual despotism.

The main political problem, therefore, is the protection of the people against any and all unnecessary and unauthorized govern-mental activity.

c. Liberal Arguments Against Censorship

All classic liberals and juridical positivists of the nineteenth century favored unlimited freedom of speech and the press. They all believed that there could be no more powerful limita-tion upon the power of the government than unrestricted crit-icism of its activity. They all agreed with Bentham that freedom

of speech, the press, and publication, contribute to the betterment of the moral standards of society, consequently people
are happier.

Bentham deduced a constitutional requirement for freedom
of the press from the principle of the greatest happiness for the
greatest number.

Bentham's praise for freedom of speech and the press is one
of the most magnificent, and most forgotten, in history. The
government should care no more about men speaking together
in public than about their eating in private, because both functions are natural for the human being. As Bentham pointed out,
the liberty of the press should not be granted or given, it should
exist by itself. No permission should be necessary. The exercise
of the natural gift of speaking and writing should simply be
unrestricted, be it in private or public. We are not granted the
right to eat and sleep by the government; we simply exercise
these faculties. Any restrictions upon this natural gift are artificial,
against nature, and oppressive.

Bentham mentioned that freedom of the press could cause
certain inconveniences. But the evils of censorship and suppression far surpass the minor evils of freedom, he insisted. The
genuine evils of the elimination of freedom of thought are immeasurable: they can stop the entire progress of human thought,
because every new and important truth must have its enemies. If
the advance of the human mind had depended upon the good will
of those in authority, he argued, then legislation, morals, the
physical sciences, all would be in darkness.

Freedom of the press meant for Bentham, specifically, the
freedom to criticize the government as a whole, its general
policy and particular activity, and the freedom to criticize the
government's functionaries. The situation in the United States
should prevail everywhere.

In this spirit he interpreted the First Amendment of the
American Constitution. According to his philosophy, the U. S.
Constitution does not confer liberty of the press upon Amer-
icans. It simply affirms its existence and prohibits anyone,

especially the Congress from restricting the human faculty and potential of speech and writing.

Bentham wrote that one of the greatest differences between the American constitutional system and all other forms of government is the fact that American officials enjoy no special privileges or immunity from criticism. Their reputations are not protected by special laws, usually known as libel laws. Let us put aside the question of to what extent Bentham's interpretation and presentation of the American legal and political system is correct. Important are his legal and political ideas, which he decided to illustrate by using American examples.

Bentham was not a utopian thinker and he understood the practical problems that could arise if the government and its administrative institutions were irresponsibly or viciously attacked. The principle of the greatest happiness also might be violated. Should the respective employees suffer for the sake of the "greater happiness" of others? Would the interests of the "greatest number" really be served in this way?

Every criticism of the government, Bentham argued, conveys "an imputation on *reputation*" of a person taking part in the government. An innocent criticism, a victimless criticism, does not exist. Bentham accepted this fact, but still defended the liberty of the press and criticism, taking into account all the social circumstances and political implications.

According to Bentham, the rights and freedom of those who criticize a government are of paramount importance. Even if a critic should be sued by the bureaucrats, the government should protect the critic; it should preserve all possible privileges and rights of a defendant; he should even enjoy the privilege of a presumption that he, the *critic of the government, is right and innocent.*

The court should judge the case in the usual way: no special tribunal and no *special* form of procedure should be applied. Even more: Bentham understood how difficult it is to win a case when the government as a whole, or even one member of the establishment supported by the whole power of the centralized

bureaucracy, is the plaintiff and has practically unlimited resources to support his case. Bentham, therefore, recommended
that the defendant should be at liberty to make proof of the truth
of his imputation; for that purpose he should be entitled to
extract evidence from the person who is the subject of it, and any
other person at large.

Bentham understood and took into account the *code d'hon-
neur* of the establishment and understood that it will be fighting
tooth and nail to protect its "reputation" and its own interest. He
therefore recommended that the defendant should have the right
to "extract evidence" from it. It is not without significance that
Bentham used the word "extract" instead of the more polite
expression "obtain" or "have access to" the available evidence.
He knows that especially where an agency of government is
interested, a defendant must "extract" evidence he needs
from it.

It seems that—according to Bentham—the critic of government enjoys the presumption of good faith whereas the government is always "suspected" and has to prove its innocence. The
government has no right to withhold from the public documents
which could damage its reputation including those that might
support the allegations of the critic.

Bentham is not far from Kant's assertion, that the degree of
openness in governmental operations is a measure of a government's morality. The point of departure for both is different, the
conclusions the same; darkness, says an old French proverb,
gives birth to crime.

Any restriction of the freedom of the press could *EVENTUATE
MISDEEDS AND CRIMES BY THE GOVERNMENT.*

* * *

Karl Wilhelm von Humboldt (1767-1835), a philosopher,
educator, and statesman of the Prussian monarchy, was only
twenty-five years old when his main treatise was written: *Ideen
zu einem Versuch die Grenzen der Wirksamkeit des Staates zu
bestimmen.* The book was published posthumously for the first

time. Its content was so unsettling that even he himself, though a minister and founder of the University of Berlin, was unable to induce the censorship to pass it.

Von Humboldt was the German equivalent of Jeremy Bentham* and Benjamin Constant. He too argued that the main purpose of the government should be to protect the interests of its citizens and to expand and promote their freedoms. Freedom, according to Humboldt, makes creative activity possible which does not, however, mean that people will be creative. Generally speaking, the longing for freedom is stronger, he maintained, than the will to take advantage of the opportunities it affords.

The government, according to Humboldt, can secure freedom in a negative way only, by guaranteeing the life and property of the citizens and non-interference in their private affairs. The authorities cannot assure the happiness of the people. They can only improve the external conditions conducive to it. When a state assumes too many duties and expands its sphere of administration, freedom suffers.

In every goverment institution, the spirit of power with its tendency to standardization and routine must prevail. Goebbels called it *Gleichschaltung* 150 years later and regarded it an advantage. Von Humboldt argued the opposite; he believed that the state in that way eliminates diversity and restricts initiative and the entrepreneurial spirit. Excessive tutelage by the state debilitates the morale of the people. They lose their independence, become morally irresponsible and slowly begin to believe that once they dutifully follow orders they are released from all responsibility and will not be blamed for the harm they inflict.

A thoughtful human being, Humboldt stated, will work with diligence only when he knows he can accomplish his purposes. When he fulfills orders given by the state, he becomes passive; he feels as if he were being led by the hand; he is not emotionally

---

*Bentham's philosophy of freedom in general, and of freedom of the press especially, was extensively analyzed in my previous book, *Juridical Positivism and Human Rights* (1981), pp. 9-65.

involved, therefore he becomes indifferent. Tutelage by the state requires definite instructions. When various personalities are all carrying out the same orders, they lose their individuality through lack of exercise.

Humboldt made an observation which has a special topical meaning for today: once the state issues ordinances, it creates a need for further clarifications, for additional instructions, for new institutions and new ordinances. It begins a vicious cycle. In order to avoid such a bureaucratic trap the first step must carefully be avoided. It seems Humboldt was the forerunner of Parkinson's law. Humboldt's conclusion is: whenever the government tries to achieve ends which are not directly connected with external and internal security, it defeats its proper ends; people are transformed into automatons, making them unhappy.

Humboldt interpreted the security of the state in the classic, liberal way: legal and political protection of the rights of the citizens and respect for their individuality and personal inclinations. He rejected the concept that the security of the state is an idea and a value in itself. On the contrary, the security of the state is inseparable from the happiness of the citizens. Obviously, this was not the *Staatsphilosophie* of the Prussian rulers.

Humboldt regarded freedom of speech and the press one of the guarantors of a legal order in a liberal state. But contrary to English, French, and American thinkers, he was unable to imagine a state in which no administrative or juridical censorship existed.

He elaborated reasonable arguments against preventive censorship and favored court supervision after publications by the press. He argued (among other items in the letter to Chancellor Hardenberg, January 9, 1816) that preventive censorship is indeed harmful to the government because readers would think that all that was printed had the approval of the authorities. Such a suspicion may even prove detrimental to external relations.

Court supervision is based on the principle that free citizens are responsible and able by themselves to understand the good and the bad. The court should start to exercise its supervisory power when the state's interest is being endangered, and especially law and order.

There is a discrepancy between Humboldt's general ideas of freedom and his thoughts on free press and government security. As he began to consider the latter problem, he departed from the type of philosophy so unequivocally expressed in the First Amendment to the Constitution of the United States and so highly praised by Jeremy Bentham. Humboldt became a Prussian bureaucrat, albeit an enlightened one, for whom *raison d'etat*, the interest of the state and its security became independent values in themselves, notions separated from the individual and his liberty.

Herein lies the difference between Humboldt's philosophy of state, law, and freedom and that of his French, English, and American counterparts. Freedom, which for the latter was unlimited, had definite limits in Humboldt's philosophy. He was a personal friend of Friedrich Schiller. Nevertheless, as a statesman, he was unable to draw the right conclusions from Schiller's pronouncement in *Don Carlos:* "Geben Sie was Sie uns nahmen wieder . . . Geben Sie Gedankenfreiheit!" (Give us what you have taken away . . . Give us the freedom to think.) That was the Marquis von Posa's plea to King Philip II of Spain.*

* * *

The differences between Constant's and von Humboldt's arguments represent the difference between French and German development. At the same time, Bentham's arguments were theoretical and juridically practical, being based on the English experience.

Benjamin Constant wrote that censorship always helps to preserve despotism and arbitrariness. Even the courts cannot remain independent without freedom of the press, he main-

---

*Friedrich Schiller, *Werke in Drei Barnden, "Don Carlos"* (Muenchen: Carl Hanser Verlag, Band I, 1966), p. 445.

tained. Napoleon many times violated legal due process but society was unaware of it because public opinion was manipulated; all publishers were supervised by the imperial authorities and there was no way to print any truth which the government regarded inconvenient.

Neutral phraseology is used in laws concerning censorship: truth should be protected, extreme criticism is to be prevented, misunderstandings are to be avoided; Constant wrote that such phrases deceive the people and may even serve as self-deception for their authors. According to Constant, it is not an impersonal institution or law which "defends," "protects," "fights," or "reduces"—it is human beings. The existence of censorship means that there are people who exercise power over the thoughts of others. Whoever maintains this power may use it to protect against lies as well as truths. Whenever a government has such power it will employ it to suppress information and limit information available to the public.

One of the results of censorship, Constant wrote, is that authors may reach a state of desperation. They are constantly under pressure, fearful that censors might disapprove of their ideas. Consequently, they lose their moral and intellectual independence without which an intellect cannot work creatively. Of course gifted and courageous authors might find ways to transmit their ideas by innuendo and allusions that may be more poisonous than the unvarnished truth. At times authors are compelled to print their works in a clandestine manner, under pseudonyms, which is as dangerous for the government as it is for the authors themselves. At times mediocre underground literature becomes sensational and creates an unhealthy interest; it may become far more influential than it would under conditions of freedom. Prohibitions draw increased attention to confiscated pamphlets, permitting falsehood to invade the minds of readers. It is a paradox, Constant wrote, that censorship often achieves the opposite of what it seeks. It dignifies lies, and undermines truth.

People's reasoning usually is simple and logical: If hundreds of censors and policemen use all the power of government to suppress certain ideas, they must have some value. Otherwise why would all that effort be expended.

Constant regarded freedom of the press to be the basic guarantee of legality, civil and political rights, and the independence of the courts. Without freedom of the press all of them become ephemeral. One should repeat a thousand times, Constant argued, that opinions repressed by the government or voluntarily rejected because of social bigotry and contempt will not remain in oblivion forever. They may be buried temporarily, but they will be resurrected in the future and their influence multiplied. An idea can be defeated only by another idea, Constant wrote; false reasoning can be defeated only by correct reasoning. Iron has no power over the mind.

According to Constant, there is no truth in the concept that physical violence can be justified in any fight against politically inconvenient theories or philosophies. Any violence against any thought must hurt truth generally, yet, paradoxically, truth persecuted is invigorated by violence.

There are times, Constant wrote, in which people become tired of philosophy and endless controversies. They are even happy at times that they are saved from having to listen to sterile discussions. But after a relatively short time the philosophical and moral controversies re-emerge; people discover the eternal truth that they cannot live by bread alone; they realize that philosophy is necessary in order to understand the meaning of life. Many are ashamed of having abdicated their intellectual responsibilities. They reawaken and search for metaphysical truths. If no meaningful philosophy is found, they will turn to wrong, shallow, superficial theories. They accept them uncritically for lack of anything better. They turn against the government with contempt and fury. The rulers then find themselves in trouble. The results of intolerance are most harmful for the intolerant; that was Constant's ultimate conclusion.

d. The Philosophy of John Stuart Mill—The Crowning Point of Liberalism

Liberalism reached its apogee in the works of John Stuart

Mill. He gave the final polish to the ideas of his predecessors and collected them into one logical entity. He reached the limits of this social theory and he demonstrated his true greatness when he did not hesitate to cross the Rubicon. He entered the realm which his fellow liberals meticulously avoided: the relationship between freedom and tolerance, class stratification, the system of government, technical progress, and the development of the working class. He is still underestimated as a thinker who threw the first bridges across from the nineteenth to the twentieth centuries.

The central political problem, as John Stuart Mill saw it, is the notion of freedom in general, and the question of the limits of governmental activity in particular. The struggle between freedom and the usurpation by government, he observed, is characteristic of the history of mankind. Since ancient times, Mill wrote, people have believed that government is necessary to protect them against foreign aggression. They were also aware that the same weapon in the hands of a ruler can be directed against his own subjects as well as foreigners. Throughout the centuries, therefore, reasonable citizens have been trying to restrict the power and the privileges of government in order to guarantee their own rights and freedoms.

Various measures were used to achieve this end. There have been societies which in various periods tried to receive from the ruler certain personal guarantees of their rights. Due to the further development of civilization and culture, nations found that, instead of personal guarantees, entire populations were to be granted constitutional liberties and rights. They considered that measure to be more effective and safer than the previous arrangement.

The next step was the realization that all public officials should be elected and made responsible to the voters and that the duration of their tenure should be limited. Ultimately, it came to be held that a government of the people, for the people, and by the people, would be the best guarantee against encroachments by governments.

The history of political evolution shows, Mill wrote, that

those thinkers were right who argued that every government, even the most democratic and truly popular, should be restricted and its competence limited. One should remember that such phrases as "autonomy," "power of the people," "government of the people," and "rule by the people," are very appealing but do not really mean much. Under any government, including a people's government, there is a great difference between those who are ruled and those who rule. It is an illusion that the government of everyone is truly a government under which everyone is autonomous and responsible for his own affairs; experience shows that under any so-called people's government it is not everyone who is a ruler; quite the contrary.

One of John Stuart Mill's basic conclusions is his recommendation that in order to preserve and to protect individual liberties it is necessary to guarantee them against any government, democratic or undemocratic, a government of the minority or of the majority.

Mill's second distinction is that not only may governments be tyrannical towards individuals but also society itself can be despotic in its relations with its individual members. Tyrannical oppression is not the exclusive monopoly of political and governmental functionaries; tyranny can also be exercised by the majority and almost all the members of a society.

Government and society must learn that there is a certain limit beyond which they may not extend their will and activity. Within these limitations, an individual must be free; no one is entitled to cross that demarcation line and an individual can be free only within that legal framework and structure of rights.

One of the first spheres in which the tyranny of government and society was limited was freedom of conscience. According to John Stuart Mill, whoever was in favor of religious tolerance was also convinced that no individual should be condemned or suffer discrimination because of his inner beliefs. Mankind, however, according to Mill, is basically intolerant and freedom of religion has never been fully realized anywhere. People felt free in their religious convictions only during short periods in which religious indifference prevailed. In those short periods people believed that social peace was more important than theological truth.

Tolerance has been accepted only with reservations, Mill wrote. It has not been regarded a good in itself. Many, therefore, are in favor of religious tolerance with qualifications; they do not want to extend it to papists or unitarians. Many believers do not want to tolerate those who do not believe in life after death. Many of those who truly and deeply believe, Mill observed, believe that others should follow them in their faith.

In order to avoid misunderstanding, usurpation, encroachment, and violations of individual freedom and social tolerance, the limits and purposes of a state's activities must be defined. According to Mill there is only one reason to justify the activity of a government or the pressure of the public on an individual, and that is the defense and protection of individual rights against pressure by members of a society or the agents of a government. No one has the right to interfere with the private life of an individual in order to protect his moral or physical well-being. Everyone should pursue his own good and happiness and no one is entitled to make an individual happy against his own will.

The activity of governments, therefore, should be negative rather than positive. It should not be expanded but limited as far as possible.

The classic liberal understanding of freedom is this: every individual should care for his own interests and mind his own business. No one should deem himself his brother's keeper unless his brother unequivocally asks him to. Every individual is a world unto himself, is a being in himself and is presupposed to be the best judge of his own affairs; everyone should respect the wishes, beliefs, and way of life of others. Privacy is sacrosanct and no intrusion upon it should be tolerated because that is the way general tolerance comes into being, it is its *modus operandi.*

Mill added, however, that this concept can only be realized among a people who are relatively civilized and educated. In his treatise on representative government, Mill argued that the liberal doctrine and ideals cannot be applied to the peoples of a lower stage of culture. He admitted in not so many words that despotism is acceptable in societies of barbarians. He did not justify that political system, he was merely prepared to accept it (for others) for a short period provided that the despot tries to achieve the ultimate goals: freedom, and progress. The eternal political question is: when is a given society sufficiently developed and civilized? Even more important: who should decide this question?

According to Mill, people will reach the level of intellectual maturity when they are able to exchange ideas as one equal to another, when they are able to discuss important matters without cutting each other's throats; at such a stage of adulthood, people will be free to decide what kind of reforms and laws should be instituted. However, neither Mill nor any other philosopher has answered the question of who will be the judge, who will decide when the period of barbarism is over. Once the decision is reached that the period of savages and ruffians has ended, who will explain to the barbarian despot that his time has come to an end and therefore he should abdicate in favor of an enlightened democratic regime? History knows few or no benevolent despots who voluntarily stepped down in favor of democracy and freedom. Neither does history know any philosophers or rhetoricians able to persuade the tyrants that it would be in their own best interest to surrender their power.

Mill argued that it is wrong to suppose that truth has a magic power which will overcome persecution, imprisonment, and torture. It is a sentimental belief, in his opinion, that error lacks power and will, therefore, fall of its own weight. History shows that people have been as zealous to serve untrue ideas as they were the true ones, that they fought for the errors which today we regard unreasonable and superstitious with the same fervor as partisans of truth and freedom. Historical experience also indicates that whenever the freedom to disseminate falsehood is curtailed, the freedom of truth is also limited. The only "innate," "natural," privilege which truth enjoys is the prospect that once defeated, once its followers are exterminated, truth will inevitably be resurrected, after a time. The suppressed surely will be rediscovered once more and after its second or third reemergence it will finally prevail.

Persecution can deprive contemporary people of the benefit of knowing and understanding truth when it is announced for the first time. All mankind loses when a lack of freedom and tolerance bans the truth for any length of time.

English society comforts itself with the fact that it no longer kills false prophets. That is an issue which Mill took on next. He asserted that it is an illusion to believe that a decisive step toward freedom of thought and speech had been undertaken in England because the severity of the punishment is not the decisive factor in the suppression of freedom. The essential element of freedom and tolerance is "absence" of all discrimination and persecution of those who hold different views. Even the slightest act of discrimination or even the fear of possible discrimination can be as harmful for the discovery of truth as are bloody executions.

One of the remnants of the period of religious persecutions is the requirement that those who erred make public confessions and public recantations of their previous ideas. These acts are facile for those who decide to be liars and hypocrites, whereas those who are decent and want to say what they really think have to suffer. Such a practice is indeed lethal for the doctrine in whose name the acts of compulsion are made. If one is afraid to express one's doubts or publicly disagree with a given doctrine, if one is compelled to express what one does not believe, then the priests and authors of the given religion or doctrine deprive themselves of the knowledge of who their friends are and who their enemies are, who truly believe and who are the skeptics.

Heretical ideas are beneficial for truth itself. During the fight against wrong perceptions, truth not only preserves its vigor but develops and reinforces itself; establishes itself while better and deeper arguments are elaborated.

Social intolerance, as it is practiced in England now, does not kill anyone nor does it eradicate adverse ideas. Intolerance only encourages heretics and all those who think independently to hide their beliefs. Suppressed beliefs can remain in the pro-

verbial "closet" for many years; the non-conformists are isolated. One day, however, when circumstances become more favorable, the suppressed ideas suddenly erupt.

Intolerance can hurt moral and civil courage. Under the rule
of intolerance people become the slaves of rhetoric. Many
become opportunists; they even repeat arguments which they
know cannot persuade the listeners but they want to pretend that
they are truly orthodox.

One cannot even estimate how much mankind loses to intolerance. It is possible that there are many more innovative and
creative minds than we dare to dream of, but they are afraid of
persecution; their characters lack strength. It would be difficult
to blame them for it. Of course, truly great thinkers usually are
deeply convinced that they should publicly announce what they
truly believe in. They have enough inner strength to disseminate
their ideas. One can therefore even argue that freedom is more
necessary for the average mortal than it is for the great. Unusual
people have unusual minds, unusually strong characters and
wills. Obstacles only serve to reinforce their convictions and
their ability to fight and win. But the average lack such unusual
drive and power of resistance. When they know that something
is going wrong, that an adversary can hurt them, they decide to
submit; they are not prepared to start a fight against an enemy
who for the time being is stronger.

Freedom and tolerance exist in a perpetual struggle. Mill
discovered and rediscovered this truth which today is almost
self-evident: freedom and tolerance, political and social freedom, should not be regarded under any regime or in any society
as something that has at long last been achieved, established,
guarded, and exercised; freedom must constantly be fought for,
continually be re-established.

* * *

John Stuart Mill more than any other liberal author understood that freedom can best be guaranteed by that form of
government which he called "representative." No one can truly
restrict or define the limits of a despotic government.

There are many zealous and impatient reformers, Mill

wrote, who are anxious to change social institutions with the help of a more "efficient" and "expedient" autocratic government. Being able to do so is an illusion, Mill observed, because people cannot be governed well when they do not have a part in their government.

It is also illusory, Mill argued, to distinguish between so-called good and bad despots. Perhaps a mild despot is more dangerous than an obviously evil one. "Good" despotism deceives and depraves the people. It poisons their thoughts, feelings, and talents. The good despotism of Caesar Augustus prepared the Romans to accept the horrendous acts of Tiberius.

Representative government must be based on the support of the people who are moral and active. Indeed, a good government can exist only in a society of people who have reached a certain level of culture and civic responsibility. Despotism dislikes people who are active, intellectually independent, full of initiative and an entrepreneurial spirit. All these features demand a democratic government in which people participate. The mere existence of freedom of conscience, thought, speech, and assembly encourages citizens to cooperate with one another, to take initiatives and develop private morality. They are united because they search for new horizons together, in contrast to a despotic government which tries to transform society into a herd of sheep which peacefully roam in the pastures marked out for them.

One of the basic premises of Mill's political philosophy is the conviction that there is a close and direct interdependence between the form of representative government and the consciousness and morality of a society. He stressed many times (and concluded by using many methods of argumentation) that in order to institute and preserve a representative government people must have the will and ability to do what is necessary to sustain such a government. People must be able to pursue not only their narrow and selfish interests. Their egoism must be enlightened and they should realize that there are certain common interests which are indispensable for achieving their particular interests. Mill did not condemn selfishness, in fact he felt it is a passion without which nothing great can be achieved. Rather, he argued, that citizens of a well governed country must represent a higher form of selfishness, a kind of enlightened egoism.

How can people be elevated to a higher form of social consciousness? Mill rejected any form of preaching or moralizing. He observed that in a society in which economic and political arrangements demoralize those who exercise power, the people as a whole will be demoralized. But in a society that is organized in such a way that decency and initiative are rewarded, the people will be frugal, honest, and entrepreneurial.

A special role in this process of elevation of the people can be played by a group of enlightened, well educated individuals who understand the nature of political systems and can share this knowledge with the rest of society. Such a method of education is proposed by Mill. He became one of the most powerful proponents of the idea that the intellectuals have a special, historical mission.

Unfortunately, the concept that the intelligentsia is the best guardian of democratic liberties has never been realized. It may be that the final blow to this concept was struck by C. Wright Mills in his works, *The Power Elite* and *White Collar*. Variations of the special concept of the mission of intellectuals are the convictions of Plato (the special role of philosophers and the "true politicians") and Lenin (the revolutionary vanguard of the proletariat can lead the people to their earthly salvation).

The strong element of Mill's theory is that he realized that there is an interdependence between the economic and social structure of a society and the ideas and beliefs of individuals. He also understood that the social structure determines the ambitions and the morality of the people. Nevertheless he was unable to elaborate a consistent theory as to how to change social and economic systems to make them more humane and compatible with the higher standards of morality which he himself recommended. The most important deficiency of his theory is that he was unable to determine realistic means for the transfor-

mation of despotism into a democratic government. Should the
people rely on the good will of an enlightened despot? He himself rejected as basically unrealistic the idea of a benevolent despot. Should citizens revolt and employ violence in order to
achieve a free society? One can argue that Mill never condemned revolution as a matter of principle, as something evil in
all circumstances, nevertheless, he never recommended it.

There are of course new elements concerning these problems in his later writings. He introduced them in the 3rd edition
of his *Principles of Political Economy.* There he analyzed the
role of the working class and concluded that it is a new social and
moral phenomenon, that workers have their own special interest
and a new social consciousness. The evolution of the working
class is the result of technical progress and the immense development of industry. The wealth produced by society becomes enormous but one should not suppose, Mill warned, that
wealth should be produced for the sake of the wealthy; that is not
the ultimate aim of society. The end is to reduce the numbers of
hours which employees spend in factories and offices. Until
now, Mill insisted, no correlation exists between the growth of
wealth and the standard of living of the workers and the amount
of free time they have at their disposal. The future of freedom
depends, Mill wrote, on the elevation of the social and intellectual standard of the working class.

How can these benefits be achieved? There are two ways, as
usual, Mill answered. One is through the tutelage of the upper
classes who in a paternalistic way teach the lower class. The
second way is self elevation. The first way has become obsolete,
Mill wrote, and the workers expect no gratification from any
rich, self-proclaimed benefactors. The second way, however, is
feasible.

The workers had already learned to read and write. They
had access to books, newspapers, and the parliamentary de-
bates. They already understood more than any of the lower
classes that had ever preceded them. As a group they were able
to acquire the necessary knowledge on their own. The upper
classes had but one truly reasonable way to influence the work-

ers: good literature should be made available because otherwise the workers would learn from poor sources.

In this way Mill reached conclusions which went beyond the horizons and expectations of bourgeois society. He was the first great liberal author who realized that there would be basic changes in the future society based on private property and free economic initiative. He also realized that new social forces had entered the social and economic arena. The problem which was of greatest concern for him was not the decline of the then upper classes, but the question of freedom and tolerance as understood, guarded, and developed by the new social strata and the new political systems. Will they be able to continue the historical trend of progress and freedom? Mill basically was an optimist, but with many reservations.

TOLERANCE

1. Tolerance of the Sin or Tolerance of the Sinner

The word tolerance comes from the Latin word, *tolerare* (to put up with). It can be defined very simply as: "the attitude of a person who will bear with the philosophical and moral convictions of others which he considers to be false or even objectionable; nor will he try to suppress their legitimate expression. Such a position means neither the approval of such convictions nor indifference with regard to truth and goodness, nor is it founded necessarily on agnosticism."[1]

This simple definition is only one of our points of departure. It is incomplete and for today's needs, inadequate. Walter Brugger, S.J., writes that the necessity for tolerance in modern society is based on (a) freedom of the person to decide what is good or false; (b) justice, whose basic maxim is that each one receive what is his due; (c) the human "almost universal capacity to err." And he immediately adds a distinction: "This right is not a right of error (for rights inhere in persons), but of the erring person or of the person whom many others think is in the wrong."[2]

This old distinction (right of error versus right of the erring person), presumably introduced into Christian philosophy and theology by St. Augustine, has had a long and bloody history. The differentiation between the rights of sin and of the sinner may be catchy and appeal to many minds, but it is basically wrong. There are no sins without sinners, and once we agree that the sinner has rights we should also admit that there may be a grain of truth in the sinful, condemned belief. To love the sinner but hate the sin is a moralistic and theological construction; it might be a good theme for a sermon, but it is no guide for conducting social relations or political activities. From the standpoint of the person charged with sinning, the most important issue is whether he, the sinner, is tolerated, whether he has the legal and moral right to freedom of thought, speech, and appropriate, legally protected activity. If he does not enjoy those elementary liberties, then the assurances of "love" from his oppressors are cynical hypocrisy. *It is better to be hated and enjoy freedom than to be loved and be gagged and bound.*

Therefore the maxim, love the sinner but hate the sin, is no friend of freedom or tolerance.

Tolerance not only means tolerating, it also encompasses attempts to comprehend the origins of different views, persuasions, ideologies and very often also irrational interests and inclinations. Any explanation, even incomplete, but based on rationalistic reasoning, can be helpful.

Sigmund Freud described certain types of dreams as childish: one realizes the fulfillment of one's daydreams, desires, and ambitions in the subconscious, while asleep. But people seek fulfillment of their daydreams. Therefore, they are attracted to television shows which give them a chance to forget about their daily misery in favor of an operetta of smiles, friendship, and beauty.

Tolerance includes an understanding of human escapism and irrationality. Dreams for betterment and happiness are endless; therefore, tolerance for such dreams and respect for subrational behavior must also be inexhaustible. One must tolerate the symbols which replace reality.

One could argue that people who are more civilized, educated, and cultured, will feel less need for symbols. Reason can dictate—in theory, at least—what is proper or improper, real or unreal, true or untrue, pleasant or unpleasant, without resorting to myths, taboos, holy pictures, paradisical joys, and other symbols. In practice, however, people still need symbols.

Carl Rowan was theoretically right when he announced on CBS-TV (Saturday, August 1, 1981, Agronsky & Company) that there is no reason why people should be more interested in the marriage of Lady Diana and Prince Charles than in the marriage of any 19 to 20 year old girl. But almost 700 million TV viewers were interested in this public relations performance of the royal family. Why? Are there so many people who are simply irrational? empty? nostalgic? looking for odd sensations? driven by vanity? Would it not rather be more correct to accept the view of Rebecca West that the "royal scene simply is a presentation of ourselves behaving well. If anyone is being honored, it is the human race . . . when they mind their manners." Was there not a grain of truth in Flora Lewis's comment: "What is left is simple acknowledgment that *symbols* are cherished still, because faith and hope remain and need to be embodied . . . So it was that the very futility of the pomp, the play of *extravaganza in a hard and uncertain world*, made the spectacle satisfying and exposed its meaning." (Flora Lewis: "Sharing the Royal Fun and the Significance," *The New York Times*, July 31, 1981, p. A 23, emphasis added).

The people who observed the wedding were not just curious, irrational, or vain. They watched the symbols of things which they miss in their lives: affluence, courtesy, good manners, kindness, civility, decency, and beauty. In their daily lives they are surrounded by ugliness, rudeness, exploitation, and poverty. Symbols, including fairy tale weddings, are nothing more than flowers embellishing their chains.

The interest accorded the famous wedding, the celebrations, the joy gained from it by so many non-and-anti-royalists, is a sign that on our overcrowded continents the chains are heavy and there is little hope to diminish that burden.

Hence, the escape from reality to the world of illusion.

Tolerance of illusions is human, because in inhuman conditions illusions are a consolation.

Tolerance requires understanding of human weakness, motives, irrationalism, failures, "bad days," unreasonable longing, pluses and minuses of mind, will, and character.

Tolerance is more important for those who are poor, meek, and weak, than for those who are mighty, proud, and rich.

We have already argued that the modern ideas of tolerance

and freedom are inseparably connected with the rise of humanism.

Humanism also has a history. This notion became renowned all over the world as the negation of the feudal subjugation of the individual to the secular and church hierarchies. With the evolution of the new social and political regimes, with the economic transformations and the new interpretations and application of religious doctrines and moral norms, the content of humanism has changed as well. Humanism has always had a positive meaning while at the same time being directed against its most dangerous adversary during the given epoch. Every humanistic idea results from social oppression, political antagonism, and struggles; it is also an assertion of the actual, positive programs which tend to expand freedom and to overcome the obsolete heritage.

Although notions of humanism and tolerance throughout the centuries have acted to preserve certain important features common to both, in every era they have also been enriched by new notions. They had contents similar in some respects and differing in others in the ages of the Renaissance, the Enlightenment, Liberalism, and in the age of contemporary totalitarianism. For instance, *socialist humanism,* so much acclaimed after World War II, is a philosophical and political reaction to the Stalinist bureaucratic type of communist despotism, and against right wing authoritarian regimes. Socialist humanism continues the traditional humanistic ideas, and democratic, individualistic, egalitarian demands; it adds to them a specific note stimulated by the new totalitarian forms of oppression.

The simple truth that both humanism and tolerance develop simultaneously and dialectically, that they represent an amalgam of traditional and new elements at every stage, is often underestimated even by the most outspoken and ardent representatives of today's humanistic movement. The reflections published by Stephen S. Fenichell, treasurer of the American Humanist Association, are so concise and appropriate that they are a good example for the presentation of our point.

As it is understood in the modern philosophical sense, humanism is our intellectual heritage from the 18th century rationale, skeptical, ironic, and dedicated to recognizable human goals. The basic tenets of humanism are quite simple. First, what is good for the people is good for society (and the state). Second, our judgements on morals, government, law, economics and education are to be based upon human reason and not on supernatural intervention or divine guidance. Third, humanism believes in individual freedom of choice as opposed to religious determinism, and so every individual is responsible for his or her actions.[3]

Of course, what the author states in points one and two is correct but point three is, in its inferences at least, incomplete and therefore partially misleading.

Not all modern religions and theologies are so deterministic that they completely deny individual freedom of choice. Catholicism, Judaism, and various (not all) Protestant denominations have for a long time been able to overcome fatalism; they reject any philosophy which could be interpreted as radically deterministic, leaving no free space for the human intellect and free will to maneuver or for people creatively to influence the course of events and be responsible for what they do. It is true that one of the philosophical foundations of humanism, tolerance, and freedom is dialectical determinism. It is opposed to both the religious and the secular concepts of fatalism or predestination. Dialectical determinism as the philosophical basis of humanism recognizes human will and activity as one of the essential factors influencing historical development; will and activity are regarded as an essential link in the chain of events.

The traditional disputes between the secular humanistic concept of determinism (not fatalism), and the religious notions of determinism (leading very often to some sort of predestination) are not the most topical controversies today and they by no means should be regarded as constituting a specific difference between these two philosophies.

If a believer in God agrees with the first humanistic premise (the good of the individual is a basic criterion which should be used to determine what is good for society and the state), and if he partially agrees with the second humanistic premise (our judgments should be based on human reason which can function independently of divine intervention), then he deserves to be called a humanist because in our epoch, characterized by a historical battle between freedom and totalitarianism, a religious man usually stands on the correct side of an invisible barricade. Very often he is for freedom and tolerance not despite of, but due to his religious beliefs. Ever more and more frequently, Christians and Jews oppose despotism, absolutism, and totalitarianism not despite, but because of their religious convictions.

All forms of totalitarianism or creeping totalitarianism constitute a total, comprehensive danger to every form or shape of humanism, tolerance, and freedom. Many philosophies, religions, theologies, political doctrines, fideism and atheism, can lead to total oppression. Whoever is against these new dangerous absolutistic trends and despotic ideas, whoever is against actual or creeping totalitarianism, is a modern partisan of humanism, tolerance, and freedom. For these purposes it does not matter what one's philosophical or ideological credo is, because today a person's attitude toward any religious or secular totalitarian oppression and barbarism serves as a sort of litmus paper to be used to distinguish friends of freedom tolerance and humanism from their adversaries.

Stephen S. Fenichel—as any contemporary humanist should—understands this problem very well and therefore, notwithstanding his previous general remarks, correctly observes:

> "The issue is whether we want to give political and economic power to fanatic, electronic evangelicals who think they have a divine, Biblical mandate to rule over the minds (and souls?) of us lesser mortals."[4]

This is the crucial problem for defenders of American tolerance and freedom in the early 1980s: to avert the danger created by the "fanatic, electronic evangelicals" and the millions of people misled and led by them in order to defeat the simple requirements of reason, dignity, and morality. In order to succeed in the new battle for humanism, for a traditional way of life and liberty, the small group of organized humanists must act in unison with all those who want to defend and to preserve the soul of the American constitutional system, the Bill of Rights. After all, "humanism is pervasive in the civilized world."[5] It happens, however, that many people may be partisans of a true moral majority (without a capital "m") who do not even realize that the struggle for the traditional western democratic, parliamentary liberties is, in its very essence and roots, a fight for humanistic ideals.

Humanism has many roots and, therefore, it may be that even secular humanism has strengthened its fiber due to the openness of certain theologies and the rationality of certain religious interpretations. Whatever the source of its vital social and intellectual juices is, they never should be rejected; they should be properly identified and absorbed.

2. Tolerance as an Attitude

Whenever we speak of tolerance, two divergent thoughts come to mind: either tolerance as an idea, or tolerance as a practical mode of behavior.

Reinhold Niebuhr wrote that tolerance may be described as "the ability to get along with people who are different. . . ." Tolerance, therefore, may be defined as: "the inclination and capacity to establish and preserve community with people who differ in some respect from the general type or consensus."[6]

Tolerance has sometimes been identified with freedom. Tolerance as a mode of behavior is a description of the pattern of real behavior on the part of individuals, social groups, political and social organizations, and especially governments. Bearing this in mind, we come upon the following paradox: a government proclaims tolerance officially, but the members of the society may be intolerant. Individuals may be antagonistic (if not downright hostile) towards all those who "differ in some respect from the general type or consensus." The opposite may also be true.

The government of the ruling party may be based on intolerance, may officially proclaim intolerance, and yet the people in daily life may practice tolerance and not, as Pericles said in his Funeral Oration, give black looks which are unfriendly and insulting; they do not mind that someone lives his life according to his own wishes as long as he harms no one; and of course they do not mind that a person has his own peculiar religion, philosophy, political convictions, or sexual preferences. Tolerance differs from freedom but the two are closely related.

Freedom as interpreted in the broad Renaissance sense, enriched by the traditions of Hegel and Dewey, determines the place of an individual in society. Economic and political factors may be decisive, but they can never encompass all the components of freedom. One of those components is tolerance.

Tolerance (or intolerance) is an idea and a way of behaving on the part of individuals and social groups, and therefore it constitutes one of the basic components of freedom at every stage of social development. A society which enables the majority to become relatively influential and allows individuals to participate in making major political decisions may be politically democratic, but the freedom of those individuals may be restricted because of the intolerant attitude of the majority towards all those who are "different." Perhaps the first step towards freedom and tolerance is the attitude of forbearance, on the part of the majority of the people, to those who are different—the mental disposition that "strange" persons should not be persecuted, nor even put in a situation which they may perceive as uncomfortable. The next step on the road to tolerance is a positive appreciation of those who differ, on the part of the majority. The majority should learn to recognize that those who are "different" make an important contribution to the general good. No progress would be possible if everybody thought and acted in the same way.

When Reinhold Niebuhr wrote in praise of tolerance that "toleration is the necessary price of social peace in any creative community."[7] he made a basic and common mistake. Tolerance should not be regarded as an exaction or burden; it is not something evil in itself. It is nonsense to assert that tolerance must, unfortunately, be practiced. On the contrary, tolerance is a vehicle for the social, political, and spiritual development of any society. It is easily demonstrated that the golden age in the life of every nation was always an age of relative tolerance—and periods of decline are often periods of intolerance, witch-hunting, bigotry, and the persecution of those who deviate from the norm of mediocrity, and oppose organized stupidity or prevailing ignorance.

Let us mention Athens under Pericles, the Roman Republic in the Second Century B.C., the Roman Empire under the Great Caesars, and Poland during the sixteenth century. The last country, in her golden age, was almost the only European country which was a haven for persecuted dissidents; it was a genuine commonwealth (*Rzeczpospolita*) of many nations, and because of that it was a European superpower at the same time.

Let us also remember that Western countries developed their cultures, civilizations, and industrial power while establishing and practicing political democracy, while expanding political liberties and all forms of political, religious, intellectual, and moral tolerance.

Indeed, every period of intolerance is expensive for humanity. Political and social decline is accompanied by intolerance and by broken lives, personal unhappiness, cultural decay, demoralization, and the loosening of social ties. It is of course possible that in such a period an intolerant government can promote technological progress, develop a new architecture, and build new industries. But the price paid for intolerance will always be exorbitant. Those affected by intolerance are victims, but very often in order to defend themselves they become persecutors, too. In this way vicious cycles of intolerance and persecution begin.

Tolerance is a value in itself. This theme was developed in a speech by George Washington, the first president of the United States. In his address to the Jewish Congregation of Newport, Rhode Island, in August 1790, Washington said,

"The citizens of the United States of America have a right to applaud themselves for having given to mankind examples of an enlarged and liberal policy—a policy worthy of imitation. All possess alike liberty of conscience and immunities of citizenship. It is now no more that toleration is spoken of, as if it was by the indulgence of one class of people that another enjoyed the exercise of their inherent natural rights. For happily the government of the United States, which gives to bigotry no sanction, to persecution no assistance, requires only that they who live under its protection should demean themselves as good citizens in giving it on all occasions their effectual support."[8]

The distinction here made by George Washington is very important: Tolerance is sometimes interpreted as a result of an indulgence, as if it was *gratia principis* (a grace of the prince), a kind of grace granted to the subjects by "his royal highness." The concept of tolerance as an "indulgence" is alien to the American Constitution, at least according to the tradition represented by George Washington.

The Constitution does not grant any indulgences or immunities, but it does guarantee political liberties, including the liberty of conscience, which is regarded as a natural and inherent right to be enjoyed by all who live in this country. The constitutional principles are the grounds of the right to demand respect, and not only condescending, grudging "toleration."

The use of the word "toleration" by George Washington in this case is very specific because he wanted to make his own particular point. Tolerance should not be placed against or opposite to freedom. It should be regarded as one of the forms or components of freedom, and one of the pre-conditions of the emergence and existence of freedom at the same time.

Washington's speech was, of course, not a philosophical treatise, but an important political pronouncement. It was his intention, when addressing the Jews of Newport—the most persecuted fraction of the population living among the Christians—to proclaim that a truly new era had begun with the foundation of the United States, the era of freedom, not of grudging acceptance.

3. Tolerance Misconceived

One should distinguish legal tolerance from social tolerance. These two notions are often interrelated—sometimes they are barely distinguishable—but the difference between them is substantial from both the practical and theoretical viewpoint.

One should also distinguish tolerance of the public expression of one's opinion and tolerance of acts, practices, and attitudes (which last is the least defined notion).

One should exclude from the general philosophy of tolerance (especially tolerance of opinions) the juridical question of libel. But the distinction between "impersonal" doctrines and opinions on one hand, and opinions concerning living persons on the other, cannot be too precise, and the limits of tolerance in this respect must be flexible. One thing seems certain: any overstrict interpretation of the concept of libel by authors, public figures, or institutions, can curtail freedom of discussion and tolerance of expression concerning topical problems, living thinkers, and active politicians.

One should deal with the problems of libel separately. Political, philosophical, and religious tolerance, rightly understood, should not be confused with "tolerance" or indifference to acts of intolerance and attempts to destroy the system of political freedom. As Byron observed:

And I will war, at least in words (and—should
   My chance so happen—deeds), with all who war
With Thought;—and of Thought's foes by far most rude,
   Tyrants and sycophants have been and are.
                        —*Don Juan, IX, xxiv.*

Byron is right when he further observes that one must fight actively "Thought's foes" with *words* and *deeds* (when necessary), because the result of this long struggle is not predetermined. The partisans of freedom and tolerance may at any time suffer defeats.

I know not who may conquer: if I could
   have such prescience, it should be no bar
To this my plain sworn downright detestation
   of every despotism in every nation.
                          —*Don Juan, IX, xxiv.*

When Byron confesses his "plain, sworn downright detestation of every despotism," he expresses the feeling of all the true
and thoughtful friends of freedom: enemies of "thought's freedom" are contemptible and detestable creatures—whose right
to think and to express their opinions should nevertheless also
be assured and protected by legal and political means. At the
same time, they should be actively criticized and fought as enemies of humanity. So long as they use intellectual means to
oppose the principles of freedom and tolerance, one should
"war... in words" (Byron); when they start to use other means,
then one must defend freedom, not by turning the other cheek
but by warring against them with "deeds."

Let us analyze two examples of tolerance misconceived. At
the beginning of the 1930's, the Weimar Republic had already
been infiltrated by Nazi activity and ideology. Hitler's cohorts
were well organized in various para-military organizations; they
were receiving regular military or para-military training that
would allow them to eliminate their adversaries. The troops of
the SS and SA were conducting illegal, anticonstitutional activity which could have been prohibited by recourse to existing
laws, in keeping with the requirements of justice and morality.
The juridical and moral questions that arose in this period of
German history have been too well analyzed to require any
specific arguments, theories, or details here. From the viewpoint of the philosophy of freedom and tolerance one can say
that the partisans of freedom and democratic liberties had no
excuse for tolerating the physical excesses and outright crimes
committed by the members of Hitler's organizations. Those
persons should have been arrested and punished immediately
upon the commission of the crimes; their organizations, their
statutes, their official and secret instructions should have been
judicially assessed in order to denounce them and punish the

conspiracy and the direct attempts at criminal activity. All these available legal measures were deliberately neglected by the German authorities. Even more, those who were financing these illegal Nazi forces and activities (German bankers, steel magnates and the war industry) should have also been prosecuted as accomplices and instigators. Before and after the seizure of power, Dr. Joseph Goebbels, Hitler's infamous propaganda chief, used to argue that the freedom enjoyed by the Nazis was in accordance with the rules of rotten liberalism, parliamentary democracy, and effete tolerance. They, the Nazis, were using those available institutions and freedoms for their own purposes, but they never promised to respect them after their victory.

The interpretation of democracy, freedom, and tolerance presented by Goebbels may be in accordance with the ideas of some liberals and partisans of tolerance. But those ideas can only be a *caricature of the true traditions, theories, and experience of tolerance.*

One should, first of all, distinguish between tolerance of thought (ideas, theories, philosophies, persuasions) and practical political activities which are either criminal or tend, through illegal or half-illegal methods, to destroy the existing social and constitutional system of democracy, freedom, and tolerance. Activities alone can be and sometimes must be prohibited. Freedom of thought and speech, never.

The difference between freedom of speech and freedom of activity was well understood by Lenin, the founder of the Bolshevik Party. From the numerous writings of Lenin concerning the problem of political liberties and their limitations, let us in this connection analyze his famous expression after the communist takeover at the beginning of the civil war: "Words today are more important than the bullets and guns. Words are like bullets."

There is no doubt that during intensive internal struggles ideas become almost a "material force" (Marx's expression). Their importance increases when the outcome of the historical competition between contradictory social forces depends on the support of almost every active member of society. But can such repressive measures as silencing the opposition, never more than partially, increase the persuasive effect of the progressive revolutionary party? Can prohibitions enforced by the police, which limit the scope and depth of the dialogue with the "masses," help the "progressive" propagandists and agitators who claim to represent the future of humanity? Why in a period of such intensive military, ideological and spiritual hostilities should all the arguments in favor of freedom of thought and speech elaborated by Spinoza and Mill suddenly become invalid? On the contrary, when the dice are cast and the issues suddenly seem clear, freedom of dialogue can help the freedom-fighters and harm the defenders of the kingdom of darkness. When the partisans of freedom start to restrict freedom, they signal that they do not believe in their own cause.

Suppression of freedom of speech can be useful to fanatical religious groups and political parties of the Nazi type. They appeal not to reason but to people's fears, emotions, prejudices, and illusions. They are not interested in dialogue or in reasoning. They want to present their ideas in the form of dogmas, which were described by Thomas Hobbes as pills which must be swallowed without biting or chewing.

If it is true that words can be like bullets, then the conclusion should not be that a truly democratic, progressive, humanistic "revolutionary" party that appeals to reason and higher principles of morality ought to favor banning the "ideological weapon" of the enemy. On the contrary, the party of progress and democracy should always fight for enlightenment in every situation, under the most dangerous circumstances, because darkness can serve only those who represent obsolete, anti-democratic, anti-humane interests. They are afraid of justice and truth; they prefer to fight in the dark.

In *Mein Kampf* Hitler wrote with his typical cynicism that most people do not like to think independently, that they are prepared to believe everything that they read (if he had known television he would have added: what is shown to them on the TV screens), and therefore they should be given only "correct" information and ideas. The form of presentation should be adjusted to their low level of intelligence; he took it for granted that most people are mentally lazy or incompetent.

When one shares Hitler's point of view, and tries to spread an ideology of hatred (the myth of the superiority of the Aryan blood and race) one must also favor the suppression of democratic liberties. Every word pointing out that there are no differences in human blood among the people living on various continents shakes the foundations of this absurdity. Therefore, fascists had to oppose democratic liberties, including freedom of speech and tolerant behavior.

A similar situation exists in the Soviet Union. The authorities there, for instance, claim that collectivized agriculture is superior to the system that exists in the West. The absurdity of these assertions could be proved by simple statistical data based on the practical experience of Soviet or Polish citizens seeking food. In this situation the government must be oppressive—it cannot "afford" freedom of speech and press, it cannot even tolerate discussion about the importation of American grain—because this very fact constitutes evidence against the government. Under the regime of total lies, the suppression of freedom must be total.

In Western parliamentary countries those who are interested in suppression (intolerance) of truth do not necessarily favor state censorship.

There have been many political parties, social groups, and religious orders—others are still in the process of formation—which, after World War II, have had an interest in limiting democratic liberties. In Western countries they do not have to change the democratic constitutions or attack civil rights guaranteed by them. Certain vested interests, thanks to their access to money, can dominate the news media and silence the opposition not by political, administrative, police, or military means, but by the sheer weight of their financial power. This is another question that ought to be discussed separately.

Any restriction of freedom and tolerance is harmful to the cause of democracy and freedom; that sounds like a tautology or a platitude, but it is neither. On the contrary, the followers of doctrines which are irrational, anti-humane, and anti-intellectual cannot operate under conditions of free dialogue and criticism. They are like those parasites that shun daylight because it is lethal to them.

The most difficult problems facing those who uphold freedom and tolerance are caused by themselves, when they do not understand their own interests and the dangers that they expose themselves to when they *try to defend democracy and freedom with the means used by their enemies.*

4. Tolerance and Decency

Tolerance is always connected with questions of normal human decency. The observation of propriety both in private and public life is a precondition of a tolerant attitude toward critics and political opponents. The famous principle that only decent people are reliable should apply to the public authorities as well.

No military junta, no dictatorship, be it leftist or rightist, can be decent. Such a regime must be corrupt because of its very nature, and therefore intolerant. Intolerant rulers will gradually become even more corrupted, more unreliable, more oppressive. There is a vicious cycle of intolerance and corruption.

A confirmation *ad oculos* of this thesis happened during the undeclared war between Great Britain and Argentina over the Falkland Islands in the spring-summer, 1982. During recent years, Argentine juntas used to present themselves as heroically anti-communist, as a fortress fighting against the evil Soviet penetration into Latin America. These pronouncements ingratiated the Argentine juntas with many anti-communists all over the world including all American administrations since World War II.

Both Democratic and Republican administrations in Washington were prepared to forgive the Argentine military rulers their collaboration with Mussolini and Hitler, even the hospitality which they extended to the Nazis who managed to escape to South America. The loud Argentinian anti-communism has been regarded a value in itself, a good reason for complete absolution.

During the feud between Argentine expansionism on the one hand and the rights of the English Commonwealth and the population of the Falklands on the other hand, the Argentine dictatorship sought and accepted Soviet assistance. The Buenos Aires-Moscow alliance (factual, without legalistic forms) was as immoral as the famous Molotov-Ribbentrop pact dividing Poland in 1939. No decent Argentine government would have maneuvered itself into a position in which the whole Western world was hostile to it, while their most powerful and staunch ally became the Soviet Union.

In this way, the value of a despotic government as an ally in an anti-communist crusade was revealed. A government which oppresses its own citizens, which does not tolerate any criticism, must be corrupt to such an extent that it cannot be a reliable partner. Democratic governments suffer from the same disadvantage as decent people do; they can never profit from a pact or alliance with criminals or organized "indecency." It does not matter whether they deal with an illegal, underground "Mafia," or with a "Mafia" organized as a government, in the form of a dictatorship or junta. The administrative titles or military ranks should not be misleading.

The "worst," the most "capricious," the "weakest" democratic government is a more reliable ally of any democratic government than the "best" dictatorship. Every dictator is ready and able to sell his allies out because he has done it a hundred times to his own nation.

A government which does not tolerate any opposition or criticism must also have lost the understanding of what decency means.

* * *

Intolerance induces people to act in a way which could be called dishonorable. Sometimes intolerance creates circumstances which are so conducive, or almost compelling, that people who are decent under normal circumstances suddenly start acting immorally. One such an example was analyzed by Morris R. Cohen in his essay: "A Scandalous Denial of Justice: The Bertrand Russell Case."[9] The Board of Higher Education in the City of New York broke its contract and denied professorship to Bertrand Russell. When the case reached the Court, Judge McGeehan decided against Russell and the Corporation Counsel of New York City refused to appeal the case. Morris R. Cohen commented:

> It is, frankly, hard to believe that an honorable legal official of a great municipality could thus be willing to participate in a grossly *dishonorable* (if not illegal) procedure, if he were not under some pressure not referred to in his letter to the Board. And indeed there is some evidence of intervention by the Mayor, who gave the identical advice to the Board.[10]

The important facts behind the affair are now well known. Bertrand Russell was denied professorship at the City College of CUNY as a result of a well organized, noisy campaign of bigotry and prejudice against the liberal scholar defying tradition. Bigotry also influenced the judge whose decision, as shown in *The Harvard Law Review* (May, 1940), was illegal and absurd. In this situation, elementary justice would have required the lawyer representing New York City to appeal the case. A lawyer must make his independent determination whether he should appeal any given case. Probably either decision, affirmative or negative, could be regarded as legal. He did not appeal and although that was formally legal, it was ". . . dishonorable." It is obvious that he should have appealed a decision which by all standards of civilized nations (including, as Morris R. Cohen pointed out, *Magna Carta*, Sec. 39) deprived a man of his property and reputation without ever giving him a chance to be heard. The judge usurped rights which he did not possess; he made certain statements blatantly untrue, they were prejudicial, because he himself was subjected to adverse and intolerant opinions.

Any New York City corporation counsel should have appealed even if he were not convinced that the higher court would be more decent, just, or reasonable. But he did not do so because he was under pressure: the press, the clergy, and the politicians who were afraid of the gallery which was intolerantly shouting, "Crucify him," about Russell. In the atmosphere of witch-hunting, one *nolens volens* makes dishonorable decisions. Morris R. Cohen commented:

> Strange, how men zealous for public morality will so often be disdainful of honest truth in their arguments.[11]

Unfortunately, the phenomenon analyzed by Cohen is neither strange, nor rare, but rather normal. Whenever and wherever problems connected with public morality are dealt with it can happen that, in a tense period, some vestiges of legality can be preserved, but virtue, decency and honor are too often replaced by servility.

Even more: legality itself becomes endangered because one cannot effectively realize "due process of law" ("legality") without being decent.

Intolerance is opposed to legality, whereas tolerance gives additional and necessary assurances that all aspects of a case will be given due attention, will be impartially weighed and evaluated. Maybe in an atmosphere of tolerance certain cases would not even have arisen. In a more tolerant atmosphere, such a case as Bertrand Russel against the Board of Higher Education in New York City would not have arisen.

This analysis leads to the following conclusion: an atmosphere of intolerance certainly creates problems and cases which should not arise in the first place; once they have emerged, the prevailing atmosphere prevents their fair, just, decent, truly legal evaluation. Tolerance is a necessary remedy against possible injustice and "errors of justice." Intolerance creates injustice, perpetuates it, and begets further escalation of injustice.

5. Reflections on the Maxim: Whoever is Not with Us is Against Us

One of the ideas which played an especially pernicious role in the history of intolerance and persecution is the famous alternative: *Whoever is not with me is against me.* (Luke 11, 23). This maxim must already have been known in ancient times, because Jesus, according to the New Testament, referred to it, and admonished his disciples with the words, *"Whoever is not against us is for us."** (Mark 9, 40)

It is a historical paradox that Janos Kadar, leader of the Hungarian Communist party, repeated this Christian formula immediately after the seizure of power and the suppression of the Hungarian uprising in 1956 by the Soviet troops. While denouncing various Stalinist crimes and dogmas, he stretched out his hand to the opposition and started to repeat that whoever does not fight against the socialist state, "objectively" supports it.

***

This is not the place to present the history of the interpretation and application of the maxim cited above. If we are to find any reasonable elements in the concept, it must be interpreted from the broad pluralistic point of view. It seems certain, however, that if one is convinced that progress and social and individual happiness arise from many roots and quite varied premises, if one agrees that people should refrain from unnecessarily interfering with one another and, rather, secure the right of all to pursue their own personal goals, then one would also agree that the mere alternative, "with us, or against us," is in itself the product of an intolerant attitude.

Intolerance starts in *public* life when one is forced to choose between alternatives. In this connection, we may observe that the famous maxim, *e pluribus unum*, may also have an anti-pluralistic and intolerant meaning. Social development depends on multi-faceted progress and on the continuous diversification of culture, activity, and goals, whereas the mere concept of unity is undefined and is, at best, a subjective perception. Usually, even worse, it is identified with uniformity. One could argue, of course, that unity should be interpreted in a very broad sense

---

*Although both these statements are found in the Bible and although the difference between them is substantial in the Biblical context, no distinction is made between them here because none is appropriate in the present discussion.

only, as for instance, the unity of a nation determined to defend its independence and its pluralistic democratic institutions. Unity so conceived is praiseworthy and in agreement with the best democratic traditions.

The origin of the Soviet notion of political and moral (or politico-moral—Stalin's expression) unity reflects the traditional and uncritical way of thinking that regards unity as a virtue in itself. Such unity has generally been either subconconsciously or deliberately identified with uniformity if not with *Gleichschaltung*, which we can truly describe as an evil in itself.

The previously quoted statement by Janos Kadar reveals that he had decided to renounce in very few words the whole communist dogma about the "unity of the people."

Part of that dogma is the Stalin-Zhdanov theory that after the successful proletarian revolution society will unite so closely that people will form a single entity, a political and moral unit. That unit—and not the antagonisms and contradictions that so many philosophers from Heraclitus to Marx regarded as necessary—will be a source of further progress and the triumphant construction of communism. This is one of many Stalinist premises and predictions which were philosophically wrong and were contradicted by the actual course of events in every country in which the communists seized power.

In reality, the people in communist countries have preserved their old moral norms, political persuasions, and religious beliefs. They did not spontaneously and uncritically embrace communist ideology, although of necessity they do cooperate with their governments and participate in economic, cultural, and social activity. The Soviet ideologues never admitted that such a miracle (i.e., practical cooperation without ideological, "moral," and "political unity") could happen. Accordingly, all the public professions of faith in the dogma of the "leading role" of the party and its official philosophy, are so important to them that they have decided to impose them with the sword. Sometimes they grudgingly admit that perhaps for the time being not all the people have achieved the full perfection of political and moral unity, but add that they have already begun to approach it.

The official Soviet concept, "He who is not with us is against us," leads to a fundamentally intolerant view of national unity.

At first, during October, 1956, and then in August, 1980, the Polish communist government rejected the simplistic conception of moral unity. The authorities were so weak that they had to appeal to all sections of the population. Any government, including a communist one, which sends messages to all the members of the nation, sooner or later must appeal to patriotism. It asks help in order to preserve national sovereignty, it begs the people to participate in the development of the national economy and culture. Even the church hierarchy, including Pope John Paul II and the Primate of Poland, were so pressed by the urgent requirements of the new *raison d'état*, that they decided to help the leadership of the Party and, on their own, issued one manifesto after another urging the Poles to be industrious and frugal. The Party, on the other hand, thanked the hierarchy for these admonitions, and made concessions unheard of in any other Communist state. The Party and the government instituted a consistent policy in keeping with the old Polish proverb: *Jak trwoga, to do Boga* (in a panic you turn to God). When they were unable to maintain their power and feared a Soviet invasion, they asked the Church for help. In this way the Poles dealt the final blow to the communist concept of moral and political unity. In communist terms, they created an anti-communist unity. The dogma of uniformity collapsed. Both Church and State pretended to preserve their respective ideological purity and virtue. They were competing for the souls of Poles. Both powers suddenly found that it could better serve their ends not to claim that they were presiding over a spiritual unity or uniformity, hence they became the strangest bedfellows in the world. For more than a year they both presided over an officially pluralistic society. Of course there are, somewhere in the hidden and forgotten Party and Church halls, pitiful remnants of those who believe in the old maxim: "*whoever is not for us is against us.*" Reality outwitted the obsolete theorists and theologians. As we write these lines, this strange marriage has been shaken, but it has by no means collapsed.

Real life has proved many times that anyone who tries to exercise a monopoly over souls will be thwarted. There is no reason to persecute those who are not with you. The sooner people come to understand that humanism and progress presuppose tolerance and pluralism and that the two latter concepts are mutually dependent, and the sooner they leave the one-track way of thinking and understand that for effective cooperation it is sufficient that one is not physically or militarily against you, the better for the preservation of humanity and freedom.

One may argue, without too great oversimplification, that the development of tolerance and the art of discussion went hand in hand in human history. Their coexistence is a necessity. Walter Bagehot argued that an uncivilized man is incapable of discussion. Savages, Sir John Lubbock observed (in his *Prehistoric Times*), have "the intellect of children" with "the passions and strength of men.'"[12] One could retort that there is a logical contradiction in this statement, because human society does not exist without communication, and where there is an exchange of thought there must be some kind of dialogue. On the other hand, a genuine discussion, presupposing tolerance, is an expanded form of the exchange of arguments which concern "speculative" reasoning, "metaphysical" ideas, and practical decision-making, followed by unity in action. True human communication and discussion concern general problems and not only exchanges dealing with narrow and immediate practicality.

Taking into account all the above reservations, one must nevertheless agree with Walter Bagehot that before speculative arguments (in the sphere of politics, ethics, religion, or economics) were possible, humanity had to come a long distance from savagery. Weak-minded people cannot be tolerant because they are unable to engage in dialogue. Insecure, they feel vulnerable morally and intellectually; they can only feel hatred and contempt for those with ready, "glib" tongues.

Tolerance is not a gift like fire, which was said to have been stolen from the gods and offered to humanity by Prometheus. On the contrary, tolerance is a product of long evolution; intolerance is more "natural" and better suits mankind at certain stages of its development.

Intolerance is an unavoidable by-product of darkness, ignorance, prejudice, and fear. Therefore, when the human intellect develops, when intellectualism and intellectuals (as a special social group) come to existence, intolerance inevitably directs its poisonous sting against a new target, reason.

Intolerance always accompanies anti-intellectualism, and vice versa.

Anti-intellectualism has existed throughout the centuries. In every epoch and in every nation it takes on a different political meaning and a different name. Whereas, in the United States during the 1950s, the political and intellectual Neanderthals felt and expressed contempt for the "eggheads," at the same time in communist countries the intellectuals were threatened with "gas-pipes" (the threat spelled out in the name of the "working class" by the infamous "Gas-Pipe General," Kazimierz Witaszewski). During the same period in the Soviet Union and People's Republic of China, an intellectual represented abstract knowledge alienated from the workers and peasants, a person by definition dangerous to the "people's power." Therefore, the *"Gang of Four"* mercilessly sent such people away to the factories, mines, and agricultural cooperatives.

Intellectuals, who are capable of engaging in discussion, who understand the need for discussion and cannot do without it, are inevitably an object of hostility on the part of those whose case is too weak to be defended, or who are not sufficiently intelligent or educated to engage in the battle of ideas. Whatever the objective or subjective reasons for intolerance, it seems that there is a general rule: those who favor intolerance feel some sort of insecurity or inferiority, and they do not believe that they can prevail without physical force in a duel with intellectuals.

In the last resort, intolerance is an integral part of the general battle waged against human culture. Field-Marshal Hermann Goering and several rebel generals in the Spanish Civil War are all variously credited with the words: "When I hear the word culture, I reach for my pistol." Sooner or later, the adherents of intolerance, who do not want to give up their intellectually indefensible cause, follow the precept of Goering and use the force of the pistol against the power of the brain.

6. On the Maxim: Primum Tolerare

One of the milestones on the road to political freedom and to tolerance has been the transformation of the personal allegiance due to the ruler, into an allegiance to a "nation," "state," "constitution", "humanity," or some other such impersonal entity.[13] This achievement has been such a great leap in the field of politics, in practice and in theory, that it can be compared only to the previous emergence of the idea of the impersonal omnipotent god, who can be neither located nor seen, neither painted nor sculptured.

The Judeo-Christian abstract God had to wait thousands of years until the western societies were able to create His earthly social counterpart in the form of impersonal and incorporeal ideals which are political, philosophical, and moral. In western industrial and parliamentary states, the ultimate success of "political monotheism" has taken place since the 1900s. As yet, however, it is limited in space and time: nations and political regimes continue to return to the cult of the political "golden calf." Every "cult of personality" or "*Fuehrerprinzip*" (including to a great extent the "imperial presidency") is a retreat to political pagan idol-worship.

When in the fascist and various authoritarian states the persons of the "duce," "caudillo," "presidente,"or a "maximus leader," are surrounded by a special protocol and ceremony, when they are proclaimed "saviors," "brightest," and "noblest"—that means that political culture is in full retreat. There is almost no room for political tolerance under such circumstances. It can be practiced *privately,* in certain social groups, but officially it is an undesirable burden. The very existence of such a phenomenon as a "cult of personality" is repugnant to freedom, reason, and decency.

After Stalin's death, his successors and critics introduced the expression: "cult of personality" into the communist political vocabulary; it has served as a code word to describe certain characteristic political and ideological features of the Soviet regime as it has evolved since 1917.

The emergence of such a phenomenon in communist countries has been a clear sign of the degeneration of the communist government into a new form of autocracy combined with a totalitarianism of unprecedented rigor. The official materialistic philosophy and secular political ideology in the formative years were replaced by a new fideism which could not afford to be as tolerant as even traditional regimes, based on well established religious beliefs, had been. Stalinist terror, before and after the death of the dictator, has been especially vicious, encompassing every sphere of life, including the most intimate. The fideistic ideology and allegiance to a mortal because of their nature must be so petty, so internally inconsistent and absurd, that only the strictest forms of totalitarian terror could assure their continued existence.

Democracy, free competiton among political parties, parliamentary elections, and the responsibility of the government to the electorate have been the result of a relatively high intellectual level of people who are able to believe in an abstract ideal, in an impersonal socio-political entity which appears to be as real as the Judeo-Christian unseen deity. At times the impersonal "nation" or "constitution" seem even more abstract than God himself, because we have not produced in the politcal realm anything which enjoys such authority or concreteness as, for instance, the Holy Scriptures do in the sphere of religion.

Only people who consistently believe in parliamentary democracy and political competition, who are able to live within such a system and to sustain it, apart from its irritating inefficiencies and faults, can be intellectually and politically mature enough to practice tolerance and to assure political and personal freedom.

In every historical period and in every state, freedom and tolerance have a concrete intellectual meaning. At the same time freedom and tolerance have been and will forever remain abstract ideals. They can be fully appreciated and pursued only by those who are able to raise themselves, at least partially, above the concreteness of reality, who are able to overcome the physicality of their existence and can devote themselves to theoretical speculation.

Freedom and tolerance are ideals which require people to pledge their allegiance to such abstract ideals as "humanity," "humanism," the "general good," "individual happiness," and lastly, or rather predominantly, to "man," the "person," the "individual."

Political and social freedom and tolerance cannot by themselves assure personal happiness. But a civilized human being cannot achieve very much happiness without a certain sphere of freedom, privacy, and a spirit of tolerance prevailing in society. Respect for humanity, which constitutes such an important ingredient in western, Judeo-Christian civilization, in our humanistic culture, requires tolerance towards all people everywhere, together as well as singly. If the commandment, "love thy neighbor," so important in both Testaments and in *many other non-religious ethical reflections*, can have any practical sense and application, then first of all it must be contained in the maxims: *be tolerant toward your neighbor*, respect his personal wishes, *"lass ihn leben,"* (let him live his own way)! Let us observe that the rule, *"primum tolerare"* (first of all tolerate), has no negative content. The same can be said about the analogous Hippocratic rule in the field of medicine: *primum non nocere* (first of all, do no harm).

Negativism is only the form in which these rules were expressed. In fact, they are positive, they require due caution in acting and in nonacting. One should refrain from doing anything which would be harmful to the neighbor or the patient.

Something even more substantial could be said concerning the foregoing rule of tolerance: the mere allegiance to the idea of humanity, to the "individual," to one's "happiness," requires that one should refrain from doing anything that might be perceived either by others or by interested persons, as hurting their feelings or interests.

In order to practice the maxim, *primum tolerare*, one must first reject any idea of a "cult of personality;" any glorification of any earthly rulers, governors, or lords; any kind of impersonal "general good."

7. Fear and Tolerance

According to the widely known maxim of Epicurus-Lucretius, fear created the gods. At the beginning of the existence of humanity, fear was aroused by the forces of nature, unknown, unpredictable, powerful, able to destroy man and his environment. But in modern times, social and political forces have become the chief sources of fear. Crisis, alienation, war, concentration of economic power in the West, total concentration of both political and economic power in the East, all these factors threaten to undermine the established patterns of life, personal well-being, and security. The new forces are as threatening to laborers as to the middle class, although the latter live in a world of their own illusions, as if they were something "better" and "higher" on the social ladder than traditional proletarians or "blue collar" workers. Fear is not only the source of religious beliefs (and—in broader terms—of many forms of irrationalism), but also of intolerance. Those who are fearful cannot be tolerant. Politicians who are weak and vulnerable cannot endure any opposition, any criticism, any dissent, because they are always insecure. Intolerance rescues those who are afraid of the danger of defeat in open competition.

According to the popular truism, rulers who are deeply convinced that they are right and strong can afford to be more tolerant than petty tyrants who are afraid of their own shadows. A ruler who has a strong police force at his disposal can allegedly afford to give a broader leeway to his critically minded citizens than an embattled and threatened despot. An efficient governor, secure in his authority, argued Adam Smith, knows that at any time the limits defined by him are violated, he can draw the reins in order to curb the transgressors. This time, common sense, as often happens in politics, betrays us. Adam Smith's remark is either a half-truth or it is so a-historical that it is practically useless.

It is also a matter of historical experience that guardians of law and order who become very strong are never satisfied; they always seek even more power, they shun no stratagem or argument to justify their importance and their need for more and more power and more and more money. Every police force in every country, even the most democratic if not properly checked, will easily and speedily transform itself from a necessary instrument for the protection of life, property, and freedom into a tool of oppression, including provocation and witch-hunting. Why this subtle dialectic of development of the official, organized armed guardians of law escaped Adam Smith is beyond the scope of this treatise. History shows that moral, intellectual, political, and ideological (including theological) "weaklings" (policemen who commit crimes, or engage in provocations or torture-always feel weak) are by their very nature intolerant, afraid of any challenge, criticism, independent research, or innovation.

The people should be taught tolerance—as the French Encyclopedists used to proclaim; but a mass society cannot be taught to practice it without the necessary social and political conditions. Even if changes in living conditions and the absorption of certain knowledge relieve people from one type of fear (and the corresponding forms of irrationalism and intolerance), they usually fall into other traps and become fearful once more in a short time. New anxiety and dread create new gods, new prejudices, and new myths, which inevitably result in new intolerance.

Let us analyze one of the latest examples: the Soviet efforts in 1980-1981 to suppress the newly acquired Polish freedoms, the mobilization of their army and a chain of warnings and threats issued by them. The reasons for avoiding a direct invasion were obvious. Poland would have been destroyed and with that, a partner in the Soviet bloc would have disappeared; anti-Soviet hatred would have burgeoned all over the world and even Communist parties of Europe themselves would have suffered splits and dissension. The price of a "covert" invasion, i.e. the martial law imposed on Dec. 13, 1981, was not so high as it would have been in an overt invasion, but Soviet foreign policy suffered enormously.

The list of negative consequences was endless, nevertheless the Soviets seriously considered an invasion. Whenever one of its "captive nations" starts actively to struggle for elementary liberties, ". . . there is really only one Soviet argument in favor of attack, but it is one filled with *anxiety:* If Soviets let the Polish virus linger, sooner or later it can destroy Soviet Communism, too. For the Poles are not challenging Soviet foreign policy or Moscow's buffer zone of pliant neighbors. They are challenging the Central Soviet idea—the idea that a minority party of self-perpetuating oligarchs can steer a nation to prosperity . . . Poland's is the most virulent challenge to this orthodoxy—because it grew up from below . . . the stronger the Russians become militarily, the weaker they grow ideologically. If they move against poor Poland now, it will be not because they failed to hear the warnings from the West, but because they could not conquer *the fear in their hearts*"[14]

Fear is one of the chief motives for the actions of many modern autocratic rulers and it is always the stupidest motive. Fear is the source of intolerance because a fearful person or government cannot tolerate anybody who dares to think independently and be different, or who might provide intelligent and objective advice and analysis.

No existing administrative and military apparatus is sufficient to relieve a government of anxiety over its security. One must perceive one's own strength and power, one must understand and estimate the moral value of one's own cause and be persuaded that one can easily regain control even after a serious challenge. In politics, even more than in an individual's life, possession of real power alone is not sufficient to lessen strain or relieve terror and dread. The powerholder (in the case described above it was the Soviet Government and its satellites), must also be internally ("in the depth of his heart") convinced that his power is unshakeable and that it is morally and legally justified. Such a conviction can hardly be deeply rooted in the minds of leaders who falsify the results of elections or refuse even to hold them.

Those who commit political crimes cannot afford to be tolerant. One of the reasons why *Macbeth, Hamlet, Julius Caesar, Richard III*, and *King Lear* are great plays is because Shakespeare had a deep insight into the souls of usurpers. They live in perpetual fear; they are afraid of every decent person, not to mention those who might justifiably be suspected of seeking revenge.

The world of criminals, generally speaking, is not and cannot be tolerant. But political criminals must be intolerant not only for personal but also political reasons. The sources of their intolerance are multifarious and deeply rooted. One factor is especially important and attention worthy: politicians become political criminals by being drawn to commit or participate in the crime by specific political circumstances.

Political criminals are not created by crimes alone and political crimes are not committed by criminals only. Such crimes usually occur and proliferate in a particular social and political climate, in circumstances which require illegal acts in order to promote political careers and to achieve desired ends. The deepest source of criminal intolerance in totalitarian countries is the monopoly of political power, the interference with all the aspects of public and private life which causes popular dissatisfaction and contempt toward the governing elite. On the other hand, in Western democracies, the social source of intolerance is the political bureaucracy and the increasing economic power of the monopolies and giant corporations with their gradually growing bureaucracy and the bureaucratization of an increasing number of social and political fields of activity; side by side with these phenomena are the rising sense of popular injustice, inequality, and needless deprivation. All these developments contribute to the upsurge of fear, irrationalism, and intolerance on all sides of the social spectrum.

Third World countries are plagued by their colonial past, by the vices of both capitalism and communism, exacerbated by tribalism; therefore it is much more difficult for them to eliminate political and religious murder and cruel tribal and factional acts of mutual extermination from their social and political fabric. The general instability, killing, sometimes genocide, are the roots of oppression, persecution, and outright fanaticism.

One of the results of these facts is that a mere exposure of the roots of intolerance and fanaticism is powerless to convert people, and especially politicians striving for power, into partisans of freedom. Explanations must be accompanied by deep changes and improvements in the real world of politics in order to extinguish the sources of fear and cruelty. Such changes cannot be achieved in the near future. We should prepare ouselves to live in an intolerant world for a long time.

8. Lord Acton's Maxim Reconsidered

Today the famous expression of Lord Acton: "Every power corrupts, absolute power corrupts absolutely," should be supplemented by a more precise thesis, which Terence Des Pres, in his Introduction to the book *Treblinka* by Jean-Francois Steiner expressed in the following way:

> The Holocaust is an unparalleled example of power run wild, which is to say that once evil on this scale picks up enough momentum, once it establishes itself in a system of functioning structures, it cannot after a certain crucial point, be stopped by any counter-force within itself. The greater the concentration of power, the greater the paranoia it generates about its need to destroy everything outside itself. The worst thing that can be said of vast power is not that it inevitably corrupts its agents, but that after some point its deployment becomes greater than the will of the men who serve it. What can be destroyed, will be destroyed . . . [15]

This is the difference between Lord Acton, a nineteenth century liberal who still entertained certain illusions, and a twentieth century author who has experienced everything that totalitarianism has been able to produce. Acton's description of absolutism and corruption are obsolete when faced with genocide and a total, systematic destruction of everything that can be destroyed. Now we are nearer and nearer to the point in human evolution when the choice is not between democracy and absolutism (especially absolutism of the old Austrian type, *"gemildert mit Schlamperei"*—softened by disorder) but between freedom and totalitarian devastation and destruction.

In this connection, an important and timely question which demands clarification is the following: is it possible that a domestic counter-force might be able to rise and develop within a totalitarian system? Is it inevitable that what can be destroyed will be destroyed? How long can or must the paranoia of omnipotent power be tolerated by those affected by it? Any careful student of history and philosophy would admit that we have enough evidence indicating that even the most solid and best organized tyrannies, including totalitarian tyrannies, produce the seeds of their own destruction within themselves. The same superconcentration of power and the subsequent paranoia which tends to destroy everything outside the government at the same time starts to infect the regime itself. Absolute power produces an *immoral majority* and, for some profit, many are prepared to saw off the branch they are sitting on.[16] The real trouble in the twentieth century is caused by the fact that humanity does not have so much time as it had in previous centuries to wait till the inevitable internal collapse of the totalitarian regimes occurs. Before the beast dies under the burden of its own crimes and inefficiency it might exterminate millions of people and even worse, it may even blow-up our planet. Although most despots still lack these means, they will sooner or later be able to buy them. Conditions have become so demonized that competition has arisen recently on who should supply the means of world destruction to the eager purchasers.

The danger generated by the new totalitarian depotisms has

surpassed the old traditional intolerance. "Absolute" corruption reaches the dimensions of "paranoia," and paranoiacs destroy without any rational reason, end, or profit.[17] Today, absolute power, being totalitarian at the same time, destroys absolutely because it is like a vampire: it is nourished by the process of destruction and self-destruction.

9. Right of Assembly and Association

The freedom of assembly and petition to the government, guaranteed by the First Amendment of the U.S. Constitution, can be regarded as extensions of the freedoms of speech and of the press.

In this respect, the Constitution incarnates traditional ideas of the classic philosophers of freedom, especially Spinoza, who argued that freedom of speech without freedom of association and assembly would be meaningless. Freedom of speech makes sense only when it is used in communication with other people. Associations and assemblies are prerequisites for any public dialogue.[18]

Freedom of association can be treated as derivative and ancillary to freedom of speech and assembly and also as an "independent right," possessing the same status as the other rights enumerated in the United States' Bill of Rights. The United States Supreme Court decided:

> "It is beyond debate that freedom to engage in association for the advancement of beliefs and ideas is an inseparable aspect of the liberty assured by the due process clause of the Fourteenth Amendment, which embraces freedom of speech . . . it is immaterial whether the beliefs sought to be advanced by association pertain to political, economic, religious or cultural matters."[19]

Any governmental or private action tending to abridge the right of association should be subject to the same close scrutiny as an act to restrict freedom of speech, press, or religion.

It might sound like a paradox, but in our age of newspapers, radio, and television, the right to assemble and associate may be more important than ever. Although ours is an era of mass-media, only chosen and limited groups have practical access to them. They have all the available means to present, publish, and broadcast their views, whereas ideas which do not belong to the official mainstream have no practical possibility of being presented to the public or to influence it.

Meetings and assemblies have always been used to propagate views which were not widely accepted. Meetigs are almost the only forum available for expressing controversial attitudes and defending unacceptable values. In the 19th century, meetings were the weapon of abolitionists and suffragettes. In the 19th and 20th centuries, meetings also were the basic weapon of labor leaders and trade-union movements in capitalist and in some communist countries. In the United States, the public assembly has had a very special place in the civil-rights movement, the anti-draft and peace organizations, the New Left, and new religious cults.

Assemblies, meetings, demonstrations, associations (more or less loosely knit or organized) have been indispensable instruments of social change throughout political history, but especially in modern times.

Although there is a "close nexus" between freedom of speech and press, on the one hand, and freedom of assembly and association on the other, they cannot be treated in the same way either philosophically or legally.

U.S. Justice Goldberg, in *Cox v. Louisiana,* distinguished between a "pure form of expression," such as newspaper comment or a telegram, and an "expression mixed with particular conduct."[20]

U.S. Justice Marshall, analyzing a question of picketing which he regarded as a specific problem of "conduct," wrote that it intermingles both speech and action, the former being protected by the First Amendment, the latter, rather not. The possible conflict between the elements "protected" and "unprotected" by the First Amendment, should be resolved in favor of the First Amendment rights.[21]

Very colorful is the expression of U.S. Justice Douglas:

"Picketing is free speech *plus,* the *plus* being physical activity that may implicate traffic and related matters. Hence the latter aspects of picketing may be regulated."[22]

Using the picturesque description of Justice Douglas, one can state that freedom of association is also "free speech *plus,*" and sometimes even more: free speech *plus* mixed with freedom of assembly *plus*. Therefore, there can be various elements, various "pluses" which can be regulated without infringing upon especially "protected" freedom of speech.

We are concerned in this book not with all aspects of the freedom of assembly and association, but with two only:

—How far can various forms of freedom and tolerance accorded to the members of an organized private association be stretched?

—What kind of freedom—protected? curtailed? unprotected?—should "enemies of freedom" enjoy?

As is true everywhere in social life and politics, there are qualifications and limitations in the enforcement of rights. In order to safeguard freedom of association (union, club, circle, name them as you will) and regard associations as one of the incarnations of the ideas of freedom and tolerance, there must be distinct, positive, affirmative features in the ends and activities of any given organization, and also there must be certain elements which must be regarded as alien to the given association and unacceptable for it.

From the abstract point of view one should not question the right of a private organization (any church is a private, nongovernmental organization from the American legal point of view; that, however, is not the opinion of other governments and not the exact attitude of the Roman Church itself) to reprimand or even exclude its members. The most touchy point is the following: once a powerful, influential, international organization, such as the Roman Catholic Church, has a disagreement with one of its members, should it be able to influence the secular society to be hostile to the member as well? If the answer is positive, then the affair of Dr. Hans Küng ceases to be merely an internal case of the Church; it becomes an object of interest for all. Such a conclusion one could deduce from the book of Leonard Swidler on Dr. Hans Küng.[23] This is the reason why the book has occupied such an important place in the intellectual struggle for freedom in our decade. Küng was deprived of his license to teach Catholic theology in a German University because the Roman Catholic Church authorities found that his views were incompatible with the official doctrine of the Church, Nevertheless, he preserved his position as a University Professor, because it was the German government that conferred that title on him and Dr. Küng had not violated any German law which could serve as a basis to dismiss him from his position.

The case of Dr. Hans Küng is connected not only with Roman Catholic intolerance of ideas regarded as erroneous, but also with most complicated aspects of the freedom of assembly and association. Once we recognize that any group of people has a right to set up an association to perform certain functions and strive to achieve their ends, why should the group not have the right to exclude those members who disagree with its doctrine, ends, or activity? It might seem like a paradox, but exclusivity of private associations should not be regarded as a threat to the ideas and attitudes of tolerance, but as a necessary means by which freedom and tolerance can be realized—provided, of course, that private exclusion is not followed by acts of discrimination by public authorities. Associations which are hostile to democracy, religious freedom, and racial and national equality, must have the right to exist under a democratic constitution, because this is the nature of democracy. Once the government has the right to discriminate concerning what kinds of social, political, or intellectual activity should be legal or illegal, sooner or later the result will be arbitrariness and capriciousness in the interpretation and application of all those liberties which were proclaimed by the U.S. Bill of Rights or by the Universal Declaration of Human Rights and the subsequent international documents. A democratic government must tolerate any organization, including those which do not contribute to the promotion of the ideas of freedom and tolerance. The ideology and activity of organizations which promote racial or religious hatred, or claim a monopoly of theological truth always must bring about certain effects harmful for progress and tolerance. Nevertheless, a democratic regime of freedom and tolerance may and should survive such ideological attacks so long as the bigotry, lies, and hatred are not supported by the whole or large segments of the government; as long as the state does not give any exclusive rights to any political, secular or religious, organizations; as long as other social and political organizations have the right to exist and enjoy freedom to promote liberty and tolerance and can actively criticize and denounce "enemies of freedom." Under such circumstances, the ideas and systems of freedom and tolerance can usually survive, develop, and even grow stronger. But the effective functioning, and even the survival of a system of freedom and tolerance when threatened by an organized governmental monopoly or ideology, supported by police terror or unlimited money supplied by special interest groups, is practically impossible.

The famous saying of the Jacobin, Saint-Just, "no freedom for the enemies of freedom," is, in essence, inimical to freedom if it means that the ideological, philosophical, or political opposition should be suppressed by using the police, the military, or administrative forces. There is, of course, another way to interpret and apply Saint-Just's maxim: the "freedom-lovers," the "*bon citoyens*," the "good guys," should be so active under the law and the democratic constitution that a handful of enemies of liberty, decency, or reason would be ashamed to raise their voices or to act openly against freedom and reason, for fear of public contempt. After World War II, it had been regarded dishonorable to be named a "racist" or an "anti-Semite." Hitler's racism and genocide caused deep social, political, juridical, and psychological transformations and, therefore, there was a short period in which such an atmosphere of contempt and intolerance toward Nazis and fascists prevailed that they did not dare to raise their voices publicly. Such "intolerance" which surrounded the fascist remnants constituted a contribution to tolerance rather than the reverse.

There are well known arguments that the Weimar Republic's tolerance of Nazism enabled Hitler's cohorts to seize power. These assertions have been especially well publicized in the Soviet Union and in the East-European "People's Democracies" as a justification of their own laws that freedom cannot be used for "antidemocratic" and "antisocialistic" purposes. On the basis of this sort of "militant" democracy, the *Brezhnev doctrine* was finally elaborated proclaiming the right of the Soviet Union in cooperation with other brotherly socialist governments to intervene in the internal affairs of any other "socialist country" troubled by a "counter-revolution" and the specter of fascism. Both doctrines, that of "militant democracy" and of Brezhnev, are unacceptable from the viewpoint of the philosophy of tolerance.

Let us recall two examples: The Nazi minister of propaganda, Dr. Joseph Goebbels, was asked by a Western journalist why the Nazis were using the liberties guaranteed by the democratic Weimar Constitution and at the same time they were criticizing its democratic spirit. His answer was significant and memorable: the Nazis are openly against democratic freedoms and regard them as a sign of liberal weakness and decadence; but the nature of democracy and liberalism requires them to grant freedom even to the enemies of freedom. Everybody has to act, concluded Goebbels, according to his own nature. The Nazi Party has taken advantage of these avenues which were given by the existing liberal regime, without endorsing them.

In his last speech to the XIX Congress of the Communist Party of the Soviet Union (1952), Stalin announced that the bourgeoisie had thrown overboard "the standard" of democratic liberties and the communists in the capitalist countries should pick it up; it is their turn to become the standard-bearers of constitutional freedoms and legality. Obviously he meant that the communists should learn to use the democratic liberties for their own purposes; they should take advantage of the existing constitutional liberties to seize power, to liquidate the same liberties under which they were fighting for the "dictatorship of the proletariat," interpreted by Stalinists as a higher type of democracy, that has to be defended with all available police methods against its relentless and implacable enemies.

The reasoning of Goebbels and Stalin reveals the traces characteristic for all the adversaries of democracy who meticulously prepare an assault against it: use the democratic liberties to promote your own ideology and program, to strengthen your party organization, and to prepare your own activity in order to seize power—legally, half-legally or illegally; then be prepared to suppress democracy and extirpate "rotten" democratic legality. Victors are not judged because they establish the new rules, they support and invigorate them with the *ultima ratio* of any law: force!

The problem of freedom and tolerance towards Nazis and their successors emerged in the United States with unprecedented intensity at the end of the 1970s. A small group of Nazis planned a rally and a march in Skokie, Illinois. This is a suburb of Chicago inhabited predominantly by Jews, including a substantial group of survivors of the Holocaust, the ghettos, and the concentration camps. The courts and the American Civil Liberties Union insisted that there was no legal basis to deny one group of citizens their democratic rights, even if they favored racism and anti-Semitism. In its support of the decision to grant the Nazis the right to assemble, demonstrate and march, the ACLU stressed constitutional liberties and warned that once the authorities started to abridge the civil and political rights of any group, they would sooner or later start to restrain the rights of other organizations, even "innocent" and democratic ones found unsympathetic by the existing authorities. In this way the great system of American liberties would be endangered, begin to disintegrate, and gradually disappear.

Those who were against granting the neo-Nazis permission to march and rally at Skokie used many arguments including: the neo-Nazis, like the old Nazis, are extolling Hitler's crimes to the skies and are inciting new acts of racial violence. Genocide, and even praise of it, are forbidden not only by the internal law of civilized countries, but by the new international law accepted by the United Nations. Anyway, the internal law of many civilized nations regards the praise of crime, exhortation and incitement to crime, as crimes in themselves. If one allows the Nazis to commit this kind of crime, one does not act in the spirit of tolerance and the maxim of the maximum happiness of the greatest number of people; one does not defend the U. S. Constitution; on the contrary, one allows the Nazis to violate the law. One does not give them equal rights but accords to them privileges, one confers on them especially favorable treatment which should not be granted to any one.

And another argument: the neo-Nazis deliberately chose a town inhabited by people extremely sensitive to the Nazi uniforms and their ideology of hatred; they were all directly or indirectly affected by the Nazi crimes, their families were murdered. Therefore a rally of official Jew-haters must reopen unhealed wounds, must evoke repulsive emotions; many people would be so deeply hurt that they might be unable to control themselves and might answer with violence against such deliberate provocation.

Tolerance should not be interpreted as the right to wound elementary feelings and offend basic human emotions. One who wants to use the principles of tolerance for such ignoble purposes, in order to satisfy his own base dispositions and perverted inclinations, does not deserve to be tolerated by decent people and should not be given an opportunity to exercise freedoms which in the final analysis were fought for and proclaimed in order to be a source of human dignity and happiness. Freedom should not be abused and transformed into a tool for hurting, humiliating, and degrading people.

It is indeed easier to defend the ban of the Nazi demonstration from the general point of view than from the legal one. Many people who might agree with the above reasoning would feel uneasy about the juridical aspects of the question. They could ask with anxiety: Should the authorities (be it federal, state or local) really have the right to decide which ideology or political program is "antihuman"? Where will the exercise of such a right lead? Can such a privilege be compared with the right of the authorities to prosecute a man who cried "fire" in a crowded theater? (This is the famous classic example used by U.S. Justice Holmes to illustrate the limits of freedom of speech.).

There are those who would even argue that there are no laws to prohibit the Nazis from marching and rallying, although the people—not the authorities!—have the right to regard such activity, attitude, and behavior as violating basic, moral, religious, philosophical and social principles of freedom and tolerance and therefore decent people, who feel justifiably emotionally offended and morally insulted, have their own right to take the case into their own hands. If that would lead to physical violence then the Nazis should be blamed; it is better to have a brief disorder and street fighting than to give the police the right to abridge democratic liberties. It is better that private citizens teach hoodlums a lesson beside or apart from the existing official law and order, than to allow the police to violate the law.

One can also argue with justification that law and law enforcement organizations cannot resolve all the disputes and controversies in a democratic society. If the number of people in a society who are hostile, or at least indifferent to freedom and tolerance, increases, as if they represent a majority, however transient, then the continued preservation of democracy becomes doubtful. Unwanted democracy and freedom cannot work. All attempts to defend democracy by curtailing democracy in order to fight an inimical antidemocratic majority will, sooner or later, prove fruitless. This is what Hegel had in mind when he wrote in his *Philosophy of History*: Napoleon was unable to compel Catholic Spain to become free; and vice versa, nobody was able to impose chains on the Netherlands in the seventeenth century.

In our century the people usually do not feel that they have any legal or moral obligation to tolerate any forms of discrimination, humiliation, or insult based on racism, religious hatred, or nationalistic prejudices. Those who are unable to get rid of their own prejudices and bigotry must face the consequences of their own intolerance, they cannot ask for tolerance, although it may happen that their victims might decide to tolerate them for a time.

Intolerance sometimes can be and should be tolerated, but always only to a certain extent. The limits are not fixed; they are socially determined, politically movable. Once they are largely transgressed by an active majority, then the friends of freedom can do very little except to follow the tragically witty advice given by Bacon in similar circumstances: Pray for good weather.

V.

CAUSES OF INTOLERANCE AT THE END OF THE TWENTIETH CENTURY

In previous chapters we have discussed the various causes of intolerance and the arguments for and against tolerance. Many of those basic arguments and counterarguments have already been analyzed many times throughout the centuries and yet they have lost neither their validity nor their vitality. Indeed, it often appears that only the forms of the arguments and counterarguments have changed, not their essence.

Unfortunately the old saying, *the more things change, the more they remain the same,* does not apply to the philosophy of freedom.

At the end of our century we are witnessing a new wave of intolerance and an accelerated "escape from freedom," as Erich Fromm described it. The same forces which either work against freedom or are hostile to the ideas, feelings, and attitudes of tolerance, bear a fatal deficiency in themselves: they beget their own antidote.

We know, of course, the famous Newtonian rule that every action gives rise to an equal and opposite reaction. This observation applies both to nature and society. The powerful forces of intolerance have always been met by new and ageless resources of freedom and tolerance; the struggle between Ormuzd and Ahriman is endless.

The purpose of this section is to examine the economic, social, and political forces which are especially active in promoting the new era of darkness in our century and the kind of opposition these forces may engender.

1. Bureaucracy

Bureaucracies are increasing all over the world. Increasingly bureaucrats infiltrate nearly all spheres of life. Perhaps most frightening is that bureaucracy no longer is confined to government, but now is becoming an essential element in economic management, political parties, and even universities and research institutions, the news media, trade unions, and the churches.

Every day in thousands of periodicals and books readers will find data on the aggrandizement of bureaucracy all over the world. From the point of view of freedom and tolerance, human initiative and the fulfillment of personality, it is clear that the unregulated realm is diminishing. The promises of every American administration, and every communist government to struggle against bureaucracy are worthless. Even if centralized governments temporarily reduced the number and levels of bureaucracy, that would not mean that bureaucracy would in fact be reduced. Certain functions are merely shifted from a higher to a lower level, from the national to the local level; sometimes it is a shift from political bodies to economic specialists; even if the numbers of white-collar workers were actually reduced for a time, the bureaucratic spheres of interference might be expanded.

Bureaucracies are typically hierarchical. From the point of view of freedom and tolerance it does not matter whether the head of the bureaucratic pyramid consists of one or more persons. Collegial bodies act as arbitrarily as individuals, because it is in the nature of hierarchy that decisions are made by few and carried out by many, under penalty of exclusion. Uniformity must be preserved.

Capitalism began by defying feudal hierarchies, and the modern concept of freedom is connected with the ideas of individualism, private initiative, the spirit of enterprise, and the courage to make decisions and take risks. All these features were accompanied by the widely proclaimed spirit of industry and self-discipline. Protestantism became the most eminent religious incarnation of these attitudes and demands.

At the present stage of the evolution of capitalist governmental and corporate bureaucracies, most of the features have ceased to be useful; they are intrinsically antagonistic to bureaucratic order. It may be that at the higher reaches of the bureaucratic ladder some of those features and qualities are still in demand, but we already have thousands of examples that even executives have found that, in order to protect their own interests, caution and the "team spirit" favor their private interests more than initiative and taking chances. It is significant that during the discussion about a new American banking law which, according to many students of world banking systems, would inevitably lead to elimination of small banks, expanding the super banks, the proponents of free competition suddenly became mute. In a short time in the United States we may reach a situation similar to that prevailing in Europe: a group of banks which has remained on the battlefield does not want to take chances; venture capital is practically unavailable. It is needless to speculate what this development and concentration of economic power would mean for the spirit of enterprise in the United States.

The prevailing feature of every bureaucracy, from top to bottom, is caution and obedience, sooner or later indistinguishable from cowardice. This is a new kind of cowardice, not to be compared to military cowardice. Hierarchy and bureaucracy stifle dissenters and innovators.

A bureaucratic apparatus cannot have a soul; human feeling must be eliminated from it. The larger the bureaucratic operation, the more cruel must be its struggle against everything that is internally or externally unacceptable to it, as Reinhold Niebuhr observed.

Ancient Rome had a popular saying: *Senatores boni viri, senatus bestia* (senators are good men, the senate is a beast). Ancient Romans knew two main collective bodies, the senate and the emperor's court. They were blessed that there were only two dangerous beasts among them. Modern societies are cursed with unlimited numbers of bureaucratic institutions: administrative, financial, trade unions, universities, churches, professional, and so on. In all these institutions the individual participants are usually well-intentioned and humane, but as members of an institution they form a "beast" which is alienated from all other members of society. They impose requirements, they supervise performance, they threaten to punish the reluctant or disobedient; for their own self-preservation they must persecute those who dare to violate their rules. Even if they wanted to, they would be unable to examine case by case the personal intentions of those whom they persecute. They deal with quantities and numbers. Nearly everyone participates in the hunt and is himself hunted by the increasing numbers of hunters. What Kafka presented in *The Castle* and in *The Trial* is becoming increasingly typical and general. The helpless hero in Kafka's *Metamorphosis* turns into a cockroach. In the bureaucratic world the individual does not have to undergo a real metamorphosis in order to be regarded as an insect. Once the manipulated opinion of the official public calls him a bug, he will be treated as one; finally he will behave accordingly. In the bureaucratic world subjective opinion or prejudice can become more real than reality itself.

Bureaucracies everywhere are governed by heartless rules. In western democracies a citizen has rights and really can defend himself against certain encroachments made by governmental institutions. But the same citizen who can help to vote a president or a congressman, a mayor, or a prime minister out of office, who can sue the government for compensation, is helpless in his lonely fight against a powerful corporation which employs or destroys him, against a trade union, or against a university or a party or caucus which has put him on a black list. Usually he is also helpless when he is a whistle-blower, calling public attention to his superior's misconduct.

In any despotic country, be it communist, fascist, or any other dictatorship, an individual is helpless in all his dealings with bureaucratized institutions. Where every institution, including the courts and churches, is a part of a hierarchical system, tolerance can hardly be detected. It may be officially proclaimed in ceremonial speeches, but it cannot flourish in reality.

In the modern western bureaucratized democracies, the intolerance ingrained in the hierarchical structures is less visible, is more civilized, has better manners, but it grinds effectively nonetheless.

Bureaucracy has become a cancer which grows incessantly, and eats away the most precious western values of tolerance and freedom.

2. Nationalism

Nationalism has become one of the most powerful and important phenomena of our century.

There are familiar opinions, often repeated, that nationalism may not only be influential, but even progressive, under certain circumstances. What is progressive from the historical viewpoint? The answer depends too often on carefully selected philosophical premises and political opinions. Eschewing detailed considerations, we use one criterion only, decisive for the subject under our examination: how do the given theories of social and political change contribute to the development and realization of the ideas of freedom?

We argue that nationalism has not been a constructive or progressive force in the history of modern societies; in our century it has become one of the most important sources of animosity, war, and intolerance.

Modern western nations have emerged as a result of long historical development. We will not discuss that process here or whether the concept of nationhood is a recent or ancient phenomenon. We stress only that the old national entities lacked many of the distinctive features which characterize modern nations.

We are also inclined to accept the opinion of many historians that modern European nations started to take final shape and form with the development of modern capitalism, the creation of national economic markets, and the evolution of modern means of communication and information, especially printing. The formation of modern European languages was a function of the development of nations, simultaneously one of its causes and one of its effects. In the eighteenth and nineteenth centuries, the process of formation of European nations had come to an end (with a few exceptions). The Reformation followed by the English and French revolutions, accelerated the development of European nations. The American revolution, with the rise of the United States, became a milestone along the road of the unification of diverse peoples into single national organisms.

Historians and philosophers usually stress that the most characteristic features of nations are a common territory, a common language (at times several languages), a common cultural heritage, economic ties, and feelings of being separate and apart from other nations and nationalities. It is quite possible that a nation can exist in the absence of some of the above features; as we know, exceptions confirm the general rule. Nations usually try to create their own states which encompass the entire territory on which the majority of the given nation lives.

The existence of an independent sovereign state is not necessary for the existence of a nation, as many historical examples confirm. It is quite possible that the existence of an independent state contributes to the final development of national unity, but it is possible that the formation of a nation might precede the emergence of an independent national state.

Here we shall examine only these elements of national life, which pertain directly to the questions of freedom and tolerance.

The French revolutionaries are credited with the creation of the idea of patriotism. Patriots were people who were prepared to fight for the ideals of the revolution: liberty, equality, and fraternity, and defend them against internal adversaries and foreign invaders. Foreign enemies not only constituted a threat to the independence of France, but also to the newly acquired freedoms won against the opposition of the monarchy, the feudal aristocracy, and the Church. Therefore, the idea of a patriot has encompassed two elements: a desire and will to defend the independence of the fatherland and the preservation of freedom, more humane institutions, and more democratic laws.

Within a short time the French revolutionaries transformed their patriotic wars into acts of aggression. Napoleon never lacked arguments to prove that new acquisitions were necessary in order to reinforce the security of the French state and territory. The result of the Napoleonic wars was mixed. The French army exported progressive ideas and it was welcomed by many as an army of liberation. On the other hand, there were people in the occupied countries who resented their new French rulers, precisely because they were foreigners, although they might have been sympathetic to their progressive ideas. The surge of national feelings took its most dramatic form in the territories inhabited by the Germans. Although a unified German state did not exist, Fichte's *Letters to the German Nation* were well understood by Germans. The importance of the growth of German national feeling and mentality may be compared only with the more or less simultaneous growth of Russian nationalism compounded by Pan-Slavism. Soon it became evident that these new emotions were ominous for further historical development.

It would be unreasonable to argue that within the framework of national states, tremendous progress has been achieved. National feelings have often stimulated great achievements. These are historical facts. Nevertheless, one may speculate whether without the formation of nations and national states, with the nationalistic hatreds which inevitably accompanied them, progress might not have been greater and more humane. Every desirable element in the development of the nation state was accompanied by irrational ideas and emotions. It may be that the most disastrous phrase of this evolution turned out to be the *"Geist,"* or Russian *"dusha"* (spirit, soul) of the nation (or "people," in German also "Volk," in Russian, "narod"). These unclear, irrational, and unscientific ideas have been exploited by skillful demogogues and politicians in every way. Historical experience shows that in the nineteenth and twentieth centuries these were predominantly right wing, conservative and militaristic parties that exploited the national feelings with demogogic phraseology for their own egoistic purposes.

The very idea that a particular nation has been predestined to fulfill a specific global mission either creates or at least stresses a division of the world, a separation from other nations. The old Stoic and Roman ideas of universalism, of the unity of humanity, were rejected. Instead of finding out and emphasizing what is common to all human beings, nationalists stress what is different, what makes their nation superior to others.

Nationalists portray themselves as true patriots. Indeed, they represent a patriotism that is distorted, if not degenerate (in German we would say: *ein entarteter Patriotismus).* Nationalists do not care for the progress, democracy, tolerance, or freedom which should be secured for every individual member of the nation. They operate with general terminology. The well-being of the individual was replaced by the idea of the interest or greatness of the nation or people. This, precisely, is the reason the nationalists hated liberalism and the liberals like Bentham and Mill, because they developed their theories as humanistic philosophies tending to serve each individual. They wanted to help all of society and all of humanity while protecting the interests of every single person.

Nationalism and traditional individualistic liberalism are incompatible.

Eighteenth century culture was rationalistic and philosophers attempted to explain everything by the help of reason. The Cartesian requirement that truth is what one sees "clearly and distinctly," obviously could not have been accepted by the representatives of the mysterious and mythical national soul. The emotional nationalistic authors who wrote avidly on the German and Russian soul were simultaneously passionate adversaries of French clarity, the Aristotelian concept of truth and rhetorical dialogue, and Anglo-Saxon common sense.

At the end of the nineteenth and the beginning of the twentieth centuries, national souls demonstrated their disastrous role in political life. The feelings of separateness and superiority were accompanied by a surge of intolerance toward all aliens and toward all those of a given nation who refused to accept the standards of national stupidity (especially in the form of inherent "superiority" and special "mission") wrapped in the form of national interests. After World War I, all the nationalist parties began a fight against liberalism and democracy. The right-wingers embraced fascism (in Germany: national socialism), the radical left-wingers, various forms of Stalinism. The importance of clashing economic interests in both World Wars being granted, there is no doubt, however, that without the appeal to nationalism, without demogoguery which used the concept of "national interest" and "soul," it would not have been possible for despotic governments to seize power and push their nations into the butchery of war.

The western democracies used nationalistic prejudices in order to conquer vast territories in Africa, Asia, and other parts of the world. Nationalism was accompanied by imperialism and colonialism. The result of imperialistic domination and oppression could have been foreseen from the beginning. The colonial powers consolidated local populations on the basis of hatred against the metropolitan nations and evoked local nationalisms. The oppressed colonial peoples were deprived of freedom and treated intolerantly. They were taught intolerance. No wonder they responded to their conquerors with intolerance.

Those who were oppressed did not practice tolerance after liberation either. Quite the contrary, they have been at least as intolerant as their previous masters. Although these actions have the appearance of a paradox, they represent a certain historical logic. The colonial oppressors did not practice and did not teach tolerance and therefore they were requited measure for measure. They should blame themselves for the excesses perpetrated by the first generation of the liberated colonial peoples, although that is no excuse for the brutality which took place in Africa and Asia.

In politics *tout comprendre* is not *tout pardonner* (to understand all should not be identified with forgiving all). The followers of freedom and tolerance observe with awe that nearly a hundred newly formed independent states, representing many nations, nationalities, and tribes, practice intolerance in their internal and international relations. The existence of so many countries in which intolerance prevails cannot but harm the development of the small group of western nations with parliamentary governments which practice tolerance, at least to some extent. Nationalism of the newly developed nations, being one of the sources of their own intolerance, endangers the global environment.

Western nations do not behave like sheep either. Today, because of the narrow nationalistic perceptions of their interests, they are unable to form an efficient alliance to defend themselves against the dangers threatening them, their style of life, and relative affluence. Nationalistic aims are exacerbating world economic competition, they cause customs wars, erupting again and again among states and groups of states which in this way defy the free trade principles they profess.

Nationalistic political parties, with the help of military establishments, are organizing people to achieve various irrational purposes, such as "liberation" of the Falkland Islands by the Argentinian ruling junta.

Nationalism has been harmful to the western parliamentary democracies in their mutual relations and in their internal policy. Nationalism and democracy are incompatible in the long run.

In the short run however nationalism can be useful to any authoritarian and totalitarian regime, communist and noncommunist alike.

The Bolsheviks seized power using the slogan "war against war," recommending defeat rather than senseless death for workers and peasants on both sides of the front lines. It took only several months before they announced that they were in favor of a patriotic war in defense of the people's fatherland. It took several years more and the Soviet government started to espouse the old Russian patriotism and nationalism. The peak was reached during the Second World War in the fight of the Red Army against the German invaders.

In every communist country, but especially in the Soviet Union, China, Vietnam, Cuba, and Yugoslavia, nationalist slogans and ardor have been more and more important. Every abandonment of the egalitarian and libertarian traditions of nineteenth century socialism, every betrayal of the old internationalist concept of fraternity, has accentuated the intellectual poverty of the refurbished nationalism.

In all communist countries the renovated nationalism (not patriotism!) is not only a reaction against the internationalism of the original socialist theory, but it also constitutes a step backward on the road to the democratic development of every nation.

Russian neo-nationalism prevailing everywhere in the Soviet Union and its dependencies helps to cement the Union and the Empire. This type of nationalism appeals to Russians, to their traditional superiority-complex, to their old beliefs that they have to fulfill a messianic mission of showing the true path to salvation to the whole world.

Russian nationalism which has been so helpful in mobilizing Russians, fails completely when it is used to appeal to other nationalities of the Soviet Union. Outside the Soviet Union, it is met with familiar and open hostility in the People's Democracies, especially in China, Poland, Hungary, and Czechoslovakia. The Brezhnev Doctrine, authorizing the Soviet Army to intervene in every Communist country (including Afghanistan) is an old Tsarist, Great Russian principle expressed in communist jargon. No wonder this type of ideology and nationalism will ultimately contribute to the disintegration of the Union and Empire. Local nationalisms constitute a reaction against Soviet nationalism and they find their staunch political and social adherents in the ideology which was betrayed by the bureaucratic super-nationalists: *liberté, egalité, fraternité*; the Declaration of Human Rights; the democratic rights proclaimed by their own Constitutions.

There must be at least partial truth in the utopian vision of the Soviet historian, Andrei Amalrik, who predicted that the final decline of the Soviet Union would be accomplished by the nationalist forces let loose by the Soviet authorities themselves.

For the time being the nationalistic smoke-screen is a convenient tool to suppress any endeavors to regain freedom, to stall any efforts to relax the tense atmosphere of terror, and to undo any human striving for tolerance.

3. Communist Parties and Stalinism

The Marxian concept of freedom was discussed in the previous chapters. As history has proved, the victory of the communist revolution in Soviet Russia and other countries has not been a great leap from the realm of necessity to the kingdom of freedom. What were Marx's and Engels' miscalculations and why was their forecast wrong? An exhaustive answer is beyond the purview of this book. But one of the answers should be that the economic factor was not as pervasive as they had anticipated and the expropriation of capitalist property did not effect the disappearance of all political elements interested in authoritarianism.

It seems certain that the seizure of power by the communist party in a country without any democratic traditions could not produce democracy and tolerance because political liberties and democratic attitudes are the result of a long historical nurture. It may be that we have one more example to confirm Hegel's observation that one cannot be forced to be free.

Among the factors which contributed to the lack of freedom in the Soviet system and the prevailing intolerance is simply the structure of the Communist Party and its ideology. The organizational and ideological foundations of the communist parties were not established by Marx and Engels and their successors in the Second International, but by Lenin at the beginning of the twentieth century, further to be elaborated by Stalin in the Soviet Union after 1917. Those principles were generally accepted by all communist parties around the world. If there are any exceptions, they are unimportant and rather connected with terminology and semantics than substance.

There were endless discussions concerning whether it would be possible to overthrow the Tsarist government and seize power without a party, of the so-called Leninist type. We are merely suggesting that if a ruling party has such a structure and ideology, intolerance must inevitably follow with all the negative consequences caused by it.

In his three fundamental books, *What is to be Done, One Step Forward, Two Steps Backward,* and *Two Tactics of Social Democracy in a Democratic Revolution,* Lenin laid the foundation for this concept of a revolutionary party. According to him, a party must be built on the principles of what Lenin called democratic centralism. Every member of the party must be a member of a relatively small cell and all the cells in a given territory (city, county, state, region) must work under the leadership of a regional committee. These regional committees were to work under the leadership of the higher committees and they, in turn, under the leadership of the central committee. In this structure, according to Lenin, democracy is shown by the fact that all party authorities are elected and that the central committee is elected by the highest authority in the party, the national conference. Delegates to this conference also are to be elected. Every member of the party has the right and duty to participate in the party's deliberations and should actively participate in the elaboration of the party line, but once this party line has been adopted by higher party authorities, disputes must end and all party members must follow the rule of iron military discipline in word and deed. If a member disagrees with a party decision, he may preserve his ideas, but outwardly no deviation from the party line may be tolerated.

Lenin's concept of the party is closer to that of an army or bureaucratic hierarchy than to a living organism consisting of autonomous and independently thinking people. He obviously was influenced by earlier Russian experience provided by many conspiratorial and terroristic groups. He criticized and rejected terrorism in principle as a political tactic and ideology, but he was influenced by the terrorists' organizational principles. Among his predecessors, whom he highly extolled before and after the revolution, were the French Jacobins. It seems however that he had forgotten that the Jacobins lost their political battles because of both the deficiencies in their political philosophy and their political tactics and organization.

The opponents of Leninism, including the Mensheviks, Rosa Luxemburg, Plekhanov, and even, for a long time, Leon Trotsky, argued that Leninist principles would inevitably lead to the ossification and dogmatization of the party. They argued further that the party would cease to be a living, thinking, social organism, and would turn into an organization of robots and automatons blindly and unquestionably executing the will of the congress imposed by its leaders. Sooner or later however they argued, the will of the congress would be transformed into the will of the central committee, and then their will would be reduced to the will of a few leaders. And finally one great leader would emerge whose will would be proclaimed the incarnation of the party's will. It did not take long for the prophesies of the social democratic opponents (including a group of Bolsheviks, as well) of Lenin to materialize. In the years before the revolution, the dangers of the bureaucratization of the party were scarcely evident. This happened because at that time the leaders of the party could not be very severe with critics and opponents. Even more important, perhaps, was the fact that the party consisted predominantly of young idealists and intellectuals who were well trained in theory and had had an opportunity to observe and know western democracy and parliamentary debate and customs.

The seizure of power in 1917 changed the style and thinking of the Bolsheviks. Former prisoners, refugees, and outcasts became the rulers of a vast empire. Daily they were obliged to make decisions which would affect civil and military administration. The new rulers were obliged to create a new apparatus which never before had existed in the history of the world: a party apparatus which officially consisted of professional revolutionaries; they soon turned into professional bureaucrats operating in the field of administration. Their most skillful manager and manipulator was to become Stalin.

It took no more than half a decade following Lenin's death for bureaucrats to control every sphere of Russia's life. The new rulers lacked true education, culture, political, or social experience. They had never lived in a democratic state. They did not have the vaguest idea of parliamentary procedures or of political freedom and tolerance. No wonder that the hidden cancerous elements of Lenin's concept of centralization soon became evident.

Stalin was able to transform his office of general secretary of the party from a relatively unimportant administrative post into an omnipotent position. The old Bolsheviks did not understand the new spirit of the times and had illusions about their party's ability to resolve problems through discussion. They soon learned that a centralized bureaucracy does not make decisions on the basis of the power of intellectual arguments, but only upon the physical power of the factions. Stalin and his cohorts first expelled all those unable to divest themselves of individual thought, unable to become faceless cogs in a faceless machine. Later, all those suspected of having been in opposition were slandered, defamed, arrested, tortured, tried and finally, killed, at times without the dubious benefit of a show trial. The mechanical uniformity of the party had been achieved.

In this way the most powerful political and bureaucratic machine ever established was founded on the principle of intolerance. It is not only the leadership of the party which is unable to tolerate deviation from the officially imposed standards of thinking, speaking, and behaving; even the rank and file cannot act otherwise. The word tolerance was officially identified with ideological and political weakness. Those who had been identified as being tolerant were considered at least ideological, if not genuine, traitors and "objective" agents of imperialism. The Bolshevik Stalinist ideology was the first since the time of the Inquisition in the Middle Ages to pronounce intolerance a political and moral virtue.

In the nineteen twenties and thirties, the Fascist parties adopted certain organizational principles from Bolshevism. Just how much and to what extent the new Fascist, and especially Nazi, ideologues were influenced by the Leninist and Stalinist experience and to what extent by Prussian Militarism would require a special study. There is no doubt that they were well acquainted with both.

The Stalinization of the Soviet communist party went hand in hand with the Stalinization of all the communist parties around the world. The exportation of the revolution which had become the official goal of the Third International (Comintern) was carried out by exporting Leninism and the Leninist principles of party structure. One may argue that in many countries these principles helped the revolutionary movement to seize power. The best examples were China and Vietnam.

The Leninist principles of party organization were also exported with the aid of Soviet tanks to the so called peoples' democracies in central Europe and into Asia. The Leninist principles also were adopted or imposed on the left wing parties of the Third World. The communist parties of the western countries (with few exceptions) also adhere to the Leninist organizational and ideological dogmas.

The fact that the Leninist-Stalinist principles of intolerance are officially proclaimed and practiced by a substantial segment of mankind, constitutes one of the most dangerous sources of intolerance at the end of our century. These principles have a deadening effect on the population of the countries which are subjected to them. Whatever the old philosophers wrote of the political and moral results of intolerance is multiplied by the fact that these principles are now observed in a totalitarian way. Because they are totally adopted in a totalitarian society they are the source of total demoralization and hypocrisy.

In this process of demoralization everyone is affected, the rulers as well as the subjects, the oppressors and the oppressed. And lastly, it is difficult even to distinguish between the victims and their oppressors. As disclosed by Krushchev himself, even the powerful members of Stalin's Politbureau, who were a

source of threat, intimidation, and fear for everyone, were themselves afraid; they knew their homes and conversations were
bugged. One of the presidents (Edward Ochab) of the Polish
Peoples' Republic had the distinct honor of having bugs implant-
ed in his bedroom—we cite this because it is one example of tapping a chief of state which has been publicly admitted.

The pyramid of intolerance is poisonous for everyone within
a given country, but it is also the source of a general pollution
throughout the world. The contemporary world cannot further
develop and practice tolerance so long as it is contaminated by
that type of organized intolerance.

Lenin, in his book *Materialism and Empiriocriticism,*
introduced a new special kind of intolerance in the sphere of
philosophy and theory. In this book he undertook the task of
defending materialist philosophy against criticism made by
modern European philosophy (neo-Kantianism, positivism)
and by a few social democrats who decided to develop or modernize Marxian dialectical materialism. This attempt was used by
Lenin to dogmatize the differentiation which Marx and Engels
had made: that there are two basic trends in philosophy, idealism and materialism. Lenin stated that materialism is unequivocally connected with the revolutionary, progressive social
movements, whereas idealism is a convenient tool of conservatism, political reaction, and all types of beliefs in the kingdom
of darkness. Lenin dotted the "i" in a way in which Marx and
Engels themselves never had. He proclaimed that any mistake
in the interpretation of materialistic philosophy must sooner or
later have practical political consequences.

Once the inevitable natural controversies in the sphere of
ideas, opinions, theories, and philosophies are regarded as an integral part of the political struggles—little room remains for
intellectual freedom or for the practice of tolerance. Their future
under such circumstances remains bleak.

4. The Resurgence of Religiosity

A resurgence of religiosity began all over the world in the

1970's. This phenomenon has been an unexpected one so that it requires special analysis. So far we do not have any sociological data based on modern sociological research. There are good reasons to suspect that the lack of progress in this research area is, at least partially, due to political and ideological causes.

Even less explored is the resurgence of religiosity in communist countries.

Sociological research in the communist bloc is still in its infancy. It is not so long ago that no communist government would tolerate sociological exploration. Whenever a study showed results at variance with the official party line, the messenger was punished for the bad news he brought. The upsurge of religious beliefs which is evident to every student of eastern affairs is officially taboo. Hardly anyone writes about it. According to the official view in every communist country, religion is a remnant of the old society based on exploitation, influencing, only the older generation; the younger generation is defined as basically atheistic, although sporadically young people may be found who are contaminated with the old beliefs. No wonder the resurgence of religiosity caught the rulers by surprise; they were unable to cope with it creatively. When the chiefs do not know what to do with an unpleasant phenomenon, they simply deny its existence. In this respect, they continue to adhere to the advice given by a bureaucrat described by Chekhov. An official troubled with the existence of America, simply ordered: cover America up. Even more surprising is the fact that in the West no serious sociological research has been undertaken concerning the social causes of the new religiosity in its unexpected forms of "cults" and "sects" and of the new political influence exercised by certain leaders who pretend to be nonpolitical because they are clothed in ministerial robes.

It would seem that we should once more return to the ancient wisdom of Epicurus and Lucretius, that fear creates the gods. We live in a world in which new fears beset mankind. In western countries it is the fear of economic disaster, unemployment, dependence on the arbitrary judgments of the omnipotent state and corporate bureaucracy, and the constant threat of new crises. In the communist countries, economic fears are accompanied by the arbitrariness of political terror in the face of which an individual is defenseless. In third world countries, people live in permanent fear of hunger, privation, and police terror. Democracy, legality, and due process of law are almost unknown in that part of the world.

Throughout the modern world another source of fear exists which was unknown to older generations, the menace of nuclear annihilation. Previous generations knew of the disasters of war, but former wars were incomparable to the present possibilities of general extermination.

The European experience from the period of the holocaust indicates that people facing extermination either give up their faith, or become even more religious. Some people renounce the existence of all moral values and others adhere to them even more faithfully. The omnipresent, perceptible, oppressive fear of death, be it conscious or subconscious, influences a person's way of thinking and behaving; it may cause contradictory feelings. It can contribute to religiosity or atheism simultaneously even in the same individuals, because despair does not adhere to the principles of Cartesian logic or rhetorical argumentation.

We live in a world in which predictability is becoming less and less possible. And the options a reasonable person can take into account fade further and further into the distance. This is the ground on which anxiety and loneliness fester, as has so well been described by the existentialists.

The growth of religiosity must lead to various forms of fanaticism which is irreconcilable with reason and tolerance, as so often stressed by Voltaire and the Encyclopedists.

The Soviet and Chinese examples show that atheism which is not connected with democracy, tolerance, or true rationalism, can also become the source of fanaticism. Atheism without free dialectical argumentation becomes an ideology. This ideology is also replete with dogma and sooner or later its purity is guarded not only by a new sect of high priests, but even by special rituals, such as parades, singing, choral shouting and a public oath of allegiance, exorcizing the "demons" (one of the popular methods used during the Chinese Cultural Revolution).

In the communist countries one can observe the upsurge of two kinds of dogmatism: the traditional *theistic,* and a new *atheistic.* Both are based on dogma, both restrict the use of reason. Each feeds the other; they form the Hegelian unity of contradictions, they fight each other and they support each other. They are both cause and effect of intolerance.

In the western world, the resurgence of religiosity is connected directly with recent economic and political difficulties. The new religiosity is more conservative (if not reactionary!) than that represented by the Christian-democratic parties immediately after World War II. In the 1940's and 1950's, Christian Democrats in West Germany, Italy, France, and Belgium, helped to rebuild the democratic institutions destroyed by fascism, they presided over the process of reconstruction of the economy and education; they contributed to the development of the social institutions and programs which tended to make the life of the people more stable and secure. They acted in alliance with various social-democratic and liberal parties. Even though these alliances were not always formal and political coalitions often collapsed, there was a certain consensus and cooperation which presupposed as well as practiced tolerance.

The religiosity of the end of the 1970's is politically opposed to the great achievements of the Welfare State and New Deal, it is less charitably minded, more primitive and more belligerent, less sophisticated and less tolerant. The American "Moral Majority" is a good example of this new trend. And the American religious sects which are mushrooming in the country and allegedly encompass ten percent of the population, revive the worst traditions of blind beliefs and prejudices.

Western societies are of course developing; they are becoming more and more educated and aim towards a powerful era of rationalism. In the present period, however, they are less resilient as a totality, more exposed to the germs of religiosity combined with neo-conservatism and the seeds of creeping totalitarianism.

American religious pluralism was one of the sources of social and political pluralism and a spirit of tolerance never yet surpassed anywhere. The increased irrationalism and fanaticism, which started to evolve in the traditional denominations occasionally but most often in the new sects and cults, undermines religious pluralism and constitutes a powerful threat to tolerance.

The Rev. Moon of the Unification Church stated that America is sick and that whenever someone is ill, the family invites a physician who is not a member of the family. He announced that he was the savior-physician. This insult to reason in a more sophisticated form is repeated by every leader of every sect. The TV preachers also present themselves as the new redeemers of mankind. If they are better received than the Rev. Moon, it is only because they are better able to sell the same commodity, in a more colorful wrapping better adjusted to the American mentality. The essence, nevertheless, remains the same. Selected quotations from the Bible serve as postulates for economic and political directives. The substance of this intellectual trick is old, well-known, and worn thin. Believe, do not think, they insist. Instead of searching for facts, search for quotations, they say. Whoever is against the policy they espouse is against God himself. And that is the very essence of intolerance.

***

Such religious leaders are of course digging their own philosophical and political graves. After their political recommendations fail to produce the fruits of paradise, people will not only turn against their policies, but also against the preachers. Once people see that the crusades against abortion, the liberation of women, and the new sexual morality fail to produce positive results, they will turn about and return to the true American traditions and values such as the separation of church and state, respect for privacy, and tolerance.

There are periods of social crises when religiosity is in a state of upheaval. But whenever the high priests try to exploit religiosity for political purposes, they sooner or later become victims of their own politics. They should long ago have learned that the capricious goddess of political success helps to provide quick political achievement, but the same Fortune is quick to discard its blind devotees. The same fear which begets gods and false prophets, also creates new apostles of freedom and tolerance. The driving wheels of dialectical contradictions are incessantly turning and sooner or later doom all who are careless and presumptuous.

5. The Rise in International Tension

Almost immediately after the end of World War II, a new war started, the Cold War. The result of World War II was the division of the world into the eastern and western blocs. There were many reasons for the Cold War and several phases of its evolution. The short periods of lesser tension and of detente were indeed a cold war as well, but fought in a different way.

The most characteristic feature of the Cold War and the armed peace is that both sides are able to destroy each other, as well as the entire world. They can do so, many times over, perhaps at least fifty, probably hundreds of times over, according to various estimates.

Fear of mutually assured destruction influences public, social, and private lives in ways so numerous that for the time being we cannot even comprehend them. It is inevitable that the growth of the military establishment must attenuate the preservation and broadening of democratic liberties, democratic institutions, and a spirit of tolerance. According to the old Roman maxim, *inter arma silent Musae;* we have no reason to doubt that during the cold war certain muses in both camps were gagged, or at least were bound.

The military preparations of the western bloc were presented throughout the Soviet bloc as the cause for international tension and the justification for the enormous expenses of the communist military buildup. War preparations also are blamed for the low standard of living and for the shortage of all commodities. These shortages have been the source of almost open dissatisfaction in the communist bloc. The authorities responded to such recrimination in their usual way, with police terror. The communist party functionaries, military establishment, and the political police cannot tolerate even the slightest dissent, because from their viewpoint every dissent, however trivial, endangers the whole power structure.

The military buildup in the communist countries always is accompanied by ideological and militaristic indoctrination of the entire population. Communists drew all the conclusions, favorable to themselves, from Karl von Clausewitz's famous maxim: war is politics continued by other means. The communist authorities, therefore, prepare for war by ideological and political means. They feel that without ideological strength they would be unable to resist or prevail. In a totalitarian state, an ideological offensive means the elimination of all unofficial points of view. "Revolutionary vigilance" is not directed so much against the legions of alleged spies, as against all those who dare to think independently and have the temerity to express their thoughts.

The Cold War and the preparations therefore were also used by the Soviet Union as an argument for the imposition of strict orthodoxy on their satellites in the peoples' democratic countries. The military aspects were officially quoted as a justification for the military interventions in East Germany, Hungary, Czechoslovakia, and the military maneuvers and imposition of martial law in Poland (1956, and 1981—1982).

Preparations for war and international tension are used as a pretext for exporting Soviet intolerance, Soviet orthodoxy and the Soviet suppression of creative research in the social and political sciences.

This situation is not new. One of the first to point out how international tension affects domestic freedom was Aristotle. He drew his conclusions from empirical observations. His is the famous statement that every despot is interested in international tension and preparations for war in order to be able to present himself as the savior of his fatherland, as the indispensable leader of his army, as a man of providence whose power should not be questioned or impugned.

Because the communist leaders have total power, they demand total obedience and conformity for the sake of the defense of their fatherland when pronounced to be endangered by class enemies and imperialist encirclement.

The western countries also must pay dearly for preparations for war in abnormal international situations. The period which in American history is known as "McCarthyism" is one of the products of the anticommunist fervor prevalent in the United States. There were, of course, many reasons for this phenomenon, including economic difficulties and political antagonisms, but it seems certain that without the prospect of war against the communist bloc, Senator McCarthy's successes would not have come so easily and its impact been so profound.

This was a period in American history when democratic institutions and the famous American traditions of tolerance characteristic in all aspects of life in the United States had begun to erode.

The war in Vietnam, with all its unhappy effects, was also one of the results of the general hostility toward an arms race and toward the Soviet bloc. The distortions of the democratic process caused by the Vietnamese war are well known. Even a "cancer" (an expression used by John Dean) which became known as Watergate and the humiliation of President Richard Nixon were further outgrowths of warlike antagonisms.

An imperial presidency is not only an American phenomenon; the unusual, extra-parliamentary concentration of power manifested itself also in France and in West Germany and in one way or another in the whole Western world.

Needless to say, any far reaching centralization of political and administrative power, especially in the period of war preparations must cause uniformity and various forms of *"Gleichschaltung"* ("equalization") which will pervade all of life. Freedom and tolerance are undermined, suspicion begins to reign and garners its victims.

It would seem that the western countries which fight for freedom against the communist bloc would need to cultivate and expand their own traditions and norms, their own political liberties, religious and political tolerance, and the great right of privacy which is so unique in the world. Unfortunately, the phenomenon of osmosis exists not only in nature, but also in politics. The struggle against Communist intolerance weakens traditional western tolerance. Efforts to fight the communist terror contribute to the curtailment of western due process of law and parliamentary liberties. Soviet vigilance and assaults compel westerners to become more vigilant. Where vigilance develops, individualism and freedom are in danger.

These are the main international reasons why an endless cold war between the east and the west, the vision of mutual destruction, create new dangers which threaten democracy, freedom, and tolerance all over the world. Never has a period existed in human history when such a monstrosity of military forces and ideologies has constituted such a total danger to human freedom and tolerance, their roots and traditions.

6. The Emergence of the Third World

We decided to use the term *Third World*, although it is one of the most confusing notions. It is not very clear which countries the term encompasses. Should it be reserved for states and nations which have been liberated from colonial rule and have formed their own states since 1945? Should it include Latin American countries? Should Cuba and other communist-dominated states be included? Should they not rather be listed as socialist states?

Many doubts of the same kind could be expressed in regard to the states of the so-called First and Second World. For instance, the communist bloc obviously does not embrace Yugoslavia. The Peoples' Republic of China, which was so important in the communist bloc and in the western political imagination during the McCarthy period, is still a communist country, but from Moscow's point of view, China is a liability to their bloc rather than a support. Japan, however, belongs to the western world. The same could be said about Israel, because it and Japan adopted a parliamentary, constitutional form of government.

All these doubts could easily be dispelled by terminological and political clarifications, but the essence of the problem would remain.

When we speak about the countries of the Third World we include all countries which emerged from colonial rule and cannot be identified as western democracies or communist regimes—we adopt this classification for the practical purposes of this book only.

A political feature of all these countries is a lack of democracy in the traditional western understanding of the word. The regimes in all these countries are more or less despotic. The Anglo-Saxon rule of law or the European system of legality are either nonexistent or in their infancy. All these countries are economically undeveloped. Perhaps the word, backward, would be more appropriate, but it is not used because of its pejorative connotation. Nevertheless, there is no question that it will take a long time for these nations to reach the industrial and educational level known to the West and to most communist countries.

Nearly all Third World regimes have been unstable. Political opposition is usually illegal. Tribal differences and political conflict very often take forms more savage than even under colonial rule.

Poverty, political conflict, tribal rivalries, and animosities, are so intertwined and intermingled in those nations that it would be very difficult to detect any signs of tolerance of one group toward another. The low level of popular education and the political inexperience of the ruling groups are an additional hindrance to democracy and freedom.

In the Third World, extermination of whole social or tribal groups or genocide is a common occurrence. The massacres in

Uganda, Biafra, Ethiopia, the empire of Central Africa (Bokasa), Zaire (Congo), Arab countries (Sudan, Iraque, Syria, Lebanon and Iran) were given the greatest amount of publicity in the western world, but this list is far from complete.

The majority of the people in these countries and their rulers do not even know what patriotism, as understood in the West, implies. We already mentioned that patriotism, if exaggerated and transformed into nationalism, can, in itself, become a source of persecution and intolerance. On the other hand, it may have a mitigating influence on the rulers who would hesitate to exterminate their own. For the time being, in most Third World countries, the process of forming nations has just begun. Patriotism, therefore, cannot be a source of dignity and respect for fellow patriots. Where the idea of human dignity is unknown, tolerance cannot exist either.

It has already been pointed out that a strange political osmosis exists: despotism in one country poisons the atmosphere of freedom and tolerance in the democratic countries. Such an osmosis exists also between Third World and western countries. It is difficult immediately to recognize or feel the chilling effect which hundreds of Third World countries have on the western democracies.

It has been observed that, in 1848, the political despotism prevailing among Slavic nations froze the peoples' upheaval in central and western Europe. We now observe a similar phenomenon on a world scale.

So far the western democracies, in spite of intensive searching for an adequate solution, have been unable to solve these strange political dilemmas: how should they treat a despotic, inhuman regime? Should they preserve diplomatic relations? Should they continue business as usual? Should they sell armaments? Is it possible that through the development of mutual relations and inter-dependence they would be able to influence the tyrants, lessen terror, and finally open the jails?

All these decisions must be made in a situation of fierce competition between the western countries themselves and between the western bloc, on the one hand, and the Soviet bloc and

the Third World on the other. A human rights policy mixed with
a foreign policy is often criticized as "moralistic." Even more
criticized were the examples of the amorality of western foreign
policy. After all, we already have had the Munich betrayal of
Czechoslovakia in 1938-39. Immoral decisions do not save—
as Winston Churchill expressed it—either peace or honor;
yet they continue to be made.

The controversies and inconsistencies in the foreign and
human rights policy characteristic of every American administration (perhaps most evident under Carter and Reagan) portray
the genuine difficulties encountered by politicians. Of course,
vested interests of various western, including American, groups
also influence the political zig-zags. They could not have
spoiled so much, however, if the difficulties in developing a consistent political line were not genuine.

The discussion in the U.S. Senate (1981) concerning Ernst
Lefevre, nominated by President Reagan to head the human
rights division in the State Department, is a reflection of the hard
dilemmas which must be resolved by any western
democracy.

One can argue, of course, that the close and reliable allies of
the western states should not be publicly condemned, should not
be put under public pressure but should rather be admonished
quietly. Jacobo Timmermann observed that "silent" or "quiet"
diplomacy cannot work because "silent diplomacy" is simply
silence and nothing more, and "quiet diplomacy" usually
amounts to surrender.

It may be that this observation constitutes the best philosophical characterization of this controversy: silence and surrender can dignify terror in other countries and they can also
undermine freedom and tolerance in one's own country. It does
not take too much imagination to understand what the ancient
authors had already known: whoever condones a crime, unwittingly becomes an accomplice. Freedom and tolerance can hardly survive among accomplices to crimes. Therefore, the despotism of Third World countries has had a chilling effect on the
western democratic countries.

* * *

In 1980 an event marked a new stage in the baneful influence of the Third World on the political development of the United States and Western systems. The U.S. State Department and a large group of politicians and super-rich businessmen officially bowed before the pressure of the Saudi Arabian Government and tried to cause United States TV networks to refuse to air the British film, *The Death of a Princess.* It was a story of a romance between a Saudi Princess and a European Christian. The illicit *Romeo-Juliet* relationship was discovered, the lovers were tried and beheaded in the 1970s. The film also depicted the Saudi brand of Muslim fanaticism, bigotry, backwardness, cruelty, and hypocrisy. The Saudi rulers felt insulted. The film also denounced the Saudi *noveau riches,* who are still sticking to the ancient barbarous mores but adulterate them with Western luxury. The Saudi governing group wanted to avoid bad publicity for many reasons, the most important being their aspiration to be the spiritual leader of the Arabs and all other Muslims in the world.

Because of its basic truthfulness, the film was perceived by the Saudis as a mortal affront. No wonder they started to move all the levers which could be reached by the use of money, bribes, and threats. They approached the people who dealt with them and they opened all the channels sensitive to Saudi political and economic pressures. The results in the United States were not so apparent, because in spite of the pressures the film was broadcast.

The U.S. State Department transmitted to the networks the Saudi protests and implicitly asked that the decision to broadcast the film be reconsidered. If the Department of State really respected American sovereignty, the American Constitution, and especially the First Amendment, it either would have rejected the Saudi demands out of hand, or at least put the letter asking for illegal action on their part, silently, into the files.

At the same time, *Mobil* published one of its advertisements supporting the Saudi request, thereby effectively recommending introduction of preventive censorship into a country which should be proud of its legal tradition, elaborated by its Congress and Supreme Court, guaranteeing the freedom of press, speech, and assembly, without a peer in the world. Both the State Department, *Mobil,* and other big oil corporations doing business with the Saudis were objectively abdicating American freedom and sovereignty by voluntarily subjecting themselves to the self-appointed supreme censor residing outside the United States, but acting through his unregistered agents. There was only one state in the United States which obediently took on itself the indignities imposed by the foreign power: Texas. Suddenly a group of the Texas oilmen disclosed an unusual *delicatesse des sentiments:* they felt compassion with the hurt feelings of the Saudi sheikhs. Their whims became for them more important than the American artistic and political liberties. When the Saudis' voice resounded, some of the famous, powerful, proud, resourceful Texan businessmen and politicians became humble and meek. Suddenly the critics of Washington bureaucracy, who pretend to be so brave and who so courageously fight the Federal Government as the main enemy of Texan and national liberties, lined up to defend the Saudi effort to impose their customs and caprices upon a nation so deeply attached to its Bill of Rights.

This example shows how many people, including well established and educated American citizens, are prepared to trade their birthright and liberties for a mess of pottage. Of course, one can always find rationalization for such actions: profits for freedom! The arguments used by the Saudis' agents were appealing: The Americans have to choose between oil or their "excessive" liberties. One can not resign from oil, because it is necessary, therefore, it is better temporarily to give up individualism, independence, and "excessive" liberties.

Does it pay to solve energy problems by becoming, "in the meantime," a servant of those foreigners who happen to have been awarded oil-fields by nature but not, for the time being, culture? Is not this lack of dignity exposed by the businessmen, editors, and a group of State Department employees, a phenomenon which shows that there are many people, even in the most democratic and powerful states, who are "escaping from freedom"? Even more: they are doing it with an elan and carelessness that would have amazed Erich Fromm and the most pessimistic thinkers.

This example shows how bad the influence can be of countries on a lower stage of political and cultural evolution on peoples with more mature democratic traditions.

7. Contemporary Anti-Semitism and Questions of Freedom and Tolerance

a. The Modern Problem

Anti-Semitism is a specific prejudice we have decided to analyze more closely. Anti-Semitism has been prominent in the Western world from feudal times to the present. Soviet bureaucratic communism has also inherited it. In the recent years of economic recession, international tension, and the energy crisis it has waxed more and more. Israel has been the only nation singled out for censure often and severely by the majority of the United Nations.

Anti-Semitism is not just another sort of bigotry. Moreover, anti-Semites are not of one kind only. Anti-Semitism may derive from religious, racist, economic, social, political, ideological, moral grounds; it may be "inborn," "inherited," or caused by social contacts and "contamination." Anti-Semitism may even be conscious or subconscious.

Twentieth-century political anti-Semites succeeded in achieving certain results unknown in previous eras. They combined anti-Semitism with many modern political ideologies: criticism of and apology for the rich, belief and disbelief in the mission of the proletariat, anti-imperialism and anti-communism, colonialism and anti-colonialism, national chauvinism and cosmopolitanism, pacifism and militarism, support for the West and the undermining of its values, communist dogmatism and its "liberal" renewal.

When Hitler and Goebbels claimed that it was "Jewish power" which cemented the incredible anti-German war alliance between the western plutocrats and the eastern Bolsheviks, they were simply turning the age-old accusations that the Jews are behind every evil to their special purposes.

After 1945 it was believed that the horrors of the Holocaust had buried anti-Semitism together with Nazism. That was one more illusion nourished by incorrigible believers in the idea of perpetual progress.

Thirty, forty years after the end of World War II we witness a renaissance of anti-Semitism; it is not just because the memory of the Nazi Holocaust is fading, as even serious analysts seem to believe;[1] the soil which nurtures this growth is not just a climate of general insensitivity and deterioration of morality and customs, as is often also suggested.[2]

The roots, sources, and patterns of anti-Semitic bigotry are manifold and complex. The ends of anti-Semitism are immediate and far-reaching, calculated and irrational, religious and political. Although anti-Semitism is historically complex, politically tangled, and morally intricate, it is possible to distinguish common features of every anti-Semitic trend in any historical period: to fight progress, to restrict liberty, to impair vision, and to enhance irrationalism.

It is the general decline of contemporary political and economic systems and the disintegration of modern ideologies that have evoked old prejudices and revived the ghosts once believed to have been exorcised forever. This political and social decline is accompanied by the deterioration of moral attitudes and a general drift towards various forms of totalitarianism all over the world in the last decades of our century.

—Western people's attitudes towards the Jews is a barometer of European culture—today this famous observation of Albert Einstein sounds more and more like a warning than an observation.

b. Communist Anti-Semitism and Its Role in the Suppression of Freedom in the Soviet Bloc

Various latent forms of anti-Semitism have existed in Soviet political life ever since the beginning of the struggle between

Stalin and Trotsky. After 1945 they promptly appeared in the people's democracies. The intensity of these anti-Semitic tendencies has differed from country to country and from time to time, but they have never disappeared altogether and are politically significant still.

1. From 1917 until the death of Lenin and the beginning of the struggle between Stalin and Trotsky.

2. The rise of Stalin and the fight against the "Jewish" opposition in the Party, 1925-1939.

3. The second World War, 1939-1945.

4. The struggle against "cosmopolitanism," the extinction of Jewish culture in the Soviet Union, and provocative trials of Jewish communists, 1946-1956.

5. Anti-Semitism in the form of anti-Zionism and anti-Israeli policies following the Suez (1956) and Six-day (1967) wars.

During the first phase which lasted until 1924 and the death of Lenin, to be a socialist or communist was generally considered incompatible with any sort of nationalistic, particularly anti-Semitic, prejudice.

The socialists who grew up at the turn of the century knew two provocative anti-Semitic trials: those of Dreyfus in France and Beilis in Russia. Both trials were arranged by reactionary forces which sought to re-introduce the "*ancien régime*" in France and to preserve the corrupt Tsarist police regime in Russia. European socialists regarded anti-Semitism as a vicious device deliberately created by the decadent classes of exploiters to substitute nationalistic hatred for the class struggle. They considered anti-Semitism, or any other form of racial and nationalistic prejudice, to be demeaning to the dignity of man and therefore an obstacle to the development of the socialist and revolutionary movement. Anti-Semitism, they argued, is a weapon in the hands of the enemies of progress.

—Anti-Semitism is the socialism of fools—August Bebel and the socialists used to repeat.

During the first years after Russia's November revolution (1917), Jews were granted all the rights enjoyed by other peoples in the new communist state. Even expressions of anti-Semitism were prohibited by law. Anyone who used expressions like "kike," or "dirty Jew," was arrested, could be tried, and sentenced by the new authorities. For the first time in East-European history, Jews were appointed to the highest organs of the ruling parties and to administrative offices of the army and the police. The percentage of Jews in the socialist movement (Mensheviks, Bolsheviks, and the Socialist-Revolutionaries) was high and many top-ranking officers appointed to governmental positions after seizure of power were of Jewish background.

The second phase of the relationship between the communist movement (and the communist government) and anti-Semitism lasted from the time of Lenin's death until the beginning of World War II in 1939.

During this period the official ideology regarding anti-Semitism was still in force. Expressions of anti-Semitism were considered to be a counter-revolutionary crime, perpetrators were prosecuted in the courts. Soviet authorities and the official party propaganda all over the world argued that fascist anti-Semitism was an element of the bourgeois imperialist superstructure and that only the socialist revolution would be able to resolve this problem as well as all other problems of nationalism and prejudice.

During the 1920s and 30s the Soviet authorities regarded the Jewish people as a nationality equal to all the other members of the "socialist family" of liberated nations. They respected Yiddish as a language of the Jewish working masses, but looked upon the Hebrew language as an artificial creation revived for politico-clerical reasons by the Zionist movement. This movement was described by them as nationalistic and reactionary, inspired by Jewish exploiters who wished to found their own capitalist state in Palestine.

The Soviet government supported the development of Jewish (Yiddish) schools, literature and press, theaters and clubs.

They started to build a new "Heimatland" for Soviet Jews in the area of Biro-Bidjan in eastern Siberia. For many years Jewish achievements in that distant land were advertised as an example of the superiority of the socialist solution for the "Jewish problem" over the Zionist one. During the late 1930s, it became obvious that the experiment had failed; the number of Jews who desired to settle there decreased and during the periods of hunger caused by the inept bureaucracy, extensive industrialization and collectivization, immigration ceased completely and a mass exodus from the new promised land began.

The bankruptcy of the idea of a Jewish settlement in Biro-Bidjan also marked the beginning of a new phase in the relationship between the Soviet government, the Jews, and anti-Semitism. Even official Soviet propaganda embarked on a new policy regarding the Jews.

The first signs of the new trend started earlier, of course: during the fight against Trotsky, when semi-officially and half-publicly, the argument was used that as a Jew, Trotsky should not be permitted to be the leader of the Communist Party. Until 1926-27, Joseph Stalin struggled, as a member of a ruling "troika" consisting of Stalin, Zinovev, and Kamenev, against Leon Trotsky. After Trotsky's downfall, when the troika fell apart, the "Jews" Zinovev and Kamenev joined the opposition and Stalinist anti-Semitic propaganda became more open. The words "Jews," or "Jewish" were camouflaged with synonyms. The Stalinists accused the opposition of being the "offspring" of the petit bourgeoisie of the small towns; it was common knowledge in Russia that the "petit bourgeoisie" of the small towns meant the Jews. During this period, for the first time in the history of the communist movement, a marriage was performed between Marxian sociological and political terminology and anti-Semitic slogans. This illicit and clandestine marriage became long-lasting and exists to this day.

The Trotskyites and all other members of the "opposition" (including those like Kamenev and Zinovev who had opposed Trotsky before 1927) were accused of "defeatism," of typical petit bourgeois (that is, Jewish) "cowardice" in the face of the attacking class enemy; they were accused of lacking confidence in the genius and talent of the Russian people who were capable of transforming the world. Such arguments appealed to the backward peasants and workers who grew up in an atmosphere of anti-Semitism which had been instilled in generation after generation by the clergy and the police, the nobles and the Tsar's government. For hundreds of years they had been taught that the Jews could not and would not understand the "true Russian soul" (whatever that was), that they were an alien body on the Russian soil and therefore could not possibly understand Russia's dreams and aspirations or recognize its potentialities and talents. And, suddenly, to the peasants' delight, the Stalinists reintroduced such slogans in a new form: the Jews (the opposition) cannot comprehend that the Russian people are capable of setting an example for the entire world; that the Soviet people will not have to wait for West Europeans to build a new paradise, but that it will be their own model which will be copied and their example which will be emulated by all oppressed peoples, classes, and nations.

Such specific anti-Jewish propaganda, at times subtle, at times blatant and arrogant, appealed both to the old and new prejudices, to old inherited emotions and to the new nationalistic megolomania.

In old Tsarist Russia, as in other European countries, the Jews were made the chief scapegoats responsible for all social, economic, and even natural disasters. Anti-Semitic propaganda, deliberate, political agitation and not the simplistic witch-hunting, served specific, although limited, purposes. It was an artful, narrow-minded, *negative*, pseudo-explanation for former defeats, setbacks and disasters, as for instance, the defeat of the Russian army by the Japanese (1905), or the periodic famines throughout the Tsarist empire.

In the hands of the Stalinists, anti-Semitic propaganda became a weapon for *positive* (not only negative) indoctrination. Anyone opposed to the "Jewish opposition," it suggested, also favored the victory of the Russian people over backwardness, over the usurpations of all aliens and foreigners (West-Europeans and Jews), for the Russian people alone were respons-

sible for the glorious days of the November 1917 revolution
when they set an example for the entire world.

In the 1920s Soviet anti-Semitism became an integral part
of the ideology of "socialism in one country." Stalin officially
was described as "rodnoy" which means: a native son, descen-
dant of the blood and bones of the people of the land, the
opposite of alien (like the Jews, Trotsky, Radek, or Kamenev).
It would be inconceivable for the expression "rodnoy Trotsky"
to come from a true Russian peasant. When the Stalinists started to use "populist" instead of "proletarian" slogans in their
agitation, when they began to appeal to feelings and emotions
instead of reason, to the "subconsciousness" and "irrationalism" of the masses, the speedy rise of a new anti-Semitism
became inevitable.

This camouflaged anti-Semitism did not represent the victory of the revolution, but its Thermidor, its decline. The Stalinists were not the popular heroes and beloved leaders of the
Russian people, they were hated bureaucrats. In the eyes of the
masses, they represented not popular hopes for freedom and
affluence, but endless terror, unjustified persecution, arbitrary
arrests, annihilation of all democratic liberties, a low standard
of living, new waves of coercion, and later, bloody collectivization, extermination of millions of innocent peasants and intellectuals, and famine to an extent heretofore unknown even in
Russian history.

Anti-Semitism became a part—using the Marxian terminology—of the new "ideological superstructure" in a period
which might be likened to similar phases in the history of other
societies and states: phases of economic, political, and moral
crisis, of growing antidemocratic, antiparliamentarian tendencies. Phases when the military, the police, and the intelligence
cliques seek to get the upper hand in a country in order to suppress all enlightened and independently thinking people.

The mere fact that Stalin and his lieutenants had to resort to
the old discredited methods of anti-Semitism proved that Stalinism was the result of a deep internal crisis and was fighting
desperately for survival.

There were occasions when Stalin and his followers not only

used camouflaged forms of anti-Semitism, but overt, blatantly offensive forms, some borrowed from Nazi Germany. The most significant occurred during the purges and trials; publications of the Central Committee, official press and propaganda releases, emphasized the previous, obviously Jewish family names of the defendants, the "traitors" and "spies." This practice was used at the same time by Julius Streicher's *Der Stuermer* and other Nazi publications inspired by Propaganda Minister Goebbels. Incidentally, this infamous device was used again by the Stalinists during the "anti-Zionist" trials in Hungary and Czechoslovakia in the 1950's and throughout the entire Soviet camp during the anti-Jewish purges which followed the six-day war in 1967, the March demonstrations in Poland (1968) and the invasion of Czechoslovakia in August, 1968.

Trotsky, Zinovev, Kamenev, *et al.* were known in the Party under pseudonyms only. In the underground, during the revolution and in the years following, they never used their real family names, their "legal" names remained unknown to the Soviet people. During the trial of Trotsky's son, Leon Sedov, the latter was referred to in the press as Bronstein, a name he had never had. Thirty years later, Wladyslaw Gomulka followed the same pattern in his speech of March 19, 1968, when he named one of the leaders of the demonstrators and added to her true legal name the Jewish name which she had never used and was not even entitled to use.

Stalin played with the Jewish problem in the international scene as well. The famous Soviet minister of Foreign Affairs, Litvinov, was dismissed in 1939 when the rapprochement between Stalin and Hitler began. So as to express genuine interest in the talks, Stalin decided to drop from his cabinet the minister the Nazi press referred to as Litvinov-Finkelstein; Stalin dismissed a cabinet minister merely because the Nazis regarded him as a member of the "inferior" race. Neither Stalin nor the Stalinists harbored the slightest misgivings about Litvinov's ouster to satisfy Nazi racist prejudice. Litvinov's functions were assigned to Vyacheslav M. Molotov, who signed the infamous "non-aggression" pact with Joachim von Ribbentrop, the Nazi Minister of Foreign Affairs. This pact contained secret clauses for the division of Poland; the eastern portion of Poland was to fall under Soviet domination.

During the two years of the "accord" (1939-1941) it was difficult to find any official Soviet enunciations or publications which criticized Nazi ideology or policies. Quite the contrary, there only were published indications that the Western powers were even more aggressive than the Germans. Although the nature of the war was imperialistic, it was England and France who had provoked the outbreak of hostilities was the constant drumbeat of the Soviet propaganda machine.

When the German troops invaded the Soviet Union in June, 1941, the Soviet propagandists argued that the war had become imperialistic only on the side of the Fascist states, while on the side of the Allies it had become a just, defensive war for the liberation of occupied nations and the triumph of democratic principles and international legality all over the world; it was the new Soviet ideological explanation.

For the Soviet Union, one of the first tangible results of the Molotov-Ribbentrop treaty was the acquisition of Eastern Poland (Western Ukraine and Byelorussia) and the occupation of the three small Baltic republics, Lithuania, Latvia, and Estonia.

The Soviet press presented the occupation of these territories as a great victory of the "wise, Stalinist foreign policy" and as the liberation of oppressed peoples and nations. The Jews in the former Polish territories were told that the period of oppression by Polish fascists, "colonels, capitalists, and landowners" now was over and that at long last they would have a chance to live freely and peacefully. Attempts were made to organize Jewish schools, publications, and artistic ventures.

When the war against Germany started, the Soviet authorities gave some prominence to propaganda articles on the extermination of Jews, but soon discontinued this policy. They wanted to forestall possible charges that they were fighting to defend the Jewish people. Instead, the Soviet government stressed the victimization of Russians, Ukrainians, Byelorussians, and other Slavic peoples.

The war against Germany was declared a national war, a

war as holy as the struggle against Napoleon's invasion in 1812. The Soviet government and the Party stressed the defense of the Fatherland and dropped the slogans about Socialism or the world revolution. In this new situation, the Soviet Communist Party started more and more to conform to old anti-Semitic prejudices. They used anti-Semitism to prove they were true Russians and patriots. The Soviet army, security police, party apparatus, and civil administration began a genuine anti-Jewish purge. Although these purges were at times carried out with silk gloves, they were mostly done in a brutal and merciless fashion. The explanation always was the same: the masses do not like the Jews, do not trust them, and therefore the Party, as the people's party, must take these feelings into consideration. The Party cannot and should not go too far ahead of the masses, should not lose touch with them and must adjust its nationality policy to popular emotions and wishes.

These new practices were a product of, as well as a powerful stimulant to, the revival of the old popular anti-Semitism. The most important expression of the policy was the dismissal by the Communist Party of Jews from official positions and responsibilities; the fact that they were Jews, or rather regarded as such by the authorities, precluded their being permitted to act "for the people." Soon these facts were used as a basis for the new ideology.

This policy towards the Jews was not the only departure from the original official "Marxist-Leninist" national policy. During the second World War the Communist Party and the Soviet authorities began other widespread racial persecutions. Minority national groups such as the Crimean Tartars, the Chechens, Ingush, and others were charged and punished for having collaborated with the Germans and although innocent, were scattered and banished as a group to Siberia. The same happened with the German population which had lived along the Volga since the time of Catherine the Great. The Jews were neither the first nor the last victims of communist nationalistic persecution. But it was a matter of sociological rule and almost a historical necessity that once racial, national, or religious discrimination took hold, the Jews would inevitably be one of the important victims in the chain of persecution.

* * *

The Second World War prompted considerable change in the Soviet Union as well as in the world Communist movement. Under direct pressure from the Soviets, new communist states were established in central Europe; the Communist Parties of Italy and France recruited millions of members and received substantial voter support.

The Jews had almost been exterminated in the Nazi occupied countries. The greatest concentration of Jews, approximately 3.5 million, had resided in Poland; they were reduced to about a quarter of a million. The Jews of the famous little settlements ("shtetls") of Russia, Ukraine, Byelorussia, Lithuania and Poland, had been exterminated and the same fate befell those of Czechoslovakia, Yugoslavia, and Hungary. A relatively large segment of the Jewish population survived in Rumania and Bulgaria.

The Jewish population in all the people's democracies constituted but a fraction of one percent of the entire population, but the "Jewish problem" there has existed since the very beginning of the emergence of the new regimes. Anti-Semitism, in the form of the old hatreds and prejudices, lived on and within a very short time after the Communist takeover it once more became an important ideological and political element of the new political systems.

From 1945 to 1949, a relatively great number of Jews held prominent positions in the Parties and governments of the people's democracies, a new phenomenon in the history of those nations. The natives were predominantly anti-Russian, anti-Soviet, anti-Communist, and anti-Semitic. Several years later, the Soviet Party and Government decided to exploit these anti-Semitic feelings for their own purposes.

One reason why there were relatively many Jews in administrative and Party offices in the Peoples Democracies during the first years after 1945 was that these Jews, especially those who survived the war in the Soviet Union, were of the old "communist guard" who had joined the Communist Party either before or during the war, at any rate prior to the seizure of power by the Communists (1944-45). Often they came from bourgeois families and were better educated than the rank and file of non-Jewish workers and peasants who had joined the Communist Party later. These Jews were therefore appointed to high responsible positions within the governments, the Party, trade-unions, security police, and the army. The idea of putting the old communists in the governments because they were trustworthy was consistent with the logic of the "dictatorship of the proletariat;" to put it more pointedly, the dictatorship of the communist vanguard.

Although few in number they were still very much in evidence to the people who were not used to seeing Jews in positions of power but rather were accustomed for centuries to look down at them and to blame the Jews for all disasters which befell their country, be they floods, epidemics, or military reversals. The methods of terror and economic pressure imported from the Soviet Union and adopted by the bureaucracy of the people's democracies were genuinely disastrous and caused immeasurable grief. A goodly measure of the local population's indignation and antagonism, justifiably, was directed at Communism and Russian-Soviet oppression, but it focused upon the individual Jews who happened to carry out that oppression. The native population finally realized that Soviet interference and the basic deficiencies of the communist system were responsible for all their economic and social disasters, but Moscow was far away, whereas the Jewish officials were on the spot. Within a very short time it became evident that the Stalinist bureaucracy would exploit this new wave of anti-Semitism. The crucial moment arrived during 1948 and 1949.

During these years, Stalin and his chief ideologist, Andrei A. Zhdanov, commenced their campaign against what they called cosmopolitanism. The reasons behind, and purposes for, this campaign were, as usual, manifold. Persecution of the Jews and extermination of the best Jewish writers and artists was not the chief purpose but became part of the campaign.

The general purpose of these actions was Stalin's drive to tighten up the so-called "ideological front." His intention was to eradicate the expectations and hopes for prosperity and freedom inspired during World War II. The Soviet bureaucracy was unable to fulfill these popular aspirations and the people's hopes and dreams had to be shattered and their illusions disspelled.

The campaign against cosmopolitanism aimed at persuading the Soviet people that the ideal of a higher standard of living was a product of petit bourgeois consumerism, incompatible with socialism. The Soviet people were urged to concentrate on the greatness of the Fatherland, on the historical mission of its people, and to ponder the grandeur of the Russian nation which enjoyed the capacity for great exploits and selfless suffering beyond that of any other nation in the world.

At the same time the Russian people were informed of the general crisis, which included unemployment, poverty, demoralization, prostitution, corruption, crime, lawlessness, and neo-fascism supposedly prevailing in the capitalist world and were told to believe that the capitalist world was decaying. These allegations were presented as unquestionable facts subject to no discussion.

The Soviet people, however, as well as the people of all other nations under Communist rule, knew that the "decadent" capitalist world was not crumbling. They knew that compared to themselves the people even of relatively poor capitalist nations enjoyed a higher standard of living, were more fashionably dressed, had cars and owned houses, and did not have to wait on long queues for food and other household necessities. They also remembered that during the war these "decadent" systems had supplied the "invincible" Soviet Union with many things—from war materials to consumer goods. The exploding of the A-bomb during the last days of the war convinced them that the United States was far advanced in the scientific and technical fields and had far surpassed the socialist camp in achievements.

The ruling bureaucracy was unable to explain away such facts. Questioning of any kind, even logical and reasonable inquiries, were regarded as dangerous. Trapped in their own lies by truth and reason, they felt compelled to attack this very truth and reason directly.

Whoever doubted that Western capitalism had one foot figuratively in its grave was considered to have been infected with "cosmopolitanism" and beguiled by the witchcraft of imperialism. Such a person was unworthy of membership in his own great society for obviously he lacked the capacity to trust in the Party's genius.

Only such people, the official propaganda asserted, who felt no deep attachment to the Nation, the Party, to Socialism, and whose roots were not within the Russian soil, were capable of admiring the West and criticizing the communistic paradise. And, who were these benighted individuals who could not feel their roots in Russian soil, could not feel attached to and committed to their "Mother Russia?" Of course, the Jews led the list! They were looked upon as classic cosmopolitans; they were the ones who called no land their own; did not feel committed to the Russian cause; they were the ingrates of the Land, the Nation, and the Fatherland that had afforded them such great opportunities and boundless prospects. The Jews, it was concluded, were neither patriots nor communists; they were not builders, not true believers in the socialist or the communist society. The Jews were not loyal citizens; they had no country of their own, they represented many cultures, professed a multitude of national and political allegiances, and were by their very nature "vagabonds without credentials," in brief, non-Russians, non-socialists.

These allegations were the new, so-called "Marxist," "Leninist," "Communist" forms of anti-Semitism. The theory was looked upon as a contribution to "Marxism-Leninism," a creative development of "historical materialism." It was, however, no more than a repetition of the old Tsarist and Nazi anti-Jewish propaganda, albeit garnished with a "socialist" sauce. Legally, anti-Semitism was still prohibited, therefore, it was only "cosmopolitanism" against which the crusade was declared.

The Jews were the first victims of this campaign against cosmopolitanism, but not the only ones. The main target of this campaign of terror was intellectualism and creativity. All true, honest, creative scholars, writers, scientists, and journalists all over the Soviet Union and the "people's democracies" were terrorized and demoralized anew. They were under constant suspicion and were mercilessly hunted down, arrested, and either shot or sent to labor camps such as those so eloquently described by Solzhenitsyn in *The Gulag Archipelago, One Day in the Life of Ivan Denisovitch*, and *The First Circle*. Jewish culture in the Soviet Union was destroyed; the art and culture of all the other Soviet nations was decimated. A new era of corruption commenced as the authorities tried to convince the Soviet people that the Russians truly were the "chosen people," that they, of all nations, had made the greatest contribution to world civilization, that they had invented automobiles, radios, the law of Lavoisier, that Moscow was indeed the "Third Rome." Only anti-communists and the enemies of the Russian people could doubt these official contentions.

The campaign against cosmopolitanism was equated with anti-Semitism. Official Communist ideology of this period, still considered to be a development of "Marxism-Leninism," lost not only decency, but also logic and good faith.

Why had the Stalinists decided to resort to anti-Semitism? The Stalinist bureaucracy decided to exploit the well-rooted and vital popular anti-Semitic prejudices in an effort to recover at least some popularity and credibility for themselves.

They needed the Jews as visible scapegoats. They might have repeated the words of Hermann Goering: "If the Jews did not exist, we would have to invent them." The Stalinists, like the Nazis, believed that the masses could only understand a visible, palpable danger. Invisible abstract threats would influence them only for a short time. They believed that if they were to control the masses through fear, they would have to point to a live, clear-cut, and definite source of danger. This was the tradition of the Inquisition, whose masterminds understood that the mere image or idea of a devil would not effectively influence the people for long. Therefore hundreds of innocent people, predominantly women, were accused of having close relations with the devil and were made to serve as visible proof of Satan's detrimental effects.

The Jews of the Soviet Union and of the entire Soviet bloc were to play the role which for centuries had been played by the witches in all "civilized" European countries. Now, as in Tsarist Russia, people were in effect, told: do you see evil all around you? Is your life difficult? If so, let us show you the source of all your difficulties: the cosmopolitans! Let us get rid of them and their non-Jewish supporters.

Communist anti-Semitism as a new essential element of the "super-structure," also added a significant dimension to the condemnation of the Yugoslav heresy by the Cominform in 1948. Among the most noteworthy results of this excommunication was that the Stalinists in Moscow then usurped the power to denounce not only the persons, but all the Communist parties and governments involved. Moreover, since the imperialists were able to get the upper hand in one party, the official reasoning concluded it must be presumed that there were many other secret, high ranking agents in all the parties which had taken power in the other people's democracies.

In keeping with this theory, every Communist Party in the people's democracies was obliged to find the hidden enemies among its highest ranking officials and to prove to the people that they were in fact agents of imperialistic secret services. The presumption that there *MUST* be foreign agents in every Politbureau was created by Stalin and his Politbureau; anyone challenging it became suspect himself.

After 1948, a wave of arrests and show trials commenced in all the people's democracies. The most infamous and tragic were those of Laszlo Rajk in Hungary, Traicho Kostov in Bulgaria, and Rudolph Slansky in Czechoslovakia. During these show trials the accusations were alike:

— the accused were bound up with the Titoist traitors;
— the accused planned to alienate their country from the Soviet Union;
— the accused wished to restore capitalism step by step through use of the ideas of the right-wing-deviation, thereby

fighting socialist industrialization and collectivization;
— the accused, or most of them, were part of the world Zionist conspiracy.

From 1948 to 1952, particularly during the show trials, the
"communist" theory of a Zionist conspiracy was elaborated.
Israel and the Zionist movement were described as a strong-
hold, albeit one of the last, of imperialism within the socialist
camp and in the Middle East. The Zionists, so went the theory,
used their influence among the Jews who had remained in the
socialist countries. These Jews, the theory held, came from the
bourgeoisie, or from the middle classes and therefore had a
natural affinity for capitalism and the ideology of Zionism.
Those Jews, alleged the Stalinists, who had relatives abroad or
had been abroad themselves were most dangerous; the fact that
the relatives had escaped to France or England to avoid extermination by the Fascists should not mislead anyone. The imperialist chieftains had laid their plan long ago, before the Holocaust, and even before the seizure of power by the Communists
and had trained their agents in preparation for the future so they
could place them in strategic positions in socialist governments.
The Jews and their Zionist inclinations of course fit best into the
imperialists' schemes and that is why they should be looked
upon as the most dangerous element in the Socialist camp, the
Soviets maintained. They must be eliminated from the newly
created communist administrations.

The anti-Jewish purges and show trials were given enormous publicity throughout the entire communist bloc. Within a
short time, thousands of essays, articles, pamphlets, and books
about them were published and disseminated throughout all
Communist states. The Party propagandists delivered speeches
at meetings which everyone had to attend.

What purpose was served by this anti-Zionist campaign
which was not only political, but also theoretical and
doctrinal?

From 1948 to 1949, it became obvious that the achievements of the new Communist governments had fallen far short of
their promises. Dependence on the Soviet Union was increasing; sovereignty, to all intents and purposes, did not exist. Eco-

nomic plans were not realized, production in agriculture declined, the housing problem became more acute every day, the stores reported shortages of supplies and the standard of living fell lower and lower. The security police, trained and directed by Soviet advisors, made arbitrary arrests, had their prisoners tortured and denied them their right to defend themselves. This crisis in the Soviet bloc was not only economic, it was doctrinal as well. These pressures and the generally dismal outlook, prompted the Stalinists to begin the anti-Zionist purges.

The Jews were held responsible for all the failures of the system, for the setbacks in industry and agriculture, for the catastrophe in foreign trade, for the low standard of living.

The anti-Zionist campaign and ideology worked to terrorize the entire population. Humiliation of the Jews, as the Nazis knew, was an important element in the process of humiliating and demoralizing all the "Aryan" nations. The rule of terror can act as an effective and stabilizing force when the nation is corrupt and deceived and does not know the true causes for its misery. The anti-Zionist campaign was an insult to both reason and morality. The Stalinist lies were horrendous, but as Hitler so often repeated and expressed in his *Mein Kampf*, the bigger the lie, the better. The more incredulous the people, the better are the chances for convincing them of the propagandist viewpoint.

The zenith of the anti-Jewish campaign was reached in the case of a group of the most eminent Jewish physicians and professors of medicine in Moscow in 1952. They were accused of a plot to kill the leaders of the Soviet Party and government while the latter were being examined and treated. This plot was an invention, of course, but the lie was swallowed by many.*

---

*On July 11, 1952, a group of Jews was accused of being "enemies of the USSR, agents of American imperialism, bourgeois nationalist Zionists...who sought to separate the Crimea from the Soviet Union and establish their own Jewish bourgeois nationalist Zionist republic there."

The accusation of the Jewish physicians of plotting against the life of their patients was not the first in history. The personal physician of Elizabeth I was a Spanish Jew, Lopez. Accused of conspiring against the queen, he was hung and quartered.

The arrest of the Jewish physicians was accompanied by a new campaign of "revolutionary vigilance." It was brought home to everyone that the foe could be anywhere and anyone.

The fabricated "doctors' plot," became the occasion for a new Stalinist theory concerning construction of communism. According to this new development, the class struggle sharpens not only during the building of socialism, but also after the socialist victory, during the period of immediate construction of the classless Communist society of the future. This theory was the last contribution made by Stalin. He died some months later, but his political philosophy has endured.

To sum up the foregoing, cosmopolitanism and afterwards anti-Zionism became a mask for anti-Semitism. In political practice however, Soviet anti-Semitism was overt.

Anti-Zionism was an integral element of the anti-cosmopolitan campaign, but it was the latter which justified all the persecutions of non-Jews, and of all other Russian and non-Russian undesirables (especially Ukrainians) as well.

Cosmopolitanism and anti-Zionism served as visible confirmation of the theory that the "class struggle" had become so intensified and acute that it required the use of terror and torture.

* * *

In the period of the cold war, the Communist authorities started the anti-western campaign which was not to the people's liking.

The Stalinists, so as to make their propaganda more effective, resorted once more to the old method: they accused the Western governments of world Zionism (Josef Goebbels used to write of the *"Welt-Judentum"*). This accusation started a vicious circle: Zionism was the tool of Western powers while the Western governments were lackeys of the Zionists. The Stalinists were not concerned over such petty inconsistencies. Their purpose was to present their battle against the Western countries as a battle against the Jews.

And lastly, it was during this period that the Soviet govern-

ment anticipated an era of new relationships with the governments of the Muslim countries. The identification of Western
capitalism with Zionism and the identification of the Soviet bloc
with anti-Zionism, became an important element in this new
turn of Soviet foreign policy.

After Stalin's death the process of de-Stalinization began
slowly. It was the period the writer, Ilya Ehrenburg, called
the "thaw."

The *thaw* started in all Communist countries, but de-Stalinization never was completed. After a brief, somewhat warmer
and sunnier period, the cold winds inevitably followed. After a
few steps forward then a few backwards, "historical necessity"
manifested itself in more reasonable approaches and a scant
measure of legality.

The Jewish doctors were rehabilitated and released from
prison. Although the Jewish artists and writers could not be
brought to life and no attempts were made to restore Jewish culture, the anti-Semitic campaign ceased for several years. The
prospects for a new anti-Jewish extermination, this time in
Siberia, were not deemed as imminent as during the last years of
Stalin's life.

Anti-Semitism ceased to be an important ideological instrument in the Soviet bloc for a short time. Nonetheless, there were
many instances of chicanery and persecution, such as the strict
quota for the admission of Jews into the universities. In accordance with the well known, although still-unpublished slogan of
N.S. Khrushchev, the same percentage of Jews was to be admitted to the universities as worked in the mines.

The workings of Khrushchev's mind were an excellent example of how the old anti-Semitic tendencies were appearing in
the entirely new social, political and ideological situation.
Khrushchev was the gifted mastermind of de-Stalinization; he
was able to develop new practical ideas and even managed to
apply the old routine in a more elastic way in both domestic and
foreign affairs. But his manner of thinking was still too primitive
to change his obsolete attitude toward the Jews.

* * *

In 1956, anti-Semitism once again became an important

ideological and political issue for the entire Soviet bloc, but especially for Hungary and Poland.

In those two countries the process of de-Stalinization and democratization had developed more quickly, thoroughly, and deeply than in any of the others. The reasons for this evolution in Poland and Hungary were various, some historically determined, some determined by the turn of events, the dogmatism or flexibility of the leaders, the emotions, and experiences of the nations, and as always, through accidents.

In both countries, nonetheless, anti-Semitism played an important role after 1956. The traditional right-wing elements pointed to the crimes of Stalinism and averred that Jews had participated in them. The conclusion therefore was simple: to avoid the perpetration of the Stalinist-type crimes in the future, the Jews (the instrument of the Soviet government) should be purged and punished, then banished from the country and sent to Israel, or at least to begin with, be removed from all responsible political, social, and administrative posts.

This idea was a revival of the old right-wing and Fascist views which had held that the Jews were responsible for Communism, that they had invented it and tried to promote it; that they had made the Russian revolution, and that they therefore were responsible for new Russian imperialism. The only difference between the Nazi concept (and that of the pre-war Hungarian and Polish anti-Semitic parties) and the new "anticommunism" was that after 1945 the right-wing elements were working within the framework of the Communist system since they believed that it would not be possible to abolish that system in the near future. It was their intention to achieve the old ends with the help of the Communist system itself. The new idea was to transform the Communist regime into a *"Judenrein"* system, one cleansed of Jews.

Because of a strange twist of history, anti-Semitism also became the most important ideological concept in the hands of the old Stalinist "Aryan" guard. When the crimes of Stalinism were officially revealed and denounced, the Stalinists in Poland and Hungary, and to a lesser degree in other Communist countries, began accusing the Jews of having been responsible for those crimes. This anti-Semitic ideology was elaborated in Moscow. Soviet agents brought it to Budapest and Warsaw and spread it throughout the people's democracies.

In an article submitted to the liberal weekly, *Poprostu* in September, 1956, I described the sources and purposes of the new anti-Semitic ideology in the following manner:

> Stalinism, as an ideology and a system of government, is in retreat throughout the entire socialist bloc. However, if I might make use of a witty Warsaw expression—Stalin's orphans and posthumous children have survived. They represent not only their poor and mischievous personalities, but a whole social stratum which owes its prestige, standard of living, clandestine connections, and social influence to the system which one used to describe as a "system of the cult of a personality." The bureaucratic elements which constitute a very specific new social class unprecedented in history form a powerful conservative social bloc with an external and internal support which is much farther reaching than we had ever suspected. From the point of view of political traditions and social theory, as well as parliamentarian terminology, these *communist conservatives* in the socialist system play a role analogous to that of the right-wing reactionary parties in the capitalist parliamentary democracies. Their vested interests lie in the preservation of the social and political status quo. The neo-conservatives, or the "communist" right-wing parties, or simply, the Stalinists, have to elaborate their own ideology in order to justify their activity and anti-social, counter-progressive purposes. They cannot bring up anything new, they do not have the "brains" in their ranks as for instance the editors and contributors of the French *Le Figaro* do, they do not have the tradition of European rightists, but only their own past which is worse than one could possibly imagine. The "communist conservatives" have to defend their very simple and prosaic interests and therefore their ideology of defense must be equally simplistic. The logic of social relations compels them to look for examples in the ideology of the traditional right-wing parties—but even the traditional rightist ideas are too sophisticated for communist conservatives. There is indeed one set of old reactionary ideas which the Stalinists could borrow from the armory of their right-wing predecessors, the shield of

anti-Semitism. Stalinists had to refer to this bankrupt ideology of
their fascist forerunners in order to avert their own bankruptcy.
The mere fact that anti-Semitism is the only ideological residue
of the bureaucracy, is an admission in itself that their cause is
historically lost, although politically they may be as successful
as was General Gallifet (commander of the French army of Ver-
sailles who suppressed the Paris Commune and started the reign
of terror).

The uncomplicated ideology of "Natolin" (Stalinist group in
Poland in 1956-57—M.M.) can be expressed in one sentence:
the Jews are responsible for the crimes of Stalinism, therefore let
us purge out the Jews and the lost communist paradise will be
restored.

Even more important is what the Stalinists do not do: they do
not try to analyze the Stalinist system, which sociologically is
the basic cause of the crimes; they do not analyze the problem of
bureaucracy, although Lenin himself (do not they call themselves Leninists?) recommended a fight against it; they do not
even admit the existence of the problem of alienation; millions of
examples of Stalinist genocide are simply "irregularities" for the
bureaucrats and trivial "abuses" of power, which allegedly have
nothing to do with the "essence" of the power-structure. They
are playing loose with the notion of "essence", because they do
not know the observation of Hegel and Lenin: essence must be
formed, whereas form is essential—one more example that the
Stalinists did not even read . . . Lenin.

It is sufficient, according to "Natolin," just to preach that it is
not nice or fair to torture and to murder innocent people, and all
the troubles and difficulties will be overcome—according to
their primitive reasoning. Who should repair the damage? the
broken administrative engine?—as the intellectuals and workers in Warsaw used to ask. The "Natolin" group replies: the
same engineers who damaged the engine, because they have
experience in dealing with it. New engineers should not be
allowed in, shout the Stalinist conservatives, because we have
no proof that they know the engine as the present ones did. There
should be one exception only concerning the old crew of political
engineers: the Jews as incurable, incorrigible, spoilers should be
excluded from the privileges of Stalinism; only the "Aryan"
Stalinists should be given a new, unrestricted opportunity to continue their blessed past activity.

The concept that Jews must be punished for the crimes of Stalinism is an imported ideology, alien to the Polish people. It is an old ideology indeed, dating from the period of Houston Chamberlain, *"The Protocols of the Elders of Zion,"* and of Hitler's *"Mein Kampf."* According to this ideology, there exists a Jewish supra-international center which directs the activity of every Jew in the world. Therefore, any Jewish official who might have committed a crime in one country should not be looked upon as one individual, but as the collective Jew; and his crime is a collective Jewish crime.

The British Prime Minister Disraeli, and the Polish-German communist Rosa Luxemburg, were both members of the Jewish world-conspiracy, fascists contended. The Jews therefore should be punished for imperialism as well as Communism. And therefore also, all the Jews of all countries should be punished because the notorious sadists and murderers Rozanski and Romkowski stemmed from Jewish families.

This is not the end of Stalinist provocative assertions, however (all Stalinists are trained in the School of Provocation— they cannot act otherwise). They accuse the Jews of having invented the ideas of a liberal, democratic, humanistic socialism. That is, they allege, the ideology of imperialist diversion propagated by Jewish writers, scholars, and journalists. And they conclude: let us purge those Jews, let us introduce good Aryan peasants and workers to the Polish editorial boards and universities. People then will stop dreaming about Jewish liberalism and humanism—by the way, the Nazis also used to accuse the Jews of being the authors of decadent liberalism.

The best expression of "Natolin" ideology was the speech delivered by Zenon Nowak during the VII Plenary Session of the Central Committee in summer 1956. But the same group prevented the publication of the speech. Why were they afraid? They love darkness and they fear the truth. In order to describe the Stalinist anti-Semitic operations, the old Nazi term would be appropriate: *Nacht und Nebel* (night and fog).

Every reasonable citizen, were he given the full text of the speech, would have been able to draw his conclusion concerning the alliance of the Stalinists and the old *"Black Hundreds,"* or the Polish *Falanga.* In 1937-39 this Polish equivalent of the German SS was led by infamous *Bepcio*, who after 1945 be-

came the Stalinist protegé. Boleslaw Piasecki and Stalinists—
what an alliance! Anti-Semitic ideology plays the same role in
the Stalinist conspiracy as it did for many centuries: it is the
ideology of the reactionary, conservative, obsolete, status quo—
it is the ideology of deceiving the people; it is the ideology of the
brutal, physical repression of the Polish Nation who desire
enlightenment, progress, freedom and legality.

At the beginning of October, 1956, my article was "withheld" (not confiscated) by Censorship for purposes of further
"clarification." Some weeks later, when Gomulka's new leadership took power, I again asked for permission to publish the
article (November 1957). Instead, the editors and I were invited
by the "number two man" in the Party, its chief ideologist,
Zenon Kliszko, to have a talk. "In the name of the first Secretary, Wieslaw Gomulka," as he put it, he tried to persuade us
that the article would be detrimental to Poland and to its relations with Moscow. Kliszko admitted (albeit as a "Party secret") that Natolin's ideology had been elaborated in Moscow,
that Zenon Nowak had discussed his anti-Semitic speech with
the Soviet Ambassador, that Moscow had recommended an
anti-Jewish purge, instead of a purge of Soviet military and
security advisors who had been "asked" by the new Polish
government to return home.

In such a situation, Kliszko stated frankly, one must understand that it would be impossible to publish such an article; it
would violate Polish *raison d'etat*. Furthermore, everything
must be done to prevent a bloody intervention such as took place
in Hungary.

I describe this episode in such detail because this story better
illustrates "communist anti-Semitism" as a Soviet and neo-
Stalinist tool than any scholarly treatise possibly could. It also
illustrates the liberal atmosphere prevailing in Poland at the end
of 1956.

Nonetheless, this ideology of "people's anti-Semitism" won
its victory some years later. It triumphed during the March
events in Poland in 1968 and the invasion of Czechoslovakia in
August of the same year.

In the years of the half-hearted "de-Stalinization," and after the 20th Congress of the CPSU, two sets of events became most relevant for the future development of "communist anti-Semitic ideology:"

—the rapprochement between the Soviet Union and the Arab countries;

—the regression toward Stalinism.

The drift towards neo-Stalinism from time to time was discontinued during the short periods of thaw (including the XXII Congress of CPSU in 1962). Neo-Stalinism had been a continuous source of the same social, economic, and political contradictions characteristic of Stalinism. But neither in the Soviet Union, nor in the people's democracies did the hopes and aspirations for a better, more humane, democratic way of life diminish. We observed acute struggles in those countries between "liberalism" and Stalinist "dogmatism," between humanistic and terroristic tendencies.

The great confrontation of those two trends took place in 1968.

The anti-Semitic trend of the new post-October (1956) regime started to appear in Poland within a very short time. The supporters of this trend were not only the old Stalinists whose ideology and politics were described above, but also other conservative elements of the new ruling groups. Among the most progressive and liberal elements of the new ruling coalition were several Jews. So as to be able to suppress them, the dogmatic, bureaucratic elements, usually without education, started to use the traditional means: anti-Semitism. In Poland, in the 1960's it was the minister of security, General Mieczyslaw Moczar, who formed a bloc of old Stalinists under Gomulka's supervision and the hard core officers of security, Party officials, army bureaucrats, demoralized individuals from combatant organizations, and faceless "youth leaders." The purpose of this bloc which acted like the "Mafia," was to exterminate the survivors of "October 1956," the liberal democratic upheaval in the Party, the Government, the press, publishing houses, and the universities.

In March 1968, Moczar's agents infiltrated students' organizations, and helped to organize a meeting feigning a protest against political reprisals, censorship and degradation of Polish culture. The peaceful meeting was used as a pretext for ruthless purges and persecutions all over Poland. Thus an anti-Jewish campaign started. The Jews were once more accused of the well-known sins:

—Jews are not loyal Polish citizens because they are more committed to the cause of Israel;

—Jews do not support the foreign policy of the Soviet Union and Poland, they are hostile to the Arabs, they supported Israel morally and economically during the Six-day war (1967); allegedly they had transferred millions of dollars to the US embassy so as to help Zionist aggression (a rumor deliberately spread by Party and security officers);

—Jews were responsible for the crimes of Stalinism, for forced collectivization of the Polish peasantry, but now they had changed their tactics and were posing as liberals and democrats;

—Jews will always be enemies of the people;

—Jews, and especially the Jewish intellectuals and liberals, will always be a "fifth column," they are the spies and agents of imperialism;

—Jews are Zionists and Zionism is an agency of world imperialist subversive armies;

—Jews slander the Polish nation by circulating false rumors blaming Poles for anti-Semitism;

—the Jews are responsible for the recent economic difficulties in Poland, for price increases, and for the deficit in foreign trade.

It was a paradox that the Jews suddenly were regarded as the most dangerous enemy of Communism although for years the traditional right-wing anti-Semitic parties had charged that they had invented and been the chief promoters of Communism. The sociological, ''Marxist'' explanation of this paradox set forth in detail in a pamphlet written by one of the Polish Party's lesser ideologists, Andrzej Werblan, was:

The Jews, as a persecuted minority, tend to support and to join the Communist parties in countries in which they are persecuted by reactionary governments like those in pre-revolutionary Russia, Rumania, Hungary, and Poland. The Jews never were proletarians; even poor Jews were lower middle class, and therefore after the socialist revolution, their old class alliances and non-proletarian consciousness revived in the atmosphere of communist "freedom" and equality. The Jews who had come from rich bourgeois families and had even been prominent in the underground communist movement, discovered during the period of the dictatorship of the proletariat that communism was not for them. They became frustrated, became the promulgators of right-wing petit-bourgeois deviations, and therewith covert imperialistic agents. After some time, several actually were recruited as conscious agents of imperialism, on the payrolls of CIA, British Intelligence Service and French Second Bureau. After the creation of the bourgeois state of Israel, according to Werblan, and other ideologists of neo-Stalinism, the Jews, including those who had been long-term members of the Party, experienced reborn nationalism and felt new nationalistic commitments to that country. They were therefore more than other citizens inclined to betray their socialist fatherland. The non-Jews, however, feel a natural affinity for their country, their people, soil, culture, customs and families. The Jews are aliens who do not have these natural commitments. The non-Jews are patriots by nature and therefore not inclined to collaborate with foreign intelligence services, whereas the Jews have no innate patriotic feelings, no patriotic emotions, and therefore, when frustrated, they become "treason-prone."

And, finally, Gomulka himself expressed this argument: the people do not like the Jews, therefore Polish communists must take this fact into account, remove the Jews from their functions and help them to leave for Israel.

In this way the old anti-Jewish arguments with the so-called Marxist sociological analysis were combined.

This elaborate communist anti-Semitic ideology also was

used in order to justify the invasion of Czechoslovakia in August 1968. The neo-Stalinist ideologists used to present Poland as a positive example to be followed: the Zionist agency in Poland was liquidated in time, that is, in March 1968; this move enabled Communism to "recover" within a relatively short period and without foreign aid. In Czechoslovakia, however, the influence of the revisionists, liberals, and dissidents organized and led by the Zionists had gone too far, Stalinists maintained; military intervention was necessary and justified. The Zionist movement and the State of Israel, according to the official propaganda, compelled the Soviet tanks to enter the city of Prague.

This ideological justification of the invasion further revealed that communistic anti-Semitic ideology had acquired another important aspect: it served as an ideological underpinning of the "*Brezhnev doctrine*"

* * *

In conclusion: in 1968, the March events in Poland and the August invasion of Czechoslovakia, created a background on which the final touches of the "communist anti-Semitic ideology" were elaborated. Whatever happened afterwards is just a practical application of the previously worked out basic elements:

The United Nations resolution of 1975 equating Zionism with racism has been a further evolution of the previously expressed Soviet ideas. This "obscene" (expression of the then U.S. Ambassador to the United Nations, Senator Daniel P. Moynihan) accusation was already ingrained in the "communist anti-Semitism."

Communist anti-Semitic bigotry became an indispensable means to fight the ideas of freedom, tolerance, justice, peace, and even independence of nations.[3]

c. Anti-Zionism: The Latest Form of Anti-Semitism.
A Phantom Revived.

The creation of the independent state of Israel had many

consequences. One of these was a change in the structure of Judaism itself associated with the new development of Zionism, the Jewish movement for the resettlement of Jews in Israel. Anti-Semitism consequently, also assumed new aspects. It turned into anti-Zionism as Jews became part of the international community.

Israel has its own army, diplomatic corps, international relations, alliances, and last but not least, its own *raison d'état*. For the first time in modern history a strange possibility has arisen: one may be an anti-Semitic ally of the State of Israel and vice versa. One can morally, intellectually, and emotionally be indifferent to Jews and Judaism, yet be an enemy or friend of Israel for political and economic reasons.

***

Nevertheless, there is no impenetrable wall between traditional anti-Semitism and the new anti-Israeli attitude. We have no intention of analyzing the complexities of the relationship between these two attitudes here, because the scope of this chapter is limited. Our general thesis is that nowadays anti-Israeli politicans take into account existing anti-Jewish prejudices and try to win support from that segment of the public which harbors the old prejudices. A modern politician does not have to be anti-Semitic himself when he exploits existing prejudices; the logic of certain political decisions pushes him into such an attitude. This logic is not a deliberate creation of sophisticated political strategists working in secret; it has emerged spontaneously because of the strange alliance which recently came into existence between semi-feudal sheiks, capitalist super-monopolists, Third World dictators, and communist rulers. This unwritten pact was never negotiated or discussed among them. Its very existence is vehemently denied by all. They genuinely despise each other politically, perhaps personally as well, but for the present they collaborate loyally because it is to their advantage. They have a common economic purpose: the accumulation of wealth and the use of economic leverage for their own individual political ends. They all are interested in softening resistance against them and in weakening their adversaries and their friends. They all agree with DeGaulle's remark that war is waged against adversaries, while peace is conducted against friends.

No alliance can rest on greed and rapacity alone because antagonisms and competition can undermine any community of interests. Such a strange, informal alliance therefore must be bound together by something more cohesive: a mutual enemy, either genuine or fabricated. It was easy to find a suitable villain: Israel. And, by extension, Israel's co-religionists all over the world.

Every member of the alliance denounces Jews as trouble-makers and wages his own campaign against them. Jews are accused of being stubborn, arrogant, unwilling to sacrifice their territory in order to enable the West and the Arab countries to cooperate. The fact that Arab countries deny Israel's right to exist is played down. Jews are held responsible for interruptions in oil supplies, for the disruption in East-West cooperation. They are even accused of dangerously playing with the idea of war.

The more nonsensical the charges and imputations, the worse it is for the accused because proof or logic are unnecessary and even undesirable. We are once more facing the situation which was described by Anatole France in connection with the Dreyfus affair: nothing undermines obviousness more than an attempt to prove it. Every member of the alliance needs the Jews in order to blame them for disasters to which they themselves have made the greatest contribution.

In the Soviet bloc Zionists are used as a visible sign of imperialistic aggression, a fifth column, treacherous conspirators who intensify the "class-struggle."

Arabs need the Jews in order to unite themselves, to silence their free-thinking intellectuals, also their poor and oppressed who are deprived of elementary rights, and in order to present the super-rich oil barons as respectable freedom fighters. Should Israel catastrophically perish, the sheiks would be the

greatest losers. They would lose their best, most suitable scapegoat. The sheiks' moral turpitude, ignorance, indolence, wastefulness and inability to organize anything truly creative would
be unmasked and apprehended by even their lowest servants
who are now kept in ignorance and illiteracy. The Arab oil
moguls have not had time to learn traditional capitalistic dil-
ligence and industry; the Protestant ethic of frugality is unknown to them. They have learned from their super-rich counterparts only what is characteristic of modern Sybarites: luxury,
wastefulness, a lack of sociological imagination, and of feelings
of compassion and responsibility. Even a concept of limited
political liberties serving as a safety valve is unknown to
them.

Arab sheiks, more than anyone else, should be interested in
the survival of Israel. However, they belong to those doomed
nouveau-riches whom the gods have deprived of reason after
having decided to punish them. The basic immorality, if not
crime, of the Arab rulers is that for political reasons they keep
their Arab brethren in refugee camps instead of providing them
with the necessities and opportunities such as the West German
authorities accorded the German refugees from Eastern and
Central Europe. The German refugees were integrated into
German society and given new opportunities.

The attitudes exhibited by Germany and the Arab states
toward their poor compatriots is a good illustration of the difference between civilization and barbarism; between freedom
and responsibility on the one hand and political callousness on
the other. It also illustrates the moral decline of the Western
democracies who finance the continuation of the suffering of the
poverty-stricken refugees condemned in the camps instead of
looking for a realistic and permanent solution to the problem.

Western support of the anti-Israeli course is conditioned by
reasons more important than general insensitivity. Certain
branches of big business, specifically the oil and armaments
industries are also interested in the existence of the new anti-
Semitism. Their goal is to maximize profits. The existing state
of affairs is shaky at best; someone must be found who can be

blamed for the economic and social difficulties into which the West has maneuvered itself.

Who could better serve as a scapegoat than a small nation burdened with prejudices, past and present, that have been mounting throughout the centuries? If the Jews did not exist, they would have to be invented. The simplistic concept that there will be "normalization" in the Middle East after an Israeli withdrawal and that Western motorists will once more be able to drive their cars at low cost and without interruptions, is a semi-official political program, unofficially whispered, but never explicitly publicly formulated. Some conservative, energy related, industrial, and financial figures, are as interested in the preservation of the existing energy impasse as are the Arab and Soviet oil exporters: no new technologies, no energy-saving devices, no progressive changes in the tax-structure, no innovations in renewable sources of energy are sought because any new idea might endanger their monopolistic earnings and political privileges. Of course, they must admit that something has gone wrong in the Kingdom. But their answer is the same as was given by the Stalinists when criticized in the Soviet bloc: we alone have the experience, only we can get you out of this mess, because he who damaged the machine knows best how to repair it and should be entrusted with the job. That is the new motto of many influential energy officials on both sides of the iron curtain. It demonstrates how certain establishments of the East and the West "converge." This perhaps explains why businessmen like Armand Hammer of Occidental Petroleum feel so comfortable in the company of the Soviet leaders and why these leaders prefer their company to that of trade-unionists, liberals, socialists, or progressive Christian statesmen. It also explains, at least in part, why the Soviet government and the Argentine military junta were able to cooperate so closely during the Falkland crisis and U.S. grain embargo. Birds of a feather flock together.

A modern method to annihilate certain social or national groups has developed. The old barbarians murdered or enslaved their enemies at once. In the modern world, because of many social, moral, and psychological reasons, this process must be divided into two stages: during the first, the victim must be clearly singled out and isolated from the rest of world society. During the second stage, the physical "processing" of the victim begins.

It took the Nazis ten years to prepare the world and their victims for their fate. During those years the world got used to daily scenes of brutality and murder. They ceased to be news. They became boring statistics. During those years the world accepted Goebbel's dictum that the Jews were *"unser Unglueck"* (our misfortune). People grew accustomed to Hitler's message that Jews were responsible for all Germany's disasters, even syphillis (Hitler's assertion in *Mein Kampf*). Little by little, step by step, Jews became socially, morally and physically isolated.

It was during the second stage that Jews were sent to camps and to the gas chambers in a state of despair and humiliation. They were regarded as untouchable pariahs, as *"Untermenschen"* (sub-human).

The majority of the victims understood or felt that their ties with the world had been cut, that no one would stretch out their arms to welcome them, that no one wanted them. There was no escape, no hope, there was nothing to look forward to. They suffered a fate worse than cattle who are swiftly brought to slaughter. They were worn out morally and gradually prepared for death, too exhausted to continue a hopeless struggle. Every beast of prey instinctively perceives when its victim has reached this stage of exhaustion, then it moves in for the kill.

To outsiders, on the other hand, the act of mass destruction seemed more like the continuation of the first stage. It was nothing new, it was an old phenomenon, although conducted on a wider scale. By and large, those who knew of the first stages and had been able to stomach the first individual tortures and murders found themselves able to accept more and more, their senses had become dull—provided they were persuaded that peace and prosperity would ensue and that the atrocities were only a temporary means toward that end. Those who believe that sacrifices are required on the altar of peace and prosperity can easily find the strength to endure the sufferings of their neighbors, as de la Rochefoucauld observed.

The Holocaust started many years before the mass murder of its victims. The decade preceding the "Final Solution" was a period in which the victims, the public, and the hangmen, were readied to play their respective roles in the drama. No one is born an executioner and there are no academies to teach the profession. One must learn the craft while practicing on victims. When a regime creates the need for them, candidates with sadistic instincts seem to arise with alacrity. Civilized society is only required to witness the incomprehensible gradually; it is gradually attuned to live with the inexpressible.

* * *

The first stage of a New Holocaust has started. The victim has been singled out and clearly marked. The world knows the nation and the state by name. Its geographical location is defined. The bill of indictment has already been made known to the victim, to the future executioners, and to the more or less indifferent onlookers and bystanders. The remaining task is simple. The propagandists will day after day repeat the charges in order to assure that at the decisive moment no one will doubt that the death of the victim is a necessity or represents eternal justice and that it will bring relief and benefit to all. The Swiss playwright Duerrenmatt depicted the entire process with the vision of an artist in *The Visit.*

The endless resolutions passed by various agencies of the United Nations including the General Assembly, the Security Council, and UNESCO concerning the alleged crimes of Israel and Zionism should be understood from the viewpoint of "processing" the victim and the executioner. It should be no consolation that the infamous resolution which equates Zionism and racism has nothing to do with reality. What counts is the number of the resolutions and their continuity which, as Senator Patrick Moynihan phrased it, are "obscene." The bigger the lie, the better, Hitler remarked in *Mein Kampf.* When the lie is so big that it seems no longer credible and almost mind-boggling, then the public will be inclined to believe it and to doubt the veracity of any denials. It is beyond the comprehension of a normal, decent human being to imagine that anyone could be so shameless as to fabricate such an enormous lie.

Once the lie is invented, agreed to by all who are interested in it, and published, it must be repeated in various ways. As Propaganda Minister Goebbels, admonished, "lie, lie, something will always remain." Four hundred years before the Nazi takeover, Niccolo Machiavelli observed with melancholy (but not approval) that so many princes were able to persuade their subjects that they (the princes) were well-intentioned and only their enemies lied. There is no reason to think that the successors of Machiavelli's "simulators" and "dissimulators" will be less successful in this respect.

Every resolution of the United Nations with anti-Semitic or anti-Zionist overtones plays its historical role, no matter how small. It confirms over and over that Israel and the Jews are responsible for an illegal occupation, for racial and religious persecution, for changing the character of the Holy City, for the extermination of Arabs, for tortures, for expropriation without compensation, for arrogance, for sowing animosity between nations, for the tensions in the Middle East and all over the world, and lastly—it goes without saying—for disruptions in the oil supplies. Israel is denounced as a troublemaker, as an enemy of modern civilization, of free enterprise, and, of course, of socialism.

Multiplication, duplication, and endless repetition itself becomes proof in the public perception. Perhaps even more important are the numerous condemnations and "regrets" issued by the Department of State of the United States, by other Western ministries of foreign affairs, by the Socialist International, and by religious leaders. Anyone with a vestige of common sense must be surprised that the foreign offices of the greatest powers in the world have the time, patience, and interest to comment about every new or enlarged agricultural settlement, the size of a small or medium American farm. The monotonous repetitions by Western authorities are even more ominous: they may be regarded as an ideological preparation for future attempts to push Israel into the sea.

Two UN resolutions were especially important in promoting anti-Semitism and isolating Israel: 1. The resolution equating Zionism with racism (1975), with many Western countries voting against it, 2. The resolution of the Security Council (March 1, 1980) *unanimously* condemning Israel.

The endless flow of anti-Israeli resolutions from the United Nations and the statements of the State Department and other Western and Eastern ministries of foreign affairs are twins from the historical and political perspective. They both lead to the same result, although by different paths. They complement each other.

The final, and possibly the main result of the flow of resolutions is simple: The sponsors add one more stone to the piles of condemnations. Quantity can sooner or later be transformed into a new quality.

When President Franklin D. Roosevelt prevented the Jewish refugees from Germany from landing under the shadow of the Statue of Liberty when they arrived on the ship *St. Louis*, his administrative order meant more than a death sentence for a thousand people. Roosevelt's decision was interpreted by the authorities in Berlin as a sign to go ahead. In effect they were told that they had a free hand, that the West had been numbed sufficiently and would not do anything substantial to block their further plans.

The Western votes in the UN are indeed an improved edition of the *St. Louis* affair. The signals are clear. The persecutors can continue to haunt and harry their victim; the victim was warned that he should be humble and accept the verdict. The main question however remains unresolved: will the victim once more be willing to enter, without any resistance, the trains leading from here to eternity?

One could argue that it is indeed the unreasonable politics of the Israeli government which constitutes the cause of the "universal" condemnation and relentless criticism, because the Israelis continue to build their settlements on the territories acquired in 1967. The wisdom of such a policy can of course be questioned.

But it does not make any difference what the Israeli people and their unrecognized state are doing or not doing because their antagonists would have found or invented many other arguments. For instance:

— Israel is even accused of preventing access to the Holy shrines—this is an obvious lie, every visitor from any country can confirm it, but it is endlessly repeated.

— Israel is accused of rendering inferior medical care to the Arabs; in fact the Arabs get the same treatment as the Jews and in the same hospitals and medical centers.

In the world of organized political bigotry and witch-hunting the mere fact that the victim is still alive is sufficient proof of its criminality. And, if the victim does not want to confess its criminality this is an additional argument proving arrogance and contempt for those rules of the game which were invented in order to entrap the hapless. Since Joseph Heller published his best-seller every schoolchild calls such an arrangement, *Catch 22*.

The Jews are not the only victims of this *Catch 22* rule. The American Blacks, the Czechs in the 1930's before and after the Munich Pact, the Polish *Solidarity* leaders after December 13, 1981, and finally every social, political, cultural, or religious group accused of heresy and victimized in a totalitarian way, find themselves repeatedly in similar situations.

The Jews have the privilege that all the new "traps" and "tricks" are at first tested on them, they are improved and later in perfected form applied by other bigots to other victims. *Anti-Semites are usually the vanguard of world intolerance.*

Anti-Semitism was and remains one of the important instruments to suppress the freedom and sovereignty of nations.

Although the question of anti-Semitism is so important in the internal policy of many countries it is sometimes even more important in the international arena. It is never an independent autonomous problem. Anti-Semitism is always part of one of the most important unresolved social and political questions of our era: racism and religious prejudice. In the world of racial and religious bias the existence of anti-Semitism is inevitable. And vice versa: the existence of anti-Semitism is an indicator that there are other racial, national, and religious groups which also suffer discrimination.

Any act of discrimination in any country should be condemned. What is needed is not a general condemnation which may be simple and unhelpful, but a condemnation of the specific forms of racism and religious prejudice existing in one's own country at the given time. An American or South African should loudly and unequivocally condemn anti-Black racism, whereas an East European, Frenchman, or German should loudly and repeatedly condemn anti-Semitism. From the moral and practical political viewpoint only those who have the civil courage to criticize the racist excesses of their own neighbors and countrymen have earned the right to throw stones at others.

Every act of racial or religious discrimination (including anti-Semitism) diminishes the sphere of freedom of the victims and in the final analysis of the oppressors as well. Whenever a victim of racial prejudice is silenced and compelled to retreat, is prevented full participation in the creative effort of the whole society, it is the whole community that loses.

Today, as we have pointed out, racism, religious fanaticism, and various forms of nationalism are important in war preparations and in alienating and exploiting foreign peoples and countries. In our century any form of racism is an enemy of humanity. Today one can observe racism and anti-Semitism in their naked forms, and evaluate the nature of the adversaries of freedom, justice, progress, and tolerance.

8. Factors Conducive To Tolerance At The End of The Twentieth Century

We have discussed the main causes of intolerance at the end of our century. These factors do not function in one direction only due to a strange dialectic of politics. It frequently happens that the same causes are a source of strength and of weakness simultaneously for a given social and political system. Everything depends on the totality of the elements involved and especially on the will of the principal actors.

Sometimes the same social conditions discussed in the previous chapter contribute to the process of broadening and strengthening freedom and tolerance as well as the reverse.

Bureaucracy, which is increasingly sweeping the world, infiltrating nearly everything in life, is frightening of course, but it contains the seed of its own future destruction: its own inefficiency. An efficient bureaucracy can be more dangerous to freedom than an inefficient one. Everything depends on the programs administered by it and on the general internal and international situation. A bureaucracy which has been set up to exercise terror, when inefficient, makes terror less efficient. An old observation expressed by the people of the old Austro-Hungarian monarchy was: *Despotismus gemildert durch Schlamperei* (Despotism tempered with disorder). The Prussians, and their military establishment in particular, looked at their Austrian comrades-in-arms with contempt. History punished them for their love of discipline and efficiency: the German Democratic Republic is the most efficient totalitarian state of all the peoples' democracies. The loopholes and *Schlamperei* which provide Poles and Hungarians with some breathing space are not available to the East Germans. A virtue turned out to be a vice.

After World War II, a number of books were published which, in a scholarly and satirical way, depicted the dangers and pitfalls of bureaucracy in government and industry. In the famous laws of Parkinson, Murphy, and the principles of Peter, reality was described in a humorous way. Indeed, the most serious problems were discussed. Satire very often portrays real life more concisely and truthfully than a long scholarly treatise. Even if certain features are exaggerated, this exaggeration serves truth and understanding.

The above mentioned authors and their "laws" have taken the place in our century of the famous maxims and anecdotes of de la Rochefoucauld, Chamford, and de la Bruyere in eighteenth century France. The decomposition and decline of their social systems are reflected in them.

Parkinson, Murphy, and Peter (even if Murphy did not exist, he should have existed and will be treated here as though he did), became household names because they appeal to the experience and common sense of ordinary people. People know that bureaucracies are becoming more and more inefficient, that something always unexpectedly goes wrong. Responsibility and responsiveness are less and less to be seen; there are no immediate connections between reason and success, morality and promotion, income and efficiency, wages and results.

Careers are less and less based on competence. Things remain undone and, as one retired professor of Columbia University, Alexander Rudzinski, used to repeat to his students and friends: "Today there is only one universal sociological law: everything is getting worse." We know that not so long ago this pessimistic opinion would not have been popular in the United States. On the contrary: people used to believe that everything would improve and all difficulties could be overcome. A hundred years ago gloomy prophets and authors would have remained unheeded. Today they are highly respected, and for good reasons.

The disintegrating bureaucracy still tends towards uniformity, conformity and *Gleichschaltung* (the English equivalent: "equalization" or "levelling" do not hold the same ominous connotation as the word *Gleichschaltung* coined by the Nazi minister Josef Goebbels). People and objects of bureaucratic manipulation are not as controllable as they appeared to be. The demands of progress and the welfare of the greatest number of people work against uniformity and conscienceless officialdom.

Let us point out once more that whenever one attributes to the bureaucracy such features as ruthlessness, carelessness, consciencelessness, one speaks of the features of the apparatus, and not of the individuals of whom such bureaucracies are composed. The officials working in these institutions may be reasonable, sensitive human beings, but the principles of organization

and law compel them to act like robots. Their subjective intentions too often remain in striking contrast to the results of their
activity. Whenever they want to act reasonably and humanely,
they frequently act against their official obligations. When they
adhere to their duties strictly, they harm people, the human
cause, and the interest of the state. It may be that the most
flagrant examples have been supplied by French customs officials. When they decide to strike, they do not neglect their
duties. On the contrary, they fulfill them to the letter in a "zeal"
strike. On these days thousands of cars and people on both sides
of the frontier have to wait to cross it. The delays hurt
everybody.

A time is coming when the most efficient bureaucrat must
act unbureaucratically. That does not portend a new respect for
law and order. Bureaucracy can exist thanks to constant deviations from the principles of its functioning.

The Soviet bureaucracy reached unprecedented levels in its
fight against its own ties. Thousands of examples are well
known when economic administrators, wanting to fulfill their
plans, entered into conspiracies with the local chiefs of security
and the Party's secretaries, they had to bribe another team of
respected technocrats, because that was the only way to receive
supplies for their enterprise. The people on both sides act immorally and illegally, but for good, moral purposes: to fulfill
their plan, which according to the official slogans "is a sacred
obligation," a legal duty, and a constitutional requirement.

Western countries have not as yet attained these new levels
of bureaucratic efficiency, but one can easily see the germs of
the future. When cities and states hire their own lobbyists in
order to protect their interests in higher levels of the government, including state assemblies and the Congress of the United
States, they do not instruct them to act in accordance with the
principles of puritan decency, protestant frugality, or the traditional conservative work ethos. We know how the demarcation line is undefined between legal or illegal, moral or immoral
activities of lobbyists and the "lobbied."

We have already mentioned that bureaucracies produce mediocrity and require mediocrity. Anyone who stands above mediocrity and wishes to make a career must follow the recommendation of Chamford. He wrote about one of his heroes who was a decent and sensitive man but pretended to be a roué in order to impress women.

During the discussions to confirm one of President Nixon's nominees to the Supreme Court, Senator Roman L. Hruska of Nebraska expressed a memorable opinion: it may be that the nominee is mediocre, but mediocrity also should be represented in the Supreme Court.

This defense of mediocrity correctly reflects bureaucratic mediocrity and the general decline of values. Indeed, in order to preserve its existence mediocrity requires gifted representatives. Karl Marx understood this problem when he wrote that Jeremy Bentham was a genius of bourgeois stupidity (by the way, Bentham did not deserve such a slur). Marx, in this way, pointed out the strange dialectic of bureaucracy. In order to survive, bureaucracy sooner or later must produce individuals who will be like the powerful personalities described by Callicles, or a *"Blonde Bestie"* as publicized by Friedrich Nietzsche. The supermen of both authors will be able to cut all ties imposed on them by society. They will trample on all limitations and will be able to lead their nations to their destinies. There are already more and more indications that in order to survive, societies will have to learn how to tolerate non-conforming individuals and reward creativity. Conformity and bureaucratic *"Gleichschaltung"* dig their own graves.

* * *

Nationalism was one of the factors which led to two world wars in our century. It was one of the decisive feelings and ideological elements which accelerated the decomposition of the colonial empires. Nationalism is also important in communist countries. It takes on the form of super-nationalism in the Soviet Union and People's Republic of China. On the other hand, it reinforces patriotic feelings and tendencies towards national liberation among smaller nations under communist rule.

Nations in the two blocks, communist and the western alliance, have reached a stage in which the old nationalism has begun to be transformed into a new social quality. It is more and more becoming clear that no nation can survive without close cooperation with other nations. They must do it not only to preserve peace, sovereignty, and their very existence, but in order to secure the wellbeing and high standard of living of their own citizens. The old nationalism tended toward isolation and autarky. It consequently has fostered intolerance towards aliens and its own citizens who deviated from the accepted paradigms. Nowadays when the nations must cooperate one with another, they have to learn how to work together with different peoples having different customs, ideologies, religions, and mores— toward common goals. Briefly: the new elementary requirements of life, of trade and commerce, cultural development and tourism, push people toward tolerance.

Tolerance extended towards aliens inevitably contributes towards shaping new more tolerant personalities. This fact must influence the domestic life of nations, relaxing the old rigidities.

Traditional nationalism used to produce a specific form of isolation and intolerance. The new nationalism can reach its fulfillment only in cooperation with others. The logic of development leads towards universalism and cosmopolitanism.

Every national state has become a member of the international community and has thereby taken on obligations based, first of all, on the Charter of the United Nations and on many international conventions including those which concern human rights. The existence of the United Nations and various international institutions is partly based on an anti-nationalistic presumption that all nations are equal in some sense, no one should enjoy special privileges, they all have duties, and no nation can claim it is predestined to carry out any special historical mission. In this way the traditional nationalistic claims and traits and the roots of nationalism are undermined. Whenever nationalistic governments and nationalistic parties proclaim their traditional nationalistic slogans and demands, they do so at the expense of logic, of international law, and their own foreign policy. Today there is a discrepancy between nationalist ideology and foreign policy, between tendencies to isolation and participation in international cooperation.

Such a discrepancy between internal and foreign policy cannot last long. Such antagonism must erode intolerant nationalistic prejudices and attitudes. Whether erosion of the basis of intolerance will by itself lead to tolerant attitudes is, of course, doubtful. The dissolution, however, of the grounds on which intolerance grows and thrives, is in itself a step forward.

Nationalism within communist nations is consciously used by communist governments for political manipulation. They do not even care that their own official ideology is incompatible with nationalism of any kind. All communist governments and parties stress the equality of nations and claim that in the bright future, after the successful overthrow of imperialism, all nations will live in peace and harmony and exploitation will be replaced by brotherly cooperation. Every nation, the official theory and propaganda stress, will be free to preserve its identity, customs, and mores and will be able to develop its own national culture. Communists hope that in the distant, golden future, nations and states will "wither away."

Although the word "tolerance" was banned from their vocabulary, it appears in disguise. Terminology, as usual, is not the most decisive factor: the substance of such mass indoctrination and propaganda is, nevertheless, important, because the official rejection of nationalism lays foundations for tolerant education, behavior, attitudes, and finally for a new more tolerant ideology and politics.

VI.

THE STATE AS LEVIATHAN: ENDANGERING AND PROTECTING FREEDOM

1. The State and Social Antagonisms

The State is a result of the historical evolution of society. There are many theories and definitions of the state, but it would be fruitless for the purposes of this book to enter controversies connected with them. For our inquiry into freedom and tolerance the state should be regarded as the special apparatus which has evolved as a consequence of the economic contradictions and social divisions in a society. The existence of private property and of various privileges result in social antagonisms which can be kept under control only with the help of governments.

The state is necessary in order to preserve order not only in relations among individuals, but also among various competing social strata seeking to preserve and enhance their privileges. A state, as Francis Bacon observed in his essays, must preserve a balance in the society and be able to navigate safely on the stormy waves of the political ocean. Machiavelli stressed that if it were impossible to be an impartial arbiter, the Prince, the government, should strive at least to appear to be neutral and just.

Since the period of the Greeks and Romans every realistic thinker agrees with Aristotle that the basic source of the disturbances and rebellions in a society is economic and social inequality. At times a superficial observer may cherish the illusion that there are other more immediate reasons for social and political upheavals. Aristotle enumerated many of them, such as envy, love affairs, pride, and unrestricted competition among power seekers; however, he stressed that they are only secondary causes for rebellions. Inequality is at the basis of the competition and change-over of governments. No wonder that "the worst are the rebellions of the belly" (Francis Bacon).

Freedom and tolerance, according to the same ancient wisdom, can be preserved only in such a state which does not permit inequality and disparity between rich and poor to go too far. Few dispute that the main task of a state is to preserve and protect life—this task includes not only law and order, but also the creation of economic conditions in which elementary human needs can be satisfied. What these needs are depends on the social and cultural development of a society. Even the Roman mob demanded not only *panem* (bread) but also *circenses* (shows). The Greek democrats paid people to attend theatrical performances. In this way they ensured the cooperation of the Athenians. The hard-line aristocrats did not understand the social meaning of this collective bribery and contemptuously called democracy, theatrocracy. They could not comprehend that social peace and political collaboration had a price.

Privileged groups in a society often forget the simple truth that sometimes an apparently unimportant injustice can stir people up to such an extent that they start a rebellion. Because political blindness seems to be incurable and therefore repeats itself, it may happen that conservative rulers will react in a similar way to similar events in various countries and periods. For instance, both Louis XVI and Czar Nicolai II, naively asked similar questions while observing demonstrations of people marching before them from the windows of their places: is this a revolt? In both cases, according to historians, the courtiers answered: No, sire, it is no revolt, it is a revolution.

The struggle between the have's and have-not's was not invented by Marx and Engels. Many philosophers and historians before them analyzed the inequalities they observed. Maybe it was Heraclitus who first drew attention to the struggle of various social strata and transformed this observation into the foundation of his dialectical method. Democritus, Plato, and Aristotle continued in this spirit, made many determinations concerning the course followed by political struggles, and made recommendations for what was to be done in order to preserve the unity of society. Aristotle elaborated his idea of *Politea* and Plato of communism in his *Republic*. Aristotle harbored the illusion that a powerful middle class would be a buffer between the very rich and the very poor. Plato did not believe that private property can be distributed evenly and he, therefore, preferred to abolish it altogether among the rulers; the combination of economic communism and political despotism (a forerunner of totalitarianism) would ensure social stability, Plato believed.

The intellectual trend initiated by the Greeks and Romans has continued through the centuries. Machiavelli wrote the history of Florence as if it were a history of economic and social struggles. Constitutions and forms of government were interpreted by him as a result of the balance between hostile social groups. The same might be said about the historical considerations of Bacon and Hobbes, of Diderot and Jean-Jacques Rousseau. And it was James Madison who connected the phenomenon of social struggles with the question of freedom.

* * *

Whatever philosophical background might be the basis for explaining the nature of class conflict—be it that of Karl Marx or Ralf Dahrendorf—one may agree that the foundations of the conflict between employers and employees consists of at least two basic elements:

—property relations;

—the place in the process of production, or—in social and political terms—the position in the structure of authority.

There are widespread theories that in the new "industrial," or "post-capitalist society," the conditions which used to form the basis of classes and class-conflicts have diappeared.

One of the most quoted arguments is that of the "bourgeoisification of the proletariat," the substantial improvement of the standard of living of the industrial workers. Ralf Dahrendorf correctly observed that the economic situation of the workers is not directly connected with class conflict. Economic satisfaction (we prefer to say, *partial* satisfaction), continues Dahrendorf, does not eliminate the causes of conflict.

> Social conflict is as universal as the relations of authority and imperatively coordinated associations, for it is the distribution of authority that provides the basis and cause of its occurrence.[1]

This assertion is true with one qualification: the manner in which "authority" is distributed in any enterprise depends upon property relations. Sometimes a worker can have an illusion that he is dealing with authority only, with his "administrative" superiors and he loses from his sight the owner, the proprietor, who seems to be hidden behind the hired manager. Illusions, however, should not be a basis for sociological conclusions.

> . . .the replacements of functioning owners or capitalists by propertyless functionaries or managers does not abolish class conflict, but merely changes its empirical patterns. Independent of the particular personnel of positions of authority, industrial enterprises remain imperatively coordinated associations, the structures of which generate quasi-groups and conflicting latent interests.[2]

We live in an era of new forms of the old conflicts between the owners of the means of production and those who lack them. One of the problems is the scope of the disparity between them. Even if one rejects the oversimplified assertion that poverty is the main reason for the conflict, there still remains an endless list of social and moral problems which can trigger or exacerbate conflicts.

Another question is who is a superior and who is only a subject? In the new complicated hierarchical organization of enterprises (including international conglomerates) many answers cannot be categorical.

These qualifications cannot undermine the basic observation that freedom and tolerance always exist in the midst of conflicts, they result from social, economic, and political antagonisms. They are not an effect of peaceful cooperation based on any imagined unity of interests.

Legal and political administrations are always dangerous to freedom and to the spirit of tolerance. But freedom and tolerance could not exist without the powerful Leviathan, without whose protection they both would have perished. Freedom and tolerance are a result of social (class) conflict and they are also political instruments, used by parties in modern democratic states. When conflicts become too acute the very foundations of freedom and tolerance become endangered.

* * *

One of the most important sociological stimuli fostering intolerant tendencies is the decline of the middle class.

What Shorris described in regard to an enterprise,[3] was analyzed in hundreds of publications in reference to the middle-class in general.

Middle class decline in the United States has become so dangerous that even *US News and World Report,* a careful, conservative, and objective publication, wrote: "they are angry, frustrated and losing ground. They're the latest have-nots—families of moderate means whose anxieties, some fear, could prompt a new kind of class struggle."[4]

It is significant that such a serious, conservative periodical should be writing about "class struggle." "Class struggle" seems to have become a respectable social, economic, and political term. Even more: without reference to class struggle it would be impossible to describe the existing social processes, political struggles, or divisions.

In recent decades an accelerated anti-middle class trend has been occurring in all western countries, especially the United States. The middle class is falling victim to inflation, the concentration of wealth, mergers, high taxation (the tax loopholes were created for the truly rich). The middle class has entered a period of creeping pauperization and is losing its social status, no longer being able to "keep up with the Joneses," becoming salaried employees. The middle class is already a mass of proletarians with high but frustrated ambitions and unsatisfied expectations. They cannot afford to buy good houses in good neighborhoods any longer, they cannot invest so as to lay a basis to build future fortunes, indeed they are losing real value on their savings accounts. They cannot take vacations abroad or in fancy resorts, they have to buy mass-produced clothes in second-rate shops. And finally, they cannot afford to send their children to the best schools and universities.

People who are "losing ground," who are "angry" and "frustrated," are not inclined to be tolerant. They discontinue discussing and exchanging ideas, they start looking for scape-goats instead of for the causes of their troubles. A victim of de-spair can easily become a pawn in the hands of demagogues who offer not a solution but an outlet for anger and mindlessness. Those who do not think cannot be tolerant; they are longing for a strong hand and revenge.

These are the basic reasons why so many members of the middle-class turn either to the left (mostly in poor countries), or—in many Western countries, included the United States and England—to racial and religious bigotry; they are inclined to be-lieve that the poor and the social welfare programs to assist them are the causes (whereas they are the results) of the decline of the middle class status.

Tolerance, as it has been known and practiced in the West, was born and flourished with the advent of the middle-class. Because of its specific economic and social situation, this class has always been interested in freedom and tolerance as a means of defense against the extremism of the super-rich (including remnants of the feudal aristocracy) and of the disquieting ple-beians. This is the middle class which is truly interested in the peaceful preservation of the *status quo,* because it is afraid of any radical or, God forbid, violent changes. In the event of unex-pected and far reaching transformations, as a whole social group and as individuals, they must be the losers. They are unable to confront and survive either the cruel terror of the extreme right, or mass expropriations and police assaults administered by the radical left.

* * *

William Howard Taft, in his book *Popular Government* (Yale University Press, 1913) wrote:

> Unfortunately, the Government can wisely do much more than the (laissez faire) school would have favored to relieve the oppressed, to create greater equality of opportunity, to make

reasonable terms for labor in employment, and to furnish vo-
cational education of the children of the poor. But on the other
hand, there is a line beyond which Government cannot go with
any good practical results in seeking to make men and society
better. Efforts to do so will only result in failure and a waste of
public effort and funds. But many enthusiasts, whose whole
attention has been so centered on the poverty and suffering in the
cities or elsewhere as to lead them to disregard the general
average improvement of the individual in the community. . .have lost their sense of due proportion and spend their
energies in pressing forward legislative plans for the uplifting of
the suffering and the poor and for the muleting of the fortunate,
the thrifty and the well-to-do that are impracticable and will only
result in defeat, and increased burden of taxation.[5]

It would not be difficult to counter argue that the "fortunate"
are not necessarily "thrifty" and the "thrifty" are not usually the
most "fortunate." This question, however, is beside the point
here.

The identification of virtue with *Fortuna* is one of the oldest
ideological arguments used since the beginning of social stratification. Needless to say, contemporary communist rulers have
taken it over and argue the same way in order to justify the
privileges of their own bureaucracy and especially of the party
apparatus. According to the official ideology the members of the
Party form the most conscientious, experienced, dedicated, and
gifted vanguard of society and, therefore, they deserve to be
apportioned a larger share of the national income.

This type of argument, which seeks to justify prevalent inequalities, has been used by ruling elites throughout history. The
forms and the specific reasons change, the propositions tending
to demonstrate the underlying causes undergo mutations, but
the essence remains the same; the "fortunate" possess certain
qualities which are so beneficial for all that they deserve to
be rewarded.

Difficulties begin when the social distinctions cause a high
level of "poverty and suffering," as William H. Taft phrased it.
At a certain time in any social system, beginning with societies
based on slavery and ending with modern capitalism and com-

munism, the underprivileged find that their situation becomes *intolerable* from the social and moral point of view and they start to rebel.

The intensity of social conflict may increase or decrease. In old capitalist society the factors increasing intensity were material hardship, "super-imposition of authority,"[6] low social status, and no accepted modes of conflict resolution in industry and politics.[7]

After World War II the intensity of the class conflicts decreased because absolute privation gave way to relative privation, the partnership between industry and the state dissolved to some extent, and methods for regulating the conflicts were elaborated.[8] How long can these arrangements remain effective without further development and improvement?

There are certain rules and factors which heavily influence the patterns of these conflicts and their sudden eruptions.

When people feel that economic deprivation and social and political oppression have been made worse by the moral turpitude of the ruling elite, they lose patience, they refuse to accept or tolerate the status quo; they perceive it not only as *unacceptable,* but as *intolerable.*

In social and political terms there is a vast difference between *acceptable* and *tolerable.* Acceptable is a social, economic or political condition which one does not regard as entirely justifiable, but still finds in it certain favorable elements which at least somewhat counterbalance the undesirable.

"Acceptable" could also describe such a state of affairs as when people feel restraint at breaking the law and using violence in order to make changes, although at the same time they feel that there is insufficient justification to continue the *status quo.* It would be less evil to tolerate the unacceptable situation than to fight against it with extraordinary or "illegal" means ("illegal"—from the point of view of the existing government).

But societies from time to time, inevitably reach a stage when a substantial (if not majority) segment of the population becomes deeply convinced that they cannot and should no longer *endure* and *tolerate* their circumstances. Their patience has been exhausted. People as a rule are conservative and resist radical change because they harbor an instinctive fear of the unknown and unpredictable. The feeling that a situation is *intolerable* stems from a long period of "poverty and suffering," and finally from moral indignation (a *sine qua non* before any possibility of confrontation can arise). When many individuals reach such a frame of mind, the storm (Bacon's expression) becomes inevitable.

Freedom is always at stake in such a situation according to the official pronouncements of the social groups or parties having decided to carry out economic, social and political reforms. Violence in these circumstances becomes a necessary means to achieve the end—although with violence, freedom becomes hostage at the outset.

Whenever changes are brought about by violence and terror, the seeds of new violence are planted, developing a new threat to the newly acquired freedom.

The resistance of the old regime and its supporting forces obstructing any necessary, meaningful and peaceful change creates a danger not only to existing freedom, but conflict will, by itself, hamper or even thwart any future evolution toward freedom.

2. Transformation and Expansion of the State Functions

At the end of the 19th and beginning of the 20th centuries a liberal theory that the state should only be a "night-watchman," was developed. The concept was at the same time political and economic, moral and philosophical. Adam Smith, Jeremy Bentham, Benjamin Constant, Wilhelm von Humboldt, James Mill and John Stuart Mill, believed that free economic initiative, consistent governmental *laisser-faire—laisser-passer,* would result in such an enormous growth in labor productivity accompanied by such a growth of riches and affluence that every member of society would profit from economic freedom. Therefore, any governmental interference must be harmful and indeed immoral because it would prevent the arrival of maximum happiness for the maximum number of people. Free competition, as the essence and foundation of freedom, should prevail every-where, even among teachers, professors, and clergymen, the liberals argued.

The ideal of the state as "night watchman" or referee was never fully realized anywhere. At the end of the 19th century it came under criticism—from the left (socialists and communists) and right: a wide spectrum beginning with christian democrats, followers of a democratic welfare state, and the New Deal, through the old and new conservatives, including fascists.

After the second World War this liberal notion of the state was reconsidered and re-named as the theory of the minimal state.[8]

The old liberal ideal of the state was a reaction against the absolutist *ancien regimes* and their unhampered intrusions into individual lives. The concept of a minimal state is a reaction against right and left wing totalitarianism and against the real proliferation of all spheres of activity of the contemporary western democratic parliamentary state. The extent of the almost cancerous expansion of government and its activity can be illustrated by the following data concerning the United States.

In the 1982 budget year, governments in the United States at all levels—federal, state, and local—will spend nearly $1.2 trillion. That is, $5,138.00 for each person, or $14,334.00 for each American household.[9]

These figures reflect, first of all, the fact that taxes paid to various levels of government constitute such an enormous burden that they compel people to work for almost half of every year to support the public authorities. These figures show that on average the American citizen has to work for his public master for as long a period as the average European serfs used to work for their feudal masters in the middle ages (the feudal work obligation for serfs varied from country to country and century to century).

One can, of course, argue that the citizens receive many benefits for their financial contributions, such as protection against domestic criminals and foreign aggressors, subsidized education, partial support in case of unemployment, sickness, and old age. To what extent the compensation for material sacrifices is just, proportional, and equitable—is, of course, debatable. But even if there were a reasonable return in the form of public services, it is still true that the citizens are not working for their own account for almost half a year, but for the public authorities, The modern tax system is in itself a restriction upon freedom for the majority.

In West European countries the tax-burden is even heavier.

These facts constitute the background on which the theory of a minimal state has developed.

The ideal of the minimal state can be expressed as follows: the best and surest way to secure individual liberty is by reducing the functions of the state to the bare minimum necessary to preserve order within and freedom from foreign attack. In all the writings of the proponents of this ideal, two basic elements remain unresolved and ambiguous: a) what is this "minimum" and what criteria should be applied to determine what it is. b) what is freedom and what actually is meant by the rights of the individual?

The ideal of the minimal state has been revived in recent years not only in the theoretical literature; it has become one of the most important political slogans of many political groups which are usually—correctly or not—listed to the right of center and rarely at the center. In the United States, the ideal of the minimal state constitutes the philosophical underpinning of the attacks against the "federal bureaucracy," "federal interference," and "federal omniscience," which allegedly is the cause of crisis, inflation, demoralization, laziness, irresponsibility, and atheism ("Let us take the federal government out of the schools, and God will return there. . ."—Ronald Reagan repeated this statement in his standard speeches during the presidential campaigns of 1976 and 1980).

All over the Western world the ideas of the "minimal state" (expressed in various forms and wordings) can be regarded as a social, political, and ideological reaction against: a) fascist and

communist totalitarianism and supercentralization of the omnipotent government; b) the expansion of the "welfare state," the
expansion of the functions of the state, and the intrusion of the
laws into spheres which until now were free of legal and administrative regulations.

The point of departure in considering the form and the
functions of the state should not be pure theory or utopian ideas,
but reality. Analysis of the evolution of the functions of states in
western countries shows that the expansion of state activities is
inevitable at this stage of historical evolution. Even those who
favor the old narrowly interpreted ideas that states should confine themselves to the role of watchman, refraining from all
activity other than: "protecting all its citizens against violence,
theft, and fraud , and to the enforcement of contracts, and so
on. . ."[10] should be aware that in the twentieth century even carrying out these functions calls for further-reaching and more
complicated activity than the old nineteenth century liberals
could have anticipated.

Even at the turn of the century, German military authors had
observed that the preparation of a nation for modern warfare
cannot be limited to military service and the procurement of
armaments. It demands cooperation between the military and
the centers of scientific research and industry. Preparation for
war also calls for coordinated effort between the armed forces
and educational institutions, including the secondary and high
schools. Even the general culture and the technical skills of the
population bear directly on the strategy and tactics to be used in
a future war. The general staff must take all these elements into
consideration. The interdependence and interrelationship between the war effort and civilian institutions have become even
closer and more pronounced during the second half of the twentieth century. A state that carries out the idea of the minimum
state to the limit would guarantee its own defeat by a foreign
challenger today. This is no crackpot militaristic idea (C.
Wright Mills), but a statement of fact.

Technological development in the second half of the twentieth century was one of the results of scientific progress; and

the advancement of science was in turn furthered by technological developments. All these facts determined that the continued development of technology and science nowadays depends on enormous investments which can be made either by the very rich centers of industry, or by the government, or by the laboratories, institutes, and universities subsidized by either or both of them. Governments all over the world promote technological and scientific developments in their countries. The application of atomic energy to either peaceful or wartime purposes would have been impossible without direct government intervention with enormous public resources. Hence it seems that the augmentation of governmental activity is historically inevitable and independent of the subjective wishes of the most ardent partisans of the idea of the minimal state. The intrusion of government into the sphere of science and technology is increasing throughout the entire western world. This policy has long since been an accomplished fact in the Communist and Third Worlds. In the foreseeable future one does not see any possibility of reversing this trend.

Innovations in the second half of the twentieth century arise every day in the production of consumer goods and their marketing which cannot remain free of government inspection and supervision. The drug and chemical industries, for example, develop new products which very often are found to be unhealthful and even harmful to people and the environment alike. Liberal theorists like Adam Smith or John Stuart Mill did not foresee that rivers, lakes, and even oceans might become contaminated by the products of industry. These facts are only some of the reasons showing that governments must develop their own capacity to supervise and test. To do so, of course, adds to their budgets and to taxes. Such services are a modern expression of the traditional protection of the lives and wellbeing of citizens that governments, even minimal governments, must supply. This protection cannot be furnished by policemen and nightwatchmen alone. New dangers require new forms of protection.

Let us also remember that in this age of enormous technological progress when new and complicated products are advertised and marketed, consumers really have no chance to verify the truthfulness of statements made by producers as the contemporaries of Adam Smith could. Who is able to protect the public against the new forms of "fraud" and "theft?" It can only be a special public organization, which for the time being must be directly or indirectly related to the government. The need for such an organization multiplies governmental functions and surpasses the ideals of the new minimal state.

In the 1970's, mankind faced its first energy crisis on a global scale. Whether this crisis was real or artificial is still questioned. One thing that is certain, however, is that new sources of energy must be developed. The problem is so difficult and complicated that without direct government interference it cannot be solved. This fact is acknowledged by all industrial nations; only in the United States are voices raised favoring leaving energy policy in private hands. Nevertheless, it is the prevailing opinion that the wellbeing of every industrial nation depends on general technological and scientific progress in the sphere of energy and also on the activity or inactivity of governments. The energy crisis in the 1970's is undeniable proof that there are spheres of industrial activity in which progress must be promoted by governments. Once more we realize that governmental functions are not the product of a false philosophy or any subjective political ideas, or—finally—statesmen deluded by megalomania, but are the direct result of objective necessity.

The number of similar examples could easily be multiplied. These provide sufficient ground, however, to conclude that we have entered a period in which expansion and multiplication of the activities of the state have become inevitable. Instead of discussing unrealistic, utopian, ideas on the minimal state, we should rather discuss what should be done to organize governments so that they become more responsible and more responsive to the needs of the people and what should be done to afford public control over bureaucratic structures. One should, of course, be aware that the unnecessary expansion of the functions of a state and the proliferation of other administrations can lead to the bureaucratization of all society. A governmental or any other bureaucratic apparatus which is expensive and alienated from society can do more harm than good. But the realistic solution lies not in absolute and uncritical condemnation of bureaucracy, but in acknowledging its existence in order to find ways to prevent damage and increase public benefits.

One could argue that the implementations of new social and economic tasks need not be carried out by the administrative organs of the state, but can sometimes be performed by various social institutions. This possibility does not change our basic thesis that the expansion of the functions of the state is inevitable today. All such social institutions will be acting under the law and in the final analysis their exposures of wrongdoing and their recommendations for reform would, in any event, have to be acted upon by governments. Their affirmative social activities would have to be approved by governments, if only in the form of exemption of their incomes from taxation. The mere existence of laws in such matters means that the given sphere will not be free of juridical interference, but be regulated in one way or another by the state.

The government is not the only bureaucratic apparatus in the modern world. At least two others can be named: the large corporations and the trade unions (in Communist countries, the Party, as well). These powerful organizations also delimit the sphere of the free creative activity of an individual. There are corporations and trade unions able to dominate a greater number of people than do many governments. The economic decisions made by them are, at times, even more important than governmental decisions.

Everyone in our century who wants to increase the freedom of the individual and overcome the process of alienation should take these additional bureaucratic structures into account. Discussions about a minimal state which disregard the existence of such powerful organizations as giant corporations are obviously one-sided. The idea of a minimal state diverts attention from the complexity of modern bureaucratization and focuses on one problem only, which may be the most important but remains only one element of reality.

The proponents of the idea of the minimal state did not elaborate the theory of freedom. They interpret freedom chiefly from the negative point of view, as a lack of impediments. A lack of constraints constitutes but one aspect of freedom. The tradition of western civilization—as we wrote already—identifies human freedom with power and creativity. A free man is one who has the opportunity to develop all his natural gifts and talents. It is not sufficient that he not be constrained; he must be afforded the genuine opportunity to act.

We have also argued that "reality," if it is not "reasonable," (so called by Hegel) should be replaced by another reality, more reasonable and more civilized.

Every step forward in the evolution of mankind must be and should be a new phase in the development of human creativity. This trend of development does not preclude gigantic leaps backward. We now live in an epoch when the maximalization of state functions will bring us into a new phase of the evolution of mankind and freedom. It will either be a step forward or we will drift into totalitarian slavery. Either the new social, technological and economic forces and the expanding state apparatus will be subjected to the enlightened will of the people and transformed into a means of their freedom, or these forces will dominate people. This is the real problem which should be analyzed and solved. From this point of view the idea of a minimal state is not very helpful because it simplistically rejects what exists.

The ideas of the "minimal state" could of course be useful as a warning signal: "Stop! Do not go too far in adding functions to the state." But the tenor of these ideas is too pretentious to serve such a limited purpose.

3. Fighting Crime and Creating Criminals

The main function of government is the protection of life,

bodily integrity, health, and property of the citizens against any internal or external danger, is agreed upon by most people. In industrial countries, especially the performance of this function is becoming more and more complicated. It takes new means and methods to achieve the desired results. Police departments are expanding and modernizing, they create highly specialized units, they act under a shroud of secrecy. It is no wonder that those police units are particularly prone to the peculiar sickness of every administrative body: corruption and a blind ambition to expand. All over the world police forces suffer from this special professional disease: they chase the criminals and they also manufacture them. Therefore the police in any social and political system, while providing the necessary protection of property, freedom, and security, are becoming a source of danger to freedom and to democratic and civil rights. What is even more significant, the police have a "natural" inclination to produce criminals. There are many causes for this tendency, including social, political and psychological.

The main cause is the best known: society is willing to pay more and more for protection at a time when dangers appear to be more and more threatening and overwhelming, while the victims feel more and more helpless. More crime means more money for police and means more promotions, higher salaries, better benefits, higher social and political prestige; and finally, immunity from criticism.

The manufacturing of criminals serves the self-interest of corrupted and careerist elements in police departments. It is easier to "succeed" in convicting a criminal conspiracy which was set-up by police themselves than to investigate the intricacies of real gangs. And, finally, there is often a link between police provocation and politics. In despotic and totalitarian countries the political police (often known as security police-there are usually many kinds of rival security agencies) must for political reasons discover plots, conspiracies, and acts of sabotage from time to time; if they cannot find them they must invent them! Their existence and to a great extent the stability of the totalitarian dictatorships depend on endless discoveries of "antipatriotic" plots. In democracies such events are not unknown either.

In the United States the most famous recent incident was an FBI operation known as ABSCAM—a trap set up to probe the "morality" of a group of US Congressmen.

Government-manufactured crimes are always morally and legally wrong and they create a direct danger to the personal freedom of citizens. Government which tempts people is perilous to the well-being of the society as a whole and of every individual in it.

In the case of Richard Kelly (former Florida Congressman involved in the ABSCAM affair), U.S. District Judge William B. Bryant (Florida) ruled that the Government tactic entrapping people into criminality was "so outrageous that it transcends any standard of fundamental fairness."[11]

There can be no justification in a democratic state for the use of methods which are "outrageous" or transcending the standards of elementary decency. The resort to such methods proves that a given branch of the government does not regard itself a servant of the society, but its moral judge and master. Although governments officially exist for their societies, they very often raise themselves, as experience shows, above society, above the citizens and their interests. In despotic and totalitarian states police provocation is a normal outgrowth of the absolutistic ideology according to which it is the state and its law and order which are values in themselves, they are the ends and the means to the well-being of the citizens. Therefore, people in totalitarian states are trained to observe patterns of behavior prescribed by the omnicompetent authorities. Provocation and the existence of numerous groups of professional *agents provocateurs* are facts which are well known officially and unofficially to citizens of despotic states. To help create an atmosphere of fear the regimes themselves do not conceal these gruesome facts.

Universal fear undermines any thought of freedom. Therefore the authors of the Atlantic Charter during World War II were right when they proclaimed freedom from fear as one of the four most important freedoms which humanity should enjoy. One of the substantial ingredients of freedom from fear is freedom from being subjected by the government's *agents-provocateurs* to clandestine procedures of "virtue-testing."

Concerning ex-Congressman Richard Kelly, Judge William B. Bryant wrote:

> A person corrupted under circumstances which only police officials can create, or by a process which only the authorities are licensed to use, has been made into a criminal by his own government.
>
> Where the government's overtures to the defendant fail substantially to model real-world behavior, the results of government conduct, while satisfying the technical elements of the bribery statute, constitute a crime which never otherwise would have occurred. I do not believe that testing virtue is a function of law enforcement. But this personal belief aside . . . the method of testing must be fair. If after an illegal offer is made, the subject rejects it in any fashion, the government cannot press on.
>
> In ordinary real-life situations, anyone who would seek to corrupt a congressman would certainly not continue to press in the face of a rejection for fear of being reported and arrested. The FBI, of course, had no such restraints in this case.[12]

What Judge Bryant described as his "personal belief" is indeed one of the philosophical pillars of any democratic theory of state, law, and constitutional freedom: when the government starts testing the morality of the citizens, the result must be terror. When the Jacobins proclaimed the rule of virtue, the effect was the reign of suspicion, denunciation, arbitrary persecution, fear, and terror.

During the debate concerning Senator Harrison Williams' conviction stemming from the FBI ABSCAM corruption probe, Senator Daniel Inouye (Democrat, Hawaii) stated that it was the government's conduct which added up "to encroachment of the legislative branch that we can not tolerate if we are to be a separate but equal branch of government . . . None of us is safe . . . This could have happened to anyone of us."[13]

Senator Daniel Inouye was right that a corruption probe of the members of Congress with the use of police provocation undermines the independence of the legislative branch of the government. The introduction of such an imbalance must be dangerous for freedom and constitutional rights in any western democracy. The system of parliamentary democracy is on shaky ground when, as was observed by Senator Alan Cranston (Democrat, California), the independence and integrity of Congress is threatened.[14]

This may be the most essential political and constitutional argument against the practice of the "corruption probe" with the use of police *provocateurs:* the agents do not improve morals, but they do endanger the "independence and integrity" of the mainstay of a democratic system and democratic freedoms, the parliament.

Whenever a government tries to elevate people morally by use of the police and their specific methods, the result must be an infringement upon privacy and violation of the liberties protected by the American Bill of Rights, the Universal Declaration of Human Rights, and every modern democratic constitution.

Whenever the police start to undertake to probe the morality of the people they enjoy a license which an ordinary evildoer trying to corrupt public officials could not have.

Agents provocateurs are more powerful than ordinary malefactors. They have more means at their disposal because they enjoy a special immunity. The struggle against such sophisticated forms of temptation is especially difficult for the victim. The marked person is *a priori* in an unfavorable position. These considerations should by no means be construed as an apology for those who let themselves be trapped. Our critical reflections are presented to show that no type of police provocation can improve morals, but instead demoralizes everybody and creates an atmosphere hostile to the enjoyment of freedom. Expansion of the police functions and privileges is charged with endless threats to normal social life, democratic values, freedom, tolerance, security, and mutual confidence.

* * *

When it comes to their security and their perception of freedom from crime, people are prepared to make tremendous sacrifices of their own, but especially of the basic interests, liberties, and dignity of their neighbors. One bizarre example: it was found at the end of 1980 that the police in the Indian state of Bihar were blinding their prisoners during interrogation. Prime Minister Indira Gandhi commented in the Parliament: "I felt physically sickened when I heard. What are we coming to in this country? That anyone can do such a thing is beyond my comprehension."[15]

But, as the journalists report, many Biharis do comprehend and approve these police actions. The state is impoverished, many peasants are landless. The area is bedeviled by "crime, caste and religious clashes, where bandits subject people to daily terror."[16]

When the guilty police-officers were suspended, 5000 Biharis protested and sat on rail-roads. Protest strikes were announced. Why:

> One Bihari woman, whose father had been robbed twice, insisted that something must be done to stop the crime. What if the accused are not guilty? She shrugged. "If police arrested them," she said, "they were probably guilty."[17]

Westerners usually console themselves that the woman represented an oriental "subculture," that in the West *habeas corpus* is so deeply ingrained in the popular psyche that such indifference towards human fate (tortured, blinded with pin and acid, and innocent) could not be accepted by people brought up in the Judeo-Christian tradition. Indeed the Indian woman's reasoning is more typical than many people are inclined to believe or admit. Whenever and wherever the government or political parties are able to instigate paroxysms of fear of danger, imagined or real, the people are prepared to give up much of their own liberties and guarantees of due process, but they are even more eager to sacrifice such guarantees for their neighbors, especially those who belong to the lower classes. The proverbial platitudes: where wood is cut, chips must fall; or you cannot make an omelette without breaking eggs-are solemnnly repeated as proof, as if popular old sayings could justify governmental crimes.

There are many people, even in Western democracies, who are so naive that they believe that groundless arrests and accusations can only happen to others, not to themselves. Many victims of lawless regimes found too late that every victimization of one innocent person and any relaxation of the strict rules of legality is a direct menace to everybody's freedom. The bell which tolls for one victim of police arbitrariness tolls for everybody.

* * *

Power in itself is a source of intolerance—this sentence is another way of expressing the famous observation of Lord Acton: every power corrupts, absolute power corrupts absolutely. The corruption of power manifests itself, first of all, in attempts to suppress criticism, to "get even" with the critics, and, inevitably, in the suppression of the flow of information concerning the activities of the government. Intolerance in politics is a sign and a manifest result of governmental corruption. Intolerance is an unavoidable effect of the personal and political fears of the corrupted persons and branches of governments.

The ancient Epicureans and Stoics used to recommend decency as the best way of life for private persons, for politicians, and for governments. Their arguments were not based on philosophy alone, but were also utilitarian, if not outright pragmatic: whoever committed an illegal, immoral, or vile act, will live in fear that it will become publicly known, disgracing him for life. Therefore, in the final analysis, they used to teach, it is better to refrain from the short-term advantages achieved by ignoble means, restrict one's desires and live more modestly.

No government yet has been willing to accept these ancient recommendations. Corruption is inseparable from any form of government. It is the nature of every government to impose secrecy so as to silence its critics.

Intolerance of any government increases with its corruption; the more corrupted it is the more fearful; gradually it becomes more intolerant, secretive, and absolutist. Political absolutism and intolerance are closely connected with the same social phenomenon: political and moral corruption.

Totalitarianism

a. The Essence of Totalitarianism

At the end of the 1950's Karl Jaspers wrote that the world is divided into three great spheres: free states, totalitarian ones, and an enormous group of states and nations which are neither totalitarian nor free. In the next three decades the situation changes, the frontiers of the spheres changed and within every block important, sometimes essential and drastic, changes took place. Some of the totalitarian states became even more terroristic; some of them partially lost their grip over their own population and became less venomous. In many democratic, free countries on the other hand, liberty was undermined because of the growth of governmental bureaucratic interference and the power of private monopolies; the un-free countries of the third world oscillated and drifted rather toward despotism and totalitarianism than toward democracy.

Mussolini expressed the essence of the idea of a totalitarian state in an unusually frank and precise way: no organization and no movement can exist outside of the state or independently of it; all parties, organizations, clubs, ideologies, spiritual trends (including churches and religion) must act within the state, according to its will, plans, and objectives; an individual derives the meaning of life from the totality of a state. Stalin expressed a similar idea in one of his first pamphlets, *Anarchism or Socialism,* with the oversimplification characteristic for him: the point of departure, according to anarchism, is the individual; according to socialism, the masses. Mussolini similarly argued: the most important factor for liberalism is the individual; for fascism—it is the state.

These are ideological and philosophical premises of any totalitarianism—of the right or the left, fascist or Stalinist (the only existing form of communism although there are variations of Stalinism). Even more important, there are also economic, social, and political foundations for the drift towards totalitarianism.

Totalitarianism in the "classic"—Nazi, fascist, or Stalinist form can hardly be reproduced. There are various new kinds and "degrees" of totalitarianism. But one totalitarian feature seems ubiquitous, undeniable, and ever growing: expansion of the internal and very often of the external functions of the state. Any totalitarianism feels threatened even by the existence of an organization not totally subject to or controlled by it.

Plato was right that any loophole favoring freedom in a closed hierarchical society threatened the whole of such a regime. Even freedom of art, including music, might be a menace. Plato was possibly the first to point out the dangers posed by creative art to spiritual slavery. According to his reasoning, those who have freedom of choice to applaud or not to applaud an artist or musical composition, will sooner or later become "arrogant" (Plato's own expression) so that they might try to assume the right to determine which laws are good and which are bad. Today perhaps we would be inclined to consider Plato's reasoning to be simplistic, but there is a rational element in it.

Every form of art (music is no exception, but rather a notable confirmation of the general thesis) being individually perceived by every member of the audience, inevitably arouses very personal feelings, emotions, and thoughts. Art penetrates into "minds and souls," it stimulates individual spiritual powers. Even narrow-minded persons have their soft spots, and can be reached by stimuli which evoke personal reflections.

Reflection is the mental process that totalitarian regimes chiefly fear. Therefore, the authorities directed by Josef Goebbels, Andrei Zhdanov and their successors still issue instructions to orchestral conductors, music directors, and composers. No totalitarian regime since Hitler's and Stalin's death has been able to impose such strict control over all kinds of spiritual creativity, but once the pattern elaborated by Goebbels and

Zhdanov was put into practice, once it proved to be workable, it can be duplicated in the future.

The existence of any form of freedom, even in its passive, non-militant, "benign" form, even in the form of an inconspicuous diversity from the prevailing uniform pattern, is a threat to totalitarianism and it is as such perceived by all totalitarian rulers. This is the nature of every contemporary political despotism or autocracy: it seeks conquest, at least over its own subjects and "total rule by terroristic subjection."[18]

With these features and distinctions in mind we can analyze the alleged differences between various forms of autocracy and totalitarianism.

The characteristics of a totalitarian state can be described in the following way:

1) All power is concentrated in the bureaucratic administrative apparatus which is centralized and the top leader at the apex of the pyramid is the ultimate source of all or at least the most important decisions. No political prerogatives or legal privileges are reserved for the lower echelons of government; higher authorities can at any time interfere with the activity of the lower levels, they can issue binding instructions or take over any case for special further handling.

The concentration of power in the administrative bureaucracy means that the legislative bodies (if they exist at all) and the courts are just auxiliaries to the administration, they are not independent; whatever is under their consideration can at any time be taken over by the administration without explanation or any delay.

2) In the administrative apparatus and the civilian bureaucracy the political police are always present. It is unimportant whether these two departments are combined into one ministry of "internal" affairs or divided into two or even more ministries or departments. It is also unimportant whether the internal security forces are combined with the army or the army remains relatively separate, because in the final analysis the supreme boss (leader, Fuehrer, duce, generalissimus, el Presidente or the

like) is the commander-in-chief of all of them. But there is always enough room for rivalry, intrigues, and merciless power-struggles always at the expense of the rest of the population.

3) The monopoly of political power is connected with the monopoly of one party. This theory was elaborated by Lenin and taken over by the fascist leaders, beginning with Benito Mussolini who as a former socialist activist and journalist was well versed in the history of the socialist movement, socialist ideologies, and heresies. The monopolistic position of one party does not necessarily mean that only one party may exist. In Communist China, Vietnam, and the European people's democracies many parties are legal, but they are not independent socio-political movements, representing various social interests or ideologies. They are, as the communists used to say during Stalin's life, mere transmitting belts between the "vanguard" and the masses who are the object of manipulation.

The monopoly of a single party is a matter of fact which is sometimes openly admitted and boasted about or hidden behind hypocritical phraseology and legal fictions. Very often the ruling group does not call itself a party, but for political mimicry they call themselves: a "non-partisan block," a "united" or "national front," or a "patriotic movement."

4) The monopoly secured by the centralized police and military forces is always associated with some sort of "ideological superstructure." This ideology or political philosophy is presented in a more or less systematic and coherent manner explaining historical, social, and political phenomena in the form of primitive theses and meaningless, universal, eternal, "absolute truths." They are usually undeniable truisms connected in a chain of assertions which are presented, on the one hand, as a key to the kingdom of happiness (a special "theory" similar to the old Christian heresy of "gnosticism"); on the other hand, these simplistic ideas are proclaimed as the answer to all the knotty questions posed by all other political, social, or religious philosophies, always considered to be basically false and having been produced by evil internal and international enemies, plotters, and conspirators. Modern, updated editions of St. Augus-

tine's idea that there is an eternal struggle between the Kingdom of God and the Kingdom of Satan constitutes an essential element of any totalitarian ideology, although not always expressed with such classic clarity as its gifted creator phrased it.

Inability to elaborate a comprehensive theory of totalitarianism is one of the greatest deficiencies in Western political science. John F. Kennedy remarked that victory has many fathers, defeat is an orphan. This time the orphan was fathered in the East and West by innumerable progenitors who have one common feature: they deny their fatherhood.

In any historical period, a lack of philosophical explanation of currently important social phenomena has many sources. Such a deficiency today cannot be caused merely by a lack of scholarly curiosity or talent. The causes are always social and ideological; they can also be a result of manipulation by some vested interests which discourage attempts to find out deeper and more penetrating explanations.

The distinction made by Jeane Kirkpatrick between despotism and totalitarianism became so popular and politically influential partly because the general theory of totalitarianism has not been sufficiently explored.

The communist theorists of state, law, and politics do not analyze the problem of totalitarianism as a matter of principle. Officially they claim that totalitarianism is either one of the features of a fascist state or that this term is just a synonym for fascism. About fascism they do not write too much either, holding that it is not a theory but merely a terroristic form of the bourgeois state during the period of imperialism, itself being, as Lenin wrote, the last and the highest stage of capitalism. Using this oversimplified reasoning, in their own official opinion, they are relieved of the duty of serious scholarly analysis.

The reasons for the inability of communist scholars to analyze the essence and forms of the fascist state are of course political: how can a Soviet scholar, without blushing, criticize a one-party system or the transformation of a parliament into a rubber-stamp? How can they describe and criticize the fascist mockery of a system of justice, corrupted by the direct influence of politicians? or show-trials? or concentration camps in which people are detained and killed without due process of law? or the unlimited power of censorship? or the existence of a single privileged, monopolistic ideology?

It is obvious that no communist could even describe all these facts and fascist-totalitarian institutions without alluding, even unintentionally, to the reality in Communist countries. For such political and ideological reasons, explorations in the theory of the totalitarian state remain *terra incognita* in Soviet and Chinese political philosophy. Whatever they can write truthfully, the reader will say: *de te fabula narratur* (the story is about yourself).

When Communist ideologues write about totalitarianism it is usually part of their campaign against "imperialist anti-communist propaganda" which dares to call the Soviet system totalitarian.

While the explanation of why communist thinkers abdicated their responsibility to analyze totalitarianism is relatively simple, the failure of their Western counterparts to dig into all the available material is more complicated.

One of the reasons for this negligence is the simple-minded identification of the communist system with the fascist (Nazi) type of totalitarianism. Although there are striking similarities between them, the differences are so essential that without their analysis comparisons remain empty. These differences are in the sphere of philosophy, ideology, education, politics, economics, and the social organization of society.

One could start with the simple observation that no fascist system has ever survived its leader. Hitler and Mussolini died during the war. The victory of the Allies destroyed the fascist states and parties. But death and military defeat are by no means all the reasons, not even the most important, for such a total collapse of these regimes and the quick disappearance even of their vestiges.

One should remember that with the death of the super-leaders no real replacement existed and no serious observer or student of politics believed in the durability of their heritage.

Let us take another example. General Francisco Franco died during peacetime, his departure from the political scene was well planned and prepared, he appointed his successor, King Juan Carlos, who succeeded him peaceably. The result: an almost total departure from the totalitarian system which had been consolidated for four decades with an unusual effort and talent.

Similar observations could be made about Peron and his regime in Argentina.

Communist regimes, however, have not suffered this fate. When Lenin and Stalin died there were inevitable personal fights and changes, but the basic structure of the regime remained intact. The state and the party did not disintegrate after Stalin's forty-year-old dictatorship. On the contrary: the basic political institutions preserved their vitality, the successors proved to be shrewd and capable organizers, who were able to preserve and to reinforce the political institutions they inherited. They saved the regime as a whole in a way which was almost bloodless (the only exception was the killing of the high-ranking security officers and their chief, Lavrenti Beria).

The removal of Khrushchev took place almost without any serious convulsions or noticeable repercussions.

Similar observations are in order in connection with the death of Mao Tse-tung, President Ho Chi Minh, Marshall Tito, Leonid Brezhnev and their successions. The situation in China improved, in Yugoslavia and Vietnam it remained stable.

We do not mention other communist countries because they are not as independent as People's Republic of China, Vietnam, and Yugoslavia. The ability of a satellite's regime to survive is directly dependent upon Soviet influence.

The survival of a regime after the death of its leader is one of the most convincing evidences of how different communist totalitarianism is from fascist totalitarianism.

b. Totalitarianism and Alienation

Totalitarianism is a political system in which political liberties by definition do not exist, although their existence may be proclaimed hypocritically in various legal acts, including constitutions.

There are, of course, various forms and degrees of totalitarian restrictions, as there are various forms and degrees of political rights and liberties.

Poles, Yugoslavs, and Hungarians enjoy more freedom of conscience, religion, and scholarly research than the citizens of other communist countries, especially the Soviet Union, East Germany, and Czechoslovakia. There is more freedom from arbitrary arrest in the first group of countries than in the second. The atmosphere in the Polish universities, even after the 1982 purges, is still more open and free than that in the Soviet Union or Cuba.

Similar comparisons could be made in reference to various Latin American countries ruled by "authoritarian" juntas. In every country forms of despotism, authoritarianism, and totalitarianism are more or less advanced, more or less inhumane, more or less oppressive.

Although there are various forms and degrees of despotism and political slavery, the essence remains the same. New and old forms of authoritarianism and totalitarianism are continuously changing and becoming more or less civilized or cruel.

There was a period when the old despotic, absolute monarchies were undergoing transformations into "enlightened" absolutism. The same can happen with a totalitarian government or a military junta from time to time—they might become more "enlightened," better disguised, and more devious at the same time.

What seems certain is that any "enlightened" form of authoritarianism or totalitarianism must be ephemeral. Political dynamics will force a return to "normal despotism" or progress toward democracy.

As the highest stage of deprivation of social and individual freedom, totalitarianism is inseparable from alienation. Alienation has so many meanings, that no social evil is excluded from it. For the purposes of our present analysis we will concentrate on what Hannah Arendt called "loneliness."[19]

Individuals may feel lonely in any society, even in the best organized and humanitarian, for many personal reasons including specific psychological causes. In modern industrial societies, where innumerable traditional, social, and family ties and bonds have disintegrated, a new type of loneliness has emerged. This is the loneliness caused by market forces, by heartless bureaucratic structures, and by mass-parties and organizations where only numbers count. An individual in such a system either feels completely helpless, uprooted, superfluous, or—if he has not reached such a stage of losing ties with society—he is afraid of becoming one more cypher without a recognized place in the world.

The feeling of isolation or the fear of approaching isolation, evokes an urge to join any organization or any institutionalized movement or party which promises help and cooperation, any company, which—as Mussolini used to describe the spirit of a totalitarian state and society—multiplies the forces of one soldier by the united force of the whole army. This "multiplied individual force" is of course an illusion. It is not an individual person who becomes an important member of the community, but a human being who loses his freedom in favor of illusions of being a part of the struggle for a "cause". Such a human being, as Jean-Jacques Rousseau observed, is not truly human any more, because he is not free. A lonely, isolated individual can hardly be regarded as free, because objectively and subjectively his sphere of creative activity is limited; freedom for an isolated, alienated person becomes a burden, a curse to which he is "condemned." It is no wonder that a lonely individual is prepared to trade the illusion of freedom for the illusion of solidarity in a totalitarian movement.

The free market, liberalism, and individualism, under certain circumstances can lead to monopolistic economy and monolithic political organizations, to mass culture, to supercentralized government, to political parties which are so overorganized that they become emotionally and intellectually empty, shapeless and still oppressive. In the process of evolution from economic and political liberalism and individualism to the current monopolistic stage, individual freedom which has been evolving from the Renaissance, through the Reformation, democratic revolutions, parliamentary democracy, and free market is being negated. Freedom is negated first by a mass alienation, by a process of political isolation and social loneliness. Finally, the individual falls victim to the totalitarian Molochs devouring every sign, symptom, and even trace of nonconformity.

c. Drift Toward Totalitarianism

It would be difficult to agree, without any qualifications, with what Hannah Arendt seems to declare, that totalitarianism, especially Nazism, was a system deliberately conceived and consciously constructed. Even the idea of the concentration camps as an institution of total domination was not deliberately worked out before the *Machtergreifung* (seizure of power). If totalitarianism had been the result of intellectual speculation only, it would not have had many chances of success. Actually, the power of totalitarian thinking, of totalitarian social tendencies and of the totalitarian regimes, is based on thousands of real roots, institutions, disasters and achievements, ideas and theories (including religious heresies, as Eric Voegelin asserts), which spontaneously and ceaselessly have started mankind adrift towards totalitarianism. Once such a social and political current comes to existence, the emergence of clever politicians who perceive the new opportunities intuitively becomes inevitable. They put the pieces together, they support or form the new political movements. They are not innovative, but they are able to see what others miss and to exploit existing opportunities to maximum advantage.

The danger of totalitarianism does not derive from new theoretical constructions, but from thousands of elements which were previously either non-existent or unimportant, unnoticed or sterile, but now are welded together under powerful opportunists.

The most important economic and social element in the pro-totalitarian tenor of recent developments is the concentration of the ownership of the means of production. In communist countries this trend has reached its zenith: total nationalization (the German term is more precise in this respect: *Verstaatlichung).* In western and non-communist countries there is partial nationalization accompanied by the gradual disappearance of small and middle size entrepreneurial property in favor of big corporations, conglomerates, and financial groups.

The effect of these processes in non-communist countries is the emergence and gradual increase of the masses of people who are not "independent" any more, they do not work for their own account: they have to work for faceless employers who are "institutionalized" or "incorporated." Owners are personally less and less known to their employees. The uprooted farmers, craftsmen, shopkeepers, and tradesmen are becoming employees hired by anonymous institutions. Such institutions cannot evoke in their employees the traditional feelings of loyalty toward persons; the natural feelings of personal loyalty must be replaced by loyalty to the company combined with abstract promises of appreciation on the part of the unknown captains of industry and the members of the board, who are for the most part shareholders of many enterprises; they do not care who the pawns hired by the responsible executives are and they do not even want to know about the daily activities of their companies.

The masses of people who are working are undifferentiated, deprived of the old milieu characterized by the traditional feelings of friendship, cooperation, and mutual help. Their old conservative scale of values, including the work-ethos, so often referred to, is not applicable to the new relationships. The masses of the working people are enlarging. Finally, they form a society of the masses and they constantly, objectively, prepare—with little or no knowledge or consciousness—for the stage in social evolution which Ortega y Gasset used to call the revolt of the masses.

These masses are alienated, fearful, full of anxiety, uncertain, distrustful, and finally, as Hannah Arendt eloquently argued, superfluous. Every individual is replaceable, dispensable, he is superfluous from the economic and social view points. Management knows that practically everybody can be replaced by somebody else and every employee perceives that it is his skill alone that is valuable; his personality counts for nothing and there is no objective reason for his superiors to take it into consideration. Mankind has entered the period of increasing total dispensability, of total indifference, of universal impersonal relationships.

* * *

In no country does there exist an impersonal, blind, historical necessity for totalitarianism. But in all the major industrial countries elements are increasing which can, as Hannah Arendt used to argue, "crystalize" into totalitarianism. In the end, the attitude of the most active members of a nation is decisive. Only where there is a balance of social forces, can a charismatic, gifted personality tip the scales in one or another direction. Perhaps we have entered into a period when the masses can, more easily than in any other period, be induced to give their support to somebody who is able to flatter them and become, at least for a short time, their political maestro.

Political understanding of the intricacies of the social mechanism are still so primitive, even in Western countries, that societies can easily fall victim to manipulators using modern mass media coupled with scholarly polls and public opinion research. In the past, African, Asian, and American natives were unable to cope with the firearms used by European invaders; similarly today the members of contemporary industrial mass societies, the man in the street, the little vulnerable people, are unable to cope mentally or politically with the massive assaults on their minds and wills mounted by well manipulated and orchestrated mass-media and other forms of information and communication.

The discrepancy between political illiteracy or a low standard of political education of vast social groups on the one hand, and mass propaganda (usually this word is consciously banned from the political vocabulary of western politicians), combined with the latest technological and scientific progress on the other hand, is the stuff from which totalitarianism comes. This phenomenon cannot quickly be rendered harmless; in the near future, even in relatively peaceful periods, this discrepancy will rather increase than diminish. The process of "creeping totalitarianism" will go on, but its every step forward will be generating new resistance and a new influx of energy to the ranks of the "friends of freedom."

The outcome of the battles and wars between modern Ahriman and Ormuzd is unpredictable in the short historical run. The cause of freedom and tolerance may suffer painful setbacks in the near future.

* * *

The development of new technology and of the modern financial and banking system have created new circumstances in which the freedom of citizens could be widened, but—on the other hand—new technology has also created circumstances which make possible far reaching invasions of privacy. In recent years, according to the presidential panel gathering information about invasions of privacy, the most important putative culprits are these:

1. A proliferation of files collected by the government and private institutions which contain information about citizens' work records, health problems, finances, and various law violations.

2. Computers, cable television and electronic banking help to collect and store data concerning the private activity and affairs of almost every citizen who is dealing with credit institutions, banks, issuers of credit cards, and even subscribers to press and cable TV.

3. New anti-crime technology includes electronic eavesdropping, tapping of telephones, hidden cameras and, in many states, job applicants are forced to take lie detector tests.

The United States Privacy Protection Study Commission issued a report on July 3, 1977 in which it stated: ". . . new avenues and needs for collection of information . . . multiply the dangers of official abuse against which the Constitution seeks to protect." In the 1970's and 80's more and more people in Western countries are afraid that the fictional country described by George Orwell in his novel *1984* is slowly but inevitably becoming a reality.

According to data prepared by the U.S. Federal Office of Management and Budget there are an average of approximately 15 files for each American; every citizen is mentioned, on the average, 15 times on paper sheets, tapes or silicon chips. To this number one should add the innumerable files which are held by credit bureaus, insurance companies, banks, private employers, educational institutions, not to mention the police, state and local governments. So long as all this data was on paper only, there always existed a fear that it could be stolen or photographed and used by unauthorized people. Now the dangers are even greater because the data is computerized, multiplied and more centralized, while security of computer systems is not great. Even more, information between various computer systems can easily be exchanged and abused. In 1980 students of one of the best private schools in the country, The Dalton School in New York City, broke the code of the computer systems of two Canadian firms and penetrated into them as a lark. In most states such activity is not illegal. Even if this type of penetration were made illegal it would be no great consolation for the public because of the ease with which such an act could be committed and the difficulty of detecting it or prosecuting those responsible.

Institutions involved in the protection of civil rights and privacy point out that subscription to newspapers, magazines, and cable TV companies can be used in order to write a profile of the subscribers. Such a company will know exactly what the preferences of their customers are including their preferences for X-rated movies or liberal publications. The use of electronic mail and the spread of electronic banking can also be used to describe features of individual personalities, their preferences, views, and even their activities. Of course, this data can be used for innocent purposes such as preparing mailing lists. But it can also be used in criminal and civil investigations, it can be useful even for the purposes of cross-examination and, of course, of discrimination and rewards.

Especially harmful for the average citizens is the activity of credit bureaus. These services are sought by landlords, insurance companies, merchants, creditors, governmental agencies, and of course banks and other financial institutions. Also, actual and prospective employers are asking for data concerning actual or future employees. It is estimated that private credit bureaus issue about 25 million reports on consumers' dealings yearly. Very often the files concerning consumers are incomplete; mistakes are usually not corrected and data which may be unfavorable for their subjects is sent to those who simply pay for the services and make decisions. In most cases the victims are never informed of the reasons for the negative decisions. *United States News and World Report,* July 19, 1982, quoted an example of a Los Angeles lawyer who was negatively listed in a computer, because it happened that he had helped his brother pay his rent and the brother was afterwards evicted. According to credit bureau files, it was the good samaritan who didn't pay the rent and the lawyer was unable to rent an apartment because landlords were informed about his bad record.

This example and millions of others show that such a fundamental constitutional right as the presumption of innocence until one is proved guilty after due process of law, is partially applicable in relations between citizens and the government, but it is not applicable to dealings between citizens and powerful private organizations and corporations. About a century ago, when one wanted to rent an apartment in a small American town, it was not difficult for all the interested parties to find out who was who. Today, when entire housing blocks either belong to or are managed by powerful private corporations, they must rely more and more often on doubtful data and secret investigations conducted by unreliable and irresponsible private detectives and credit bureaus. The average citizen doesn't know by whom he is being observed, when his telephone is tapped, what irresponsible employees write in their files and when and why he can be victimized. Western societies are becoming more and more "bugged," "observed," and "evaluated" societies.

These transformations have taken place mostly since 1950. In this period the political, constitutional, and legal systems of Western democracies have not changed substantially. They are still regarded free countries from the constitutional point of view. They are still considered countries in which law and order exist and civil rights are protected. Nevertheless, the nature of social relationships has changed in them to such an extent that the democratic order is gradually losing its ability to cope with new challenges.

The constitutional provisions protecting citizens were created when the abuses of power by the feudal and absolutistic despots were still fresh in the memory of the people. These legal provisions were efficient antidotes against governmental encroachments upon the liberties and privacy of average citizens. The same provisions of law are insufficient and almost helpless in the struggle to preserve personal freedom and privacy against modern encroachments.

These facts induced Earl Shorris, in his book *The Oppressed Middle, Politics of Middle Management,* to assert that big business is becoming totalitarian. According to Shorris, white collar workers and middle management live in continuous fear which deprives them of freedom to think independently. They have to adapt to the wishes of their boards of directors. They cannot question their board's allegedly total and superior wisdom. They are mere executors of higher policy and the less they think about the justification for a given policy or decision, the better off they are.

Shorris does not imply that this totalitarian structure and atmosphere was deliberately created. He only feels that the logic of the bureaucratization of the privately owned corporations inevitably produces employees who must adapt their personalities, their patterns of thinking, feeling, and reacting, to the requirements of the new hierarchical structure.

In his review of this book in *Fortune* (May 18, 1981, pp.

115-117), Professor Andrew Hacker points out that the application of the word totalitarianism to modern corporations is unfounded and any comparison of corporate structures to totalitarian systems is unreasonable.

> Totalitarianism is the evil of our time, still hugely in our midst. To equate it with routines of business offices is to turn a horror of history into a dilettante's conceit. The rather widespread acceptance of that conceit may be a greater cause for worry than the dubious dilemmas cited in this book (*Ibid, p. 117*).

The problem is not only terminological and it is not a question of the good name of the corporate institutions and their policies that are here involved.

Even if one agrees with Hacker's argument, the basic problem remains: is there any relationship between the social structure and social relations within economic enterprises and the evolution of the social and political system?

Ralf Dahrendorf rightly observed:

> Industry is the dominating order of the society; its structures of authority and patterns of conflict therefore extend to the whole society. Consequently, the quasi groups of industry also extend to the political sphere. The industrial quasi-group of capital becomes, as bourgeoisie (to use the Marxian terms once again), the dominant group of the state, whereas wage labor is, as proletariat, subjected in the political sphere as well. Since, under the particular conditions of capitalist society, conflict fronts that characterized industry and society were identical, the conflict was intensified to an extraordinary degree.[20]

Shorris tries to present empirically what Dahrendorf analyzed theoretically: what is the relationship between the social structure of the "microorganism," of an enterprise and the political system of the rest of society? There is no doubt that there is a mutual two-way influence and conditioning. The essential question raised by the authors concerns the social position of the middle class. If one is right that the position of this class is indeed insecure in its very foundations, if members of the middle class regard their situation with anxiety, fear, and despair, then there are good reasons to accept that an extremely important social pillar of totalitarianism has been established.

The roots of totalitarianism are manifold. The bureaucratic hierarchy existing in modern corporations, their economic and social power, constitutes one of the most essential elements contributing to the spontaneous modern drift toward totalitarianism. As in the middle ages, the existing social and economic hierarchical ladder was a necessary material out of which the political hierarchy was constructed, so in modern times the existing hierarchy in the economic institutions can lead to totalitarian tendencies in politics. The existence of such a trend is inevitable, but it does not mean that a transformation of the modern democratic state into a totalitarian system should be regarded as a "historical necessity." The awareness of the objective roots of totalitarian tendencies can be one of the significant factors preventing a slide towards totalitarianism.

Earl Shorris is right when he writes:

> Totalitarianism denotes a form of political . . . organization, a diminishing or absence of freedom. It does not advertise itself for what it is; in fact, the longer it remains concealed the stronger it becomes (Page 3) . . . Totalitarianism, as trait or totality, escapes social scientists because of their innocence (Page 5) . . . The first rule of totalitarianism is silence, and the isolation it implies. The traveler in a totalitarian society cannot see or hear silence. Isolated himself, he cannot recognize isolation. The surface of nascent totalitarianism appears normal. From the outside one cannot recognize totalitarianism until it reaches the bizarre stage of expansion by force, repression by overt terror, unmitigated madness. The earlier stages can only be experienced subjectively.[21]

This is a correct description of some of the inconspicuous elements composing the modern evolution towards totalitarianism. Every step towards totalitarianism is small and seems unimportant (if noticed at all). But these small changes are, as Hegel once observed, treacherous. They are hidden, unpretentious, and deceptive because of their supposed irrelevance. In fact, under the surface, they will lead to the most important outbreaks, and to a complete change of the established order. They will uproot the established stability and the official hierarchy of values. This is the reason why it is so important to notice every little change in the existing order of economic and political institutions and subsequently in the real scope of freedom and tolerant attitudes. This is what Erich Fromm had in mind when he argued in his *Escape from Freedom* that the serious threat to our democracy does not lie so much in the existence of foreign totalitarian states, but in our own internal attitudes and in domestic institutions. The real battlefield for freedom is in every single country.

In this connection, it is worth pointing out that Hannah Arendt was wrong when she argued that a fully developed totalitarian state and society cannot be constructed in a small-sized country, that it should be a state of the size of the Soviet Union or of the Third Reich after its first conquests. Indeed, totalitarian states and societies may be very small. A totalitarian regime can be very efficient in any size country, as in communist Albania and Cuba or capitalist Portugal under Salazar. Extermination of masses of people and military expansion and occupation of foreign territories are not necessary traits of totalitarianism. Totalitarianism can exist without mass extermination or military conquests. It can have a more "benign" form than Hitler's, Stalin's, or Mao's rule. But it will still be a system in which every individual is totally subjected to arbitrary rule, isolated among a faceless mass fearful of everybody, and exposed to totalitarian ideological propaganda.

VII.

TOLERANCE AND TRUTH

1. Lessing's Wisdom

The essence of the relationship between Tolerance and Truth was presented in a concise and picturesque way by Gotthold Ephraim Lessing in Act III of his drama *Nathan the Wise.*

Lessing created a unique example in the world of literature: he was able to outline a possible solution to one of the most controversial and complicated philosophical problems in a reasonable, non-pedantic way.

Nathan, the hero of Lessing's play, tells the sultan, Saladin, a tale about three rings.

An aged father of three sons was the owner of a ring which had a magic force. When the time to prepare his will had arrived, he asked jewelers to make two exact copies of the ring. Afterwards he gave one of the three rings to each one of his sons assuring each that he was the recipient of the original. After the father's death the sons started to quarrel about whose ring was in fact the original. Finally they showed up before the judge. Each son

> . . . *swore to the judge, he had received*
> *The ring directly from his father's hand.—*
> *As was the truth!—And long before had had*
> *His father's promise, one day to enjoy*
> *The privilege of the ring.—No less than truth!—*
> *His father, each asserted, could not have*
> *Been false to him;*

313

The judge's first reaction was that it was not his function to solve riddles. When he thought over the situation again, he noted that the unusual magic power of the genuine ring could be found out in some way. After all, the ring makes

> . . . . *its wearer loved,*
> *Beloved of God and men. That must decide!*
> *For spurious rings can surely not do that!—*

The results of this magic cannot manifest themselves in a short time, however; therefore the judge decided he was unable to issue a final determination, but he thought it would be advisable to give the sons the following counsel:

> *Accept the matter wholly as it stands.*
> *If each one from his father has his ring,*
> *Then let each one believe his ring to be*
> *The true one.—Possibly the father wished*
> *To tolerate no longer in his house*
> *The tyranny of just one ring!—And know:*
> *That you, all three, he loved; and loved alike;*
> *Since two of you he'd not humiliate*
> *To favor one.—Well then! Let each aspire*
> *To emulate his father's unbeguiled,*
> *Unprejudiced affection! Let each strive*
> *To match the rest in bringing to the fore*
> *The magic of the opal in his ring!*
> *Assist that power with all humility,*
> *With benefaction, hearty peacefulness,*
> *And with profound submission to God's will!*
> *And when the magic powers of the stones*
> *Reveal themselves in children's children's children:*
> *I bid you, in a thousand thousand years,*
> *To stand again before this seat. For then*
> *A wiser man than I will sit as judge,*
> *Upon this bench, and speak. Depart!—So said*
> *The modest judge.*

These rings represent the three religions, Judaism, Christianity, and Islam.

Actually, Lessing's allegory should be interpreted in much broader terms: all political philosophies and doctrines should compete in order to achieve the good ends that they promise without exterminating each other's devotees.

If all three religions regard the principle, *"Love thy neighbor as thyself"* to be the foundation of their faith, if they truly want their followers to be beloved by God and men—they should not seek to annihilate each other, but compete for "souls and minds" consistently with their principles.

Is there any way at all to find out which religion or philosophy is the truth? Lessing suggested that instead of quarreling, seeking an arbiter to make a binding award, and asking him to answer an unanswerable question, all believers should concentrate their efforts on positive activity: let all the followers of each doctrine (or *ring*) believe in their own truth and let them compete at the same time for prestige, recognition, adherence. After "a thousand thousand years" the magic powers of truth will "reveal themselves in their children's children's children." "By their fruits shall ye know them." The most important effect of such an approach would be that in the forthcoming millennia, mankind would no longer "tolerate in his house the tyranny of just one ring."

Wherever a monopoly of one "truth," one "religion," "philosophy," "ideology," the opinion of one "ring," exists—tyranny is inevitable; this is the philosophy of the wise Nathan. Which roads leading to truth, love, and happiness are correct should be decided by the people "in a thousand thousand years." Truth cannot be given in a short time one can only strive,

". . . bringing to the fore,
The magic of the opal in his ring."

One should pursue these goals, because only in the active advancement of these ends will the truth emerge.

The truth will not be pointed out, it will "reveal" itself gradually to future generations.

One of the basic philosophical and political problems is: how should truth be understood? Since the beginning of our era we have been haunted, as Hans Kelsen used to argue, by the famous dilemma posed by Pontius Pilate.

When Jesus was arrested, brought before Pilate, and asked by the procurator whether he was a king, he answered that his mission was to "bear witness unto the truth" (*John,* XVIII, 37).

Pilate, a Roman statesman brought up in the spirit of Greek critical philosophy, simply remarked: "What is truth" (*John,* XVIII, 38)?

Without waiting for an answer, which his sceptical mind would not have accepted anyway, he left the prisoner "and washed his hands before the multitude" (*Matt,* XVII, 24). The crowd was let to decide the problem of guilt by a majority which is—as Hans Kelsen observed—the only democratic way of making a decision when one has doubts about what the truth is!

And "what is truth"? And what is the relationship between truth and tolerance? Is "washing the hands" an act compatible with philosophical relativism and tolerance? Can Pilate be promoted to a symbol of democracy? or a "value-neutral" judicial system?

2. Truth. Epistemological Foundations of Tolerance

The point of departure for our reflections concerning truth will be the classic Aristolelian definition:

> For in the case of truth, affirmation is of objects which are combined, and denial of objects which are divided, but in the case of falsity, affirmation is of objects which are divided and denial of objects which are combined.[2]

Man thinks truly if he thinks as follows:

> Now it is not because we think truly of your being white that you are white, but it is because you are white that we speak truly in saying that you are white.[3]

Furthermore:

A falsity is a statement of that which is that it is not, of that which is not that it is; and a truth is a statement of that which is that it is, or that which is not that it is not. Hence, he who states of anything that it is, or that it is not, will either speak truly or speak falsely.[4]

Aristotle's definitions lay down the main lines of the theory of truth and knowledge.

Two Aristotelian premises are of great importance for our epistemological considerations: the world exists independently of us and it is perceived more or less accurately by our senses. As Francis Bacon asserted, our minds are like "uneven mirrors," but mirrors nevertheless. According to the classic Aristotelian understanding, truth ultimately is a subjective reflection in the human mind of the objective reality.

From the epistemological point of view, ideas and material reality do not represent two different universes, separated by an unbridgeable chasm. On the contrary: There is one world of things and their perception in the human brain. People therefore can be persuaded to change their minds either through real changes occurring in the social and political realm, or through appeals to their minds. Various combinations of these two methods are of course also possible.

We feel confident in dealing with the "objectivity" we more or less know; but how should we deal with the exigencies of subjectivity, especially in the field of politics, economics, and morality? In order to answer this question, we have to enter a new field: dialogue and argumentation.

The Aristotelian concept of truth should be interpreted in connection with the dialectical view of the world. The dialectical approach was presented for the first time in the history of western thought by Heraclitus: Everything is flowing. One cannot step into the same river twice. The world is ever-changing like fire. There are intermittently new flames and new extinguishings. Life and death are inseparable. Death is the source of new forms, new life. Everything fades out, but comes to life again in a new form. The universe is in flux, undergoing everlasting changes. Everything in it is inexhaustible. The epistemological conclusion is that the validity of every truth is limited.

Aristotle himself was unable to apply Heraclitus' dialectics to his own metaphysics. Nevertheless the synthesis of the Aristotelian concept of truth and the dialectical notion of an eternal and ever-changing universe leads to the conclusion that whatever we know is in fact a correct reflection of the world, albeit qualified in scope and extent, space, and time. A simple statement of a simple fact, such as "a total eclipse of the moon took place on March 24, 1978, Greenwich time" can be regarded as an absolute truth within the framework of our own planet and calendar. The number of such absolute truths is unlimited, yet they are no more than the raw material for the process of thinking and for our understanding of the world. Every general statement which tends to connect various facts opens a Pandora's box. It becomes a part of a theory, of the process of understanding, of the interpretation of events with an eventual forecast of the future. Because the universe is infinite in time and space, the interconnections also are infinite, in length and depth, in macrocosm and microcosm. Every presentation of reality while being correct must also be an oversimplification, in which the "elements," "grains," and "seeds" of objective truth are contained.

Spinoza observed that every definition is pernicious, but can we live without them? One may even consider that every explanation of events in nature and society is "pernicious," but only to a certain extent, because it is incomplete, whereas reality is multi-faceted and infinitely complicated.

On the other hand, we may conclude that every new definition, every new explanation, every new theory, being *relatively* true, contains certain elements of "objective" "absolute" truth as long as it reflects certain aspects of nature and society.

It is paradoxical that "absolute," "eternal" truth is but a process of acquiring knowledge. It consists of an infinite sum of relative truths in which grains of absolute truth are found. Is it possible for humanity to achieve absolute truth? The answer should be affirmative, with one qualification only: Humanity will achieve it in the infinite process of development, in eternity, in a "thousand thousand years," as Lessing put it. Does not this answer mean *never*, because eternity will never be? Asking such a question do we not return to the dispute of whether the bottle is half full or half empty? Any parallels to this debate would be inappropriate. The status of the liquid in the bottle is stable whereas the process of our knowledge is dynamic. There are neither pauses, breaks, nor limits.

Albert Einstein is credited with observing that our increasing knowledge is comparable to that which a man gets who is interested in having a closer look at the moon when he climbs upon the roof of his house to see that celestial body better![5]

This comparison shows that human knowledge always has limits and is in any case not great. But there are two sides to the issue. The first is our human certitude that although our knowledge is limited, nevertheless it is a knowledge of the objective truth which can be useful in practical human activity and can at the same time serve as a point of departure for further research.

The second aspect of Einstein's comparison is a stress on the incompleteness of our knowledge; however, this incompleteness is relative as well. The current incompleteness and relativism are caused by two factors.

The first is that there are no limits of time, space, or matter; matter is inexhaustible from any viewpoint; every day our knowledge of the universe expands.

The second relative boundary for our knowledge is the inevitable limitation of our perceptions and their interpretation. But time allows constant perfecting of the instruments, refining both our empirical observations and their interpretation.

Einstein's principle and these two aspects of knowledge should be understood simultaneously, because our knowledge is never a mere statement of facts, it is a process of acquiring truth. Scholars and politicians should therefore be modest because no solution is absolutely correct, although we have to make decisions and be willing steadfastly to pursue the path we consider correct on the basis of what we know.

Once we agree that the real meaning of human knowledge includes permanent growth, an endless process of acquisition, we should conclude that the relationship between relative and absolute truth constitutes the philosophical basis for the assertion that any suppression of any ideas must be harmful to humanity. Any act of intolerance interferes with the normal flow of the simultaneously antagonistic and harmonious exchange of information and the construction of the edifice of knowledge.

Tolerance should be regarded as necessary for every person in the world. Tolerance promotes advancement in science and in practical activity. The tolerant attitude also serves to warn that anything that has been achieved is far from being perfect and should only be regarded as a tiny step up an endless mountain.

The reasoning and arguments presented above are often encountered by those interested in knowledge, progress, and education. It may be argued that the terminology employed here is ambiguous. Is that surprising? Is there any philosophical or political terminology universally approved? Are there any theories upon which everyone agrees that enjoy the privilege of Cartesian clarity? There is no doubt, apart from the terminology, that there is a close link and interdependence, confirmed by history and social science and demonstrated by the great intellectual battles throughout the centuries, between progress and truth and between the evolution of knowledge and tolerance.

Tolerance is the stepping-stone which must be reached if one hopes to develop all aspects of culture, whereas intolerance produces such bitter fruits as ignorance, fanaticism, and cruelty. Again we return to the fundamental question: what are the intellectual causes of intolerance? What are the strange elements of our cultural heritage which promote intolerant attitudes? Why do people not use their common sense in this important domain, even when they are able to think rationally in so many other aspects of their private and professional lives?

Let us once more ask the simple and old question: is ignorance the only intellectual source of intolerance? Nearly all the philosophers of the Enlightenment believed that with the development of education, with acceptance of the idea that man is born free and should remain so, with the explanation of the meaning of ignorance and prejudice, humanity would become not only enlightened but also tolerant, and would reject fanaticism once and for all. Immanuel Kant, in his essay: *What is Enlightenment?* presented these beliefs with unusual fervor, with a passion surpassing many talented French authors. More than three centuries have passed since the period of Spinoza and Milton. Elementary education is compulsory almost everywhere throughout the world. In more developed countries, at least in Europe (Eastern and Western) and America, secondary and higher education is available to most. New possibilities of education for adults have been created and millions take advantage of them. Education is one of the preconditions of tolerance; it is a necessary condition, but it is insufficient in itself.

Whatever may be said in defense of the relativity of truth should not be construed as a recommendation against holding firm convictions. Nothing great can ever be achieved without a deeply rooted belief in the correctness of one's views. Mirabeau said of Robespierre that he would go far because he believed what he said.

Mirabeau's observation should be applied not only to great personalities trying to change the course of history, but to everybody who is thinking and acting, who wants to achieve something different and creative in any sphere of life, personal or professional (very often it is difficult to draw a line between the two). One who tries to achieve something new must be convinced that his decision is right, that his appraisal of the situation and possibilities was correct, the proposed solution is the best in the given circumstances, warrants effort and will succeed.

Relativism of truth does not mean that active endeavors should cease, that one can afford to be paralyzed by doubts and second thoughts. On the contrary: relativity should encourage constant corrections and modifications in what has been chosen as one's course of activity.

Robespierre was an unusual man, possessing an exceptionally strong will, an extraordinary character, and firm convictions. The obstacles on his road, criticism, and even violent

attacks served rather to galvanize his inner strength, helped
develop his political abilities and increased the effectiveness
and power of his mind and will to achieve his ends. But ordinary
people who do not possess the stamina enjoyed by unusual historical personalities can be discouraged by an intolerant environment and by hostile attitudes surrounding them. Tolerance
in daily life is not so important for great personalities as it is for
average mortals, for the smooth and happy course of their lives.
Tolerance is indispensable for their peaceful, gradual evolution.

Intolerance usually cannot thwart unusual people, but it can
change the course of their lives: roadblocks make them into har-
dened radicals, implacable reformers, and finally revolutionaries. Thanks to their genius they can cause radical changes in
the course of events; they become spiritual or political or military leaders of upheavals. Finally they are able to impose their
will on those who refuse to acknowledge or even to tolerate
them, provided of course that they represent the *"Zeitgeist"*
(spirit of the time). But that is not the fate of normal, average
people. They can breathe freely only in an atmosphere of tolerance, fear paralyzes them. They prefer gradual change, without great leaps, without gigantic efforts and tensions which must
be always painful to individuals.

An average human being cannot feel free to think and search
for new avenues when he feels censorious eyes observing incessantly, prepared to harm in case of disapproval.

The atmosphere of tolerance does not impose any special
burden on average humans when they must choose between
various alternatives. Tolerance relieves the pressure while they
are making certain decisions. They can think more tranquilly
and thereby have more chance to avoid mistakes and to correct
them in time. And even more important: they know that they do
not have to stick to their decisions and ideas, they need not
defend them at any cost, they do not have to explain their mistakes, they do not have to make confessions or apologize for
their errors. Tolerance helps to find truth, and tolerance makes it
easier to abandon false paths; it creates conditions for a more
comfortable life, with fewer fears and anxieties.

Intolerance makes the lives of people more difficult and complicated. Intolerance adds pressure while people are struggling to make choices and decisions, while leaving less time and room to correct them. It has a freezing effect on human minds when they constantly live in fear that they could at anytime be asked by the state (party or church) authorities to explain and justify their determinations, both erroneous and correct. Intolerance is an obstacle on the road to truth, it usually leads to false decisions and mistakes. The whole pattern of life under conditions of intolerance is distorted.

Intolerance is never "total," it is always selective. Even the worst satraps have had to tolerate certain ideas, groups, parties, or coteries; as in a tale of Krylov, they are afraid of certain creatures, even small ones, and must tolerate their existence. This tolerance is imposed by the power of the enemies of intolerance. Let us consider one such example:

In East European communist countries, the governments suppressed all the liberal and humanistic doctrines and associations. The individuals survived, many of them respected intellectuals, professors, authors, or journalists. Sometimes they smuggled into their lectures or writings the forbidden ideas, but they did not belong to any organized "school" or "club," because the existence of such groups is illegal.

On the other hand, the most staunch adversary of communism, the Roman Catholic Church, enjoys certain privileges and liberties, it is tolerated with more punctilio than anybody else. The people participate in religious ceremonies, they listen to sermons proclaiming God and his Son to be the only true Lord, they have a chance, especially in Poland and Hungary, to read Roman Catholic publications. Even if these liberties and tolerance are imperfect (their scope varies from period to period and country to country), they are more extensive than the freedom enjoyed by any other non-communist, non-governmental ideas or organizations. What is the source of these governmental and party concessions? They were unable wholly to suppress the church and religion, therefore they had to learn how to live with that tough institution for the sake of mutual benefits.

Possibly this relative religious freedom under the communist regimes in Poland, Hungary, Czechoslovakia, Yugoslavia, and even East Germany, reflects an old truth: *les extremités se touchent* (the extremities meet each other). Their point of contact is dogmas, unverifiable by normal logical or argumentative reasoning.

Their dogmas, even though contradictory, feed each other by their mere existence. It is only reasonable and rationalistic thinking which truly undermines all dogmas and extirpates all the residues of mythology in human minds. The dogma of the transubstantiation of the dictatorship of the party into a genuine democracy and the dogma of the transubstantiation of wine into blood as defined by the Council of Trent, are less harmful to each of the dogmatists than a critical examination of the same dogmas by a reason free of any limitations. Thomas Hobbes' observation that dogmas should be swallowed like bitter medication, quickly and without chewing, is reconfirmed. A mind captivated by one type of dogma is prone to accept either another set of dogmas uncritically or to incorporate them into the existing ones. Peaceful coexistence of dogmas is more likely than coexistence of any dogmas with reasonableness and rationality, with truths empirically discovered.

The old Romans and many Asian peoples (the Vietnamese before the communist takeover) instinctively understood that and therefore they built temples and pagodas consecrated to various gods, their statues standing one next to another. Sometimes they proceeded even more simply and inexpensively: they brought the new gods into a common habitation with the old gods, believing—as the wise judge in Lessing's *Nathan The , Wise*—that ". . .the magic powers of the stones reveal themselves in children's children's children . . ." (Act III, 7).

3. The Theory of Argumentation and the Foundations of Tolerance and Pluralism*

After World War II, the foundations of the ideas of tolerance

---

*The ideas and problems discussed in this paragraph were extensively developed in my book *Juridical Positivism and Human Rights* (1981), pp. 165-222.

were expanded by a revival of the Aristotelian rhetoric and the elaboration of the New Theory of Argumentation, also called the *New Rhetoric* by its founder, Chaim Perelman, Professor of the Free University in Brussels, Belgium.

The origins of the New Rhetoric explain its points of departure and its purposes. In his essay, "The New Rhetoric: A Theory of Practical Reasoning," Perelman told how he felt about the traditional western logical and positivistic principle that there is an insurmountable barrier between judgments of fact and those of value, between *"sein"* and *"sollen,"* that every normative system is arbitrary and logically indeterminate and cannot be subject to any rational criticism.

In this frame of mind he asked whether it was possible "to reason about values instead of making them depend solely on irrational choices based on interest, passion, prejudice and myth?"[6]

And let us add the additional question: how can tolerance be justified rationally?

The solution was the revival of the pre-Socratic, Socratic, and classic rhetorical tradition of argumentation.

From the very beginning, the New Theory of Argumentation was meant to be an analytical tool in social and intellectual life, developed as an instrument critical of all kinds of irrationalism, prejudice, dogma, and *a priori* judgments. It is a philosophical method, but it gained enormous political weight in our "times of contempt."

Perelman's research was influenced by his teacher, a Belgian philosopher, Eugene Dupreél, who opposed the concept of monism (a search for unique truths, or values) with the philosophy of pluralism.

The epistemological premise of pluralism is that every idea, program, solution, and every mind or group of minds is imperfect. Progress can be assured only through diversity and plurality.

The manner in which many imperfect minds operate is dialogue. Dialogue is a nourishment, a stimulant for the mind; it generates intellectual progress. The isolated person must be intellectually inferior to one who is a member of a community, of a "plurality of minds." Dialogue, conceived as the interaction between speaker and audience, should be interpreted in the broadest terms.

Rhetorical pluralism is consciously opposed to all forms of totalitarianism which are philosophically based on a belief in final truth, absolute value, and a notion of a unique order without inherent conflicts.

Pluralism assumes that the "best" life, the incarnation of Reason, will never be achieved, but it also urges a search for improvement, for compromises, accommodations, and syntheses.[7]

Once we agree that we should seek accommodations and compromises aimed at incremental improvement then we must also conclude that individuals should not push their interests and convictions too far: they should be moderate. People can live reasonably, as individuals, as members of a group, and as citizens of the state, in all three capacities at the same time, without endangering the foundation of the social edifice. They can live together in equilibrium, each person pursuing a way of life acceptable to all, while preserving freedom and individuality. Under any monistic, absolutistic order pretending to represent absolute values, freedom consists only in the freedom to conform, which is intrinsically opposed to creative initiative, tolerance, and a right of choice. Freedom can be exercised only in a differentiated, pluralistic society where the individual can enter into a multiplicity of allegiances and at the same time transcend every group of which he is a member.

If freedom is to have any sense, it must be "the freedom of the man who is capable of elaborating a moral ideal which gives meaning to his life, an assured direction to his action. It is the freedom of conscious man, who is not the toy of external forces." Consequently, it is misleading to say that man is born free. Freedom is not an attribute of man, "It belongs only to the one who takes in hand the direction of his life and is completely responsible for his acts."[8]

The main elements in the New Theory of Argumentation which make it a methodological basis for pluralism and tolerance are the following:

—A broader concept of the audience.

—A new interpretation of the importance of dialogue.

—A new solution for the relationship between the *reasonable* and the *rational*.

There have always been a number of intellectuals who believed that to be persuasive one must simply present a clear, faultlessly logical argument, because people are spontaneously inclined to accept the truth. If one's case is just, rational, logically grounded, then—as the well known argument goes—the power of the syllogism alone will be sufficient to sway attentive minds.

We know the famous advice of Descartes: if two men have contrary judgments about the same thing, at least one must be mistaken and irrational, although it may be that both are in error.[9]

According to the rhetorical point of view, there are many human, practical, political, and moral problems which cannot be reduced to the antinomy: true or false. Descartes' claim that any disagreement is a sign that at least one party is in error, if not both is not justified. It may happen that both parties are reasonable although they do not propound self-evident truths; such a possibility lies at the heart of the rhetorical argumentative approach, of pluralism, and tolerance.

One should therefore distinguish between the rational and reasonable. If one restricts the rational as narrowly as the neo-positivists do, then nearly all decisions concerning action (politics, morality) are "turned over to the irrational."[10]

How can one *rationally* choose between various, often contradictory, ends? If quantitative measures are the only ones to be taken into account, then "all conflicts of values would be dismissed as based on futile ideologies."[11]

The reduction of the rational to one principle is an intellectual impoverishment and leads either to irrational pluralism (pluralism without any principles or convictions), or to the monism of values. The monism of values is usually irrational and unreasonable but it can be and often has been used by authoritarian and totalitarian regimes, especially those which pretend to be based on "rationality."

One can draw logical, apparently rational, conclusions from

unjust, immoral premises, as has often been done by Soviet ideologists (what is good for the Soviet government is beneficial for the victory of communism, and this is good for the welfare of the whole human race), or by the Nazi authorities (the highest good is the preservation of pure German Blood and this should be regarded the highest criterion of morality). The Nazi, Stalinist, or racist ideologies can be proved unreasonable only by expanding the framework of reasoning by rejecting formalistic limitations on the sphere of reason.

The conclusion is that the New Theory of Argumentation is the intellectual basis of tolerance and pluralism in all spheres of social activity, in every field of political, legal, and moral ideas. The New Rhetoric does not eliminate formal logic, but reserves a proper place for it in the totality of human reasoning. The New Rhetoric does not reject the value of syllogisms where deduction and induction are necessary, but presents them in their proper dimensions, relying on the concept of the reasonable which is, in its nature, tolerant and antitotalitarian.

The question of the difference between the "rational" and the "reasonable" has been discussed since the rise of modern rationalism.

Well-known forms of presenting this problem are the popular sayings "this is logical, but not true," or "this is logically correct, but inhuman."

This example and many others like it indicate that "the idea of reason can be taken in at least two diametrically opposed ways."[12]

Both words, rational and reasonable, derive from the same substantive, both connote a conformity to reason, but they are rarely interchangeable; one would call a deduction which conforms to the rules of logic, rational, but not necessarily reasonable; a compromise thereof, however, may be called reasonable. On the other hand, a rational decision may be unreasonable, or vice versa.

Behavior may be rational when it is "in conformity to principles . . . not allowing oneself to be held or led astray by the emotions or passions." According to Bertrand Russell, the "consistently" rational man would only be an inhuman monster.[13] Such a man separates reason from his other faculties. He is a one-sided being, functioning like a machine, without feelings, he is like the officer in Kafka's *Penal Colony*.

The reasonable man behaves differently, he often feels and acts contrary to alleged formal logic. His judgment and behavior are influenced by "common" or "good" sense. He endeavors to do what is acceptable by his own society, and if possible, by all. Even more, the reasonable man takes changing circumstances into account, human evolution, human sensitivity, the development of morality, and changing standards of decency. What is reasonable in one age may not be in another. The reasonable is not fixed; it may even have different meanings for different social groups.

Without such a broad concept of the reasonable, reason would become a closed fortress, a force and an instrument of ossification rather than a basis for overcoming what is obsolete. A reasonable individual at the same time may adhere to a variety of ideals and philosophies, not necessarily all compatible. Briefly, there is no theoretical or practical reason why a person cannot be persuaded that it is good to live in a pluralistic environment.

The rational can easily lead to biased, socially inadmissible conclusions even in the framework of acceptable political and legal institutions. When the rational, logical conclusion really leads to an unreasonable outcome, we have to look for compromise, or for a re-evaluation, and even a reconsideration of the whole system. In law, the idea of "the reasonable corresponds to an equitable solution."[14]

In general, what is reasonable stands against an uncritical acceptance of established reality and always supports transcendence of an obsolete order. The reasonable points to pluralistic development; the rational pertains to stability.

This observation constitutes one of the most important philosophical premises on which political, juridical, and moral tolerance and pluralism are founded: rationalism may lead to monism and absolutism; reasonableness always leads to pluralism, tolerance, and freedom.

Rationalists can accept reality as necessary, whereas a

reasonable man tries to overcome the reality which has become obsolete, unreasonable, and therefore unnecessary. A pure rationalist must view the first signs of the future as utopian, whereas a reasonable man is able to see in them the first fruits of a new development, of the new future forms, of a new enriching pluralistic experience for society. Indeed, one could even argue that *it would be difficult to be truly rationalistic without being reasonable,* without looking forward instead of backward.

A rationalism reduced to formal syllogisms is used in our time as the philosophical bulwark of modern, "mindless" conservatism.[15]

A quarter of a century ago C. Wright Mills observed, and his words are even more topical today:

> While intellectuals have been embraced by the new conservative gentility, the silent conservatives have assumed political power ... The silent conservatives of corporations, army and state have benefited by the antics of the petty right. . .these men have replaced mind by the platitude, and the dogmas by which they are legitimated are so widely accepted that no counter-balance of mind prevails against them. Such men as these are crackpot realists, who, in the name of realism have constructed a paranoid reality all their own and in the name of practicality have projected a utopian image of capitalism.[16]

Apart from Mills' various sociological and political concepts one can agree that the above sentences describe the political sense of modern pseudo-rationalism, lacking reasonableness, which serves to justify the social and political status quo in the modern world; it justifies the modern forms of conservatism, the mindlessness of which is almost *a priori* antagonistic to any innovation, to evolution, and to democratic pluralism. Psuedo-rationalism tends toward uniformity, toward *Gleichschaltung,* and presents stability as a logical demand of pure reason; whereas the reasonable man opposes uniformity, undermines any form of absolute order, and presupposes tolerance and pluralism in every sphere of life.

Mindless rationalism and alleged realism do not reject tolerance, they only imprison it in a Procrustean bed of platitudes, dogmas, and paranoic images of reality.

* * *

The introduction of the theory of argumentation and of the notion of reasonableness into legal reasoning was necessary because legal reasoning is inevitably charged with tension, a tension derived from the need for the law to conciliate stability with change, continuity with adaptation, security with justice, equity with the common good. Legal philosophy usually minimizes the personal will, opinions, and accidental perceptions.

> But the person factor cannot be eliminated from legal reasoning. Like all argumentation, being the function of the people who argue, its value will depend, in the final analysis, upon the integrity and intelligence of the judges who determine its specific nature.[17]

A judge, or anyone who applies legal rules, is not only a mouthpiece of the law, or a preprogrammed calculator. He is a thinking being who confronts various values, he must serve them and understand their hierarchy. Every decision rendered by a judge, even one based upon explicit legal material, nevertheless remains personal. All legal reasoning bears this personal imprint. A juridical decision is not a formal demonstration, but it is always supported by arguments aiming to persuade those to whom it is addressed.

Since World War II, a judge's power over the interpretation and application of law has steadily grown in western European countries. More and more the general principles of law must be taken into consideration by judges in applying legislation to reality. In this way a rapproachement between the Continental and the Anglo-Saxon judicial systems has begun and is still in progress.

Once the demands for achieving a mechanically uniform interpretation and application of legal norms were overcome, the specifics of dialogue entered upon the scene. Pluralistic solutions openly became admissible. What is reasonable and equitable is freely asking for its due. Tolerance due to pluralism and the theory of argumentation is becoming part and parcel of democratic legal systems.

* * *

Dialogue is the form and the soul of the process of argumentation. The first precondition for the existence of dialogue is the interest of the participants in an exchange of ideas.

The second precondition is freedom for the participants. The interlocutor must feel free, he should not be afraid to raise doubts, ask questions, use counter-arguments. If he is afraid, he may agree outwardly, but his mind will remain unchanged. One cannot gain the adherence of the minds of those who fear to express their thoughts and hesitate to participate in a dialogue. The manner of persuasion can hardly be effective when the audience is not invited to participate actively, but is merely a passive recipient of the truth.

An advocate must know his audience in order to select suitable arguments and to select the right form for presenting them in order to reach his listeners or readers and to persuade them.

One of the most important characteristics of the art of true rhetoric is that it is not a *scientia male dicendi*, it is not the art of using immoral means for immoral ends. This explains why the New Theory of Argumentation introduced the idea of the *universal audience*, including present and future philosophers and scholars who can be convinced only by really sound arguments.

Only perverted forms of rhetoric can be used by despotic, totalitarian rulers. Why? Because the theory of argumentation presupposes a dialogue and any free and active audience will sooner or later detect lies and misrepresentations. When argumentation fails to persuade, that still does not mean that it was completely wrong, unjust, or unfounded. Arguments can be rejected by an audience for various reasons, but lies can be brought to light sooner in a free dispute than in any other way. There are no guarantees against deception, but it is more difficult for it to remain undetected when the interlocutor is free to think, speak, to collect material, to investigate the case, when he is free and is prepared to take part in the process of argumentation.

The New Theory of Argumentation does not take anything for granted. It does not believe in the magic force of facts, truth, or common sense. They all must be supported by arguments.

The effects of the use of common sense are especially more limited today than in previous centuries. As was proved by Voltaire in his philosophical essays, common sense could act as the sword which cuts the Gordian Knot of theology, feudalism, and absolutism. But in the twentieth century the same common sense ceased to be such an effective weapon against new attacks coming from the new irrational forces, both especially in the industrial democracies and in the communist totalitarian countries. Why? Because the New Kingdom of Darkness has started to present itself as a realm of logic and reason. Rationality is used against Reason. Reason therefore should be strengthened by the well elaborated theory of argumentation.

Mass propaganda in a mass society, the "selling" of ideas, of presidents, and even the clergy, tends to channel thoughts into a one-track, one-way flow of alleged obviousness. It is a pseudo "common sense" which, together with blatant irrationalism, has become one of the most dangerous enemies of reason in modern, industrial democracies.

Argumentation is a way of overcoming the power of appearances,[18] of dogmas, myths, and the "obvious truths" of "common sense." The rhetorical flow of arguments, the appeal to an audience and the invitation to join in dialogue—these are the tools for criticism of simplistic ideas which remain deeply ingrained in the minds of people who, generally speaking, are rather critical and creative in their own professional lives, but unable to apply the same demanding criteria to an analysis of social and political issues.

Western culture has generally held that any conclusions reached by human thought must be a personal, subjective conviction, the result of an investigation, not a blind belief.

Such is the concept of rhetorical discourse. Everything that falls into the stream of argumentation changes its meaning and place in the system of thought, invading the substance of the system itself.

Rhetorical argumentation never ceases, it does not know stops or pauses. Rhetorical truth is like Heraclitus' river: you cannot step into the same river twice; it flows continually.

The intrinsic link between rhetorical methodology, tolerance, and pluralism is that there is nothing perfect; no social group or party can have a monopoly on absolute wisdom and knowledge.

The idea of pluralism as developed here is diametrically opposed to the philosophy and methodology of scepticism or relativism, as understood by Hans Kelsen, for instance.[19] In his famous, already classical, considerations about Pontius Pilate, Kelsen argued—as was mentioned already—that Pilate's act of washing his hands was a truly and consistently democratic act because there is no valid criterion for distinguishing between the value of the life of a convicted criminal and that of a man who identified himself as the messenger of truth.

Hans Kelsen wrote that once we accept the relativistic concept that truth cannot be known, that everything is relative (except relativity), then we must also accept as justifiable the behavior and decision of the cynical Roman procurator. It may be that an intellectually consistent, logical, and rationalistic skeptic and relativist could agree with Kelsen's conclusions. But they are not acceptable to the ideas of pluralism and tolerance based on argumentation.

Pluralism and tolerance do not reject moral, political, social, legal, and philosophical ideals as senseless or worthless. They subject these ideals, their interpretation, and application to endless critical scrutiny.

The method of rhetoric is against dogmatism; it is for pluralism, for democracy, for unlimited intellectual freedom; it is against conservatism, because it finds contradictions everywhere and struggles for new solutions.

Philosophy based on argumentation, pluralism and tolerance favors reasonable compromises, to foster the evolution by critically rejecting what has become obsolete and critically defending what is developing or should be given a chance to be born and to live. From the viewpoint of such a philosophy, compromise is not unprincipled, but the contrary.

Reasonable compromise is an instrument and a generator of further evolution because it is a resolution of the conflict of opposing forces. Such compromise does not pretend to resolve all incompatibilities forever; on the contrary, it creates new sources of struggle and change; it is in itself a result of a pluralistic society. Conscious, reasonable compromises help to promote the development of democratic institutions based upon the requirements of freedom and tolerance.

The principles of argumentation, pluralism, and tolerance are meant to be a Diogenes' lamp for those who travel along a road which is dimly lit, full of hazardous curves, and traverses unknown domains.

4. When Tolerance Requires Intolerance

If tolerance is not interpreted as an acquiescence in evil (sometimes nothing short of acceptance)[20] or a feeling, reasoning, acting, or attitudes which are value-neutral[21]—then a most difficult problem arises: what actions or situations should not be tolerated in order to maintain and strengthen tolerance? Can it happen that intolerance sometimes is indispensable for tolerance?

If tolerance is a value in itself, one substantial qualification should be added: tolerance should be a means for expanding freedom and promoting progress, not a road paved—as Saint-Just used to warn—for "the enemies of freedom," who want to use the existing liberties to put an end to freedom. One cannot of course accept Saint Just's vague recommendation "no freedom for enemies of freedom," because it is the nature of freedom and tolerance that they require that even "enemies of freedom" should be free, within the existing legal democratic order. But how free? Do freedom and tolerance require the partisans of freedom to let the enemies of liberty annihilate them?

Who can be qualified as an "enemy of freedom?" what criteria apply?

—Unexpressed convictions? It would be against the very nature of humanism and freedom to authorize "probes" of one's soul.

—Speech or publication? Freedom of speech, press, publications can exist so long as it is unlimited—this is the idea of the First Amendment; once this freedom is even partially curtailed by any kind of censorship, it will fade away.

—Activity? Behavior?—This problem is real and it is most complicated. A very general rule might be: every activity should be allowed and tolerated by the government so long as it does not violate the law promulgated by a democratic government in order to preserve the lives and property of the citizens and the country's independence from foreign powers.

That implies that speeches, publications, rallies, organizations of those who are against existing freedoms and constitutional provisions should be free and legal. Only actual violations of the existing laws should be regarded as illegal and prosecuted with due process.

Any intervention, or restrictions on the part of the government, wanting to compel the people either to perform certain actions, or to refrain from them, in order to make them "happy," "good," or "moral" are unnecessary for the protection of life and property and cannot be justified.

These premises may be said to constitute a philosophical, legal, and political basis for freedom and tolerance.

Therefore when one argues that nobody needs to tolerate fraud, deception, or misrepresentation, two meanings are possible.

One meaning: under certain conditions it is illegal to commit such deeds; they are not only morally repulsive but also prohibited by law.

Second meaning: when these deeds are not illegal under certain circumstances (even if they could cause certain legal consequences), they should not be morally, socially, or politically tolerated; the people can, and even should, manifest their disgust or condemnation.

The upshot of these considerations might be summed up in the following way: tolerance can exist while an atmosphere of intolerance surrounds those who violate certain basic principles of morality, decency, tolerance, and democratic laws.

Freedom and tolerance can thrive only in a society able to construct a reasonable legal system which upholds due process, including guarantees of democratic liberties and of human and civil rights.

The "enemies of freedom" and tolerance often try to use democratic liberties to gain power, sometimes declaring that democracy and liberalism are "rotten." This is one of the points of agreement between *fascists* and *Stalinists*. They openly announce that they intend to prevent these "depraved" ideas from undermining "national unity," "state sovereignty," *"die neue Ordnung,"* or the "foundations of communism"—the number of such phrases is unlimited. True, the fascists and the bolsheviks made no secret of their intention to introduce one-party rule, abolish parliamentary democracy, and ban political opposition. But none of these parties told the whole truth, that they intended to exterminate their real or suspected opponents, that terror, torture, and arbitrary arrests of suspects, their friends, and families, would be the everyday practice.

Before and after he became chancellor, Hitler was more candid than any other politician, he openly said much more than his propagandists and followers did, he admitted even more than the partisans of appeasement, or even his future victims, wanted to find in his pronouncements. But he did not tell everything even about his immediate intentions: unlimited powers for the political police, torture chambers, arbitrary murders, and concentration camps.

German authorities in the Weimar Republic had good reason to anticipate such possibilities and take precautionary measures foreseen by domestic and international law. Our contention is that in dealings with such organizations as the fascists or the Red Brigades, the principles of political tolerance or intolerance are not applicable; there is only the problem of applying the democratic laws strictly and fairly. According to the criminal law in every civilized country it is not only prohibited to commit a crime, but even certain stages of preparations to commit it or instigate it, are also illegal.

Members of such organizations who become defendents should of course enjoy the presumption of innocence and should be guaranteed all other constitutional and legal safeguards. Of course, the courts may find them not guilty from a strictly legal point of view, but not everything that is legal (it would be better to say: not everything that is not legal) should be politically, socially, and intellectually tolerated. Society has many other ways to show its repugnance although a particular perpetrator may not and should not be behind bars.

Society can and should prove that it abhors people who openly favor discrimination on the basis of religion, race, nationality, or social origins.

Society can and should show that it does not tolerate those who praise genocide or justify it.

Society can and should shun politicians in democratic countries who promise one thing before elections and then flagrantly break these promises and turn their backs upon the helpless voters afterward.

These are only three categories of people, ideas, and deeds which should not be politically, socially, or philosophically tolerated. How can one show that such misbehavior is intolerable in a democratic society? First of all by an organized, loud, and public denunciation of their ideas and behavior. The silence of decent people is the first step toward acquiescence, exoneration, and finally, respectability.

The proposal that intolerable ideas and actions should be loudly, publicly, and in an organized way denounced as morally repugnant and politically harmful is not unimportant. This response is most essential for the preservation of a "sane society" (as Erich Fromm called it). Democracy starts with openness and cannot endure without it.

Openness should not be interpreted in a narrow, passive way, as might be deduced from Kant's remark that what is hidden by the government is presumed to be immoral. Openness in modern democratic societies should be interpreted radically:

there should be no bars against reaching to the roots and criticizing all types of ideas and activities of the government, political parties, and organizations. One should take into account all the facts, bring them to the light, draw them regularly to the public's attention. Nothing that tends or seems to be antisocial or immoral (although not criminal, because the case then should be in the hands of the police and the courts) should be left untouched, everything should clearly be presented to the public, without hiding the truth and moral judgments behind diplomatic pleasantries. On the contrary: the idea of tolerance requires that the people should be shown how misinformed, misled, and mistreated they have been; the evil-doer should not be morally and socially tolerated. The common practice of arbitrarily classifying political documents as "secrets" should not be tolerated.

These are the pre-conditions for an atmosphere of public intolerance towards ideas and activities which should not be tolerated in a political democracy. Such intolerance is contrary to any form of government-sponsored terror or intimidation exercised by bigots or other groups and organizations which do not shrink from invoking the image of Satan to frighten uneducated people in order to achieve their political and social aims.

The public intolerance advocated here is indeed a condemnation of sneaky maneuvering, of dishonest attacks on freedom and tolerance under the pretext of public interest, justice, and religion.[22] This is a democratic type of struggle against the adversaries of democracy. This is how freedom can fight and win the battle against "the enemies of freedom" without destroying itself in the process.

There is no doubt that these problems are complex. Often it is difficult to make any decision because issues pertaining to the preservation, extension, and defense of freedom are unusually sensitive. And as ever, one step too far in the defense of freedom could be more harmful than no defense at all. Using certain means to defend freedom is like using poison to produce a medicine: the right dose is beneficial for the patient, while either a lack of medication or too large a dose might be fatal. The health of freedom is always fragile, yet the difficulties which the followers of freedom are meeting must be addressed.

Freedom and tolerance, and the dangers to which they are perpetually exposed, are so intricate and perplexing that every reasonable partisan of freedom must become its active defender. At a time when there are so many internal and external adversaries of the principles of democracy, freedom, and tolerance it becomes more essential than ever before to manifest political (not administrative, police, or military) and philosophical intolerance of anti-human ideas and activities. At stake is, as we have already mentioned, not only the freeom but also the survival of humanity. Today it is especially true that the victory of evil can be achieved not so much by the activity of the evildoers as by the passivity of the good.

All the preceding considerations concerning intolerance of antidemocratic (but legal) forces apply only to democratic, parliamentary systems. What should the behavior of the followers of freedom and tolerance be in a despotic or totalitarian country? This is a problem which will be treated in the following chapters.

Our considerations concerning intolerance in a democracy, however, would not be complete without an analysis of the international aspects of the active defense of freedom and tolerance and outright condemnation of tyranny.

Almost all countries are members of the United Nations, having voluntarily obliged themselves to observe the U.N. Charter and the provisions of international law. Norms concerning human rights are an essential and integral part of the legal and moral fabric underlying modern international relations. Any violation of human rights in any country constitutes a danger to peaceful cooperation among all nations and to world peace and the security of all states.

The relationship between democracy, freedom, and tolerance and peace among nations was well known to progressive thinkers many centuries ago. Possibly the ideas developed by the

German and Polish philosophers, Immanuel Kant and Stanislaw Staszic, are most interesting in this connection.

The political program of President Carter's administration concerning the observation of human rights all over the world coupled with public denunciation of incorrigible violators was philosophically correct. Whether the execution of this policy was consistent and effective, is not the subject of this book. The main premise of his policy was that neither the United States nor any other democracy should remain silent or indifferent while people in other countries were being deprived of their elementary *human* rights, that democracies should not silently tolerate oppression, torture, arbitrary arrests and "disappearances" in other countries including, especially, those which are considered friendly. What is intolerable domestically should not be acceptable in another country, especially a friendly one.

This problem became especially important in international relations after Stalin's death in 1953. When the dictator left the scene, a period of *"thaw"* followed.

The term *"thaw"* became very popular in politics after the publication of Ilya Ehrenburg's novel of that title at the end of the Stalin era. The thaw in Soviet domestic policy was accompanied by a partial termination of the cold war. A phase of détente and cooperation ensued. This period of international peaceful cooperation has been curtailed with the tightening of political screws in the Soviet Union and other communist countries, and further acts of expansion and out-right aggression.

A very similar development took place in the relations between the People's Republic of China and the Western countries including the United States. During the Cultural Revolution, characterized by general and blind terror, relations with the West were more tense than ever before or since. With the gradual disappearance of the terroristic gangs, including the "gang of four," and with the decline of the health and vitality and the eventual death of Chairman Mao, China's relations with Western countries started to improve. This improvement finally led to opening diplomatic, trade, commercial, and cultural relations with the United States. This most recent phase took place when the situation in China had reached a new stage, still very far from any Western understanding of democracy, but nevertheless some sort of an enlightened absolutism. The Chinese domestic thaw was accompanied by an expanding exchange and cooperation with western countries.

The policy of the United States toward absolutist communist countries cannot be based on the same principles as toward allies, such as those in Latin America. Silent, benevolent tolerance of the despotic excesses of the governments which belong to the "free world" can only be harmful for the cause of freedom all over the world.

Practically and theoretically, democratic governments have only one justification for imposing an immense burden of taxes on their citizens and spending these funds for armaments: the moral superiority of the free parliamentary societies over the totalitarian regimes represented today in the most dangerous form by the Soviet Union and its militaristic expansionism. There can be no other justification for asking the people to defend themselves and die. Any deviation from the purpose, which is the defense of freedom and tolerance defeats the ends themselves.

Moreover, any betrayal of the democratic ideals by unscrupulous collaboration with dictators and any reinforcement of their rule can weaken the democratic society to such an extent that its military strength and will to defend itself could be undermined as well.

There is a well known link between the morale of an army and its military performance; today this statement has become a truism. In democratic countries infringements upon democratic principles sooner or later erode the fighting spirit of the soldiers and consequently their military efficiency.

The problem facing decent people in despotic or totalitarian countries may be reduced to the following: how far may one go in cooperating with the authorities? When does cooperation become collaboration? What forms of disapproval or opposition can be used? What is the minimum and maximum risk one can reasonably take in order to remain true to the minimal requirements of decency and morality?

It is impossible to give clear-cut, detailed answers valid in all circumstances and for every system. There are special circumstances in every undemocratic country which must be considered and which might properly impel an individual either to cooperate with the authorities (there are always certain limits) or to refuse any involvement, any kind of cooperation.

Our further considerations in this respect will be influenced by development of the situation in Poland in the period August 1980 through December 1981. The relatively peaceful, bloodless, transformation (1980) of the repressive regime proved that it is possible to advance the cause of freedom and tolerance even under the most unfavorable circumstances, such as the rule of a corrupt and repressive governments surrounding Poland. During the first period of Liberalization, 1956-1957, the Poles used to ask an ironic question: is it possible to build socialism (*humanistic*) in a socialist environment (Soviet type)? It seems that it is possible to achieve incremental democratic progress by the concerted pressure of the whole nation, by the persistent and more or less public condemnation of the corrupt officials, by making them ashamed of their participation in the ruling clique. It is possible to wring concessions when the over-powering majority reaches a national consensus which Soviet propagandists call "political-moral unity." Such a consensus has never been formed around any communist party, contrary to the insistence of the Soviet ideologues. In Poland such a unity has finally been achieved, but against the communist ruling group and its Soviet mentors.

The series of Polish democratic victories, although short lived (1956, 1970, 1980-1981), show how a nation might liberate itself without endangering its existence or even its economic and cultural achievements.

No person can be morally or even legally excused[24] for participating in crimes against humanity and his own nation, even if a government calls this activity legal, moral, and indispensable to the state. This is a maxim known since the beginning of our civilization, and long ago was expressed in literature—first of all in Euripides tragedy *Alkmeon*, which was discussed by Aristotle in his *Nicomachean Ethics*.[25] The most important contemporary moral and legal landmarks are the Charter of the Nuremberg Tribunal, its verdicts, and the United Nations convention prohibiting genocide.

The deeds punished by the Nuremberg Tribunal after the Second World War are also juridically prohibited by almost all despotic and totalitarian countries. No person should count on human tolerance and "understanding" when deciding to participate in genocide voluntarily or becoming a member of an organization which intends to exterminate innocent individuals or entire national, racial, religious, or political groups. It is inexcusable to participate in such actions as denouncing one's parents, relatives, or friends to the political police for being dissenters; such denunciations have been encouraged and praised in the Soviet Union and other communist countries as well as in all fascist countries and such "authoritarian" countries as South Vietnam under the regimes of Ngo Dinh Diem, Ngo Dinh Nhu and their successors, or Cambodia under the Khmer Rouge. Such actions tear apart the very fabric of society and demoralize everybody: perpetrators, authorities, victims, and even passive onlookers. Since the Inquisition, informers have been rewarded in the most nasty way: then they received a part of their victim's property. In richer totalitarian countries the rewards are more generous.

One of the reasons that the Soviet authorities are able to buy souls for such a low price is the low standard of living and daily struggle necessary for bare survival. When the informant is assured such a reward as an uninterrupted supply of bread, sugar, meat, milk, even in small quantities, he feels that he belongs to a higher class and is prepared to pay for that privilege with the only coin he has: his own soul. As one of the heroes of Shaw's *Pygmalion* observed: he is too poor to be moral. Poverty demoralizes in every social system; demoralization is compounded by lack of freedom and tolerance.

In every epoch, sooner or later, new ideologies are elaborated which are used as an excuse by those with bad consciences. People, as was observed not only by Freudians, cannot live long with the feeling that they are villains. They must suppress their lack of self-respect; they need consolation. Religious absolutions are important even in the lives of political sinners, but church compassion cannot be sufficient. Contemporary political villains need more: they need ideologico-political opium. Every despot tries to provide his vicious army with this indispensable medication. They hire preachers, authors, journalists, even university professors who prepare the spiritual food which is required by the collaborators.

Our contention is that people who have had the bad luck to live under despotism or outright totalitarianism must make many compromises, nevertheless all of them should observe at least the minimal moral and legal standards. They should not participate in the most heinous criminal governmental activities such as denouncing innocent people, bearing false witness, participation in torture. This is a minimal moral requirement and violators should not expect compassion and tolerance. They should not expect that anyone will say in their defense: *tout comprendre, c'est tout pardonner* (to understand everything, means to forgive everything). There are limits which should never be exceeded and violation of such rules must not be tolerated ever.

From the moral viewpoint, the question of justified intolerance is always connected with a conflict of values. The same is true for political tolerance or intolerance; this is the heart of the problem.

5. Excesses of Relativism—Intolerance and Untruth

Philosophical relativism and the relativistic concept of truth can constitute a foundation both for tolerance or intolerance. If the answer to the fundamental questions: does truth exist? is it possible to discover it? can it be given to us once and for all?—is affirmative, then there can be no surprise that there are so many self-professed possessors of truth who claim the right to suppress views inconsistent with their truth. It seems clear that anyone who is intolerant must claim, explicitly or implicitly, that since he knows *the Truth* he is entitled to stop those who disagree with him. We know, however, that belief in absolute truth does not make every self-made possessor of it intolerant.

There is still another possibility: One who believes that he has gained the truth, can be deeply convinced that his truth has such an intrinsic persuasive power that sooner or later all will accept these beliefs. One may favor tolerance because of the belief that once truth and error—as Benjamin Franklin wrote in his "Apology for Printers" (*The Pennsylvania Gazette*, June 10, 1731)—have a chance of fair play, the former is always an overmatch for the latter.

Consistent philosophical relativism can logically lead to tolerance. Usually it is the philosophers and intellectuals who are more or less consistent relativists. But they constitute a small minority in any society. Therefore, relativism cannot be a firm social basis for tolerance. Most people believe that we are in the process of acquiring truth, that some truth has been discovered; therefore, tolerance must be developed and based on a firmer and more dependable foundation than relativism.

In his book, *Escape from Freedom,* Erich Fromm observed that one of the ways to discourage original thinking is to regard all truths as relative. "Truth is made out to be a metaphysical concept, and if anyone speaks about wanting to discover the truth he is thought backward by the 'progressive' thinkers of our age. Truth is declared to be an entirely subjective matter, almost a matter of taste."[26]

To hold that all truths are relative and that there are no firm criteria to distinguish between a true statement and a false statement is not a sign of a critical mind but rather of intellectual irresponsibility if not inability to think. One should distinguish between the problem of the reliability or accuracy of a general economic, political, social, or historical theory and statements of the facts, be they social or natural. We already stated that truth, according to the best traditions of Western philosophy as initiated by Democritus and Aristotle, is connected with a reflection of an external reality in the thinking mind and to regard them as totally subjective, as matters of taste, would

completely undermine any possibility of knowledge and reasonable acting. Fromm was right when he observed that, even if it
hides behind a concern for the correct usage of words and exclusion of any unwarranted beliefs, relativism finally causes thinking to lose its essential stimulus: "the wishes and interest of the
person who thinks."[27]

Can total relativism constitute a sound basis for tolerance
and freedom of thought and research?

Relativism which denies the existence of any truths can
assist in the exploration of moral, social, and political differences but cannot serve as a solid philosophical foundation for
tolerance. Sometimes even to the contrary. When every belief
or opinion, even those empirically proven to be true (within certain limits, of course) are held to have a value equal to unfounded beliefs, that is not tolerance but rather indifference to any
progress and value in human mental endeavors. A striking example of this attitude was supplied by Noam Chomsky, Professor
at the Massachusetts Institute of Technology. The facts are
the following:

Robert Faurisson, a lecturer in classical and modern literature at the University of Lyons, wrote a book in which he denied
that the Holocaust had ever taken place. In the past few years,
he even started to deny that there were ever Nazi death camps.
He alleged that there were only crematoria, but no death
chambers.

What Faurisson denied was not a theory or hypothesis but
well established and known facts witnessed by many survivors
of World War II, who can still testify to what they know firsthand.
These facts were confirmed by the soldiers and officers of the
allied armies who liberated the death camps and by many of the
executioners themselves. No reasonable person denies such
obvious and notorious facts. Faurrison's lies were denounced
by many organizations of former resistance fighters and Nazi
victims. They sued him for defamation and "disinformation."
The University of Lyons suspended him as a University
Lecturer.

The decision of the University authorities was criticized in a

petition by about 500 intellectuals who argued that the authorities had violated the principles of academic freedom. One of
those to sign the petition was MIT Professor Noam Chomsky
who was especially severely criticized for so doing. At the end of
1980, Professor Faurisson published a new book in which he
once more denied the existence of Nazi camps and republished
various articles and clippings which were used in his defense
in court.

Professor Chomsky wrote the foreword to this book.[28]
Chomsky stressed that he did know very much about the book
but that his only concern was that the author, Robert Faurisson,
should have the right to express an unpopular thesis, that pressure against that author was unjustified. The mere criticism of
Faurisson and of 500 intellectuals who defended him was denounced by Professor Chomsky as a drastic example of intolerance on the part of French intellectuals. He also denounced
the French authors and scholars as a group of people who love to
"line up" and "march in step."

Professor Chomsky felt that the reasons for this intolerant
attitude among French intellectuals should be sought in the
French past: Feelings of guilt because of the Vichy regime, *"La
salle guerre"* ("the dirty war") in Indo-China, the impact of
Stalinism, and traditional anti-Semitism.

He went on to contrast the attitude of American intellectuals. No measures were taken against American professors
who denied the existence of Nazi death camps and Nazis were
allowed to march in Skokie, Illinois.

The French intellectuals were of course not impressed by
Chomsky's reprimand and some of them pointed out, as reported by *The New York Times* (January 1, 1981), that Chomsky
did not understand France and that he especially did not consider that totalitarianism had been a recent and devastating
experience in that part of the world. One writer published a letter
in *Le Monde* in which he argued tongue-in-cheek that World
War I was an invention of the veterans who were still drawing
pensions for their alleged services in the defense of their
countries.

From a philosophical and moral point of view, the ideas of

Professor Chomsky show that he misunderstands certain elementary aspects of knowledge, freedom, and tolerance.

Whether the death camps existed is not theoretical but an empirical question. It was a reality, it was a fact. One can and even should discuss the underlying political or ideological reasons for their creation and operation; one might discuss how many victims perished in these camps because the Nazis did not keep a complete count; there could be differences over how many people were destroyed in the gas chambers as against how many were murdered by the use of more "traditional" methods. But one thing is undeniable: the death camps and deliberate genocide existed as surely as did World War II, as does New York City, or Harvard University. Whoever denies such facts or defends the "right" to doubt that M.I.T. exists does not represent another point of view, but is either insane or simply a liar who should not be protected by any scholarly and moral theories. One who writes a preface or a letter supporting the right of a liar to lie does not serve the cause of objectivity, freedom, tolerance, or truth, but supports the cause of deception. In this case it is a deception which serves not only the interests of the immediate murderers, but of all who helped the murderers to seize power, exercise it, and wish to repeat this enormous tragedy whenever possible and expedient.

For the sake of truth, morality, and peace we should remember the warning of Santayana that those who ignore the experience of history will be condemned to live through the tragedy once more.

By defending Faurisson's right to lie, Professor Chomsky in effect denied the possibility of finding and declaring historical truth or historical facts. If everything is relative, if even undeniable facts, witnessed by millions of people, corrobated by material evidence may be denied; if any obvious, notorious lie can be accorded serious consideration as another legitimate point of view that merits tolerant reception—then truth and social or historical experience are meaningless. Indeed truth should then be regarded as a nullity, as a senseless mental conceit or play of words.

Tolerance does not mean equating the validity and value of

truth and falsehood. A person who does so is not tolerant; he is indifferent to the cause of mankind, progress, and humanism. Anyone who adds to the respectability of a liar and murderer— in this case mass murderers—does not deserve to be regarded as tolerant and humane, because he is insulting the victims and the defenders of truth and justice, he is undermining the victims' credibility, the truthfulness and the good faith of all who condemn oppressors. We do not live in a world in which everybody is interested in discovering the truth, quite the contrary.

Truth can be advantageous for one group and disadvantageous for others. Let us return to another observation of Erich Fromm:

> Actually, just as thinking in general has developed out of the need for mastery of material life, so the quest for truth is rooted in the interest and needs of individuals and social groups. Without such interest the stimulus for seeking the truth would be lacking. There are always groups whose interest is furthered by truth, and their representatives have been the pioneers of human thought: there are other groups whose interests are furthered by concealing truths. Only in the latter case does interest prove harmful to the cause of truth. The problem, therefore, is not that there is *an* interest at stake but *which kind* of interest is at stake. I might say that inasmuch as there is some longing for the truth in every human being, it is because every human being has some need for it.[29]

Sometimes it is difficult to determine in whose interest it is to conceal the truth. But in the case discussed above, however, it is obvious whose interest is served by denying the existence of the extermination camps. It is the interest of the exterminators, their ideological inspirers and political supporters that is served by untruth. Anyone who tolerates such an untruth, is not tolerant; he is serving anti-humane interests.

In our world truth is not "non-partisan." Truth may be an object of passionate struggle by vested interests. Anyone pretending that he doesn't notice these struggles is neither reasonable nor decent nor tolerant. The only excuse for such a person can be that he does not understand the social and political mechanism of the struggle for truth.

Tolerance is a way of life, an attitude, a method of thinking and of acting which tends to search for truth and for solutions which are best for the greatest happiness for the greatest number of people. But tolerance has nothing to do with tolerance of bigotry, racism, extermination, genocide, and has nothing to do with skepticism concerning their existence. It has nothing to do with the right to let somebody die in mud, as could be justified by absolute skepticism like Pyrrho's. According to tradition, when Pyrrho was slowly drowning in the mud, one of his students saw him, looked at him, and left him without helping his teacher. Pyrrho was rescued by other people who severely condemned the student. Pyrrho was the only one who defended him. One never knows what is better for one's neighbor, argued Pyrrho.

Tolerance has nothing to do with absolute skepticism.[30] Tolerance is not an attitude of indifference, it is a method of acting and living in society, a way of searching for truth, freedom, justice, peace, and happiness, an attitude of civilized people who endeavor to assure progress which would be impossible without "working truths;" be they relative, incomplete, albeit the only ones available. Tolerance is not a haven for ignoramuses and alleged scholars prostituting their consciences and titles to please the rulers, the rich, and the powerful who want to ingratiate themselves with past and future gas-chamber operators. Tolerance is the most humanistic method of denunciation of the adversaries of human dignity.

These are the most important elements which Noam Chomsky has overlooked in his preface; tolerance and freedom (any freedom, including academic) is an essential attribute of human dignity, whereas ignorance, lies, denials of facts, and ethical blindness diminish human dignity. The indignation of the French scholars condemning Faurisson and his defenders was reasonable, justified, and truly humane; whereas the defense of Faurisson, allegedly based on the unspecified requirements of freedom—is a cold blooded exercise of inhumane reasoning mixed with contempt toward mortals who express their boiling sentiments.

Tolerance should not be interpreted as moral blindness or

scholarly indifference, but as a method of defense of humanity, of human feelings, passions, love of truth, and search for happiness.

VIII.

NEW DANGERS: THE NEW RIGHT AND THE NEW LEFT

1. The New Right and the Old Right

In his review of two books that represent the New Right in the 1980s, Peter Steinfels observes: "I cannot remember a time when political commentators were not discovering a New Right."[1] He refers to a book consisting of a collection of essays under the title, *The New American Right* published by a group of distinguished authors and professors in the 1950's. An enlarged edition of that book, called *The Radical Right,* was republished in 1963. There was much talk of the New Right in connection with the U.S. Republican Party's nomination of Barry Goldwater, the political campaigns of George Wallace, the U.S. presidency of Richard Nixon, the famous speeches of then U.S. Vice President Spiro Agnew, and the emergence of the Silent Majority. One can detect a continuity from Father Coughlin to the Rev. Falwell, Paul Weyrich, Kevin P. Phillips, the presidency of Ronald Reagan, and the proclamations of the Moral Majority.[2]

The concept of the New Right has never been clearly defined, but one could always identify the principal features of their political ideology and the names of their chief representatives. The same may be stated of the latest epiphany of the New Right, although the task of their identification was facilitated by the fact that they themselves used this appellation and entitled their main book: *The New Right Papers.*

The New Right is not merely a neo-conservative movement. It represents more, and at the same time less, than that. The New Right is not a party in the traditional European parliamentary or socialist meaning. The New Right is too amorphous to be a party bound together by an organization and party discipline.

353

On the other hand, one may argue that the New Right is a cohesive social group with an elaborated ideology and a political agenda. The New Right represents a well considered political strategy and tactics and clearly sets forth its most important short and long term political ends. Although the New Right is a movement rather than a party, it still has at its disposal substantial financial resources and connections with many financial centers which can help its leaders to organize and act in a variety of ways.

It may be that the New Right movement is a new political phenomenon of the era of instantaneous mass communication. It illustrates that amorphous new movements can develop independently of political parties. In this discussion the phenomenon of the New Right will be analyzed from one aspect only: the danger it poses to freedom and tolerance.

The emergence of the *New Right* on the American political scene is significant. In this country there have always been political groups to the right of traditional American conservatives, members of both great parties. Very often they have been able to influence policy. The recently formed New Right is, however, different from traditional conservatism.

Thomas Fleming, author of an essay in *The New Right Papers* indicates one of the main distinctions between the New and the Old Right: freedom was the basic issue for the Old Right, whereas for the New Right the "social and moral" issues are fundamental.

Thomas Fleming defines freedom in a truly obsolete and restrictive way: he repeats after Sam Ervin that "the freedom of the individual. . . is simply the right. . . to be free of governmental tyranny."[3] It seems that the author did not notice that other dangers to freedom have emerged in recent centuries.

Thomas Fleming calls freedom a "capitalist idol" which is an abstraction for which the civil and constitutional rights were surrendered.

Here is the presentation of this philosophy of freedom:

> "Our capitalist friends have made an idol of freedom and have invoked its aid to solve every social ill that man is heir to.

But freedom is not god; it is not even something precious like gold, an entity like church, or a condition like goodness. It is just an abstraction—and a negative one at that.''[4]

This is the essence of the *New Right* philosophy: freedom is low on the ladder of their values—after God, gold, church and "goodness." What does "goodness" mean without freedom? Is it not an "abstraction"? No wonder that after such a reevaluation of values, Fleming concludes that the Old Right conservatives "are nothing better than 19th century liberals with a hangover," that they are nearer to the socialists than to the *New Right*.

The old Stalin principle was revived: those who are near, but not with us are the most dangerous, because they are not in the middle of the road, as they pretend to be, but are actually on the other side of the barricade. Stalin used to argue that socialists, liberals, and democrats, are fascists "in essence;" the *New Right* "bolsheviks" argue that the *Old Right "mensheviks"* are "in essence" socialists. The intolerant stance: "he who is not with us, is against us," is characteristic of all extremists.

Thomas Fleming stressed:

Still worse, our worship of the idol of freedom has destroyed the real thing, by forcing us to surrender our civil and constitutional rights to the government that enslaves us all.[5]

Thomas Fleming calls the reforms initiated by the New Deal, ''surrender'' of rights. But these reforms, although not perfect, added rights which made the "idol of freedom" more concrete and substantial, not less so. The right "to hold and dispose of property"[6] can be often regarded an important privilege of free people but by no means is it the sole guarantee or cornerstone of freedom.

The old liberals and conservatives were in favor of constitutional principles based on the separation of powers. Kevin P. Phillips argues that today the American political system as laid down by the founding fathers has become obsolete. The failure of that system produced Watergate (whereas the "liberals" and "others" contend that Watergate proved that the system works) and even worse: defeat in Vietnam and the "break-down of national security."[7]

Even Ronald Reagan's surprising success in 1981 when he had pushed his tax and budget cuts through the "awed Congress" demonstrated the fallibilities of the separation of powers.[8]

Kevin P. Phillips used these examples and numerous quotations from the writings of many authors and politicians from all over the political spectrum in order to substantiate his two theses: the crippling "mechanisms and relationships"[9] in most "American institutions and processes[10] need reform; even the American party system has become so obsolete that both the Republicans and Democrats may no longer be able to revitalize themselves"[11]; the present separation of powers "guarantees" stalemates[12]; American society has entered an era of "balkanization".[13] Therefore: "Power at the *Federal level* must be *augmented*, and lodged for the most part in the *executive branch.*"[14]

One of the means by which the federal executive authority should be augmented and the separation of powers be overcome should be bringing senators and congressmen into the cabinet.[15]

Kevin P. Phillips strikes at the heart of the American concept of separation of powers as one of the most essential arrangements to preserve and protect civil and political liberties. The separation of powers is not perfect and by itself cannot guarantee the survival of democracy in the U.S., but without this system, the framers of the American Constitution believed, individual liberty would be doomed. Kevin P. Phillips is right when he remembers Alvin Toffler's warning that in America, without reforms "bloodshed and totalitarianism"[16] might follow; but the political and institutional reforms which the New Right proposes would not save us from such a disaster. They might delay the alleged outbreak by augmenting the federal power which implies authoritarianism and might easily lead to totalitarianism.

The crisis or paralysis of the American political system is

not caused by the constitutional institutions and processes, but by the new economic forces and by social and political realignments caused by them. Instead of focusing public attention on the well known deficiencies of the system of separation of powers, one should analyze such phenomena as concentration of wealth, links between economic interests and the political process, the new "structural" or "permanent" unemployment, the decline of the old industrial and cultural centers, and the new social diversification. The new economic and social forces have provided the power promoting the pro-centralistic, pro-authoritarian tendencies. The New Right retires easily before those forces at the expense of the American system of liberties. Instead, they should try to improve and reinforce the system of checks and balances if they want to protect the traditional freedom.

"The ideologies of liberalism and conservatism both seem to lack capacity for innovation,"[17] complains Kevin P. Phillips. Maybe he is right; but at least the liberals and the "old" conservatives do not want to discard American constitutional traditions of protecting freedom, tolerance, and justice under law.

The second basic difference between the two "Rights" has to do with the relationship between the state and free enterprise. According to Samuel Francis, the New Right should *openly* reject this "classical liberal principle," the idea of the state being a "watchman," and instead embrace the tactic of the MAR (Middle American Radical) coalition and its allies in the Sunbelt: strong governmental intervention in the development of various branches of industry (energy, defense, aerospace, and . . . agriculture). Kevin Phillips, in his *Post-Conservative American* (Random House, 1983), is even more specific about this issue. He stresses that the New Right prefers governmental power over the free market as an instrument to achieve their economic goals and adds that it was not Ronald Reagan but John Connally, who was a favorite son of the New Right politicians, tried to arrange an open alliance between government and big corporate business.

One can apply to the New Right the famous words of the Republican Presidential candidate, Senator Barry Goldwater: "A government that is big enough to give all you want is big enough to take it away" (Oct. 21, 1964).

This "classic" representative of the Old Right attacked all forms of socialism and the New Deal. Today the situation has changed to such an extent that Goldwater's warning sounds more ominous when applied to those on his right than on his left.

Bruce Bartlett, in his review of *The New Right Papers (Human Events,* August 14, 1982, Vol. XLII, No. 33, p. 14-15 [706-707]), criticizes them from the old traditional conservative positions:

> "Rather than causing them concern, they rejoice at the opportunity to use state power to force people to adhere to their moral and social code."

He rejects as naive the New Right's belief that it pays to add "social and moral" issues to the free economy concept. He concludes:

> "I sincerely hope that people like Thomas Fleming are wrong when they say there are irreconcilable differences between the New Right and the Old Right on the issue of freedom. For if this is the case, there is certainly no question that I will stand on the side of freedom."

Freedom is at stake—this is the common opinion of all those who adhere to the ideas of the Bill of Rights, the traditional American freedoms, and the American way of life.

One of the further distinctive differences between the New Right and traditional American conservatism, even including neo-conservatism, is an almost total rejection of liberalism. Peter Steinfels, in his illuminating monograph, *The Neoconservatives, The Men Who Are Changing America's Politics* (New York: Simon and Schuster, a Touchstone Book, 1979), observed that American conservatism is liberal in its sources and inspiration:

I say this in full awareness of their repeated proclamations of fidelity to liberalism. It is by now a commonplace that we have worked out our history almost entirely within the framework of this one tradition, and that it is now so ingrained we hardly know how to think and talk, at least about public matters, outside of it . . . Yet it should not be forgotten that liberalism itself contains important conservative elements.[18]

It is true that liberalism which was developed in the struggle against feudalism, absolutism, governmental interference, and protectionism contained within itself elements of conservatism from its inception. Nevertheless, for the past two hundred years it has been a progressive, political, economic, and philosophical force. It helped to establish all the western, democratic constitutional political systems. As long as these traditions and constitutional rights and liberties exist, liberalism continues to be a source of social and economic progress. Although its progressive force has diminished, it still powerfully influences the course of events in a world threatened by new and old forms of authoritarianism, despotism, and totalitarianism.

The divergence of the New Right from liberal traditions is a dangerous social phenomenon which should be taken into account not only by the so called traditional Left and Center, but also by those who are to the Right of the Center while adhering to the traditional ideas ingrained in the American Constitution.

The New Right constitutes a danger because in one way or another it tries to undermine such American traditions as individual liberties, the separation of Church and State, the rejection of censorship, and reduction of interference of government in private and social life.

2. Thou Shalt Not Bear False Witness—And The New Right

Terry Dolan, chairman of the National Conservative Political Action Committee, pronounced the following as a *modus operandi* of his organization:

"A group like ours could lie through its teeth, and the candidate it helps stays clean."[19]

Terry Dolan made this candid confession explaining what his group and other similar groups currently acting on the American political scene can do. They do not give money directly to the candidate they support. In this way they bypass the 1974 law prohibiting greater contributions than $5,000.00 per candidate from the same source. These groups spend millions attacking the candidates they oppose. In the American political system where there are practically only two competing candidates, discrediting one of them means an unofficial but very effective support for the other.

Either such groups and activities did not exist before 1974 or they were politically less important. When they emerged in 1980, they immediately became known as big spenders. They injected more than $14 million into the Federal campaigns, very often changing the outcome of certain races in favor of the most "right wing" candidates for the Senate and the House of Representatives.

Although the Republicans were the primary beneficiaries of these efforts and campaigns conducted by the National Conservative Political Action Committee, many of them felt uncomfortable allied with such supporters. Their reservations were voiced by Richard Richards, the chairman of the Republican National Committee. He accused the "independent" spenders of creating "mischief" and stated: "If campaigns are going to be honest, the candidates have to be responsible for everything that is done."[20]

One can argue that there have always been lies in democratic political campaigns and sometimes they have determined results. Without any attempt to justify former lies, it can be said that while analyzing any deceit or fraud, one should always ask questions concerning their quality, quantity, degree, and the scope of their effects. One should always distinguish between an "occasional" lie in a one-to-one race in one district and a systematic campaign of lies prepared and organized nationally from a single center.

There always have been and there always will be politicians in any democracy who are, as Machiavelli called them, *simula-*

tores or *dissimulatores* (liars who assert that something took place which did not happen, or that something did not take place when it really did). There is still a difference between casual individual lying and a special organization which distorts the democratic process by publishing inaccurate information, half-truths, and elaborate lies formulated so that no simple denial will check them. A classic example in this respect is the famous question: When did you stop betraying your wife? Any short answer would partially confirm the accusation implied in the question. During his senatorial campaign George McGovern was accused by the New Right organizations of being a baby-killer. They claimed truthfulness because the senator had favored freedom of abortion, and according to the "pro-life" organizations, a fetus is a full-fledged human being, a baby. George McGovern used to answer that after all he was a happy father and grandfather of many children. His assertion was not even pertinent. McGovern had to fight against Kafkaesque accusations of infanticide while his opponent remained aloof and uncompromised.

When such an organization is free to act throughout the country, if its financial resources are substantial, if it can use news media, the churches, personal telephone calls, if it can endlessly repeat its lies and half-truths[21]—then we have entered a new phase in the evolution of American democratic society, a new period of totalitarian danger.

When Dr. Joseph Goebbels became the Gauleiter (leader) of the Nazi party in Berlin (before Hitler came to power in 1933) and began to popularize his paper *Der Angriff,* he deliberately published the most incredible and horrifying lies about his opponents. He was delighted when his adversaries started to respond or explain. In this way they contributed to his paper's popularity. He was becoming a participant in a public exchange; he gained respectability. The people who did not know very much about the Nazi Party were made to feel that this party was a power, that it was respectable, that it knew something and a prudent person should reckon with its influence.

When Joseph Stalin announced in 1930 that the leaders of

the Communist Revolution in November 1917 were traitors and agents of the capitalist governments, the accusation was mind-boggling, but possibly it was one of the reasons that so many usually critically minded people were inclined to believe it. The same happened about twenty years later when a group of eminent Soviet physicians were accused of conspiracy to kill the Soviet leaders.

When Senator Joseph McCarthy announced that he had in his hands the lists of hundreds of communists who staffed various sensitive U.S. agencies, the press, and cultural institutions, many people believed him without his having produced any evidence. Who dared to imagine that a U.S. Senator might publicly assert that he had certain documents when indeed he did not have them?

The Americans, who deserve a government as good as the people (Jimmy Carter, 1976), due to their goodness, decency, and traditional optimism, are possibly more vulnerable than any other nation when it comes to distinguishing political lies from the truth.

Free political choice can be truly free when the people know as many facts as necessary to make an enlightened decision. Political lies destroy the very opportunity to understand reality. Lies and distortions ruin the foundations of freedom.

Therefore, the tactics of political prevarication and broadcasting of falsehoods in the 1980's may be more disastrous than a superficial observer might assume. Democratic order cannot passively afford to watch or tolerate the resurgence of a Nazi-type campaign of distortion.

3. The New Right and the American Constitution

a. State and Church. Reinterpretation of the First Amendment

The dangers to traditional American liberties created by the New Right, including the Moral Majority, are manifold:

The establishment of a well disciplined centralized organization which mixes religion and politics and tries to justify many political "right-wing" demands with arbitrarily selected quotations from the Bible is an abuse of religious beliefs in itself. The claim that God supports only one special, clearly delineated way of solving existing political problems, that God is a "right winger"—is an attempt to mislead people who are usually genuine and honest believers, but lack special political education and experience to thread their way through the labyrinth of theology and politics. Their innocent ignorance is being exploited. The leaders seem to be contemptuous of their followers' intelligence; this attitude and approach are typically anti-democratic.

The spiritual leaders of the Moral Majority established their organization on the premise that they already represented the majority before their organization's inception and certainly before it was presented to the public. They used the same tactic developed and perfected by the great advertising firms: when a new medication appears on the market they announce that most physicians recommend it; when a book is going to be published and it is predestined by its publisher and his public relations specialists to be a best-seller—it is proclaimed to be a best-seller on the day of its publication and people start to buy it because they want to be familiar with best-sellers. The style of TASS or *Pravda* announcements is well known all over the world. A few hours after an event in the U.S. or Western Europe which does not meet with the Politbureau's approval, the official Soviet news media announce: "the Soviet people unanimously condemn these imperialistic claims." The Soviet people were not asked for their opinion nor did they (with few exceptions) even know that the event had occurred which had already been condemned in their name.

A similar tactic seems to be used by the "apparatchiks" of some of the New Right organizations: they appeared out of the blue sky and announced that they represented the majority of the people at a time when the real majority did not even know that such an organization had come into existence.

The main danger of the "New Right" is that the abuse of their religious beliefs confuses people and induces them to make their political decisions without understanding their substance and without knowing the key elements involved. Clergymen use the prestige of their Churches to influence, sometimes even determine, the outcome of the political process. In this way one of the basic democratic institutions, the separation of church and state, is being undermined.

This specific point was noticed by those who want the Bill of Rights to be honored in this country. Dean Norman K. Wessells of Leland Sanford Jr. University School of Humanities and Sciences stated in his address to a Phi Beta Kappa convocation:

"Our Constitution and constitutional law quite rightly protect religions from governmental or societal interference. But, I fear, they do not equally protect society and the political process when religions turn to lobbying and political pressure.."[22]

Today the First Amendment can and should be interpreted and applied in both ways: protection of the denominations against governmental interference and vice versa, protection of the public against the usurpations of clergymen and their agents. The first European settlers in this country were people who were persecuted by governments trying to impose their own religion on their subjects according to the principle: *cujus regio, ejus religio.* Sometimes the princes deprived people of their rights and privileges without saying in so many words that the purpose of the discrimination was conversion to the religion sponsored by the government. Entire generations of people persecuted for religion left old despotic Europe to come to America, perhaps the only land of liberty at that time.

That is why the First Amendment was seen chiefly as a protection against intrusions of the government. Neither the first Americans nor later generations of immigrants had any experience of being systematically persecuted by anyone other than governments and government-sponsored denominations.

The newcomers knew, of course, that there were many intolerant individuals and groups, but they also thought that these elements would be helpless so long as they lacked the support of the government. These groups after all were only local; their influence and activities were limited socially as well as politically. Anyone being disturbed by them could "liberate" himself by moving elsewhere as the Mormons did or joining another group, either more liberal or more protective.

The Moral Majority is new. Possibly for the first time in U.S. history we see a national organization united by religious precepts and a coherent political program. This is the first national organization of such a type which is seriously reaching for "rule over souls" and political power on the federal, state, and local levels. A victim targeted by them would have a hard time to find a new place to escape or to hide in the U.S. Americans who do not share the ideas of these self-proclaimed defenders of morality have never been in such a danger. New means must therefore be found to protect American freedom and tolerance. New extraordinary circumstances endangering freedom demand new extraordinary means to defend it.

First of all, the enemies of liberty should not enjoy immunity from public criticism. So long as they are on the offensive, so long as they slander certain people and intimidate others, censor libraries, TV programs, and burn books unresisted—they can continue to gain ground to the detriment of freedom enjoyed by all Americans.

The real danger of the New Right crusade depends not so much on the power and depth of the religious beliefs (and prejudices) of the politically naive people caught by surprise, as on the strength of unannounced, undeclared, political alliances.

> Our republic faces one of its very gravest crises . . . in the next two decades, because of the wedding of the very rich, ultraconservative theological groups with politics . . . The unholy merger of theological groups with politics has the potential to infringe upon our freedoms, upon the rights each of us has inherited from our ancestors especially those learned men of the 18th century who expressly separated church and state in America.[23]

The churches and the theologians should enjoy freedom of speech and activity which is guaranteed to every citizen, every group, organization, and political party by the Bill of Rights and the whole network of American jurisprudence. The denominations always participated in public life in various ways and very often expressed their political opinions, usually under cover of morality.[24] But with the emergence of the Moral Majority a new political situation has arisen. This is the first nationally organized religious and political group which has at its disposal the most powerful national media: television, radio, and the press. They can use millions of occasions to propagate their ideas, including prayers in churches and lectures at schools. They can use the most beautiful and respected buildings—the churches, temples, and other edifices.

They are richer than any other political organization and their tax exempt income is skyrocketing. And finally for the first time in the history of the U.S. they seem about to create a national alliance between organized church groups and the new well organized political right wing which encompasses not only small groups of the very rich new conservatives, but also a substantial part of the misled middle-class now in desperate economic straits.

As long as opponents of democracy, freedom, and tolerance are fragmented, a strong democratic system as in the U.S. can survive their criticism and can even become stronger. Once the adversaries of a secular state unite however and begin a concerted campaign of intolerance, then the roots of democracy and freedom are endangered.

The first victim in such a situation must be the very spirit of tolerance in this country.

Professor A. Bartlett Giamatti, the President of Yale University, characterized the Moral Majority in his 1981 address to the freshman class—let me quote him extensively, because it would be difficult to surpass his passionate appeal:

A self-proclaimed "Moral Majority" and its satellite or client groups, cunning in the use of a native blend of old intimidations and new technology, threaten through political pressure or public denunciation whoever dares to disagree with their authoritarian positions. Using television, direct mail and economic boycott, they would sweep before them anyone who holds a different opinion.[25]

And further:

> Those voices of coercion speak not for liberty but for license, the license to divide in the name of patriotism, the license to deny in the name of Christianity . . . they have licensed a new meanness of spirit in our land . . . There is no debate, no discussion, no dissent. They know. There is only one set of over-arching political and spiritual and social beliefs, whatever view does not conform to those views is by definition relativistic, negative, secular, immoral, against the family, anti-free enterprise, un-American . . . What nonsense. What dangerous, malicious nonsense.[26]

At the turn of the century the German philosophers of law introduced a term: *Die normativierende Kraft der Wirklichheit* (the normative power of reality). One can apply this concept *mutatis mutandis* to the presence of intolerant groups: the mere fact of their existence, the perceptible dangers of their attacks are slowly becoming a "normative system." People adjust to possible terror in anticipation of possible harm. This may be one of the most important, hidden elements of the effectiveness of any terror system; intimidation does not start with imprisonment in a cell with or without a number. It starts with the news or rumors that those who are not loyal to the new masters will suffer and pay for their disobedience.

Once it becomes known that somebody has been fired and the newspapers report these facts, in good faith, two purposes of those who exercise moral coercion are achieved: the immediate target is hit and, which is probably even more important, the example will influence the social atmosphere. Those vacillating will start to join the spiritual death squads; the stronger will become more careful and begin to hesitate: the meek get panicky and begin considering collaboration; one more successful blow combined with a speech which hits home and several more of those of "feeble faith" in freedom will follow the path pointed out by the self-anointed spiritual leaders.[27]

b. The Social Issues on the New Right's Agenda

The most important social issues on the New Right's agenda

are the following:

— A ban on abortion; the proclamation that a fetus is a human being who acquires all basic human rights at the moment of conception; restrictions on the sale and use of contraceptives;

— The furthering of clericalism in the school system through the use of various methods: introduction of prayers, financial support for denominational schools through tax-credits for the parents, censorship of school libraries and school-texts, ban on sex-education; introduction of the study of "creation science;"

—A campaign against the ultimate emancipation of women, a fight against the Equal Rights Amendment and similar measures.

The problem of abortion can be discussed from many viewpoints. Our main interest is the question of the freedom of a woman. Is she entitled to control the vital functions of her body, her sexual activity and the planning of her family? Every restriction in this respect (except "restrictions" concerning her physical and mental health—can they rightly be called "restrictions"?), should be regarded an intrusion into the sphere of privacy, and must infringe upon her personal freedom and her right to be happy. The ancient principle (which became popular thanks to Bentham's writings) that individual happiness should be considered the highest criterion of law and morality—is fully applicable to the question of freedom of abortion. No manipulation of the definition of the beginning of life can change the nature of the real issue at stake: the right of a woman to make the most important decision concerning her life in a manner free from governmental constraints.

Of course, a woman who makes her decisions according to her religious beliefs is as free as any other woman, as long as she sincerely believes in the necessity to exercise the requirements of her faith. One can believe that human life starts at any time, but one should refrain from imposing this point of view on others. Obviously it would be against the basic Western concepts of democracy, freedom, and tolerance to make legislative

determinations concerning scientific, moral, and religious dilemmas.

It is one of the principles of Western civilization that whenever there is doubt whether the rights and privacy of the individual should be encroached upon, the rights and persuasions of
an individual should take precedence and should be respected.
The famous argument of the anti-abortionists: if we do not know
when life begins, we should take precautions and therefore we
should protect it—is basically inimical to freedom. Such a question should be posed and solved in the following way: whenever
we have doubts about which solutions are correct, we should opt
for individual freedom, for respecting privacy, for mental and
physical autonomy, for tolerance, these are solutions that can
make individuals happy. *Primum tolerare!*—we have already
tried to substantiate this principle.

Therefore, the preservation of freedom of abortion is an
essential element of the whole process of freedom, of social and
moral sanity.

The anti-abortionists claim that they represent morality and
humanism against promiscuity and genocide. Indeed, they are
in the worst company from the historical point of view. In the
20th century the totalitarian states were the most efficient in the
terroristic protection of unwanted pregnancy. Both fascist states
and the Stalinist Soviet Union regarded the unborn as objects to
be guarded by the police. Women in all totalitarian states are
treated as child-bearing machines and the young are viewed as
future cannon fodder.

Truly civilized respect for life should include care for the
quality of the lives of those who will be born. Considerations
about human life should not be reduced to the bare physical
existence. Those who so often refer to the Holy Scriptures to
fight against freedom for woman and her right to plan her family,
do not want to remember the Gospel's assertions: a man lives
not by bread alone. In our world, in which so many nations and
so many parents are unable to secure even bread for their
children, they should not be compelled to bear the consequences
of any unwanted pregnancy.

The inevitable results of a ban on abortion have been tragic from every point of view: for individuals, for their families, and for the whole fabric of society. Such a ban is accompanied by prosecution of offenders; one set of standards is applied to the poor—another to those who are better off and can afford expensive, if illegal, medical intervention. Those who are unhappy are persecuted also: the women who had an abortion because of natural reasons are investigated—insult is added to injury.

Police all over the world are unable to check real criminals, the number of crimes is increasing; it is folly to add the burden of prosecuting artificially created offenders. Many police departments do not and will not even bother to enforce such laws—such a negligence in law enforcement must be demoralizing in itself.

Whatever the authorities are doing or not doing in enforcing anti-abortion laws, the cause of freedom must suffer; the atmosphere of tolerance is poisoned.

c. Prayers in Schools

Motto: "And when you pray, you shall not be as the hypocrites are." (*Matt. VI, 5*).

In order to illustrate the way of thinking of those who favor prayers in school, we will analyze several typical pronouncements.

Connaught Marshner, Chairperson of the *National Pro-Family Coalition* said in an interview with James M. Perry, Washington bureau correspondent covering politics for *The Wall Street Journal:*

Suppose that you are a working class person . . . you want your children to grow up knowing right from wrong. . . . you know that many schools have real problems with drug users and violent youths, and you believe with your whole heart that the schools would be better off if a prayer were said at the beginning of the day . . .[28]

The thinking here is as simplistic as that of a backward, uneducated peasant: he who prays is decent and keeps himself and others from sin; he who does not start the day with prayers is open to temptation and must be worse off, sharing the evil with others with whom he associates (especially in the same classroom). One has the constitutional right to think this way and to recommend prayers on any occasion, but one should not impose one's piety on others; nobody should be compelled either to participate in, or even to be a spectator at, religious rites. This elementary sort of freedom seems to be unknown to the *Pro-Family Coalition*. The idea that one should not be disturbed by other peoples' prayers or customs is one of the earliest achievements of our civilization. Pericles in his funeral oration, praising the Athenian democratic system, felt it necessary to stress: "We do not get upset with our next-door neighbor if he enjoys himself in his own way, nor do we give him the kind of black looks which, though they do no real harm, still do hurt people's feelings. We are free and tolerant in our private lives . . ."[29]

New Right followers should really be reminded of certain sentences from the Bible. In the Sermon on the Mount, Jesus describes as hypocrites those who publicly manifest their devotion instead of praying privately in their own rooms.

> And when you pray, you shall not be as the hypocrites are: for they love to pray standing in the synagogues and in the corners of the streets, that they may be seen of man. Verily I say unto you, they have their reward. But you, when you pray enter your closet, and when you have shut the door, pray to your Father which is in secret; and your Father which seeth in secret shall reward you openly. (*Matt,* VI, 5-6)

This is one of those great recommendations of the Holy Scriptures which makes these books a treasure not only for believers but also for all non-sectarians and humanists whose aim has always been the promotion of a truly humane relationship among people. The comparison between these ideas contained in the Bible and the ostentatious militant piety of the New Right shows that the new pharisees do not really care for their own Bible, they select from it what at the given moment fits either their simple minds or their political aims. Connaught

Marshner in a later part of the interview complained that candidate Ronald Reagan made believe that he felt the same way as the *Pro-Family Coalition:*

> "And nearly a year later, you haven't heard anything about it
> . . . A note of cynicism creeps in, and you think this President is
> not different from any other, and maybe you'll go back to voting
> Democratic next year after all."

It is significant that the author of these words, who is not a "simple" worker but the chairman of an influential national coalition, does not even mention the First Amendment to the American Constitution. Of course, she knows that the principle of the separation of State and Church does not allow prayers in the public schools. She knows also that any attempt to introduce them by the Congress or by the President would be a violation of one of the most traditional and sacred American values: the faithful observance of the Constitution. Why suddenly do we need to violate the Consitution or amend it in a way which contradicts the American way of life, the way of freedom and tolerance?

These basic questions remain unanswered. The only element of truth in the words of the chairman of the *National Pro-Family Coalition* is the reminder that candidate Ronald Reagan used to indicate that he agreed with these demands. The leaders and the foot-soldiers of such coalitions really helped him to win the nomination and the election. Now, after their victory they think they have earned the right to compensation. The question is whether the President is obliged to keep unconstitutional promises?

The problem of school prayers should also be analyzed from the point of view of an important political principle: avoid whenever and wherever possible friction between various philosophies, political approaches, and attitudes. Laws are not for angels but for real people who were brought up in many different traditions, customs, and prejudices, who have many contradictory interests; who are rather less than more tolerant and understanding. A reasonable legislator who has good will and truly seeks order and cooperation in his bailiwick will try to legislate so as to avoid divisions. He will shelve all proposals which might multiply misunderstandings and conflicts. He will do his best to diminish opportunities for misinterpretation and acts of bad will, but instead will endeavor to enhance the possibilities for friendly cooperation. Briefly, a good legislator should avoid in advance the predictable dangers and undesired effects of his acts and wishful thinking.

We live in a strange period when very often the most profound and far-seeing political analyses are done by those who are usually regarded as not very serious writers: the satirists and humorists.

Art Buchwald in a column: *Prayer in Schools* (published May 14, 1982) depicts the following possible scenario after the adoption of the constitutional amendment legalizing prayer in schools:

"All right, children, we will now open with a morning prayer. Those sinners who don't believe in God can either stand in the back of the room with their faces to the wall or hide in the clothes closet.

"Come, you little Bolsheviks, hurry up so the rest of us can get on with seeking divine guidance. Where are you going, Tony?"

"I'm going to the back of the room. I already prayed at home this morning."

"And you think that's enough?"

"It's enough for me."

"Look at Tony, children. He is a perfect example of a secular humanist. He'd rather stand in the back of the room than pray to God. Does anyone know where Tony is going to wind up with his attitude?"

"In hell."

"Very good, Charles. And who will he find in hell?"

"Satan."

"He'll make him feed the flames of a fiery furnace, and Tony will have to wear a tail, and he'll be screaming all the time and fighting off snakes, but it won't do him any good."

"That's absolutely right, Enid. Who knows what else will happen to him?"

"Blackbirds will peck his eyes out, and he'll have a stomach ache all the time, and his toes will drop off."

"Very good, Everett. Well, what do you have to say to that, Tony?"

"I'd still rather stand in the back of the room."

"Are there any other Communists in the class who would like to join him?" All right, Tony, you seem to be the only one. Go to the back, and I don't want to see your ugly face until I tell you to take your seat. Now, class, let us bow our heads and pray for Tony's soul! Heavenly Father, there is always one rotten apple in the barrel . . ."

There is hope that if the proposed amendment to the US Constitution is adopted such scenarios will not happen very often.[30] But one can reasonably assume that there are many bigots in our country who will try to impose their beliefs (and prejudices) on helpless young students whenever an opportunity is given to them. The history of religion, as we know, is a chain of persecutions and impositions. The fact that there is a new wave of religious (supported by national and racial) fanaticism all over the world, is not a good omen. It seems that today wherever a possibility exists for friction or conflict connected with religious beliefs, such friction and conflict will arise. Murphy's law applies to socio-religious relations: whatever can go wrong, will.

d. Censorship of Books

Since the emergence of the new wave of religiosity an ominous movement started all over the country—religious zealots have begun to use various institutions and all available avenues in order to censor books in school-libraries. Many classics have fallen prey to the militant bigots. For instance: Kurt Vonnegut Jr.: *Slaughterhouse-Five,* Bernard Malamud: *The Fixer,* Eldridge Cleaver: *Soul on Ice,* and dozens of others.

In several little neighborhoods the confiscated books were burned at an improvised stake. The participants and onlookers either did not know or had forgotten the wisdom which has become common today: where books are burnt, people will be burnt as well.

State and local authorities very often behave with duplicity, sometimes they facilitate and even encourage such actions.

A special opportunity to censor books was created by Texas legislators. They did it in a very specific way that is becoming more and more typical: a little known, seemingly unimportant act of the executive or legislative branch undermines the constitutional provisions and the spirit of tolerance while officially proclaiming adherence to the democratic process and praising it. When the functions of government are legally expanded in a way which is difficult to notice by an average citizen, then the New Right militants who were silently working behind the scenes in order to pass such an act step into the new opening. They are the first on the battlefield and they are well prepared to fight in the approaching campaign.

Wherever there is a loophole in the existing laws protecting traditional American liberties, the opponents of these freedoms try to squeeze in. Whenever legislators create the slightest opening to allow some kind of censorship, the censors will be born and will march in.

An opportunity to censor school-books seems to have been deliberately created by the Texas authorities.

In a Proclamation the Texas State Board of Eduction stated in 1982:

> Textbook content shall promote citizenship and the understanding of the free-enterprise system, emphasize patriotism and respect for recognized authority . . .
>
> Textbook content shall not encourage life-styles deviating from generally accepted standards of society.

These recommendations are so vague that they could serve the cause of education, freedom, democracy, and citizenship; but the same vagueness can be interpreted in the spirit of repression and intolerance. One could even argue that such vague recommendations are asking rather for an interpretation which is contrary to the Constitutional principles; otherwise no one would have been interested in pressing them. What does the expression, to promote "the understanding of the free-enterprise system" mean? Should the students at school be taught that any restrictions upon private property, even when made by Congress, are bad? Should they be taught that the ideas of the New Deal or Great Society were basically wrong? an aberration?

What are the ideals of "citizenship" which are not contained in the Constitutions of the United States or the State of Texas? Once we accept the idea that the government should not usurp any power which is not afforded to it by the Constitution, then any proclamation concerning "textbook content" can influence the interpretation and the application of the First Amendment in a restrictive way. Examples are abundant.

Norma Gabler (Longview, Texas) regularly criticizes proposed textbooks during public hearings. Her activity and her organization, *Educational Research Analysts,* have won public admiration by the New Right leaders—Rev. Jerry Falwell and Phyllis Schlafly. In 1982, during hearings, she objected to the paragraph in one of the books which listed beneficial qualities of certain drugs, like insulin for diabetes, because such information may "instill" in students' minds that "the term drugs refers to a beneficial product." She further objected to another book, because there was a chapter entitled: "When things go wrong." Her demand was that there should also be a positive chapter called "When things go right."[31]

And she also objected to a history book because of "an unnecessarily large number of pictures of people protesting."[2]

Paul Mathews, a member of the State Board of Education, and supporter of Gabler's organization, which she runs together with her husband, commented:

"I feel the Gablers are doing a great service. They're ferreting out slang, vulgarities and also things that are unpatriotic."[33]

This is a typical narrow-minded interpretation of patriotism: a patriot is a person who is optimistic, does not protest, does not even use such words as "drug," because it could evoke undesirable resonances.

There are strong indications that the procedure adopted by the Texas State Board of Education was conceived in bad faith as far as freedom, tolerance, and truth are concerned. They did not allow favorable testimony during the hearings but only critical, hostile opinions, about the proposed texts. Therefore, other organizations, such as non-denominational PFAW (People for the American Way), representing 82,000 teachers nationwide (2,500 members in Texas), had no opportunity to present their views. The board which makes the final selection of the texts, did not have the benefit of listening to contradictory opinions; such a procedure is more similar to an inquisition than a democractic hearing.

No wonder, therefore, that the intellectual quality of Gabler's arguments is so poor; where rebuttals and free exchange of views do not take place, nothing creative can be produced. The procedure for selecting texts adopted by the Texas Board of Education could rightly be called organized intolerance.

Ovida Whiteside an English teacher in Austin, Texas, commented: "We all sat back for a long time and thought the whole thing was a joke. Suddenly we realized we'd been had."[34]

One of the main reasons why the followers of reason, rationality, tolerance, and freedom lose battles and wars against obscurantism, is the fact that they underestimate the power of unchecked ignorance and prejudice.

* * *

In connection with the nomination of Sandra Day O'Connor to the Supreme Court, the anti-abortionists fervently distributed their own "Declaration of the People of America" which, according to the intentions of its authors, should be on the desk of every American judge and from which these judges would learn that they (the judges) are "ayatollahs of paganism" that they are "fawned upon by a cowardly, purchased press."

Such invective and vituperation, addressed generally to all American judges, is the result of one factor only: the judges try to observe the Constitution and rule in accordance with interpretations given by the Supreme Court. It means that judges in this democratic country are giving Caesar what is Caesar's; is that un-christian? Is it not un-American, as Senator Howard Metzenbaum observed, to judge American judges on the basis of one issue, abortion, on the basis of one arbitrarily selected criterion? How can one honestly compare the Ayatollah's type of atrocities with the American courts—one of the greatest democratic institutions ever created by our civilization?

At best, the comparisons are foolish. They are rather a product of fanaticism, of political zeal which is as extreme as it is irrational. It is madness, but there is a method to it, it is not sheer stupidity. Such methodically organized madness on a national scale, is a result of the deep economic and social, political and moral crisis existing in the western societies. In every period of decline the true social majority loses it cohesion, while others take advantage of the ensuing confusion. The new form of intellectual darkness is a reflection of the thinking—let us use the expression of McAteer—of "intellectual barbarians." The "madness" of the "new radicals" is a part of the general retreat from the Kingdom of Reason.

4. Conclusion: Is "Apple-Pie Authoritarianism" Feasible?

Kevin P. Phillips in his book *The Emerging Republican Majority* predicted that the new affluent middle-class group living in the Sun Belt is bound "to cast a lengthening national shadow" on the political arena.[35]

A dozen years later, Kevin P. Phillips elaborated that today's Sun Belt middle-class represents "a confluence of Social Darwinisim, entrepreneurialism, high technology, nationalism, nostalgia and fundamentalist religion." These social, economic, and moral features of the new "radical" middle-class determine their potential *"to accommodate a drift toward apple-pie authoritarianism." (emphasis added)*[36]

The drift toward "native," "original," "100% American" authoritarianism is perhaps authentic but it is dangerous. It is no consolation that it will be an *"apple-pie"* authoritarianism; political liberties will be restricted and mortally endangered.

A similar movement may succeed in Western Europe.

Walter Laquer anticipates a new drift toward authoritarianism in Europe. He is afraid that the European societies facing a crisis of survival "will voluntarily surrender *some of the freedom*" (emphasis added) and that a new balance will emerge "between the rights of the individual and the interests of society."

The real issue is that under the regime of new authoritarianism, societies will not merely surrender "some of the freedom," but also the basic effects of the gradual Western evolution toward freedom and tolerance, a development which took centuries may suffer a severe setback for a very long time. Even if many of the ideologues, politicians, preachers, and officers of the New Right, in the U.S. and Europe, do not want such results and would like to avoid them, they objectively help to create and support powerful social forces which no sorcerer will be able to tame or subdue without great suffering and social retrogression.

The danger of the New Right lies not so much in the power and attractiveness of its ideas as in the weakness of those who oppose it. We live in a period when the traditional political and social center is weak and unimaginative. Certain liberal concepts have become obsolete. West European socialism has been unable to develop anything new to compare with Keynesianism, the New Deal, or the Welfare State. The radical left and especially various forms of Soviet and Chinese communism are totally compromised because of their complete economic failure and totalitarianism.

In a period when democratic, progressive forces in the western world have been unable to develop a constructive program to appeal to the masses, the danger of the New Right increases.

There already are a number of authors who have observed that as an antidote to the New Right the "Left" has "virtually ceased to exist."[37]

The situation is even more complicated by the fact that the representatives of democracy and progress have been incapable of elaborating a constructive alternative to the Soviet or Chinese types of communism. We live in a world in which there are no realistic, well elaborated, and appealing alternatives to the New Right or the radical (old and new) Left. In the meantime, the two radical extremes have been feeding each other, becoming an increasing threat to democracy, freedom, and tolerance.

* * *

From the sociological viewpoint, the social basis of the New Right constitutes the MAR—Middle American Radicals, according to Samuel T. Francis.[38] MAR's characteristics are the following: A MAR's family had an average income up to $13,-000 in the mid-1970s; they usually lacked college education and high professional skills. MAR are twice as common in the South as in the North-Central states. They are less identifiable as a class from the objective point of view, but more because of their "subjectively distinguished temperament."[39] Their main political beliefs narrow down to the following:

> "The rich give in to demands of the poor, and the middle income people have to pay the bill."[40]

This attitude, argues Samuel T. Francis, expresses "a sense of resentment and exploitation" (broader than economic) directed upward and downward; they feel frustrated, mistrust the authorities, the current decision-makers and the ruling elites.

They reject socialism and liberalism; the latter is for them "semi-collectivist" and "cosmopolitan"; the "modern liberals," according to them, favor big government which manipulates social and economic processes in favor of the poor, but ultimately for the benefit of the elites in corporations and the bureaucracy. The MAR want to fight the qualities of the present social and political structures because of their: "ossification," "decadence," "inertia," and especially because of their "clearly foreign," "alien" ideologies.[41]

The remedy proposed by the New Right, expressing the wishes and interests of the MARs should be:

> In place of the hedonistic, pragmatist, relativist, and secularized cosmopolitan of the present elite, the New Right should expound *without compromise* (emphasis added) the ideals and

the institutions of the American ethos: hard work and self-sacrifice, morally based legislation and policies, and a public commitment to religious faith.[42]

How can these "ideals" be achieved? The author has only one concrete answer: the constitutional system should be changed:

> In place of the faith in congressional supremacy and established intermediary institutions that characterizes both the Old Right and the entrenched managerial elite, the New Right will favor a populist-based Presidency able to cut through the present oligarchical establishment and to promote new intermediary institutions centered on Middle America.[43]

Well, it means that America can be saved by a presidential "Duce" who will secure the right choice between "degeneration and rebirth, between death and survival."[44] The dramatization of the choice is deliberate. It indicates the sense of urgency justifying a state of emergency. The true, traditional American ideals of freedom and tolerance, of coopertion and compromise, have been lost in these diatribes.

The program of the New Right is predominantly a reaction against the social reforms started by Franklin D. Roosevelt and continued in various ways until almost the end of Carter's presidency.

Instead of appealing to the reason and conscience of the thinking voter, the New Right tries rather to play on their irrational feelings and fears; William A. Rusher's observation is very revealing:

> At bottom, however, I suspect that the most important contribution of the New Right to the cause of conservatism is neither theoretical nor technical, but emotional. There is something in the sheer passion of the members of the New Right that is impossible to weigh, but which unquestionably has an impact on events. It is related to the adjective most often applied to them as a group—"feisty".[45]

Every political party and movement appeals not only to the reason but also to the feelings of people. If the emotions can be reasonably explained and supported by an analysis which meets the logical criterion that the result can be seen "clearly and distinctly"—then the emotional attitude can be helpful in the perpetual struggle for freedom and justice. If, however, emotions are evoked by fears, prejudices, or vengefulness, then the cause of common sense and freedom is endangered and can suffer irreparable losses.

The remarks of Thomas Fleming are significant in this respect:

> "It never occurs to them (Northern capitalists—M.M.) that political man lives by *myths* . . . We have lost nearly all of our conservative *myth*. . . The only *real conservative myth* left to Americans is *the South*. It is a fairy tale place, of strong courageous men and gentle but determined ladies. . . where the Constitution is respected more than progress . . .[46]

Thus the mythology of the South was added to the glossary of such mythical ideas as the Russian "dusha" (soul) and German "Volksgeist" (people's spirit) which have evoked so many emotions, although no author or politician ever tried to explain them rationally. They occupy a special place in the history of aggression, war, persecution, and human suffering.

Therefore, one should always beware of those who appeal to and depend on emotions not supported by a rational political program, one which is able to persuade critically minded citizens.

Hegel observed that the great social and political changes marking the end of an era repeat themselves twice: for the first time they signal a new phenomenon and then they are regarded as something accidental; the second appearance persuades people that the new fundamental changes were historically inevitable.

Fascist authoritarianism reigned over a great part of Europe between the two world wars. Should the drift toward new authoritarianism of the New Right be interpreted as a Hegelian omen that the era of Western liberties has come to an end?

One can also argue otherwise: the defeat of fascism and possible end to the dangers of the New Right could serve as proof that the ideas of freedom, tolerance, democracy, and progress are invincible and are now flourishing more than ever before.

Professor Philip Green was right when he observed in his review of Phillip's book:

> Phillip's fearful scenario is not beyond possibility. It is just unlikely. . . At the moment, therefore, it would be going too far to say that the stench of an American version of fascism is in the air . . . The odor is detectable though. And whatever the outcome, along the way a lot of damage will almost certainly be done to the liberal values of tolerance, cosmopolitanism, freedom of choice and, yes, secular humanism.[47]

The forces of freedom are still too powerful in the Western democracies and the people can overcome the approaching dangers.

5. Liberation and Tolerance in the New Left Ideology— Herbert Marcuse

For a quarter of a century, a movement called the New Left has attracted attention in the West. It reached its apogee in 1968, marked by mass demonstrations against Gaullism in France and American involvement in Vietnam. The New Left started with great hopes. It promised to show humanity a new road: non-capitalist and non-communist. It promised new freedom and democracy, unknown in the East and in the West. It announced a new type of revolutionary movement without the leadership of a party and without bureaucracy. It declared a new struggle for justice and equality.

In the 1970's this ephemeral movement disintegrated. Its remnants turned to terrorist activity, which they tried to justify with an incoherent pastiche of leftist slogans picked up at random from traditional socialist and Marxist literature.

The New Left had indeed one important and representative philosopher, Herbert Marcuse. He was the only one to express in a theoretical way the most important New Left positions. He was the philosophical brain of the New Left; the movement did not survive him.

From the intellectual point of view, the New Left philosophy of freedom and liberation does not deserve the detailed analysis presented in this chapter. This doctrine is, however, historically significant because Herbert Marcuse made an effort to elaborate a leftist theory of liberation and fundamental social changes which were neither communist nor capitalist, neither liberal nor "revisionist." His total failure deserves to be noticed.

a. Herbert Marcuse as a New Left Ideologue.

After World War II, Marcuse did not confine himself to universities and libraries. He was active in contemporary political life, expressed his opinions about the most important topical issues, like co-existence between East and West, the armaments race, the war in Vietnam, the students' demonstrations, and even about the cases of Lieutenant Calley[48] and Angela Davis.[49]

He criticized without reservation Eastern and Western societies at a time when so many thinking people in both systems were disillusioned with information, interpretation, and propaganda. He praised freedom in his own way in an epoch when freedom had been endangered on every continent.

Marcuse's strong card was the ambiguity of his theories. It seems like a paradox, but every epoch adds new proof that vagueness of expression can often be helpful in winning public attention.

There is another specifically sociological reason for Marcuse's immense popularity: the public, and especially critically minded students, were bored with descriptive sociology and political science, without teeth, which then dominated the academic East as well as the West.

Marcuse did not solve the problems, but in a turbulent period he was able to pose the right questions.

There is no doubt that Marcuse's intentions were humanistic. Many aspects of his critical analysis, especially concerning American society and Soviet Marxism, are intellectually stimulating. He was an authority on the philosophy of Hegel, Marx, and Freud. It is even widely held that his *Eros and Civilization* constitutes a most radical synthesis of Freud and Marx.[50]

But the value of his books and essays must be judged apart from the intentions of their author. To assess all the aspects of Marcuse's philosophy would not be useful for our subject. Only certain crucial problems have been selected.

Herbert Marcuse regarded himself a creative Marxist. In almost every one of his books he stressed that his analysis was based on dialectical and historical materialism.

He claimed that he was not bound by the conclusions of his predecessors, but only by the "spirit" of their writings, by their methodological approach, which he himself applied to the interpretation of the new phenomena of post-industrial capitalism, of the Communist bloc, and the anti-colonial revolutions.

There were various stages and trends in the creative life of Marcuse. *Reason and Revolution* is one of the first and at the same time one of the most abstract and "Hegelian" of his monographs. His *One-Dimensional Man* was written in the period of the growth of the New Left and should rightly be considered his most important treatise. *An Essay on Liberation, Repressive Tolerance* and many articles articulate forcefully the need for an anti-capitalist and anti-bureaucratic revolution.

One of his last works, *Counter-revolution and Revolt* (1972), summarized his political ideas and elaborated them, as he asserted himself, for the period of the advanced "counter-revolution" and the decline of leftist movements in the developed Western democracies.

b. Marcuse's New Revolutionary Liberation

Marcuse believed in the inevitability of the collapse of advanced capitalist societies despite their accelerating technical progress, expanding Gross National Product, and rising standard of living. To him these elements are an obstacle to the development of the revolutionary forces.

> To sum up: the highest stage of capitalist development corresponds, in the advanced capitalist countries, to a low of revolutionary potential.[51]

At the same time he expressed a typical Marxian conviction that capitalism in any event would extend the mass base for revolution and for the revival of the *"radical ... goals of socialism."*[52]

Marcuse rejected Marx's old thesis that the working class was the most revolutionary class because this concept had become obsolete. The new working class has become part of bourgeois society, has been transformed into a conservative force. But history created *new* forces which have picked up the standard of revolution: students and national minorities.

Marcuse emphasized that in the West the "bourgeois democratic" phase of capitalism has terminated and a new period of *preventive* counter-revolution has begun. The forces of law and order have been made "a force above the law,"[53] the police in capitalist countries resemble the Nazi SS; undercover agents have blanketed countries, parliaments have been emasculated, the soil is being prepared "for a subsequent fascist phase."[54]

> Escalation (of terror—M. M.) is built into the system and accelerates the counter-revolution unless it is stopped in time.

How should one fight for the new genuine revolution and true liberation? How can the world of exploitation, alienation, and oppression be overcome? Marcuse answered that liberation will result from a *genuine* socialist revolution, from *true* socialist reforms. He presented his basic ideas in this respect in two essays: *Reexamination of the Concept of Revolution*[55] and *An Essay on Liberation.*[56]

The Marxian theory of the Socialist Revolution was, Marcuse declared, correct for previous historical periods only. Karl Marx thought that the revolution had to be initiated in advanced industrial societies, it would be a result of an economic crisis, and would be carried out by "large scale" mass action of the working class, leading to the "dictatorship of the proletariat as a transitory stage."[57] Collective ownership of the means of production by the "immediate producers" would be secured.

According to Marcuse, this concept of revolution contains two democratic presuppositions:
—the revolution would be carried out by a majority of the

population;
—political democracy offers the most favorable condition for the organization of the proletarians and for fostering their class-consciousness.

> The Marxian concept of revolution also implies continuity in change: development of the productive forces contained by capitalism, taking over the technology and of the technical apparatus by the new producers.[58]

In the second half of this century conditions changed, according to Marcuse, so radically, that the *whole* theory of revolution should be changed. Not only its separate parts or elements should be reexamined, but the entire theory, and especially the very problem of the *"redefinition"* of Socialism, of the new *qualitative notion* of Socialism as a definite negation of capitalism.[59]

The social basis for the potential revolution was recently extended as a result of the national liberation movements in the "Third World." Marcuse thought that this thesis was his contribution to an updated Marxism-Leninism. In the old Marxian theory—he pointed out—the peoples in the colonial and backward areas were regarded mainly as "adjuncts," "allies," "a reservoir" (Lenin's term) for the western proletarians and were seen as the primary historical agent of revolution.[60] Not so today:

> ... we are confronted with a *tripartite division* of historical forces *which cut across the division into the First, Second, and Third World.* The contest between capitalism and Socialism divides the Third World too, and, as a new historical force, there appears what may be called (and what is thus called by the New Left) an alternative to the capitalist as well as to the established Socialist societies, namely the struggle for a different way of socialist construction, a construction "from below," but from a "new below" not integrated into the value system of the old societies—a new socialism of cooperation and solidarity, where men and women determine collectively their needs and goals, their priorities, and the method and pace of "modernization."[61]

Let us observe at the beginning of our analysis that Marcuse here commits one of the typical errors of many allegedly "leftist," "democratic," "progressive," and "liberal" thinkers who, while extolling the virtues of the oppressed ex-colonial nations, never ask the simple question: How can it be supposed that relatively backward peoples can be an example of a *democratic* revolution (a revolution from a "new below"? what does this mean?) and of the "socialism of cooperation and solidarity," when the more developed European nations have been unable to organize such a society? It seems that Marcuse's theory is a new edition of the theory that the center of the revolution has been moving to the East. According to Lenin and Stalin it moved to Moscow; according to Mao, to Peking; according to Marcuse, it is moving to the Southern Hemisphere despite his continued insistence that the working class still remains (in essence? in potential?) the "main agent of the revolution."[62]

The second Marxian concept of revolution, wrote Marcuse, which has now become old-fashioned, was his contention that the revolution would be carried out by the *majority* of the exploited masses. Today the revolution in the metropolitan centers must be "synchronized" with the revolution of national liberation movements; there must emerge an alliance of militant intelligentsia (students) and working class groups liberated from integrated unions.[63]

The future revolution will be a result of a crisis of the system of affluence and "superfluity," which will "spontaneously" disintegrate the whole structure; there will be a "general loosening of cohesion."[64] This crisis should not be seen as a "narrow" "national" crisis within one country, but as a crisis on a world scale, because the internal contradictions assert themselves on a "global scale."[65]

There is one more difference between the concept of revolution of Marx and Engels and of Marcuse: Marx and Engels anticipated that the revolution would occur in the industrialized, developed Western countries, whereas Marcuse combined Stalin and Trotsky: he took from Stalin the idea of the general crisis of capitalism and from Trotsky the idea that the revolution must be permanent and will last up to its victory in the last country and island.

Now let us examine what economic and political changes would take place in the liberated world.

The answers of Marcuse, like those of Marx and Lenin before him, are extremely vague:

a) There will be a "total transvaluation of values, transformation of needs and goals,"[66] as for example, relating to tolerance (we deal with this point in a special paragraph later).

b) There will be a "break" and a "rupture," not only of the "continuation of domination" but even:

> a break with the continuity of the technical apparatus of productivity which, for Marx, would extend (freed from capitalist abuse) to the socialist society. Such "technological" continuity would *constitute a fateful link between capitalism and socialism,* because this technical apparatus has, in its very structure and scope, become an apparatus of control and domination.[67]

Marcuse regarded as part of the apparatus of domination not only the political and administrative apparatus of the capitalist state as did Marx and Lenin, but also the whole apparatus of trade, commerce, industry, and public utilities. Lenin even recommended that such a capitalist apparatus as the banking system be entirely preserved (except for general managers and presidents who are not employees but owners only), but for Marcuse almost every organization is entirely political, exercising "control and domination" and deserving to be *"aufgesprengt,"* blasted or blown-up. He is more radical than Marx and Lenin combined, showing in this way that he is even less practical than his intellectual mentors.

c) What will happen after the revolutionary "rupture"? *Cutting this link,* Marcuse wrote, would mean not to regress in technical progress, but to reconstruct the technical apparatus in accordance with the needs of free men, guided by their own consciousness and sensibility, by their autonomy. "This autonomy calls for a decentralized apparatus of national control on a reduced basis—reduced because no longer inflated by the requirements of exploitation, aggressive expansion, and competition, held together by *solidarity* in cooperation."[68]

It is nonsense to suppose that after "blowing-up" the technical apparatus there would be no "regression." And how should the new apparatus (—*nota bene*: it would still be an apparatus, although a new one!—) be built up in order to prevent it from degeneration into an apparatus of domination? Marcuse does not explain.

Indeed, Marcuse's concept of an apparatus that would no longer be an "apparatus of domination" is a repetition of the utopian idea of Engels, expressed in *Anti-Dühring,* that in the future Communist society control of man would be replaced by the "control of things." In the process of production there is a continuous interrelation between a) the individual and nature, and b) between cooperating persons. Even in the most rudimentary organization of labor there must be management and control which can be exercised more or less democratically or despotically, but "supervision" and "hierarchy" there must be, because it belongs to the nature of the process of production.

Marcuse calls for the decentralization of the apparatus, suggesting that decentralization would greatly promote democracy. Why? There is no direct link between decentralization and democracy. The process of centralization in the modern world was not the result of the capricious whim of big business or of Soviet bureaucracy; it has been an inevitable result of technical progress, of enormous industrial projects, of super jets, hydroelectric dams, atomic energy, and the need to mobilize millions of workers to carry these gigantic projects out. There are, of course, in the West and the East, tendencies to decentralize, but a high degree of centralization is inevitable, and what is necessary, as Hegel wrote, is also reasonable and real. Instead of denouncing centralization in general it would be better to try to find out what the relationship between centralization and decentralization should be in particular circumstances, in a given country or branch of production. Not every centralization is a step backward, not every decentralization is progress. All depends on historical circumstances.

d) Which social forces will carry out the revolution?

These forces, answered Marcuse, would not coincide with "traditional classes," they will *emerge* during the revolutionary crisis from the opposition among "intelligentsia, especially the students" and the "politically articulate and active groups among the working classes."

These two revolutionary groups are weak and their weakness is "expressive of the new historical constellation which defines the concept of the revolution;" they will fight:

1. Against the majority of the integrated population, including that of the "immediate producers";

2. Against a well-functioning, prosperous society which is "neither in a revolutionary nor a pre-revolutionary situation."[69]

The conclusion is clear: the anti-capitalist revolution advocated by the New Left would be a revolution of the *minority* against the *majority*, which is today prosperous, does not want change, and certainly does not want to be "liberated" from their ease and affluence. Will not the ruling minority be compelled by the course of events to use "revolutionary" terror and domination? In this theory of revolution much is unclear, especially its vision of the future.

How should "collective ownership" be organized and run in an "unbureaucratic way?" What are the possible alternatives to Soviet "state property" or Yugoslav "workers' councils?" And how would a "democracy" of a minority against the majority function? How is it possible that Marcuse's future government will avoid recourse to terror?

Marcuse provides us no answer in his books concerning the practical, legal, political, or institutional conclusions he has drawn from the degeneration of the Soviet-style bureaucracy. It was hardly sufficient merely to declare: "We are against these distortions, we will build a new free life in another way." A responsible thinker or a statesman should explain what he intends to do on the basis of common sense and experience. Good will counts from the moral and religious point of view, but not from the political.

The fact that Khrushchev, Gomulka, Kadar, and Husak

condemned the "errors" and "crimes" of Stalin does not mean that they were genuine anti-Stalinists, or that they had found or adopted qualitatively different theoretical or practical policies.

Marcuse seemed to be sincerely opposed to Stalinism, but his anti-capitalist phraseology offered no alternatives to "Stalinism" or to the "distortions" of Mao's cultural revolution. At the end of our century when a philosopher of revolution fails to declare what he expects the legal, administrative, and institutional embodiments of his ideas should be, his ideas should be regarded as wishful thinking and not more scientific, say, than the Holy Scripture's command to "love thy neighbor" or Kant's imperative that man should always be the end and not the means of our activity.

The theory of revolution of Marcuse, is rather a theory of rebellion, it is similar to that advocated by Max Stirner: rebellion without program, purpose, organization, or vision; rebellion carried out by spiritual necessity.

This theory constitutes the background of Marcuse's philosophy of "intolerant" tolerance.

c. Tolerance Without Freedom

In his essay *"Repressive Tolerance,"* Herbert Marcuse concluded that the realization of the objective of tolerance:

> would call for intolerance toward prevailing policies, attitudes, opinions, and the extension of tolerance to policies, attitudes, and opinions which are outlawed or suppressed. In other words, today tolerance appears again as what it was in its origins, at the beginning of the modern period—a partisan goal, a subversive liberating notion and practice.[70]

Herbert Marcuse added that the great goal of mankind should be to practice tolerance, because in the present system of bourgeois parliamentary democracy, tolerance has ceased to play a liberating, progressive role. On the contrary, it has become part of the new bondage system. Marcuse explained this conversion in the following manner:

> According to a dialectical proposition it is the whole which determines the truth—not in the sense that the whole is prior or

superior to its parts, but in the sense that its structure and function determine every particular condition and relation. Thus,
within a repressive society, every progressive movement
threatens to turn into its opposite to the degree to which it accepts
the rules of the game. To take a most controversial case: the exercise of political rights (such as voting, letter writing to the press,
to Senators, etc. protests, demonstrations and *a priori* renun-
ciations of counterviolence) in a society of total administration
serves to strengthen this administration by testifying to the existence of democratic liberties which, in reality, have changed
their content and lost their effectiveness. In such a case, freedom
(of opinion, of assembly, of speech) becomes an instrument for
absolving servitude.[71]

Of course Marcuse's conclusions are sophistical and it is
unimportant for our reflections that his interpretation and application of dialectics is arbitrary, to say the least. But it is true
that one of the elementary principles of the dialectical approach
is the recognition that reality is contradictory in itself: every
entity must consist of contradictory elements which at the same
time sustain and undermine it. Every repressive society contains inherent contradictory elements pressing for freedom and
liberation, while persistently undermining the repressive fabric
of the establishment.

In any society, not only contemporary society, it is the whole
which influences the truth, but the whole never determines
absolutely and entirely all the details of the structure and all the
functions and every element of the social relations. From any
point of view, Cartesian logic, rhetorical argumentation or
Hegelian-Marxist dialectics, positivism or pragmatism, Marcuse's thesis about the role of the whole is inadmissible.

If Herbert Marcuse felt that all the existing freedoms and
institutions in Western society are insufficient to secure genuine
freedom and democracy, then the solution should not be suspen-
sion of freedom in order to fight the repressive society, but the
extension of freedoms; if the existing tolerance is not sufficient
to secure freedom of conscience, speech, and assembly, then the
solution should be to transform the limited crippled tolerance

into a tolerance free of shortcomings.

Marcuse's proposed solution that the present false tolerance should be transformed into intolerance toward prevailing policies, attitudes, and opinions, is either a repetition of St. Augustine or of the Jacobins. St. Augustine argued that truth should not tolerate untruth, that good should not tolerate evil, that one should be intolerant in order to pave the way for truth, good, and God. According to this philosophy, tolerance is an evil in itself.

. According to Maximilien De Robespierre and St. Just there should be "no liberty for the enemies of liberty."

We know how disastrous for mankind the ideas and the practices of the Inquisition and of the Jacobin terror were.

Any responsible author proposing intolerance in order to defend freedom toward certain *"policies, attitudes, and opinions,* should at least state exactly, clearly, and distinctly which *"policies, attitudes, and opinions"* should be prohibited. The word *prevailing* does not clearly specify anything and can be interpreted in a most arbitrary way.

The next important thing which a responsible proponent of intolerance should do is to set forth clearly what means and which individuals will determine the *"policies, attitudes, and opinions"* that are to be suppressed. Does Herbert Marcuse's recommendation mean that after the victory of the New Left revolution, a new censorship would be imposed? For how long? Would it be a preventive censorship or post-publication censorship? Herbert Marcuse elaborated neither the guidelines nor the details of how, specifically, the future New Left "democracy" and "unrepressive society" would suppress undesirable *"policies, attitudes, and opinions."*

The very expression, *"policies, attitudes, and opinions"* mixes up various social, political, and intellectual categories indiscriminately. Even in the repressive, fascist or Stalinist states there are various degrees of intolerance towards various *"policies, attitudes, and opinions;"* the apparatus of terror is sometimes more permissive towards some attitudes and less permissive to certain other "opinions," and sometimes vice versa. Even the most repressive regimes or governments distinguish between terroristic suppression of practical activity and of private opinions and beliefs. When one accepts the possibility of political control over attitudes, one opens the door to all the Orwellian horrors.

d. Marcuse's Philosophy: The Ideological Weakness of the New Left

There are sociological reasons for the weakness of the political program of the New Left.

In the first decades of this century, it was socialism which was regarded as an alternative to the repulsive aspects of capitalism. The Soviet experience and that of other communist countries proved that economic nationalization is no basis for democratic development. On the contrary: the new economic system became an instrument for an arbitrary, despotic, totalitarian political system.

Because of practical communist experience—its crimes, inefficiency, and oppression—all the left-wingers, socialists, and democrats sympathetic to socialism, have been compelled to elaborate a new theory: anti-capitalist and non-soviet. All the programs of the New Left have therefore been vague, not as a result of the subjective qualities of the New Left theoreticians, but because of the objective difficulties of elaborating their ideas in such unfavorable circumstances.

The weakness of Marcuse's revolutionary program reflects the general weakness of leftist democratic ideology in a world divided into two opposed camps. The shortcomings of his political philosophy are not a personal failing; they are the result of the social and political ambiguities connected with the origins, position, and function of the New Left.

Today Marcuse and his official and unofficial followers are criticized by both left and right, by orthodox communists and social-democrats, by right-wing conservatives and by all kinds of liberals. The police all over the world, in every country, mark them as the enemies of their establishment, of law and order, and regard them as a reincarnation of Bakunin and Savinnikov.

The criticism of the ideas of Herbert Marcuse, as presented in this book, should by no means be construed as an uncritical apology for the social and political status quo. The gist of all anti-Marcuse arguments might be reduced to the requirement that every political program recommending changes and reforms should be based on the principles of common sense and experience.

Dialectics without logic, revolution without reason, tolerance without freedom, liberation without liberty, negation without continuation, movement without clearly defined purpose—this is the philosophy of Marcuse and the remnants of the New Left.

They are fighting simultaneously on two fronts—against two evils, the capitalist and the communist. They are, therefore, vulnerable on both sides, and they give an opportunity to their thoughtless adversaries on both sides to point to their difficulties as a proof that no "third road" is possible.

6. Chinese Theory of a "Hundred Flowers" and Freedom

Mao's short lived "Hundred Flowers" was significant for many reasons.

The emergence of this theory proves that no despotism can be consistent and from time to time suffers periods of "Liberal" weakness. Both government and people have to breathe. Such a time of rest must be accompanied by relative tolerance.

The Chinese experience also proves that under any despotic regime, freedom and tolerance, even limited in scope and depth, can only survive for a very short time. When the regime reinforces itself, when it recharges its terroristic mechanism, a period of "normalization" inevitably follows. Those who believed in freedom and the good intentions of the political leaders and police, have to pay for their audacity, decency, sensitivity, and naiveté.

In a short time Chairman Mao elaborated two antagonistic theories: a philosophy of contradictions and tolerance and an ideology of Cultural Revolution, the most terroristic version of bureaucratic communism.

a. On Contradictions and Tolerance

The idea of "contradictions among the people" was authored by Mao himself. It is obviously different from the official Soviet philosophy.

According to Zhdanov's theory, elaborated in the 1940's, contradictions are not always the source and generator of social development, as Hegel, Marx and Engels used to argue. Stalin and Zhdanov became "solidarists" and contended that socialism is the first society in history in which a unity of interests prevails everywhere and this unity generates social evolution. This concept served to justify the Party's use of the police to persecute anybody who disagreed with the Party's leadership. A heretic had to be condemned because in a period of officially proclaimed spiritual unanimity, whoever preserves his own opinion can never be regarded a genuine, good, loyal, or sane citizen.

Long before the victory of the Chinese Communists, Mao Tse-tung wrote a pamphlet, *On Contradictions* (August, 1937). This essay is a very rudimentary popular explanation of the basic principles of the Hegelian and Marxian interpretation of social contradictions. Mao Tse-tung studied these problems on the basis of Lenin's writings and was especially influenced by Lenin's *Philosophical Notebook*. The *Philosophical Notebook* includes Lenin's summaries of Hegel's writings concerning logic, dialectics, and the philosophy of history.

In his pamphlet *On Contradictions*, Mao Tse-tung accepted the traditional dialectical contention that there are internal contradictions in every phenomenon and these are the source of change and progress. Contradictions, Mao agreed with his masters, are universal, eternal, and inevitable. At a certain point in development a unity of opposites emerges but it is only temporary and relative; inevitably it will be replaced by a new struggle which will be followed by a new relative unity of opposites. Contradictions are universal and absolute, while unity is only temporary and relative. Mao quoted Engels that motion itself is a contradiction.

From these general philosophical considerations Mao drew

his own practical conclusions. In war and politics, he wrote, one must be able to combine two contradictory tactics, offense and defense, advance and retreat, even victory cannot exist without defeat.

Every difference in men's ideas, wrote Mao, reflects an objective contradiction.

Society is also a unity of contradictory forces and therefore, the contradictory elements of movement and evolution must be reflected in our thinking. It is also inevitable that there must be differences of opinions in the Party; its ideology also reflects the contradictions of life.

None of these considerations of Mao Tse-tung is new to students of Hegelian-Marxian dialectics. Mao's pamphlet was left in oblivion and did not seem important to Communist philosophy. It suddenly reemerged about twenty years later when Mao Tse-tung wrote a new pamphlet *On the Correct Handling of Contradictions Among the People.* This pamphlet was written after the famous "secret speech" of Khrushchev during the XXth Party Congress in 1956, after the Hungarian uprising, and after the events known as the *Polish October,* in 1956.

This was a period in China when revolutionary enthusiasm and the relative successes of the new government were overshadowed by a new political crisis in which social contradictions arose and the government had to deal with them. On the eve of the re-Stalinization of the Soviet Union and the European Communist countries, the Chinese leaders decided to choose another path which at least appeared to be more liberal.

Mao Tse-tung wrote that in the past the struggle between the people led by the Communist Party and the old class enemy had been very acute, therefore contradictions among the people did not attract as much attention as they deserved nor were they as important as they are today. The contradictions between the people and the exploiters are *antagonistic* and they can be resolved only by the use of force, by revolutionary violence, and by the establishment of a new social and political order. Contradictions among the people are also objective, but they are *non-antagonistic* and can be resolved within the framework of socialist society without the need for violence, oppression, revolution, or changing the social and political order.

Then Mao stressed that contradictions among the people, although non-antagonistic, may become antagonistic if they are not handled properly. In such circumstances it is possible that the non-antagonistic contradictions among the people will become so acute that they can be used by the counter-revolutionaries in order to act against the people's government. According to Mao Tse-tung that is what happened in Hungary, in October and November, 1956.

In order to resolve non-antagonistic contradictions and in order to handle them properly, these contradictions should be known, comprehended, analyzed, and only then can the correct methods of dealing with them be found. There is only one way to find the truth and the right political tactics according to Mao: *free discussion.*

That was the philosophical background underlying the famous slogans of the Chinese Communists from 1956 till 1959. "Let a hundred flowers bloom, let a hundred schools of thought contend" and "a long-term coexistence and mutual supervision." According to Mao, these two slogans expressed the specific Chinese policy for promoting the progress of art, science, and culture. Questions of right and wrong in art and science—including political science and philosophy—should be settled, stressed Mao, through free discussion among artists and scientists and through practical achievements. He argued that any administrative measure, any governmental imposition of style, thought, theories, or administrative prohibition of some styles or theories could only be harmful to the people and to the development of art, science, and culture.

> A period of trial is often needed to determine whether something is right or wrong. Throughout history, new and correct things have often failed at the outset to win recognition from the majority of people and have had to develop by twists and turns in struggle. Often correct and good things have first been regarded not as fragrant flowers but as poisonous weeds. Copernicus' theory of the solar system and Darwin's theory of evolution were once dismissed as erroneous and had to win through over bitter opposition . . . In a socialist society, conditions for the growth of

the new are radically different from and far superior to those in the old society. Nevertheless, it still often happens that new, rising forces, are held back and rational proposals constricted . . . it is therefore necessary to be careful about questions of right and wrong in the arts and sciences, to encourage free discussion and avoid hasty conclusions.[72]

Mao Tse-tung made it clear that even obviously erroneous, albeit popular, ideas should not be banned and even obviously non-Marxist ideas or those critical toward Marxism should also be allowed free expression. Mao wrote that being a true science, Marxism does not fear criticism having itself developed through contradictions and struggle before it was accepted by so many nations of the world. Marxists should even be grateful for criticism because it helps them to develop their own philosophy.

"Fighting against wrong ideas is like being vaccinated—a man develops greater immunity to disease as a result of vaccination. Plants raised in hot-houses are unlikely to be sturdy."[73]

Here Mao Tse-tung repeated Spinoza and Voltaire's famous arguments for tolerance which were collected in the writings of liberals. The argument comparing criticism with vaccination in order to develop greater immunity sounds as if it was lifted directly from John Stuart Mill. Mill asserted that when believers in a religion or doctrine do not have to defend their beliefs, they cease even to understand their own philosophy. What they believe in is not connected with any emotions and they do not even try to practice these beliefs—a characteristic of European Christianity, observed John Stuart Mill.

Mao wrote that his considerations about freedom of discussion, and his recommendation that the hundred flowers should bloom and the hundred schools compete—should be regarded as a very general outline, a basic rule to be applied in different ways in the construction of communism.

Liberals in all Communist countries were misled by Mao's tolerant philosophy, and quoted Mao against their own terroristic regimes. In Hungary and Poland particularly, the idea of a hundred flowers and schools competing was deliberately quoted against Stalinism, neo-Stalinism, and all the discredited ideas about "socialist realism," and the Party-spirit (in Russian: *'par-tijnost'*) in science and art.

In fact, Mao Tse-tung was very far from being a true exponent of freedom and democratic liberties. His pamphlets are extremely vague and hypocritical and could be used at any time for terroristic purposes. There are internal contradictions in Mao's pamphlets. He mentioned that no other countries and parties should or must follow the Chinese way,[74] but, on the other hand, since his arguments in favor of freedom or discussion are general, they should apply generally. If his arguments are really derived, as he himself asserted, from the dialectical considerations of Marx, Engels, and Lenin, how can other Communists and Marxists disagree with him who find their inspiration in the same books?

Mao Tse-tung also wrote that counter-revolutionaries and saboteurs should be deprived of freedom of speech, but "incorrect ideas among the people are quite a different matter."[75] It would seem that the right of free speech depends on who is speaking. If it is one of "the people," his freedom should be unlimited. But the same idea expressed by a counter-revolutionary (whose definition?) should be regarded as a counter-revolutionary, anti-patriotic act.

Mao added that the people should learn how to distinguish fragrant flowers from poisonous weeds. These latter should be eradicated wherever they crop up. To distinguish weeds from flowers, he recommended the following tests:

1. Words and actions should help to unite, and not divide, the people of our various nationalities.
2. They should be beneficial, and not harmful, to socialist transformation and socialist construction.
3. They should help to consolidate, and not undermine or weaken, the people's democratic dictatorship.
4. They should help to consolidate, and not undermine or weaken, democratic centralism.
5. They should help to strengthen, and not discard or weaken, the leadership of the Communist Party.
6. They should be beneficial, and not harmful, to international

socialist unity and the unity of the peace-loving people of the world.[76]

Mao Tse-tung's criteria coincide very well with those so ably pilloried by Marx in his first article about freedom of speech. If he could have read Mao, Marx would have repeated the denunciation he leveled at the Prussian instruction on censorship. If the purpose of the discussion is the truth, Marx would have written, then the truth should be the only criterion of correctness and incorrectness. When one seeks the truth, one seeks something unifying and beneficial, not harmful to the genuine progressive transformation and construction of a more just society. The truth should help to consolidate and to strengthen the political fabric of society. But if pre-conditions are interposed in the way to achieving the truth, these pre-conditions become more important than the truth itself. From Marx's point of view, Mao's treatise on the correct handling of contradictions among the people would only be a poor re-issue of the Prussian police instruction on the question of freedom of expression.

b. Cultural Revolution

In 1966 the theory of the Cultural Revolution was elaborated by the Chinese Communists. What the real political and economic reasons behind this concept were we still do not know exactly and can only conjecture. Mao Tse-tung was the principal ideologist of the Cultural Revolution and his then heir apparent Lin Piao was especially active in its promotion. When the convulsions of the cultural Revolution ended, Lin Piao disappeared from the Chinese political scene in a mysterious way.

The Cultural Revolution was detrimental to Chinese science, art, and culture; it was harmful to Chinese industry and agriculture. For many months and even years Chinese schools and universities were closed. The Chinese armed forces suffered great losses because in the modern world military strength is highly dependent on industry, communications, and science. Constant purges lowered morale.

During the Cultural Revolution thousands of statesmen,

military and administrative officers, scientists and managers, artists, writers and journalists were purged; if not physically, they were persecuted and humiliated morally and mentally. Even for the greatest nation in the world it would be difficult to make good such heavy losses.

The reasons for the Cultural Revolution were no doubt political, ideological, and personal.

In a country run by a monolithic Party, where all opposition is prohibited, various tendencies which are inevitably prompted by the country's internal development and change, find their reflection in the Party itself and even within its close-knit leadership. The situation in China in the 1960's was not easy. International isolation, hostile relations with its powerful ex-ally, but permanent neighbor, the Soviet Union; economic shortages, the danger of famine, difficulties and set-backs in industrialization—all these difficulties had to cause tension in the country, the Party, and within the ruling team.

Various ideas concerning what should be done to overcome the difficulties, secure smoother development, and overcome popular dissatisfaction had circulated in the ruling group. It was found that revolutionary enthusiasm and support by various, never numerous, groups among the people was declining, that the new rulers were losing popularity, and that bureaucratization and new alienation were growing.

The political and ideological differences within the ruling team were accompanied by increasing personal animosities (e.g. Mao v. Liu Shao-chi, Chou En-Lai v. Lin Piao); they added to the differences in the sphere of politics and ideology. There were indications that the power and influence of Chairman Mao were decreasing. It may be that Chairman Mao had to counterattack because he feared for his own position and continued influence. Anyway, his counter-attack against the highest governmental and Party bosses including the president of the republic, Liu Shao-chi, gave ideological shape to the Cultural Revolution. There are many indications that the Cultural Revolution in Chinese history was analagous to the bloody purges in the 1930's in the Soviet Union. One can go even further and compare the Cultural Revolution with the Thermidor period following the French Revolution. If Trotsky's charge that Stalinism represented Thermidorian counter-revolution was correct, then the Chinese purges had the same effect. If it is true that every victorious revolution sooner or later must devour its own children, the Chinese Cultural Revolution was a perfect confirmation.

In August, 1966, the Central Committee of the Chinese Communist Party decided to launch what they described as the great Proletarian Cultural Revolution. In the first sentence of their announcement they stated that the great proletarian cultural revolution was now unfolding, that it "touches people to their very souls," and that China has entered a new stage of the revolution which is "broader and deeper."[77]

The Central Committee stated that the overthrown imperialists and bourgeoisie were still very powerful in the areas of ideology and culture, the formerly exploited masses of the Chinese people were still following the habits, customs, culture, and ideas of the old classes who were still corrupting them, trying to capture their minds in order to prepare for their comeback. Therefore, the proletariat must do the exact opposite, must educate the masses in the spirit of socialism and simultaneously it should reeducate itself in the course of this new fundamental revolution in ideology. It is a very difficult revolution to win because after political defeat the overthrown classes are strong, mischievous, and treacherous. But worse than that is the fact that there were high-ranking officials in the government and in the Party who chose the non-socialist, rightist path. On the way to the victory of the Cultural Revolution there will be many twists and turns but the only way to achieve victory is through the free activity of the masses which should be boldly aroused. The true followers of Chairman Mao, whose writings are the best weapon to win the upheaval, are not afraid of any difficulties and they encourage the masses to expose "every kind of ghost and monster," including the monsters who entrenched themselves in Communist Party headquarters.

On the 5th of August, 1966, Mao himself wrote a "big-character poster" which said "Bombard Headquarters." In this way Mao not only supported the Peking University rebels, but also gave a signal to others to attack the highest party and government officials.

The ideological consequences of the cultural revolution can be described in the following way:

The communist political conceptions laid down during the last hundred years were substantially changed and transformed into the Chinese communist ideology, described as being new, creative, and constructive. The cult of Chairman Mao was bound up with the old traditions of the superiority of the great Chinese nation, the creator of the oldest culture on our globe.

The massive propaganda of the "proletarian," "socialist," "Maoist" ideas tried to influence the nation, to induce the people to think in a more uniform *gleichgeschaltet* way than at any time in history. The political, administrative, and military unification of continental China, which took place to such a degree for the first time in history, was supposed to be followed by an ideological and spiritual unification. Even if this "ideological" unification was broader rather than deep, still there was initiated, according to the promoters, a very active penetrating process of driving the minds of the citizenry into captivity. The results of Soviet and Nazi "drum propaganda" indicate that the Maoists might also have been successful. The experience of the 20th century shows that the combination of the nationalistic feelings of a great nation (e.g. Russians, Germans) with a particular social and economic ideology can lead to tremendous effects and many irreversible changes.

From the standpoint of Marxian philosophy and even of Leninism the Cultural Revolution is a deviation from the mainstream of history. According to historical materialism any changes in the psychology and mentality of society must be the result of a long evolution of the social and political structure, of a long process of education, and of transformations in culture, arts, and sciences. In the 1920's Lenin described self-appointed "specialists" in proletarian culture as "ignoramuses," and "barbarians" who neither knew nor understood the history of mankind and civilization.

Lenin described as an absurdity the idea that proletarian culture was different from the general culture of mankind.

The old Marxists and Leninists would have applied the strongest epithets to the Chinese concept of the Great Proletarian Cultural Revolution. They would have agreed with western intellectuals that only the ignorant or the politically irresponsible could think that any governmental decrees, decisions, or recommendations could drastically change the culture and the deeply rooted spiritual life of a people.

From the traditional Western and the traditional Marxian points of view, the Chinese Cultural Revolution neither favored culture nor was it a revolution. Instead, it was the worst type of terrorism, interfering with the intimate thoughts and feelings of the people. No wonder that the Cultural Revolution did not survive Mao's regime. Its successors reversed this aberration; they found that the very sanity and survival of their nation were at stake.

IX
THE VATICAN ON
FREEDOM AND TOLERANCE IN
THE TWENTIETH CENTURY

1. Preliminary Remarks

As the title indicates, the official doctrine of the Roman Catholic Church concerning freedom and tolerance will be analyzed in this chapter. Today, the Catholic world community is divided into various theological, philosophical, and political factions; a similar situation exists in every traditional community.

Every Roman Catholic trend has its representative personalities, writers, and thinkers. These tendencies draw their adherents from among millions of the clergy and lay persons.

The various tendencies can be divided into more or less conservative, more or less liberal, reformist, and progressive. No wonder that there are new theologies, as for instance the theology of liberation, which exist alongside the traditional theology, which from the social viewpoint could be called a theology of the status quo.

One should view all these terms with hesitation; each is imprecise, a partial description of reality, and may even be misleading. However, such terminology is useful in a general sense.

The Roman Catholic Church has been able to preserve its unified and centralized organization throughout the recent stormy centuries. The head of the Church, the Pope, officially regarded as the deputy or vicar of Jesus Christ on earth, still enjoys the support of the dogma of infallibility whenever he speaks *ex cathedra* on questions of faith. He also decides whether a given question is one of faith, derived from it, or neutral from the Church's point of view.

The army of Catholic clergy and involved laity is no longer as uncritically obedient to the Roman Curia as it used to be. It is by no means like a stick in the hands of an old man. Still, when it comes to the basics, they are loyal and prepared to accept the recommendations of their superiors as spiritually binding in practical activity.

The Roman Catholic Church exercises enormous spiritual and political influence in the contemporary world. One could even argue that while all ideologies are in decline, empires dissolving and every denomination is disintegrating, the power and influence of the centralized Roman Church is increasing by comparison. The Catholic Church—although far from being spiritually and theologically unified, appears to be a monolithic rock amid the chaos and disorganization of almost every other institution, party, and ideology. Even if the Church were only outwardly unified, it would still affect the course of events and impress the minds of onlookers.

If the Catholic Church had remained a bastion of intolerance and religious persecution its attitude would have had a chilling effect on the whole world. And on the contrary, when the Roman Catholic Church enters the period of its own thaw, when it officially changes the course which for more than a thousand years seemed to be unchangeable, when it officially praises democratic liberties and tolerance, when it accepts freedom of conscience and recognizes the value of pluralism, then the Church makes an important contribution to the cause of progress, freedom, and justice. One could even go further and argue that the Church's contribution is indispensable to the defense of democratic liberties today, difficult to estimate in our era of growing, "creeping" totalitarianism.[1]

2. Leo XIII and the First Aggiornamento

The Roman Catholic Church has undergone an *Aggiornamento* (updating) twice in the last hundred years.

At the end of the 19 century the Church belatedly adjusted to the era of bourgeois liberal economics and parliamentary democracy.

In the middle of the 20th century the Church once more readjusted to a changed situation: new cultural rationalistic, and secular trends in the developed industrial countries; increasing influence of social-democratic ideas and welfare-state policies; profound transformation of traditional Western moral and religious attitudes; the emergence and relative stabilization of the communist bloc; the end of the era of colonization and the birth of many new independent states; new social movements in many Catholic countries, including Latin America and the nations under communist rule; and last but not least, the invention of nuclear weapons.

Finally, the Church had to accept the fact that the leading industrial countries in the civilized and Christian world are Protestant. In our era of new dangers such as communism, fascism and various new forms of barbarism, when all democracies must cooperate in order to avoid disaster, the pretense that the Protestant states were ephemeral, could not be continued with impunity.

Pope Leo XIII started the process of *updating* in the last decades of the nineteenth century. Neither he nor his immediate successors were able to bring this process to an end. The Pope of the second *aggiornamento* was John XXIII. He had to finish what his predecessors had failed to do especially in the area of the philosophy of freedom and tolerance. He energetically started to update not only the Church's social and political philosophy but also her theology. He could not, of course, leave intact the Church's organization and her way of functioning.

Leo XIII was a great master of pretense. He concentrated on forms, on terminology, on the play of ideas and he thought that he would be able to speak to the modern world without a true compromise. To a certain extent he was right, his political successes justified the means he employed. But his convictions were not only "simulations" or "dissimulations," as Niccolo Machiavelli occasionally observed. His illusion of success was not groundless either.

To shake dogmas, dogmatic institutions and ways of thinking ingrained for centuries without, however, destroying this institution altogether or forfeiting public approval, one cannot employ frontal attacks. One must begin with incremental changes in terminology, with reinterpretation of subtle concepts while insisting that the substance has remained unchanged. Every step forward toward democracy was fortified by Leo XIII with clauses and safeguards assuring the entrenched defenders of the ecclesiastical *ancien régime* that nothing wrong had happened, that the only change was a small *regroupement* of the loyal forces.

Leo XIII wanted to preserve substance by sacrificing the obsolete harmful terminology of the *Quanta Cura* (1864). His successors up to the end of the 1950's continued this trend of the rule of form over substance. The last Pope of Leo's type was Pius XII. After World War II, he was able to use Leo's methods to save the unity of the Church and steer it through the stormy waters of criticism. But finally the resources for such efforts were exhausted.

When John XXIII was elected Pope, the world situation had changed to such a degree that it was objectively and subjectively impossible to use progressive terms without changing their contents. When the encyclical *Pacem in Terris* (1963) was addressed not only to the hierarchy, but also to all people of good will, the period of playing with words and forms had come to an end. Changes in the substance of Catholic social doctrine became essential and had to be expressed.

Until Leo XIII, the Apostolic See and the hierarchy still dreamt about restoring the Church to the place it had held in feudal society. The Church's hostility toward the French Revolution and its social consequences had not ceased. In the encyclicals and official pronouncements of Gregory XVI are found general condemnations of all rational, liberal, and democratic movements and ideas. The Church was not even able to overcome its distaste for parliamentary democracy and constitutional freedoms. The popes regarded as abominable the very ideas of freedom of the press, speech, conscience, and religion. Rome stated officially that it could not in any way compromise with such heresies. All these numerous condemnations were repeated and collected in one document, the *Syllabus of Errors,* issued in 1864.

The Catholic Church gave its blessing to the Holy Alliance and to its successors who tried to restore and maintain reactionary regimes in Europe. The logic of this policy led the Apostolic See to a practical collaboration with the Orthodox Russian Tsar even at the expense of Polish Catholicism. The uprisings in 1830, 1846-8, and 1863 of Polish Catholics against national and religious persecution by three oppressing empires were condemned by the Vatican with the use of the famous words: "For there is no power but of God . . . Whosoever therefore resists the power, resisteth the ordinance of God: and they that resist shall receive to themselves damnation" (*Rom.* 13:1, 2). The Poles were therefore officially condemned for resisting the allegedly legitimate power of the Tsar. The Polish Catholics regarded this use of Scripture as peculiar, obviously politically partisan, and as a violation of their own moral and national principles.

During the last decades of the nineteenth century it became obvious that because of the ultraconservative policy represented by Gregory XVI, especially as expressed in *Quanta Cura* and in the *Syllabus*, the Church was losing touch with society and becoming estranged from "modern civilization" (cf. the last articles of the *Syllabus*). Many enlightened Catholics feared that such a policy could finally undercut Catholic influence in Western societies. They decided that it was urgent to narrow the gap between the Church and the industrial west.

All the social and political writings of Leo XIII should be read in close correlation with the Encyclical *Aeterni Patris* (1879), which represents the most serious and successful attempt to restore and reinterpret the writings of St. Thomas Aquinas.

We exhort you, venerable brethren, in all earnestness to restore the golden wisdom of St. Thomas, and to spread it far and wide for the defense and beauty of the Catholic faith, for the good

of society, and for the advantage of all the sciences . . . Let carefully selected teachers endeavor to plant the doctrine of Thomas
Aquinas in the minds of students, and set forth clearly his solid-
ity and excellence over others. Let the universities already founded or to be founded by you illustrate and defend this doctrine,
and use it for the refutation of prevailing errors. But, lest the false
for the true or the corrupt for the pure be drunk in, be ye watchful
that the doctrine of Thomas be drawn from his own fountains
. . .[2]

Leo XIII did not want to restore the doctrine of St. Thomas
Aquinas as Thomas wrote it. He intended to revive only selected elements of Thomistic theology, philosophy, and social
teachings and adjust them to fit modern requirements. The
revival was also a revision.

This task was accomplished by Leo XIII gradually and carefully. He acted under constant pressure from both the reactionary elements and from the more liberal progressives who
warned him that unless he modernized the Church, the enemies
of the faith could use this failure to act to the detriment of the
Church's worldly and spiritual interests. Leo also had to overcome the conservative reluctance, if not hostility, of his own
advisers in the papal court. Almost a century later, similar problems confronted John XXIII and his successors.

The basic theoretical and political ideas of Leo XIII can be
narrowed to the following:
1) The Church should accept modern parliamentary govern-
    ment;
2) The Church should recognize the aspirations of the work-
    ing class and the ideas of trade unions; and
3) The Church should discontinue its criticism of demo-
    cratic liberties.

Why did the Church decide to revive and revise the teaching
of St. Thomas, a philosopher who had not enjoyed the best
reputation in recent centuries among enlightened Western thinkers? Apart from the subjective intentions of those who promoted
the renaissance of Thomism, it was necessary in the period of
relative social, political, and spiritual relaxation and flexibility to

return to the foundations in order to avoid blundering in the laby-
rinths and confusions of the modern world.

The teachings of St. Thomas Aquinas could be revived and
used because they were themselves a product of the thirteenth
century when the Church had to adjust to a new phase in the
development of feudal society. In this period the Church had to
fight against a new wave of heresies, including rationalism
based on Aristotelian philosophy, which had become newly popular. *Aggiornamento* was badly needed.

St. Thomas brilliantly performed several tasks. He laid the
foundation for the Inquisition and for the persecution of the
heretics, but at the same time he contributed to a kind of *aper-
tura a sinistra* (opening to the left). He saved the Church from a
futile fight against the development of science, from the complete derationalization of religion and in this way he saved theology. St. Thomas Aquinas also laid the foundations for the
ecclesiastical defense of private property and for the interpretation of the origins and purposes of the state and law.

The recommendations and definitions of St. Thomas
Aquinas were so flexible that Catholic theologians received an
excellent weapon with which to condemn at any time any government considered by the Church to be inimical and harmful; at
the same time they could cooperate with any form of government and with any system of law because one of the main
criteria was the greater glory of the Church, and the Church was
proclaimed the sole judge in its own case.

No wonder that Leo XIII found that St. Thomas "repro-
cessed" could be used to perform a similar task of updating in
the new historical circumstances. On the one hand he could be
used to wage the fight against atheism and the new heresies.
And, on the other hand, he could also be used to announce a formal acceptance of the parliamentary, bourgeois governments
with the simultaneous proclamation of a new crusade—this time
against socialism and communism.

Leo XIII finally accepted the concept which many Catholic
thinkers had long ago proposed: although all legitimate political
power comes from God this does not mean that absolute em-

perors and kings are the only possible agents God might choose to conduct worldly affairs. It was also found that parliaments could be regarded as the executors of God's will expressed through the people's will. Leo XIII further indicated that it was possible for the Church to take part in normal parliamentary struggles. Thus these elements of flexibility were an essential part of St. Thomas' philosophy of law and the state and they could be used against stubborn Catholic monarchists and ultra-montanes.

The encyclical *Rerum Novarum* (May 15, 1891) was a most important element in modernizing Catholic social doctrine. Leo XIII for the first time in the history of the Church proclaimed the Church the only sincere and true defender of the modern workman and condemned capitalist abuses of power and wealth:

> The elements of the conflict now raging are unmistakable . . . in the changed relations between masters and workmen; in the enormous fortunes of some few individuals, and the utter poverty of the masses; in the increased self-reliance . . . of the working classes . . . To this must be added that the hiring of labor and the conduct of trade are concentrated in the hands of comparatively few; so that a small number of very rich men have been able to lay upon the teeming masses of the laboring poor a yoke little better than that of slavery itself.[3]

After this description of the status of the workers, echoing the thundering phrases of the *Communist Manifesto,* the conclusions of Leo XIII are very moderate. He urged capitalists to honor in every worker his humanity; the governments should intervene to secure every worker a sufficient salary for himself and for his family. The encyclical even issued a warning: if governments and capitalists do not carry these recommendations out, the masses of workers will be inclined to accept the socialist demagoguery to abolish private property. Beware, curb greed, give away voluntarily something in order to preserve the basic benefits!

A substantial part of *Rerum Novarum* was devoted to refuting the arguments of the socialists that private property is the source of poverty and should be abolished in order to relieve the degradation of the poor. On the contrary, argued Leo XIII, every proletarian should become a private property owner and thus will lose interest in class struggle. The worker-owner will be as free as the capitalists and we will return to the paternalistic feudal idyll with benevolent relations between masters and their servants and apprentices. The Pope regretted that the past was irretrievable; however he continued to glorify the old social relations. This idealization of the past is not only nostalgic. It is used for new political purposes. The Pope recommended a new paternalism in the relations betwen capital and labor. In this way the Encyclical *Rerum Novarum* is a strange mixture of the modern approach and the nostalgic desire to revive the obsolete forms of the past.

In order to resolve the problem of poverty and avoid class hatred and class struggle—argued Leo XIII—there must be cooperation between Church, state, capital, and labor. In this alliance the Church must act above the contending parties, she must step in every time when the general interest or that of any particular class is endangered. In any event one must remember that strikes are harmful to the community and should be avoided. Workers should, of course, be organized in trade unions, which should cooperate with employers' associations under the state's supervision. Workers should keep away from associations directed by socialists; they should wisely be inspired and supervised by the Church and should remain in close union with the bishops and local clergy. The state, for its part, is obliged to suppress associations whose purposes are dangerous to it. True workers' associations should aim not only at material but also spiritual improvement.

The ideas of Leo XIII concerning the nature of the class-struggle are far from consistent. He regarded the class struggle as an invention of socialists, as something subjective which would disappear with the socialists themselves and their agitation. But on the other hand, he pointed out that poverty and oppression (a "yoke" which he himself compared to "slavery")

are the genuine reasons that the workers feel "broken in spirit
and worn down in body"; they think that "they have been fooled
by empty promises and deceived by false pretexts."[4]

Once the grounds for dissatisfaction are seen actually to
exist then the effects should also be regarded as an objective
social phenomenon and not an illusion created by propaganda
and artificial stimulation.

How can mankind overcome this undesirable social phenomenon, the class struggle? It should be replaced, the Pope
recommends, by cooperation under the supervision of the state
and Church. In this way, as was later observed many times, Leo
XIII laid the foundation, if only in a general way, for the future
theory of corporativism and the corporate state. This Encyclical
can also be understood as a green light for the clergy and lay
Catholics to found their own organizations and associations in
order to promote Catholic social ideals. The Vatican had finally
grasped the elementary truth that in order to influence modern
society the church would have to use means appropriate to the
changing conditions of the modern world. But the Pope concentrated once more on questions of form rather than on the questions of substance.

* * *

At the end of the 19th century, one of the crucial problems
which the Roman Catholic Church had to solve was to update its
attitude toward freedom and tolerance. The era of *Quanta Cura*
(1864) had passed for good.

Leo XIII's most important ideas about freedom and tolerance were formulated in the Encyclical *Libertas Praestantissimum* (1888).

A significant statement opens the Encyclical:

> Liberty, the highest of natural endowments . . . confers on
> man this dignity—that he is in the hand of his counsel[5]. . . and
> has power over his actions.[6]

The Pope tried to present the history of the Roman Church
in a new light:

> The Church has always most faithfully fostered civil liberty,
> and this was seen especially in Italy . . .[7]

The purpose of the encyclical *Libertas Praestantissimum* was
to persuade the world that it was a "calumny on the Church . . .
to assert that she is the foe of individual and public liberty."[8]
The Church wanted to avoid confusing "true liberty" with
"sheer" and "foolish license," which is nothing other than
following "in the footsteps of Lucifer."[9]

It should be noted that the imputation that those who had a
different opinion were inspired by Lucifer, is intolerant in
itself. Leo XIII was espousing a concept of freedom and tolerance under the precondition that those who disagreed with him
were either low or unreasonable; that they were in favor of
"license," an intolerable deviation from "right" thinking!

Especially significant is the general tenor of this encyclical.

Leo XIII openly admitted that he "acquiesces" with the
"modern liberties" not of his free will and internal conviction
but because of necessity.

> And although in the extraordinary condition of these times
> the Church usually *acquiesces* in certain modern liberties, not
> because she prefers *them in themselves,* but because she judges
> it *expedient to permit* them, she would in happier times *exercise
> her own liberty;* and, by persuasion, exhortation and entreaty,
> would endeavor, as she is bound, to fulfill the duty assigned to
> her by God of providing for the *eternal salvation* of mankind[10]
> (italics added—M.M.)

This is the essence of Leo's true attitude toward the idea of
freedom: the church has to accept democratic liberties today,
under extraordinary modern conditions, under duress, under
the compulsion of modern social pressures favoring democracy.
However, "in happier times," after the suppression of the prevailing, democratic, liberal, parliamentary regimes, and after
the eventful restoration of the *ancien régimes,* the Church would

"exercise her own liberty" which would apparently be used to liquidate the contemptible modern liberties. Then, finally, the Church would regain all the necessary, direct, unobstructed means to fulfill its duty: "providing for the eternal salvation of mankind."

Etienne Gilson in his commentaries is even more expressive and less subtle than his mentor. He wrote about Leo's concept of liberty and tolerance:

> This is entirely different from granting to all liberty to do all things, for it is absurd to maintain that error and truth, or evil and good, should have equal rights.[11]

Etienne Gilson dotted the "i": he revived in the twentieth century the old theory that freedom should be given to "truth" and "good" only. Gilson pretended that the full answer to the question of what is true and good had already been given. The problem of "freedom for truth only" has already been discussed in this book and there is no need to repeat our considerations. Facing such an attitude as that of Leo XIII one can only continue to repeat the words of Voltaire (and Rosa Luxemburg written in her last pamphlet criticizing the Bolsheviks and the Soviet Government): it is necessary to secure freedom for our adversaries for the sake of our freedom, for our well-understood interests, for our happiness and for our salvation from our errors and arrogance. This democratic, typically liberal attitude is alien to Leo XIII. Instead, he continued to condemn his whipping boy—liberalism.

The condemnation of liberalism as a political and economic philosophy and practice is fundamental to the social theory of Leo XIII. Apart from the specific arguments used against liberal ideas and their realization, the main thesis of the Pope was that, being an application of the erroneous "naturalism" and "rationalism" to the sphere of practical political philosophy, liberalism must be good for nothing. "Naturalism" should be condemned, because in the Pope's interpretation, it recognizes the existence of nature and natural laws only, without referring to "supernatural" phenomena. "Rationalism" should be condemned for similar reasons: it follows the footsteps of "naturalists." According to "rationalism" true knowledge is a product of human reason only, it is independent of the "supernatural revelation." *Ergo:* rationalistic knowledge cannot be complete. Liberalism should be condemned because as an application of "naturalism" and "rationalism" to politics, it denies the existence of natural and divine laws, it recognizes only "positive," state, legal norms.

Liberalism, as a political ideology, was interpreted by Leo XIII in a very broad and very narrow way at the same time. Basically, liberalism is an evil identified with secular power, with the separation of the state and Church. This last idea, expressed so clearly in the First Amendment to the U.S. Constitution, in Leo's theory of politics, is just as bad as original sin in theology.

Under cover of an attack on liberalism, Leo XIII continued a general offensive against the essence of the secular philosophy, organization, and activity of the modern state.

Leo XIII needed his narrowly conceived anti-liberal exhortations not only for criticism but for the sake of his political aims. He decided indirectly to reintroduce the traditional monarchic principle of "the divine right of kings." Of course, this discredited doctrine was "amended" by him and "updated" verbally. Leo's interpretation of the principle of the divine right of kings was especially influenced by the fact that elections had become a way of life in modern states.

It is possible and legitimate, he argued, to elect a president of a republic or any other ruler by electoral process; but those elected do not receive their power and authority from the electors because the electors do not possess it. The president-elect or senator-, deputy-, congressman-elect receive their power from God. The authority "flows" from Him only. Even hereditary monarchs, emphasized Leo XIII, are not vested with their authority by their predecessors, but receive it from God and remain responsible to God.

The strange "equalization" of the elected presidents with the hereditary monarchs served its purpose: the enhancement of the extremely unpopular doctrine of despotism with democratic phraseology tended to persuade public opinion that the Pope had ceased to support the traditional absolutist power, that he was prepared to accept democratic elections as a way of working for political solutions. This recognition or acceptance of democracy was only an illusion, because Leo XIII rejected the essence of democracy, that it is the people, the nation, the electorate, who are the sole source of power, of authority, of the right to create legal norms and to execute them. Any attempt to shake these premises of every democratic system, old or new, tends to undermine the foundations of democracy itself.

Etienne Gilson, editor and commentator of the social and political encyclicals of Leo XIII, made the following remarks on this point:

> At any rate, the doctrine according to which the people has no authority either to give or delegate entails this consequence, that the people has no right to unmake rulers whom it has no power to make, or, in other terms, that the electoral body has no justification for taking away from the elected ruler a political power which it did not give to him on election day . . . God alone, who gives to rulers their authority, can take it away from them before the appointed day of their lives or of their constitutional tenures."[12]

It seems that according to Gilson's interpretation Leo XIII applied the doctrine of the "indissolubility" of marriage to the state: what had been bound in heaven cannot be divided on earth. In this way, the essence of democracy was once more turned upside down; a political system in which the people lack the right or legal opportunity to terminate the tenure of the delegates whom they find negligent or corrupt, or who for any other reasons have lost their confidence, cannot be called a democracy.

About freedom of speech and press, the Pope wrote that it should not be allowed "if it be not used in moderation, and if it pass beyond the bounds and end of all true liberty."[13]

If freedom of speech ceases to be used "in moderation" and within certain "bounds," then it becomes a "mental plague," a "vice" corrupting heart and life and "should be *diligently repressed by public authority* " *(emphasis* added—M.M.).[14]

In plain political language, this recommendation means that the government should exercise censorship and they and the Church should be the sole arbiters of what constitutes freedom and what is an abuse, or "license." These authorities should have the right to decide which matters of opinion "God leaves to man's free discussion" and only afterwards "full liberty of thought and of speech" should be granted.[15]

It had been a long and tortuous way from Leo's initial proclamation in favor of freedom to the statement that one has the right to discuss only subjects which God left to man's reason and free discussion.

One comparison of Leo sounds especially ominous: "The excesses of an unbridled intellect,—which unfailingly end in the oppression of the untutored multitude, are no less rightly controlled by the authority of the law than are the injuries inflicted by violence upon the weak."[16]

Whenever material, natural changes are mechanically compared with those of the mind, it is not the physical element which is raised to the level of intellect, but vice versa: this is the spiritual phenomenon which is degraded to something corporeal.

In one respect however the Pope was right: "If unbridled license of speech and of writing be granted to all, nothing will remain sacred and inviolate."[17]

This is the end, the substance and the *modus operandi* of freedom: not to leave anything "sacred and inviolate" without critical examination and argumentation. This is the reason why freedom is so precious, why it should be fostered and protected, not criticized.

Human liberty in the final analysis, according to Leo XIII, consists of obeying God and his divine law, only a Christian, who knows the Gospel becomes a "possessor of a more perfect liberty."[18] The "supreme end" of human liberty is God himself![19]

The very idea that liberty must have an ultimate end is in

itself alien to liberty. The end of liberty, if one wants to use such terminology, is liberty itself! We cannot cease repeating this maxim, because it expresses certain substantial features of humanism and of the philosophy of freedom. The free man himself determines his own ends. In order to determine the goals and the means which should be employed to realize them, a person must be set free. Freedom is the end and the means of human activity.

Freedom is a process of liberating, an endless process of achieving happiness, an intellectual and practical process of comprehending and overcoming the conditions in which we are living; a free human being cannot be guided by some "outside," external authorities or centers. Every formal and forceful restriction of the moral and practical quest for freedom, must negatively influence the individual's handling of the available means to acquire more freedom, to extend its temporary scope. In all of Leo's writings allegedly praising freedom, we do not find even one affirmative word about the progress or democracy actually existing in the 19th century, not even one kind remark about the developments of the modern ideas of freedom and tolerance. All modern forms of democracy and liberty are treated with hostility and contempt. They are unfavorably contrasted with those patterns of true democracy and liberty which are nothing more in Leo's interpretation, than a voluntary obedience to the Church for the sake of one's own salvation.

The abuse of religion and personal faith for the promotion of a political doctrine is here so blatant that none of Leo's successors dared openly to go so far. Anyway, Leo XIII achieved his main intended goal; he rehabilitated liberal phraseology, introduced it into the Church's political vocabulary and then pronounced the Roman Catholic Church the main tutor of *true* freedom, tolerance, democracy, the well-being of the poor and oppressed. Leo XIII was able to create the grand illusion: he substituted substance for appearances, essence for forms, and came down to history as the founder of the modern social doctrine of the Roman Catholic Church.

3. Stagnation and Decline

The most significant document of the period between the First and Second World Wars is the Encyclical of Pius XI, *Quadragesimo Anno* issued on May 15, 1931, the fortieth anniversary of Leo XIII's Encyclical, *Rerum Novarum,* as the title indicates.

The Pope took into account: the victory of the communist revolution in Russia; the seizure of power by the fascists in Italy, and the growth of fascism in Europe and the Americas; the world economic crisis and the lack of stability of the parliamentary democracies, especially in Germany, Austria, and even in France. The Great Depression caused mass unemployment, sharp political tension, and much social unrest. Poverty, unemployment, and hopelessness provided a hotbed for rightist and leftist extremism.

In this situation the Vatican decided that the gravest danger came from the left, communism. They were afraid that the example of the Russian Revolution might attract the impoverished masses of workers and middle classes. Therefore, after a short period of hesitation, the Church hierarchy in Italy, and finally Pope Pius XI himself, came to an agreement with the fascist regime and became proponents of the new ideology. In the Encyclical *Quadragesimo Anno* we find very clear recommendations that Catholic political movements all over the world should favor the corporate state.

One could argue that the Church did not unequivocally endorse the Italian form of fascism and the Italian corporate state. But it is a fact that we do not find any real criticism or condemnation of the Italian concept of the corporate state. On the contrary, one finds in the Encyclical *Quadragesimo Anno* many recommendations which are most substantial: a compulsory unification of employees' unions with employers' organizations under the aegis of the existing government. In such a state, as was stressed by the fascists and by *Quadragesimo Anno,* class struggle should be prohibited. That meant in practical terms that every independent demand of the workers upon their employers could be regarded as an expression of class hatred and struggle and therefore be indiscriminately and arbitrarily suppressed.

In this period the Vatican was against the idea of independent, and autonomous trade-unions. The existence of such trade unions has been indispensable for the preservation of freedom and democracy; obviously, Western democracy did not have a friend in the Holy See.

There are many examples of how close the Vatican and the higher strata of the Catholic hierarchy were to the fascist movement in the 1930's.

The Vatican was the first state that signed an international agreement (concordat) with Hitler; Hitler regarded this pact as very important because it was a badly needed recognition of the new Nazi government after their seizure of power in 1933.

In the Encyclical *Mit Brennender Sorge* Pope Pius XI criticized the Nazi Government for its persecution of the Catholic clergy, but this criticism was very limited in its scope and purpose. Not even the existence of concentration camps or arbitrary arrests and torture were mentioned in this Encyclical which, after World War II, was sometimes praised as having been anti-Nazi. The pro-Nazi German cardinals, bishops, and even the whole assembly of the German hierarchy issued hundreds of documents, pastoral letters, and sermons in which they endorsed the Nazi-racist ideology and the concepts of *"Herrenvolk"* and the *"Fuehrerprinzip."* The Roman Curia never reproached them.

In Austria in the 1930's pro-fascist groups claiming affiliation with "Christian social ideals" were supported by the Vatican and by almost all Catholic prelates. The German *Anschluss* of Austria was not opposed. In a special message the bishops of Austria asked the people to remain loyal to the new authorities.

In Poland, the Church hierarchy supported the right-wing, semi-fascist, nationalistic parties, especially the National Democrats, and of course the Christian Democratic Party which was always more rightist than the C.D. parties in Western Europe.

During this period even the centrist policies of Marshal Pilsudski received heavy clerical criticism because he stood for a secular concept of Polish *citizenship,* not based on religion. Even very moderate peasant parties were the target of criticism by the Catholic hierarchy. After 1926, after Marshal Pilsudski's *coup d'état,* part of the Catholic hierarchy was still oriented further to the right. But another part of the hierarchy, under the influence of the Vatican which was more far-sighted than the Polish domestic clerical politicians, changed this orientation, strongly supporting the new authoritarian, military dictatorship.

In the new concordat with the Polish government the Church gained prerogatives which had long ago been abolished in Western democracies such as compulsory religious instruction in both private and public schools; a compulsory religious form of marriage; clerical participation in state ceremonies; an active role in the social and religious instruction of the army; and, finally, a special legal position for members of the clergy including special privileges even in criminal cases and exemption from some civic duties. This privileged position of the Church was acknowledged by the Constitution and the hierarchy used their position to press for a Polish form of corporativism.

The cooperation between the Vatican and the fascist states and parties was based on a similar assessment of the political situation which held that fascism and other forms of despotism should be regarded as the most effective remedy against communist aspirations.

This view implies that Western democracy had become too weak to offer efficient resistance to communism. The Vatican was unable to understand that the only truly effective alternative to communist totalitarianism *was not right-wing despotism but the full application of the Western traditions of democracy and liberty.*

There is one important distinction in *Quadragesimo Anno* which was unknown in *Rerum Novarum.* Pius XI distinguished between *communist* ideology and parties and the *socialist* ideology and parties, and stressed that the differences between moderate social-democratic parties (non-communist) and Catholic philosophy and politics had been substantially reduced and therefore the possibility of cooperation existed. In the period between the world wars these distinctions had no practical importance, but immediately after World War II the idea that the differences between Socialist and Christian democratic parties were bridgeable became an important issue, not only theoretically but also in practical politics.

* * *

After the Second World War ecclesiastical authors reassessed the ideology and behavior of the Vatican during the fascist era. They tried to reinterpret the writings and the speeches of Pope Pius XI and Pope Pius XII, to prove that they had not been uncritical partisans of fascism but, on the contrary, had tried to condemn both fascism and communism. It was during this period, 1944-47, that the new philosophy was propounded that the Church had always been *antitotalitarian* and had condemned all of its forms.

In this way at least two ideological purposes were served. First, by equating communism and fascism as forms of totalitarianism, the Vatican's earlier criticism of communist totalitarianism was also, and retroactively, directed toward fascist totalitarianism and the Church could claim that it had always favored true democracy. Second, condemnation of totalitarianism paralleled the *final acceptance* of the *Western parliamentary forms of government,* although with certain antiliberal reservations.

In the 1940's and 1950's another crucial problem emerged, that of atomic weapons and war. Basic controversies started among Catholic thinkers over the question of whether the use of atomic weapons and other weapons of mass destruction could ever be justified. There were even differences of opinion whether Pius XII, who had made many critical remarks on the use of atomic weapons, had condemned their use absolutely or only conditionally.

In these discussions the new edition of the *Code of Inter-*

national Morality (1949) prepared by a group of Catholic social researchers in Malines, Belgium, under the spiritual leadership of Cardinal Van Roey, became very important. This group concluded that ABC (atomic-bacteriological-chemical) weapons should not be unconditionally condemned and prohibited, but their use should not contradict the moral norms.

One of the most important problems discussed was the old Judeo-Christian principle promoted, among others, by Taparelli: *"Numquam licet interficere innocentes."* (No one may kill innocent people.)

The authors of the Code wrote that, in view of new developments in warfare, the concept of a *participant* must be redefined. Whereas in the past, argued the authors, armies lived on the margins of society, in modern war the power of the army depends on the material and moral support of the whole society. The difference between who was formerly considered a *belligerent* and who is now is enormous. In modern war sometimes workers and engineers who are producing new and more effective weapons are more important than soldiers. Nowadays the might of an army depends on food supplies and therefore farmers are no longer as "innocent" as they once were. Newspapermen and radio commentators contribute to the moral strengthening of the army and of the "home front;" when they enhance the morale of the society they become part of the war machine. All these categories of civilians also become belligerents in "total war" conditions and therefore should be treated as such. Those who conduct wars must draw the appropriate conclusions when they consider using ABC weapons because the concept of "innocence" and "guilt" has changed.

The problem still remains that when an entire populated area is destroyed by ABC weapons, not only belligerents who may now be legitimately exterminated, but also their families, old men, women, and children, will be destroyed. Can this too be morally justified? The authors of the *Code* answer that destruction of these innocents should be deplored, but sometimes it is simply unavoidable. The destruction of such people could be regarded as immoral only under the following circumstances: 1) If the belligerent party who used ABC weapons did so without due consideration or frivolously; or, 2) If they deliberately aimed to destroy that innocent stratum of the population.

But if the destruction of elderly and children was done after due consideration and regretfully, and it was only a *side-effect* of the otherwise justifiable use of ABC weapons, then such an act could not be regarded as immoral. Crucial here is the subjective intention: was the destruction of the innocent civilians directly intended or was it "only" an unavoidable side-effect? If it is only a side-effect then, from the strictly moral and juridical point of view, guilt is excluded according to the *Code*.

In this way the great cycle in European moral philosophy had reached a dead end. Perhaps moral philosophy started in Europe with the Sophists followed by Socrates, Plato, Aristotle, the Epicureans and Stoics, and a whole pleiad of others who argued that the essential element of guilt, justice, and morality is constituted by subjective intentions. This concept is also expressed in the Bible, according to the generations of Judaic and Christian authors who have magnificently elaborated this doctrine of morality over the past two millennia. The famous defense of Helen of Troy by Gorgias is an excellent example of how the concept of subjectivity came to be so important in the development of humanism and of the proper assessment of an individual. In the *Code of International Morality* the problem of subjective intentions was interpreted in such a way that it could even justify the use of weapons of mass destruction, if necessary. The problem is far from solved (much depends on the interpretation of the concept of "necessity") and therefore a dead end was reached: the concept of subjectivity in philosophy and theology was developed in order to defend every individual and to open the way to a just and profound assessment of each person's moral value. It started as a life-enhancing concept; it ended now as an absolution for annihilation. As a result of a curious twist in historical evolution, this most valuable element in the growth of our civilization may be used to destroy it. The authors of the *Code* unwittingly opened a Pandora's box.

The *Code* does not carry the weight that official papal announcements do, although it was written and distributed under
the auspices of several bishops and cardinals. The Holy See
never denounced the *Code*.

In the end it was John XXIII who had to clarify this and
many other delicate questions and a pastoral letter by the
National Conference of Catholic Bishops, *The Challenge of
Peace,* June 1983, opened a new chapter in the Catholic doctrine concerning nuclear warfare.

4. The Reign of John XXIII

The death of Pope Pius XII symbolically and actually ended
obsolete dogmatism. The new pope, John XXIII, evinced unusual personal qualities. He was a man of vision, able to perform
highly demanding tasks. He used to stress his lack of theological
finesse, but it was he who understood the needs and interests of
the Church and of the democratic world more profoundly than
many highly educated theologians and philosophers. He was
already known as a person of exceptional personal kindness and
humility, but he also proved to be a genius in tactical diplomacy,
able to move the generally hostile Roman Curia to carry out his
ideas. He was even able to arrange personal talks with communist leaders.

When John XXIII became Pope, a tremendous task lay
before him. He himself described it as *aggiornamento.* Everything in the Church needed to be *updated* and *adjusted* to the
requirements of modern times. The Church organization itself
had to be reformed. The supercentralization of the decision-
making powers in the offices of the *Curia Romana,* had a de-
pressing effect on the entire Church. The Church had to rely on
the efficiency of its servants scattered throughout the world, but
the latter had atrophied as decision-makers. Even the liturgy of
the Catholic Church had become obsolete; prayers in the respective national languages had become a necessity, because
Latin had no appeal for the new generation who knew no
Latin.

The Cold War period of the 1940's and 1950's had approached its demise. The old hostilities and suspicions still existed of course, but the situation was changing. The Church had to become reconciled to the fact that millions of Catholics, especially those in Poland, Hungary, Czechoslovakia, and Lithuania, would be living under Communist regimes for an indefinitely long time. The Church finally had to realize that Communist and Socialist parties in many other countries would, after many setbacks, gain influence during the coming years.

In previous centuries, the Church had traditionally cooperated with the colonial powers. Although the contribution of the various monastic orders to the health care, education, and culture of backward nations was significant, missionaries were nevertheless often identified with colonialism. The awakening of anti-colonial and nationalistic feelings and the emergence of new sovereign states in Africa and Asia posed new problems for the whole of Christianity. The Roman Catholic Church had to update its relations with the countries of the Third World.

It may have been that the most difficult task for the Church was to modernize its activity in the industrial countries. The Vatican had finally to accept the fact that in all democratic Western countries the doctrine of the separation of Church and State was generally accepted and deeply-rooted while many of those governments had been sympathetic to the interests of religion, the process of secularization had gone very far. It would appear that the seeds of secularization and religious indifference (if not overt atheism) lay in the growth of modern society.

On the other hand, Communist governments, parties, and many other revolutionary movements worked hard to eradicate religion and present it as an instrument of oppression, exploitation, and colonialization. Militant atheism had become a part of the left-wing radical ideology.

In this situation, interdenominational struggles among the Churches became more dangerous to the cause of all religions than ever before. Mutual criticism by the denominations served the atheists and was deliverately used by them to promote their purposes.

At the end of the 1950's it became imperative that the Church begin to lay new foundations for its relations with the other great world religions. It was particularly urgent to begin a friendly dialogue with the various Christian churches.

John XXIII was one of the first to understand that without a new ecumenical council it would be impossible to achieve his reforms. Nearly everyone of influence in the Roman and world hierarchy argued that it would not be possible to organize a council and bring it to a conclusion within a short time. There were those who argued that it would require at least twenty years to achieve the ambitious plans outlined by the new Pope. He, however, was able not only to break the resistance of the doubters without making them enemies, but also to inspire the reluctant to participate in his far-reaching projects.

John XXIII averted a deep crisis and opened a new important chapter in the history of the Catholic Church. Believers could regard him as a man sent by Providence. From the standpoint of the Hegelian theory of history, Cardinal Angelo Giuseppe Roncalli was one of those great men who better than any one else in his organization understood the needs of the times and the role of his institution in this time. He was better equipped than anybody else to execute the ideas whose time had come. He was endowed with special personal qualities capable of healing old wounds, overcoming long-standing antagonisms, and creating a new unity based on mutual understanding. He was a man of strong will and convictions, but easy-going, accessible, persuasive, and open to suggestions. His premature death slowed many of the processes he had set in motion, but no one would be able to return the Church to the state it had been in preceding his reign.

The decisions of the Second Vatican Council were predetermined politically and socially by two important social encyclicals issued by John XXIII: *Mater et Magistra* (Mother and Teacher, 1961), and *Pacem in Terris* (Peace on Earth, 1963). Their main ideas have been incorporated into the *Documents of Vatican II.*

John XXIII introduced into the philosophy of the Church

new concepts of freedom and justice. The encyclical *Mater et Magistra* was issued on May 1, 1961 in order to commemorate the social encyclicals, *Rerum Novarum, and Quadragesimo Anno,* and radio broadcast of Pius XII on Pentecost June 21, 1941. In the first part of *Mater et Magistra* these three documents were reviewed in a very special way. The Pope made a deliberate effort to extract from the old documents only what he considered to be relevant to the new circumstances.[19]

John evaluated the recommendations of his predecessors in the field of social and economic life as follows:

Private property is indispensable for the benefit of all of society, but owners should remember that it has two aspects, the individual and the social; therefore both liberalism and communism should be condemned. The first because of its egoistic abuses of private property, the second for its abolition of private property. John especially emphasizes that workers should be treated as human beings, with their own specific material and spiritual needs.

John XXIII recalled that his predecessors had already supported the institution of trade unions. This is a very generous interpretation of the *Quadragesimo Anno,* because Pius XI had insisted that the workers should cooperate with their employers under the aegis of the corporate states. John XXIII expressed the opposite idea by stressing that unions should represent the employees' needs.

Changes have taken place, continued the Pope, in the development of social insurance and security, in the improvement of basic and secondary education, the workers have become more socially aware, but there are still imbalances in society: between rich and poor, between agriculture and industry, and finally, the imbalance between the more or less developed regions and countries of the world.

More people from every social level participate in public affairs, governments have widened their spheres of activity, there are new supra-national institutions and the scope of their activities is getting wider and deeper. The Church should take all these new phenomena into account and apply its basic principles to the changing times.

John XXIII thought that governments of developed Western countries had new responsibilities, they should realize that their relatively high standards of living are not enough. Governments should intervene in the economic system in order to reduce social disparities.

Pope John here developed the principle of "subsidiarity" which had already been mentioned in *Quadragesimo Anno,* but for him this principle is more important than it was in the philosophy of his predecessors. According to him, the authorities should not only encourage and stimulate private initiative but also take affirmative action to achieve desirable social ends. Positive action by governments is necessary because the economy of the world has reached such a stage that there cannot be prosperity without close cooperation between the citizens, private initiative, and government.

Leo condemned liberal capitalism for its inhumane competition, as he phrased it; John XXIII condemned not only this type of competition but also the new phenomenon, the concentration of power and accumulation of wealth in a few hands, on a worldwide basis. *Mater et Magistra* should be regarded as a warning addressed to Western governments and the super rich that if they do not work toward desirable social change, an explosive political situation will arise.

Mater et Magistra defended the institution of private property, but this defense was far different from the primitivism one finds in *Rerum Novarum* where even the arguments for the preservation of private property were drawn from the Bible.

And finally John XXIII introduced into his encyclical the notion of *sozzializatione.* This expression was first used in the Italian translation of *Mater et Magistra.* Although the original Latin text does not use this word or an equivalent it is significant that the word was used in the text published by *Osservatore Romano.* There is no doubt that use of the term was deliberate. It was the first time in the history of the Church that the word "socialization" was used, not pejoratively as theretofore, but to describe a new and eventually desirable social phenomenon. It was not, of course, intended to imply socialization in the Marxist sense. It did not call for ending private ownership of the means of production. The text of *Mater et Magistra* defined socialization:

> One of the principal characteristics of our time is the multiplication of social relationships, that is, a daily more complex interdependence of citizens, introducing into their lives and activities many and varied forms of association, recognized for the most part in private and even in public law. This tendency seemingly stems from a number of factors operative in the present era, among which are technical and scientific progress, greater productive efficiency, and a higher standard of living among citizens.
>
> These developments in social living are at once both a symptom and a cause of the growing intervention of public authorities in matters which, since they pertain to the more intimate aspects of personal life, are of serious moment and not without danger. Such, for example, are the care of health, the instruction and education of youth, the choice of a personal career, the ways and means of rehabilitating or assisting those handicapped mentally or physically. But this trend also indicates . . . (that) men are impelled voluntarily to enter into associations in order to attain objectives which each one desires, but which exceed the capacity of single individuals. This tendency has given rise, especially in recent years to organizations and institutes on both national and international levels . . . (para. 59-60, pp. 25-26).

John correctly pointed out that human relationships had become incomparably more complicated than in previous periods of history, and consequently "socialization" had become inevitable. Why? There are more and more goals which people want to achieve and in order to achieve them they must not only enter into private but public associations. Moreover, some goals are attainable only through international cooperation. This idea was only mentioned marginally in *Mater et Magistra*, it was fully elaborated in John's later encyclical, *Pacem in Terris*.

Mater et Magistra was the first Church document strongly

influenced by existentialist, personalist philosophy. In it the Pope wrote that the new economic institutions could have a bad influence on the life of the workers; that there was a danger that people would become "automatons" and cease to be "personally responsible." (para. 62, p. 26). The encyclical stressed that such a possibility should be consciously resisted. Society should assist people to develop and perfect their natural talents. Workers should receive just compensation for their labor. In order to determine what is just, the following factors should be considered: the contribution of individuals to the economic effort, the economic state of the enterprise, the requirements of each community, and finally, the affairs of the state as well as those of all states.

The Pope recommended that in order to attach the workers to their enterprises, they should be given some property share in them. Each country and each enterprise should develop its own scheme by which the workers might participate in the companies in which they work.

In this way John expanded the concept of freedom and justice. Justice was to be observed not only in the distribution of wealth, but also in regard to the productive conditions under which men engage in economic activity. Freedom and justice are connected with the innate need of humans to engage in productive activity, to have an opportunity to assume responsibility, and to perfect themselves by their own efforts.

> Consequently, if the organization and structure of economic life be such that the human dignity of workers is compromised, or their sense of responsibility is weakened, or their freedom of action removed, then we judge such an economic order to be unjust, even though it produces a large amount of goods, whose distribution conforms to the norms of justice and equity. (para. 82-83, p. 32.)

This is a completely new idea for the Catholic Church. Even more, John embraced ideas which constitute a denial of the previous traditions. John's predecessors often wrote about the dignity of the human being as well as freedom, and distributive and commutative justice, but in very general terms. John XXIII was the first to stress that the requirements of justice, freedom, and dignity demand that the worker should be afforded an opportunity *to employ creativity* in the process of work. Young Marx's concept, discarded by his own Communist followers, was revived on another philosophical plane. The line initiated in the Renaissance by Pico della Mirandola found a new powerful follower.

John XXIII was also more specific than his predecessors on the duties and responsibilities of public authorities.

First of all, he recommended that the authorities should assist the rural areas and the peasants dwelling there. The government should see to it that new highways be constructed, market facilities expanded, that medical and educational services be introduced and even that pure drinking water be assured. The mission of the Church and Government should be more down to earth.

The Pope's second recommendation was that governments assure the effective participation of workers on all levels of production. Workers' associations should have legal status and workers themselves should participate in management. He even expressed his esteem for the International Labor Organization which "had done effective and valuable work in adapting the economic and social order everywhere to the norms of justice and humanity. In such an order, the legitmate rights of workers are recognized and preserved." (para. 103, p. 37).

And finally, John recommended that the government bear in mind the imbalance existing between advanced industrial countries and those in the process of development. The first enjoy the conveniences of life, the latter experience "dire poverty." (para. 157).

According to the Pope it is a moral duty of the affluent nations to help the poor nations to overcome poverty and hunger. Whoever lives under such misery is unable to "enjoy basic human rights." The more developed nations should give scientific and technical help. This aid should be rendered without self-interest and without using it to gain political influence in the poor country. The Pope warned against attempts to employ new forms of colonialism and other outdated concepts of domination. John's thoughts on international relations (North-South) were only outlined here; they were elaborated in *Pacem in Terris*.

The encyclical *Pacem in Terris* (April 1963) was published two months before the Pope's death. It should be considered the crowning accomplishment of John XXIII's brief reign. *Pacem in Terris* opened a new epoch in the Church's social and political philosophy. Almost every idea expressed in this encyclical is different—either in form, or in substance, or in substantiation—from preceding statements on social affairs issued by the Vatican: the tone, the manner of thinking, and arguing, the new spirit of tolerance, the literary style, and the conclusions. It was the first Catholic encyclical addressed not only to the clergy and to Catholic believers, but to "all men of good will."

According to many knowledgeable sources, preparations for the encyclical were prompted by the Cuban crisis in October 1962. The date of publication preceded by a short period the test ban treaty entered into between the United States and the Soviet Union. The reaction of the world to the encyclical was general acclaim. No papal utterance had ever been received so warmly. It was praised by western and communist leaders, by the statesmen of the Third World, by Protestants and by Jews.

One month later the Pope, already confined with a severe illness, spoke about his beloved document:

> And so we address our exhortation to all humanity . . . Presented to our contemporaries without partisan slant, it cannot but foster the growth in the world of those who worthily and with glory will be called builders and makers of peace.*

Pacem in Terris is an encyclical in which the Pope outlined his views favoring a democratically governed welfare state in which the rule of law prevails and constitutional and human rights are observed. In the first part, "Order between Men," he enumerated the basic human, democratic rights. John derived

*"The Pope Speaks" Magazine, eds. *The Encyclicals and other Messages of John XXIII,* (Washington, D.C.: TPS Press 1964) p 378.

them from natural law which is inscribed in man's nature by God. This traditional Thomist concept was reinterpreted. John stressed the humanistic concept that every individual is a person and that the rights and duties of a person must be universal (Jean-Jacques Rousseau's words are used), inviolable, and inalienable. able.

The first of man's rights is the right to live which the Pope interpreted in a very extensive, truly modern way. It encompasses the right to bodily integrity, the availability of food, shelter, medical care, rest, and necessary social services. The right to live also includes the right to assistance in case of old age, unemployment, ill health, and other physical disabilities.

The next right stressed by the Pope is "a natural right to be respected." (Para. 12).

Other rights enumerated by the Pope may be regarded as broadly interpreted social rights. Everyone should have the freedom to seek the truth, to enjoy the freedom of speech and publication. Every individual should have the right to choose his own profession and share the benefits of culture, education, progress, and professional training. Gifted persons are to be given the opportunity to engage in advanced study to use their talents for the benefit of mankind.

Everyone should have the right to acquire property, the opportunity to participate actively in the process of production, and to exercise personal initiative. The Pope returned to the ancient Athenian concept of the active citizen, writing that the natural consequence of men's dignity "is unquestionably their right to take an active part in the government, though their degree of participation will necessarily depend on the state of development reached by the political community of which they are members." (Para. 73).

The enumeration of these human rights shows that the Pope adopted the most modern ideas concerning democratic liberties. He incorporated into the Church's teachings the concepts of modern constitutions and of the "Universal Declaration of Human Rights" adopted by the United Nations in 1948. (Para.

143). The period of the *Syllabus of Errors* and of Catholic support for authoritarian regimes was finally ended in principle.

John XXIII also analyzed the problem of the just organization of government. He obviously endorsed the Western form of democracy as something desirable and not only tolerable. He favored the division of powers and stressed that every state must have a public constitution. The juridical system must be "a clear and precisely worded charter of fundamental human rights" which should be "incorporated into the State's general constitution." (Para. 75). Government should not be unlimited. The state has no right to interfere with freedom of conscience. Freedom of religion must be unlimited. The authorities should act to achieve the common good.

The people should have the right to choose their rulers. John explained once more how the famous words of St. Paul should be interpreted, namely that there is no power except from God (*Romans:* XIII, 1-6). These words should be understood to mean that authority as such is given by God, but not that individual rulers govern with God's authority at all times. This interpretation was given by St. John Chrysostom and developed by St. Thomas Aquinas. John XXIII, however, was the first pope to use this famous passage on authority to support a democratic system of elections.

The most topical and innovative part of the encyclical concerns relations between states. John wrote that nations like individuals are the subjects of reciprocal rights and duties. Relations between states should be based on four pillars: truth, justice, willing cooperation, and freedom. Truth calls for the elimination of all racial discrimination.

Every state and its people should enjoy the right to existence, self-development, and the means to achieve it. States have no right to oppress minorities. These should be absorbed into the majority little by little. John condemned, without qualification, all forms of racism and strongly recommended the development of friendly relations between peoples of various nations and races. In this connection he also discussed the problem of political refugees. According to him everyone should have the right to leave the country in which he lives, enter another country, and be treated with due hospitality.

> And among man's personal rights we must include his right to enter a country in which he hopes to be able to provide more fittingly for himself and his dependents. It is therefore the duty of state officials to accept such immigrants and—so far as the good of their own community, rightly understood, permits—to further the aims of those who may wish to become members of a new society. (Para. 106).

Apart from John's particular recommendations concerning the rights of emigration and immigration, his general idea that mankind be regarded as one entity and that the particular interests of nations and states be subordinate to the common good of humanity must be emphasized.

In the light of this philosophy, one should read his unqualified condemnation of war and the preparations for war. Great intellectual and material resources are wasted because they are not used for the social and economic development of the people. The Pope condemned the "balance of terror" doctrine and especially the stockpiling of atomic weapons.

It is difficult to believe, wrote the Pope, that anyone would deliberately start a war to destroy the world, but a conflagration might start by chance in unforeseen circumstances. In this situation, the Pope wrote, even the testing of nuclear devices for military purposes should be prohibited because it may be dangerous to many forms of life on earth. Mankind needs disarmament:

> Hence justice, right reason, and the recognition of man's dignity cry out instantly for the cessation of the arms race. The stock-piles of armaments which have been built up in various countries must be reduced all around and simultaneously by the parties concerned. Nuclear weapons must be banned. A general agreement must be reached on a suitable disarmament program, with an effective system of mutual control . . . Everyone must sincerely cooperate in the effort to banish fear and the anxious expectation of war from men's minds. (Paras. 12-13).

The Pope believed that cooperation among nations was possible. To secure lasting peace, the existing principles of politics should be replaced by the concept that true peace among nations "cannot consist in the possession of an equal supply of armaments but only in mutual trust." The requirements of peace, according to the Pope, are dictated by common sense and everyone must agree that those requirements are the most desirable and fruitful goals. Peace must be based on negotiations and faithful fulfillment of obligations. In order to avoid war, relations between states must be regulated by the principle of freedom which means that no country has the right to interfere in the internal affairs of another. Violations of justice should be restored by negotiation because no dispute can be resolved by war in the nuclear age.

Pacem in Terris is the first unqualified condemnation by the Vatican of the very idea of nuclear war in such strong language. The ban of these weapons is encouraged. The basic principles of the cold war were rejected in this encyclical. At the same time, John elaborated his own concept of positive international cooperation. It is obvious that he recommended cooperation between the communist and western countries; he therefore had to develop new principles for collaboration between believers and non-believers, between Catholics, Liberals, Socialists, Communists, and representatives of other doctrines. His statement had been anticipated by many other progressive Catholic thinkers, particularly those in the Anglo-Saxon countries. In *Pacem in Terris* they received the official approbation.

The Pope asked men of good will to distinguish between error and the person who falls into error. To this admonition he added his own exhortation:

> A man who has fallen into error does not cease to be a man. He never forfeits his personal dignity; and that is something that must always be taken into account. Besides, there exists in man's very nature an undying capacity to break through barriers of error and seek the road to truth . . . Catholics who, in order to achieve some external good, collaborate with unbelievers or

with those who through error lack the fullness of faith in Christ, may possibly provide the occasion or even the incentive for their conversion to the truth. (para. 158).

Pius XII, the predecessor of John XXIII, not only condemned Communism but also announced that any cooperation between Communists and Catholics would be a sin. The words of Pius XII could lead to the isolation of Catholics from various political parties and social movements, even those hostile to the Soviet Union who nevertheless profess ideas which could be denounced as communist or communist-like. In the new complicated world situation (especially in the period of deep divisions and animosities among communist parties and states) the recommendation of Pius XII had become obsolete and at times even harmful to the interests of freedom and religion.

John's approach was based on the tradition of tolerance and freedom. He had confidence in the attractive power of religion and therefore believed that collaboration between Catholics and unbelievers might prove fruitful.

Finally, John distinguished between false philosophies and their results. It may happen, he wrote, that people influenced by false ideas produce results which conform to the dictates of reason. This possibility must be acknowledged and therefore cooperation with such people may be beneficial.[20]

In this way, John XXIII urged Catholics to seek every opportunity for cooperation which might bring about good and peaceful results. In *Pacem in Terris* innovative principles of freedom and toleration were laid down which have been developed during the Second Vatican Council and especially during the tenure of John Paul II.

5. The Second Vatican Council: Freedom and Tolerance Regained

On November 19, 1963, the first schema on religious freedom was presented to the Conciliar Fathers . . .

Thus, the greatest argument on religous freedom in all history happily broke forth in the Church. The debate was full and free and vigorous, if at times confused and emotional . . . the document is a significant event in the history of the Church. It was, of course, the most controversial document of the whole Council.[20a]

These words of John Courtney Murray, S.J., the true architect of the schema, taken from his introduction to the *Declaration on Religious Freedom (Dignitatis Humanae Personae)* characterize the main achievements of Vatican II.

This is the Council which philosophically redirected the Roman Catholic Church toward the cause of freedom. Almost every document of the Council was influenced by the new theology of freedom and tolerance. It is not only the *Declaration on Religious Freedom* which deals with freedom; freedom had become the first item on the Church's agenda since January 25, 1959, when Pope John XXIII announced his decision to convoke the twenty-first Ecumenical Council of the Catholic Church. Only two councils had taken place since the Protestant Reformation, one in Trent (1545-1563) and one at the Vatican (1869-1870).

During the three sessions of the Second Vatican Council, (October 11, 1962-December 8, 1965), sixteen basic documents were issued concerning the internal life of the Church, the role of the Church in the world, and the relationship between Catholics and all other denominations. This immense work was to satisfy the fundamental demand of John XXIII that the Catholic Church be brought up to date.

There still are many eminent Catholic thinkers who are not fully satisfied with the progress achieved during and especially after the Council. Concerned non-Catholics often concur that neither the Council nor the successors of John XXIII have gone far enough.

There is no doubt, however, that the Church cast aside its most obsolete ideas and opened a new chapter in its own and world history. It would be unrealistic to assume that an organization as gigantic and complex as the Roman Catholic Church, with such old traditions and cumbersome customs would be able to put such new ideas into practice without faltering at all. Now that twenty years have passed since Vatican II it is clear that the Church has moved forward, slowly and cautiously discarding obsolete philosophy, transforming itself.

The Declaration *Dignitatis Humanae Personae* closes a long history of Catholic intolerance.[21] The Declaration makes it clear that there have been periods when the principle concerning religious freedom was erroneously interpreted and applied by Christians. These words should be regarded as a final and official renunciation of the use of the "sword" in matters of faith.

> This Vatican Synod declares that the human person has a right to religious freedom. This freedom means that all men are to be immune from coercion on the part of individuals and of social groups and of any human power, in such wise that in matters religious no one is to be forced to act in a manner contrary to his own beliefs. Nor is any one to be restrained from acting in accordance with his own beliefs, whether privately or publicly, whether alone or in association with others, within due limits.[22]

The freedom endorsed here is not only freedom of internal subjective beliefs, but also freedom of behavior, connected with the freedom of association. The argument of Spinoza and John Stuart Mill that no link in the chain of liberties can arbitrarily be broken without harming the totality of freedom, is here confirmed.

The *Declaration of Religious Freedom* is addressed to the whole world, to all denominations and to non-believers as well. This is the reason that two sets of arguments are used in it, secular arguments derived from ideas about human dignity and arguments from Scripture.

In the first chapter one reads that the right of religious freedom has its foundation "in the very dignity of the human person, as this dignity is known through the revealed Word of God and by reason itself."[23] The second source of religious freedom is Revelation, discussed in Chapter 2 of the Declaration.

Revelation gives evidence "of the respect which Christ showed toward the freedom with which man is to fulfill his duty of belief in the Word of God. . . Religious freedom in society is entirely consonant with the freedom of the act of the Christian faith."[24]

Revelation also affirms "the right of man to immunity" from external coercion in "matters religious."[25]

Religious freedom in the Declaration is not interpreted as a mere passive freedom. The Church reserved for itself the right to promote the Catholic religion and to give "testimony to the truth" which is interpreted as a correct interpretation of Revelation. Respect for religious freedom and active promotion of the faith should be the active concerns of every individual, all social organizations, and the state. The state should be obliged legally, if not constitutionally, to guarantee freedom of religion. Even more, governments should create conditions favorable to the fostering of religious life:

> ". . . religious bodies should not be prohibited from freely
> undertaking to show the special value of their doctrine in what
> concerns the organization of society and the inspiration in the
> whole of human activity."[26]

The Rev. John Courtney Murray, S.J., makes the following comments regarding this concept.

> Implicitly rejected here is the outmoded notion that "religion
> is a purely private affair" or that "the Church belongs to the sac-
> risty." Religion is relevant to the life and action of society.
> Therefore religious freedom includes the right to point out the
> social relevance of religious beliefs.[27]

Father Murray is right that freedom according to the letter and spirit of the *Declaration* is in accordance with the first Amendment to the American Constitution. There is no doubt that American freedoms were an important source and inspiration for the Council.

Although Rev. John Courtney Murray's contribution to the elaboration of these ideas during Vatican II was enormous, it nevertheless would be difficult to agree with him that the idea that religion is a private affair has become outmoded.

This concept has a long history. From the period of the

French Revolution, all progressives used to repeat this sentence to stress that the symbiosis between government and church, as it existed in feudal and absolutist political systems, was harmful to the freedom and well-being of society. This famous sentence meant that the state and its gendarmes should not enter into the hearts of the citizens and the Church should refrain from using its authority for purely political reasons. This is the historical meaning of the sentence and it has not become obsolete.

Those who believe in various religions and also have their own social, political, and economic ideas, should have the right to express these ideas and struggle to realize them in the same way every free citizen in a democratic country may. On the other hand, those who disagree with the political ideas promoted by the Church, should have the right to criticize them and deal with them as with any other political idea even if the followers claim that these political programs represent only religious and not political convictions.

There is no doubt that this question is one of the most difficult in any democratic parliamentary country. The first Amendment represents and gives a legal basis to one of the basic American traditions, sometimes more praised than practiced, that religion should not be used in political campaigns and that the religious affiliation of politicians should not be taken into account by enlightened voters.

And this is also one of the most important Western democratic traditions that religious beliefs should not be imposed on people under the pretext that they are not religious but merely ethical (for instance, abortion), or scientific as in the case of the origin of human life or the theory of evolution. The state should have only one obligation towards religion, namely, to secure freedom of beliefs and legal activities connected with these beliefs.

Franklin H. Littell, a Protestant theologian, praised the *Declaration* and quoted the words of Peter Taylor Forsyth:

> The Reformation did not propose as an end religious liberty in the political sense. It was not a battle for liberty, but for truth. It did not, and does not, care for liberty except as a product of the

truth and for its sake. Truth is the Church's aim, liberty only the means thereto.[28]

There are endless discussions in philosophical and political literature concerning the relation between truth and liberty, which should be regarded the means and which the end and whether the distinction makes sense.

From the general philosophical and humanistic viewpoint, freedom should be regarded as a human end standing in its own right. If we interpret freedom as a process of acquiring power over one's own activity and destiny, then there is no reason to degrade freedom to a means. One could even argue that it is truth which is a means to broaden freedom because one aspect of freedom is the understanding of necessity.

Apart from its theological attitude, the *Declaration* also indicated a practical solution for this problem.

"The truth cannot impose itself except by virtue of its own truth as it makes its entrance into the mind at once quietly and with power."[29]

The above discussion as to whether truth or liberty are ends or means becomes unimportant if we assume that truth may only speak for itself: it may not be imposed by fire or the sword.

The *Declaration on Religious Freedom* should be regarded as the philosophical basis of two other declarations: the *Decree on Ecumenism* and the *Declaration on the Relationship of the Church to non-Christian Religions*.

* * *

Pope John XXIII wanted the council to prepare a special statement on the relationship between Christians and Jews. The statement concerning the Jews originally was part of the *Decree on Ecumenism*. But during the later sessions of the Council the statements concerning Jews and religious freedom were excluded so as to become separate documents.

The statement concerning the Jews was the object of many political considerations and of lobbying for a change of the original draft and even its deletion. Those who opposed the statement were mostly from the Arab countries. They feared that these documents would become a pretext for anti-Christian persecutions. But the majority of the Council regarded this problem as a most important religious and moral question and voted to issue the document. Most active in the struggle in favor of the statement concerning Jews were the American bishops and most especially the German Cardinal Bea. It was he who argued against the exclusion of the statement, stressing its religious character. He even urged a special paragraph requesting forgiveness by those who were wronged in addition to condemning persecution of the Jews.

The *Declaration on the Relationship of the Church to non-Christian Religions (Nostra Aetate)* defined the attitude of the Catholic Church toward Hinduism and Buddhism, the Muslim and Jewish religions. The point of departure of the *Declaration* is Pope John's idea that there are features and affinities common to all human beings. All peoples comprise *"a single community"* because they have one origin and one final goal. In all religions men seek the answers to the most important questions: what is man, what is the purpose of life, what is good and bad, how does man achieve happiness, what is truth and what will happen beyond the grave.

> The Catholic Church rejects nothing which is true and holy in these religions. She looks with sincere respect upon those ways of conduct and life, those rules and teachings which, though different in many particulars from what she holds and sets forth, nevertheless often reflect a ray of that Truth which enlightens all men[30]

This proclamation began a new chapter in the philosophy, or at least in the policy of the Catholic Church. It is well-known that non-Christian religions were regarded erroneous *in toto et in parte* (totally and in particular). Conversion to Christianity meant a rejection of harmful errors in favor of Truth and Salvation. The declaration *Nostra Aetate* breaks with this tradition and returns to the forgotten philosophy of Justin Martyr who taught that all the truths which exist in non-Christian religions enter into the great Truth of Christianity. The revival of the transformed ideas of Justin Martyr means that the Church recognizes the values of other religions. Their unconditional condemnation becomes unwarranted, a dialogue should be commenced with them.

Concerning Jews and Judaism, the *Declaration* stressed what the two religions have in common, the spiritual bond which links the Old and New Testaments. The Church cannot forget the fact that the Old Testament was received from a people chosen by God; the Church believes that the cross of Christ reconciled the Jews and Gentiles and made them "both one in Himself."[31]

The Church recalls that Christ is of the Jewish people "according to the flesh" and that from the Jewish people "sprang the apostles, . . foundation stones and pillars, as well as most of the early disciples who proclaimed Christ to the world."[32]

With these words the Council proclaimed the existence of a unity between Jews and Christians and returned to an often forgotten but authentic, tradition of Christianity.

The authors of the *Declaration* also felt it necessary to recall that Jews in large numbers did not accept the new gospel which was, traditionally, one of the reasons for the animosity between Christianity and Judaism.

Nevertheless the *Declaration* reminded its readers that according to St. Paul the Jews remain most dear to God because of their fathers:

> Since the spiritual patrimony common to Christians and Jews is thus so great, this sacred Synod wishes to foster and recommend that mutual understanding and respect which is the fruit above all of biblical and theological studies, and of brotherly dialogues.[33]

The Council recommended a mutual brotherly dialogue, which means that there should be a two-way discussion. It also means that the Council did not recommend any special effort to convert the Jews.

One of the first effects of the Declaration was the decision of the Congregation of Rites prohibiting further veneration of Simon of Trent—a boy who was murdered in 1475; the Jews were accused of having killed him in order to use his blood for matzos. More important was the fact that Pope Paul VI ordered that the Good Friday Prayer be changed from: "For the conversion of the Jews," into: "For the Jews." Within a short time special commissions were organized, especially in the United States, to promote dialogue between Catholics and Jews and to fight against anti-Semitism.

One of the most delicate and important problems which the Council had to deal with was the old accusation that the Jews had committed "deicide" (killing of God). In the first version of the Declaration the expression "not guilty of deicide" was included in order to make clear that the Jews should not be blamed for it. In the following versions, because of various objections (among others from the Catholic representatives living in Arab countries), the word "deicide" was deleted. The final text is as follows:

> True, authorities of the Jews and those who followed their lead pressed for the death of Christ . . . still, what happened in His Passion cannot be blamed upon all the Jews then living, without distinction, nor upon the Jews of today. Although the Church is the new people of God, the Jews should not be presented as repudiated or cursed by God, as if such views followed from the Holy Scriptures . . . The Church repudiates all persecutions against any man. Moreover, mindful of her common testimony with the Jews, and motivated by the Gospel's spiritual love and by no political considerations, she deplores the hatred, persecutions, and displays of anti-Semitism directed against the Jews at any time and from any source.[34]

This part of the Declaration has truly historical meaning. Anti-Semitism based on selected quotations from the Bible has a long history in the Christian world. Throughout the centuries it was often used for economic and political reasons. There is no doubt, as Cardinal Bea observed in his address to the Council, that the Nazis exploited the anti-Jewish tradition in Christian history. Finally, anti-Semitism became one of the ideological weapons of the Soviet-type of Communism. Therefore, the initiative of the second Vatican Council to repudiate all forms of anti-Semitism is important, not only morally and philosophically, but also because of the immediate political situation.[35]

In connection with the new view of religious freedom an important movement known as ecumenism began. Ecumenism can be defined as policies which promote the restoration of unity among all Christians. Since John XXIII the Church has regarded all non-Catholic Christian communions as separated brethren and not as deviationists or sinners who should be enlightened and brought back to the one true Roman Catholic Church. In the *Decree on Ecumenism (Unitatis Redintegratio)* the Council admitted that the Catholic Church shared responsibility for the disagreements and separation which took place within the last thousand years in the East and in the West. The Decree does not analyze the historical reasons and quarrels. The separation is regarded as regrettable and harmful to the cause of Christianity:

> This sacred synod, therefore, exhorts all the Catholic faithful to recognize the signs of the times and to participate skillfully in the work of Ecumenism.

The ''Ecumenical Movement'' encompasses those activities and enterprises which are organized for the fostering of unity among Christians.[36] Judgments and actions inimical to the common Christian interests should be eliminated. All Christian communions should engage in a dialogue. They should cooperate for the common good on a national and international scale. Catholics should keep in touch with the ''separated brethren,'' and they should make the first approaches and feel responsible for the success of the new movement.[37]

The result of this recommendation was the creation of ecumenical commissions by many bishops in their dioceses. In the United States a national office for ecumenical affairs was organized. The bishops' commissions encouraged conversations with Protestants, Eastern Orthodox, and Jews.

The following recommendation is especially important:

... Catholic theologians engaged in ecumenical dialogue while standing fast by the teaching of the Church and searching together with separated brethren into divine mysteries should act with love for truth, with charity, and with humility. When comparing doctrines, they should remember that in Catholic teaching there exists an order or "hierarchy" of truth, since they vary in their relationship to the foundation of the Christian faith.[38]

The idea of a "hierarchy" of truths provides Catholics with philosophical flexibility without which "charity" and the "love for truth" cannot exist in any conversation.

The idea of ecumenism should be understood, at least on the basis of the official documents and speeches, as a policy to encourage unification through compromise, if this political term can correctly be used here. The non-Catholic communions are not simply to be "swallowed" up by the Catholic Church; partnership rather than merger is the intention. Compromise and partnership presuppose that nobody can claim a monoply of truth; mutual tolerance is required.

The political significance of the ecumenical movement is extremely great. The West represents the most important traditions of democracy and in the contemporary world democracy is in jeopardy. In order to survive, strengthen, and enlarge the sphere of freedom, democratic states must achieve some degree of unity. Religious differences dividing them should therefore be reduced to a minimum. Even if the complete unity of Christian communions is unattainable in the foreseeable future, the mere fact that antagonism and bitterness among them have been overcome constitutes in itself an important step forward politically. At any rate the religious differences among the Christians, and between Christians and Jews should be considered private family disputes in dealing with anti-democratic forces. In the peculiar world situation which exists in the second half of the twentieth century, the ecumenical movement is crucial in the cause of promoting political democracy. These are the political and secular causes which determine the world-wide importance of the pontificate of John XXIII and of the Second Vatican Council.

* * *

The Church's economic, social, and political ideas found their expression in the *Pastoral Constitution on the Church in the Modern World (Gaudium et Spes)*, addressed to all Christians and "all humanity."

We will discuss only the aspects of the *Constitution* which directly pertain to our topic, freedom.

The *Pastoral Constitution* seems to repeat many of the ideas already found in the papal messages published in this century, but it is written under the influence of existentialist and personalistic philosophy. The influence of Jacques Maritain and Emmanuel Mounier can be detected.

> Though made of body and soul, man is one . . . man is not allowed to despise his bodily life . . . the very dignity of man postulates that man glorify God in his body . . .[39]

There is of course nothing new in the statement that man consists of body and soul, but the special emphasis on bodily requirements deviates from the traditional asceticism. Therefore the council even changed the traditional arguments in favor of private ownership, stressing the thesis that private property should be regarded as a contribution "to the expression of personality . . .[40], and even to the "extension of human freedom." The Council repeated the ideas of prior popes and those of St. Thomas Aquinas, that individual ownership should not be regarded as absolute, but added a topical warning: if property becomes an occasion of greed, it will become a source "of serious disturbances,"[42] and those who are against the very idea of private property, will be given a pretext for "calling the right itself into question."[42] The authors of the *Constitution* made it clear that the greed of private owners of the means of production (they do not use the word capitalists) and the low standard of living of the workers could be dangerous for the whole existing social structure and therefore remedies should be actively sought.

Even more important are the statements about land ownership in underdeveloped countries. The recommendations of the

Council are revolutionary when compared with previous traditions and attitudes:

> In many underdeveloped areas there are large or even gigantic rural estates which are only moderately cultivated or lie completely idle for the sake of profit. At the same time the majority of the people are either without land or have only very small holdings and there is an evident and urgent need to increase land productivity.
>
> It is not rare for those who are hired to work for the landowners, or who till a portion of the land as tenants, to receive a wage or income unworthy of human beings, to lack decent housing, and to be exploited by middle men. Deprived of all security, they live under such personal servitude that almost all opportunity for acting on their own initiative and responsibility is denied to them, and all advancement in human culture and all sharing in social and political life are ruled out.
>
> Depending on circumstances, therefore, reforms must be instituted . . . Indeed, insufficiently cultivated estates should be distributed to those who can make these lands fruitful.[43].

There is no doubt that the Fathers of the Council recommended some kind of land reform. At last the Catholic Church realized that the problem of land ownership and land use is one of the most important causes of revolutions in many countries. It took at least four successful revolutions (Russia, China, Vietnam, and Cuba) to prove that the Communists, without the support of the poor peasants, could not have seized power. The pronounced inequalities in the villages gave rise to the Bolshevik idea of an alliance between workers and poor peasants and Mao Tse Tung's idea of the ocean of revolutionary peasants surrounding capitalistic urban "islands." Up to the Second Vatican Council the Church had been against land reform thus acting against the well-conceived interests of Western democracy.

These questions are directly connected with the basic human rights and democratic liberties whose value had already been declared in *Pacem in Terris.* The *Constitution* reiterates that freedom cannot be enjoyed by those who are deprived of the elementary means of support, education, and culture.

The concept of socialization, introduced by John XXIII into the Italian text of *Mater et Magistra,* was further elaborated in the *Pastoral Constitution.*

The Church finally tried to draw conclusions from the phenomenon which they themselves described: in our era reciprocal ties and dependencies increase day by day, new associations and organizations both public and private continuously arise. This development, they argued, can be advantageous for the growth of the human person and the protection of his life, but on the other hand, socialization may become a detriment to human freedom and dignity. The basic reason that something advantageous may turn bad is the fact that man, "already born with a bent toward evil ... finds new inducements to sin."[44] It is obvious that the Church could not abandon the concept of original sin, its harmful effects on human beings and social activity, although the general tone of the documents of the Second Vatican Council and their outlook concerning the future of mankind are definitely more optimistic than warranted by the traditions of original sin. Compared with previous periods, the political effect of original sin was reduced to a minimum, but it still remained a hindrance to a more profound analysis of the question: why does "socialization" endanger freedom.

The *Pastoral Constitution* discusses also one of the most sensitive problems; the freedom of scholars and the relationship between science and revelation. The progress in this area achieved by Vatican II is tremendous, although this question must always remain controversial for all thinkers who adhere to unshakeable dogmas.

> Although the Church has contributed much to the development of culture, experience shows that, because of circumstances, it is sometimes difficult to harmonize culture with Christian teaching.

> These difficulties do not necessarily harm the life of faith. Indeed they can stimulate the mind to a more accurate and penetrating grasp of the faith. For recent studies and findings of

science, history, and philosophy raise new questions which influence life and demand new theological investigations.[45]

These words should be interpreted as a demand that theology also enter the period of *aggiornamento*. Theologians are invited to seek new ways to express revealed truths. They should make appropriate use "not only of theological principles, but also of the findings of the secular sciences... Thus the faithful can be brought to live the faith in a more thorough and mature way."[46]

These carefully worded sentences indicate the care which the Council employed to avoid "double truths" which could instigate the insanity of Orwellian "double think." The following statements were written as if the Council really wanted to overcome all mental reservations in this area:

> May the faithful, therefore, live in very close union with the men of their time ... Let them blend modern science and its theories with Christian morality and doctrine. Thus their religious practice and morality can keep pace with their scientific knowledge and with an ever-advancing technology. Thus too, they will be able to test and interpret all things in a truly Christian spirit... In order that such persons may fulfil their proper function, let it be recognized that all the faithful, clerical and lay, possess a lawful freedom of inquiry and of thought, and the freedom to express their minds humbly and courageously about those matters in which they enjoy competence.[47]

Does this exhortation mean that the Church once and for all put behind itself even the possibility of a condemnation of a new Copernicus, Giordano Bruno, or Galileo Galilei? Has the period of condemnation of any "new, unorthodox" theologians ended? It even seems as if the basic ideas of the enlightened Catholic thinker, Teilhard de Chardin, have been recognized officially. The most eminent authors who promoted new reconciliation of faith and science were invited to consult with the Council, as for instance Fathers Henri de Lubac, Jean Danielou, and Yves Congar. Subsequently, the first two were named cardinals. Did they truly convince the bureaucratic hierarchy of the blessings of freedom of thought and research? The Council recommended that the new approach to science should become part of the training given to future priests: in this way at least the philosophical foundation for the updating of the Church in this respect was laid.

During the decades which have passed since the close of the Second Vatican Council many changes have transpired in the Church and in the world. There are those who believe that in this time the progress achieved is fundamental and remarkable. There are of course Catholics and non-Catholics who feel that the pace of the changes is too slow and that it should be quickened. Critics are especially dissatisfied with the inflexible attitude toward abortion in a world which is over-populated and undernourished.[48] The intolerance toward the gifted theologian and prolific author, Professor Hans Küng, one of the most creative minds of our era, evoked specters of the past.[49] And there are of course conservatives who criticize the decisions of the Second Vatican Council as too liberal. Their cause is obviously lost, but the cause of progress is not easy and the road to freedom is difficult and endless.

6. John Paul II on the Dignity and Freedom of Workers

The Encyclicals of John Paul II, *Redemptor Hominis,* 1979, and *Laborem Exercens,* 1981, opened a new chapter in the Catholic theology and philosophy of freedom.

In his first Encyclical, *Redemptor Hominis,* John Paul argued that the Second Vatican Council had stressed that the human being is the center of the universe. This assessment of the Second Vatican Council became the point of departure for John Paul's social philosophy and new theological interpretations. The mission of the Roman Catholic Church, according to John Paul, is to secure and develop human freedom and liberate the powerful forces latent in every person. Every generation should strive to create more and more humane conditions for life.

In *Redemptor Hominis* his reflections on human dignity and

freedom are very broad and general; in *Laborem Exercens,* however, they are elaborated in detail.

Laborem Exercens, obviously, is an encyclical inspired by papal experience gathered under two divergent economic and political systems, capitalism and communism. It criticizes both systems, as well as Marxist and liberal-bourgeois doctrines. John Paul II endeavors to go beyond these two ideologies. He develops answers to the legitimate questions posed, but not answered, by these doctrines. He accepts the Marxian assertion that in capitalist society there is antagonism between capital and labor. Labor is separated from capital in "primitive" capitalism. This separation originated in the economic and social practices of the 18th and 19th centuries.

In this way the dignity and creativity of the workers is undermined, according to John Paul. Work, according to the Pope, is a source of the dignity and the freedom of the human being. Experience has proved this point; also God's command that man should earn his bread by the sweat of his brow. He immediately adds that it is not a curse, but the normal need of every reasonable being. God himself worked, John Paul states, while creating the world. He rested on the seventh day, but afterwards according to the testimony of Jesus himself, God resumed his work and continues it. Man, who was created in the image of God, should also employ all his talents and be creative in the image of God, should also employ all his talents and be creative for the benefit of his own self, his family, his nation, and all humanity. The expression, "by the sweat of thy brow" should be understood as the conditions under which humans work and try to creatively overcome difficulties.

John Paul II obviously was inspired by certain theses of Marx who argued that capital is the result of the accumulation of labor throughout the centuries. Today, capital constitutes the "conditions of man's work;" it is: "the result of work and bears the signs of human labor," according to John Paul. It is "the historical heritage of human labor,"[50] he continues. Capital cannot be separated from labor, or labor from capital because production could not then take place, Pope John Paul observes. We know, however, he continues that there is an opposition between labor and capital. This opposition does not spring from the structure of the production process, but as the Pope stresses, from the "structure" of the economic process. The conclusion is that this "structure" in "rigid"[51] capitalist and communist countries should be changed.

A society in which the dignity of workers can be assured should observe the following principles: joint ownership of the means of production, a sharing by the workers in the management and the profits of businesses. Private owners should remember the social aspects of property and their personal obligations towards God and society. In communist countries the nationalization of the means of production does not imply that the workers are the true owners and managers of such property. Bureaucracy and political terror contradict the communist assertions that under their rule it is the people who own the property (the Pope deliberately avoids use of the word "communism," but describes it clearly enough).

John Paul II continues the line initiated by John XXIII in *Mater et Magistra*, 1961, where the word socialization was used for the first time in a positive meaning. John Paul II asserts that under suitable conditions the socialization of certain means of production may be advisable. Socialization should not, however, be confused with a monopoly by a centralized bureaucratic administration which acts only to satisfy its own whims and interests, giving no consideration to the dignity of the workers and violating their human rights. Socialization as recommended by the Pope is assured when:

> "each person is fully entitled to consider himself a part owner of the great workbench at which he is working with everyone else. A way toward that goal could be found by associating labor with the ownership of capital, as far as possible, and by producing a wide range of intermediate bodies with economic, social and cultural purposes: they would be bodies enjoying real autonomy with regard to public powers, pursuing their specific aims in honest collaboration with each other . . ."[52]

John Paul draws additional political conclusions from the "principle of the priority of labor over capital."[53] He stresses the special responsibility of the state and even of the international community in organizing labor conditions and pays special attention to the importance of trade unions. It is quite possible that sec. 20, "The Importance of Unions," was inserted because of the situation in Poland and the emergence of "Solidarity," the first free trade union in the Communist bloc. The Pope emphasizes that a worker's dignity requires the right to form associations for the purpose of defending the workers' vital interests. Although John Paul does not officially approve of the concept of the class struggle, he nevertheless stresses that modern unions developed as the workers, who were compelled by the immoral social structures, fought to protect their just rights against the entrepreneurs and factory owners. Trade unions have become an indispensable element of social life; they are a constructive force of the social order. They have to use various methods to protect the rights of the workers including the right to order strikes and work stoppages. He calls the strike a kind of ultimatum to those in authority, especially the employers. Although the Pope writes that the strike is recognized by Catholic social teaching as legitimate, one should not forget that it was Pius XI, in his Encyclical *Quadragesimo Anno*, 1931, who disapproved of strikes as a form of class struggle which he unconditionally rejected.

There is no doubt that John Paul II has introduced into Catholic social teaching strong arguments which are of great social and political importance. For the first time in the history of the Catholic Church the philosophy of freedom had been connected with human creative activity. For the first time the point of departure has been seen as the process of production. It is stated that an individual who is free is active, is a worker and a creator. Social and economic systems which prevent individuals from taking part in productive activity are pronounced by the Pope to be intrinsically immoral.

John Paul II, for the first time in the history of the Catholic Church, binds the creativity of a productive individual with human rights, observing that their combination determines the true freedom of the human being. In this way economic and political solutions were combined with morality and the theology of human dignity and human freedom.

The Pope's specific and positive recommendations concerning changes which should be introduced in order to assure creativity and the freedom of workers are few. Nevertheless, they represent important criticisms of both capitalism and communism.

As far as criticism of the communist system is concerned, the remarks of John Paul tend toward criticism of certain aspects of communism as largely made already by the "revisionists," "communist liberals," and the followers of the institution of workers' councils in Poland in 1956-57. *"Solidarity"* took over the latter's ideas and tried unsuccessfully to augment and update them.

Criticisms of capitalism lean toward arguments made by social democrats and trade unionists who favor worker profit sharing and co-management (*Mitbestimmungsrecht*).

The implementation of these recommendations would lead to profound changes in contemporary societies. This new philosophy of freedom opens new directions for political activism.

THE POLISH ROAD TO FREEDOM AND TOLERANCE

1. Introduction

In the years 1980-1981, the Poles became—as Hegel used to write—a historical nation. One does not have to be a Hegelian in order to agree that in certain historical periods one nation or a group of nations plays an especially important role, and becomes a generator of historical development.

The Poles have played such a role several times, but after World War II they were pushed more and more in the foreground of events. In 1980, the peak was reached.

The events in Poland have already influenced the course of history. Whatever will happen there in the future will be of great importance.

Poland became a "historical nation" because it showed that it was possible to shatter a communist bureaucratic system and gain a stage of relative national independence with an advanced internal freedom. The Poles also showed that freedom and social ownership of the means of production were compatible. And they proved that there is a possibility for fruitful cooperation between a communist government and the Catholic Church, and that that cooperation could last for more than a quarter of a century.

How did it happen? Our treatise on freedom and tolerance in the 20th century would not be complete without an analysis of the Polish experience.

2. Sovereignty and Universalism

The part of Europe inhabited by the Poles has a unique political and intellectual past in which is reflected all the major

European achievements and failures, elements of progress and retrogression, of the Enlightenment and of the Kingdom of Darkness.

The attractive elements, as has often happened with relatively small nations, sometimes shine brighter than the achievements of larger nations, but sometimes the unfavorable elements are especially repulsive. So it happened with the Poles in their political activity and in their theoretical work. Many of their virtures as well as their vices were exaggerated, and had countervailing effects. The "love of our fatherland reaches the stage of insanity; we practice it with passion." These words, written in the diary of a distinguished Warsaw lady at the end of the eighteenth century,[1] illustrate a general "insanity" with which everything Polish appeared to be tinged throughout the centuries—good and evil, passivity and hyperactivity, genius and mediocrity.

During periods of political upheaval, nothing can be considered normal in a small nation which has been condemned to live squeezed between two great nations, Russia and Germany. Events compelled the Poles either to be enormously brave and intelligent or to be defeated, corrupted, and ruled by foreign invaders.

The political and intellectual history of Poland incorporates as in a microcosm all the unusual and even the trivial trends and elements of the last centuries. Polish politicians and thinkers were an integral part of the European community, and at the same time they were original statesmen and thinkers who by no means mechanically repeated the ideas of the great, universally known French, Italian, German, and English authorities. The Poles knew them, they admired them, and they were influenced by them; but they drew their own conclusions from Poland's peculiar history and experience. The most important elements of Polish political philosophy were elaborated by the Poles independently. Polish philosophical and political ideas were part of European culture, not because of the mechanical affiliation with Locke, Rousseau, or Kant, but because the Polish theories were born and grew up on Polish soil, they were developed on the common ground of the Greek and Roman traditions and the accomplishments of the Renaissance.

The first stage of the development of Polish democratic political thought can be placed at the end of the fourteenth century and the beginning of the fifteenth. During this period the internal affairs of Poland were closely connected with the international situation. Of greatest concern was the activity of the Teutonic Order which at this time was attempting to occupy territories that were part of Poland or Lithuania or, at least, put them under their control.

The justification offered by the Teutonic Order is well known. The Order claimed to be defending the true faith; it was their mission to convert the pagans and to fight against those who were really pagans while pretending to be good Christians. In the course of justifying their actions, the Teutonic Order referred to the special prerogative that has been given to them by the Church. They also referred to various spurious documents to support their position. From the philosophical point of view, however, these factors were relatively minor.

In order to protect Polish and Lithuanian sovereignty, and the right of these two nations to organize their life in accordance with their own desires, it became necessary to fight for several fundamental principles.

The first of these principles can be expressed by posing the following questions: Does anyone have the right to use "fire and sword" to convert pagans to Catholicism? Does the Roman Pope posses such an authority, and can he rightfully delegate it to others?

This issue was intimately related to two other questions which were under discussion during this period. The first concerned the authority of the Church as compared with that of the state, or the question of whether the Church can exercise supreme power over the state? Whatever the answer to this first question, the second was: Who truly represents the Church? Is it the Pope of Rome, or the Council (Concilium) of Bishops, or even the community of all Christians?

The representatives of the Polish king, especially Pawel

Wlodkowic of Brudzewo and Stanislaw of Skalbimierz, argued that neither the Pope nor the Church had power over the sovereign king of Poland and of Lithuania; moreover, no one had the right to interfere with the internal affairs of the state.

In the process of defending the independence and sovereignty of state, these scholars and statesmen likewise had to dispute the existence of any "right" to convert forcibly to Catholicism anyone who did not believe in the Christian faith and its Roman interpretation. In this way, for the first time in Polish history, and perhaps for the first time so clearly in European history, the idea of state sovereignty was linked to the concept of religious tolerance.

It should, of course, be noted that this association of religious tolerance with state sovereignty was a specific characteristic of Polish historical development. However, it can very easily be argued, and indeed many supporting historical examples can be found to suggest that state sovereignty was used and abused in order to promote various forms of intolerance and both religious and political persecution. The Polish conception of tolerance was nevertheless born of the struggle against papal universalism and the consequent intolerance that had been imported into Poland.

The second stage of such "imported" intolerance took place in the seventeenth and eighteenth centuries. Even though Polish "democracy for noblemen" was very limited, and was really only a facade to conceal the oppression of the peasants and the burghers, it was, nonetheless, a kind of democracy and included freedom of speech, conscience, and assembly, as well as the right to engage in political discussion and agitation.

The Counter-Reformation was an international movement that carried into every country, including Poland, the ideas of intolerance. It fought for the victory of intolerance and for the supremacy of the Church's power over that of the civil authorities. Protestant intolerance was also an international movement which had its impact on the internal affairs of Poland.

The third stage in the development of the universalistic

political and ideological concepts of intolerance occurred during the period after the Napoleonic Wars and the formation of the Holy Alliance. The old reactionary ideas of the deposed regimes were once again revived and imposed upon the Poles, who were fighting for their national independence and social liberation. The struggle against those powers that had participated in the partition of Poland became not only national and international, but also social and political. It was impossible to win independence without at the same time effectuating profound social changes, in particular extensive land reform, the abolition of serfdom, the destruction of various feudal privileges and duties, and the instituting of a democratic form of government.

The Poles had to struggle at the same time against other international forces of reaction, such as Pan-Slavism, the German *Drang nach Osten,* and the global policy of the papacy. Therefore the Polish democratic and patriotic movement coincided, once more, with the development of democratic ideas in other Western countries, including the United States.

Polish democratic aspirations were a part of the broader international movement for freedom, democracy, liberalism, and national independence. But the ideas of freedom were never imposed upon the Poles by force; on the contrary, the ideas and institutions of oppression and backwardness were forced upon them by the international and internal forces of the *ancien régime.*

Finally, in the twentieth century, the development of the ideas of freedom and democracy in Poland arose out of Polish opposition to various international trends representing oppression, exploitation, and backwardness. In the period between the First and Second World Wars, Polish democracy struggled against internal fascist elements which were being supported by the international fascist movements, especially the German and the Italian. However, simultaneously, there commenced a new fight, against a new adversary on the Left, represented by an alleged internationalism which by the 1920's and '30's had clearly become a new ideological form of old Russian expansionism. Whatever may have been the source and the names of the anti-democratic concepts and activities, one thing is certain: these anti-humanistic tendencies in Poland possessed features in common with the anti-democratic forces in other European countries.

During and after the Second World War the various humanistic and liberal ideas combined once more the struggle for national independence and sovereignty. The fight against the imported, Soviet, bureaucratic, allegedly universalistic model became patriotic in form and democratic in essence. In this way the circle of the evolution of Polish philosophies of freedom was completed.

In the course of the last seven centuries the social content of various Polish democratic ideas has been transformed. The political content of anti-democratic nationalistic and universalistic tendencies has also undergone changes. Some problems, however, have remained: the interconnection of the Polish concepts of democracy and tolerance with those of other Western nations and the common struggle against the forces of regression and prejudice, social and national oppression.

The conflict of those contradictory ideas is at the same time national and international. It follows, therefore, that the contributions made by Polish thinkers in this respect have had both national and international significance and value.

The general conclusion, which will be substantiated, is that the Poles were compelled by historical circumstances to fight against international oppression, and therefore their patriotic struggle for independence and freedom became an essential part of the general struggle for democracy and humanism. The national and universalistic expressions of democracy and tolerance have constituted two sides of the same coin, and today more than ever they play the same progressive historical role.

3. The Renaissance. The Arguments for Tolerance

The sixteenth century was regarded as the "golden age" of the "Republic of Two Nations." It was a period of economic prosperity and of extraordinary development of democratic institutions and liberties enjoyed under law. Poland and Lithuania were countries enjoying widespread liberties, and the noblemen of these two nations were proud of their freedom.

Instead of recapitulating the facts which are readily available elsewhere, let us recall two often overlooked statements which would be difficult to find either in conservative or in allegedly Marxist textbooks on the history of Poland.

When King Stefan Batory was urged by Papists to use his royal power to deny freedom to non-Catholics, he replied: "Leave me in peace; I am a King of people and not of consciences. God decided to preserve for Himself three domains only: the creation of something from nothing; knowledge of the future; and the reign over consciences."

The famous Chancellor Jan Zamoyski used to insist that he was prepared to give up half of his blood to convert the heretics, but that he would be willing to pour out all his blood to resist an attempt to convert them by force or to exterminate them. He also said that it would make him happy to see heretics converted, even if he were only half alive; but he would prefer to die before witnessing the extermination of heretics or the suppression of freedom.

These two statements are characteristic of the attitude of the two nations and the Polish-Lithuanian government in the sixteenth century. It is very unlikely that either the King or Chancellor would have dared to make such statements against intolerance and for religious freedom if they did not accord with a broad public consensus and with the opinions of many clergymen.

The most significant and original thinker in the sixteenth century was Andrzej Frycz-Modrzewski. He was one of the best known Polish philosophers of politics and law during the period of the Renaissance. He was well-known among eminent European humanists, and he himself tried to combine the progressive ideas of the Renaissance with Polish social needs and political philosophies.

Frycz-Modrzewski, who had a clear and brilliant mind, was very well educated and had immense political experience; thus he was well equipped to write about the basics of affairs in

Poland, in Europe, and in the Church. One can find his personal values in the famous treatise, *De Republica Emendanda,* and in his six books about the Church.

In all his writings Frycz-Modrzewski took as point of departure the existing democratic institutions and liberties. But of course he was not fully satisfied with the European and Polish status quo and recommended reforms which he felt were necessary to strengthen and expand liberties and the rule of law.

For our purposes, however, the analysis of Frycz-Modrzewski's writings will be limited to only two points: his thoughts about the Church and the Reformation, and about freedom of conscience and religious tolerance.

Although Frycz-Modrzewski was often accused by the Catholic authorities of departing from Catholicism, and holding views close to those of Luther, Zwingli, and Calvin, nevertheless he remained in the Catholic community until the end of his life. If there was anything common to the Reformation and Frycz-Modrzewski's ideas, it was their criticism of corruption in the Church and of the abuse of Church privileges in many areas of secular life.

Frycz-Modrzewski was an early proponent of the idea of religious peace and ecumenism. He did not think that dogmatic disputes were important. Indeed, he felt that it would be very easy to reconcile the Roman Church with the reformers, provided that the discussion started with a series of strict definitions of the ideas on both sides. Most of the disputes then current, according to Frycz-Modrzewski, arose from verbal misunderstandings. Later, especially in the last volumes of his books on the Church, he declared that the linguistic problems were merely specious, and were being exploited for political and social ends and by no means in order to find religious truth.

Frycz-Modrzewski's interpretation of Catholicism was truly universalistic. He wanted the Church to become an institution for the whole of mankind, uniting all Christian churches, trends, and interpretations.

> There should be unification not only of the churches of the Roman faith but also of other churches, even those which are

fighting against us under the same sign of Jesus Christ, such as the Greek and the Ethiopian churches and the churches which exist on our territory: the Armenian and the Russian . . . There are people who feel that the Russian and the Armenian do not belong to the Church of Christ. But since they have the same sacraments as we and since they are proud and happy that they are fighting under the banner of Christ, then God Himself should protect me from any idea that they should be expelled from the common host . . . Even more, I think that without them there cannot be unity of the whole Church, and one cannot regard as a *Catholic* church only the Roman church. That which is a part cannot be the whole.[2]

During the period of the Council of Trent, Frycz-Modrzewski proposed that representatives of all churches should be invited, and not only theologians but also lay delegates who could contribute greatly to the deliberations. He also believed that the delegates to the Council should be elected by the people. They should be authorized to defend their own beliefs and should be entitled to criticize the opinions of the adversaries.

Frycz-Modrzewski emphasized that the purpose of theological discussion should be to seek the truth. Every opinion should be weighed in order to find and preserve every grain of truth while rejecting whatever is untrue.

Frycz-Modrzewski questioned the arbitrary power of the Pope in matters of faith. He did not think that the decision of Rome should be regarded as final. He felt rather that the Council should elect a panel of judges who would then resolve the most important issues. The panel, however, should be guided only by Holy Scripture. Holy Scripture should be regarded as the foundation of all religious truth. In this respect, Frycz-Modrzewski closely approached the Protestants; he differed from them, however, because he also acknowledged some traditions of the Church which were rejected by them.

Of course, in case of a discrepancy between the Holy Scriptures and Church traditions, the Scriptures should prevail. In this way, Frycz-Modrzewski felt that it would be possible to achieve the essence of Christianity—peace, concord, and harmony.

Seeking to diminish if not eliminate the sources of quarrels and disputes, Frycz-Modrzewski recommended that there should be as few dogmas as possible, the *fewer the dogmas, the fewer the quarrels!* This recommendation by the way, is one of the outstanding proposals in the history of the ideas of democracy and tolerance in Poland, even down to the present day.

In order to secure freedom of conscience, the Church ought to be separated from the state. The clergy, wrote Frycz-Modrzewski, should observe the laws of the country and they should work for the benefit of the republic.

Freedom of conscience and religion is natural, it is impossible to compel people to change their ideas by force or torture. Frycz-Modrzewski stressed that one can break the body but not the mind. He frequently praised King Zygmunt August who on August 12, 1569, told the Diet in Lublin: "Everyone should understand that I do not intend to induce people to believe by means of cruelty or severity and I do not intend to burden anyone's conscience. I assure you that such is not my intention."[3]

In commenting upon these words of the King, Frycz-Modrzewski wrote that if disturbances of the heart cannot be cured by the Divine Word then nothing will cure them, neither thunder nor condemnation, nor curses nor even death itself. Spiritual storms cannot be appeased by physical force. Error can be overthrown by arguments only. The human soul is so free that "even after torture it feels and thinks as it chooses, and not as those wish who use violence." The Anti-Christ cannot be defeated by the sword, "but only by the word of Jesus Christ."[4]

Religious tolerance and freedom of conscience and belief were interpreted by Frycz-Modrzewski as extensively as possible. He went even further than Locke: he was in favor of freedom of conscience for atheists as well.

It is no political or social accident that in Poland the so-called "Arians" or "Socinians," or just Unitarians, Anti-Trinitarians, or Polish Brothers enjoyed all the freedoms which were denied to them all over Europe, and especially in Hungary, Bohemia, Germany, and Italy.

It is useful to survey briefly the arguments developed among those groups in support of freedom of conscience, religious freedom and free speech.

In Poland they were free to organize their theological seminaries or academies. They had hundreds of students, and at their conferences and seminars there was the freest discussion of philosophical, theological, and moral problems. They were allowed to publish the results of their deliberations and they were able to develop basic arguments in favor of freedom of conscience.

We shall not name the particular authors who elaborated each specific argument for two reasons: Firstly, the same arguments were developed by many authors at the same time; secondly—and even more important—all the arguments were elaborated in various seminars and academies run by the Polish Brothers in many localities. Therefore they are the result of the public exchange of ideas in which many students, both Catholic and Protestant, took part. One should regard these elemental arguments more as a product of the Polish Renaissance or of Polish democracy than of the writings of individual members of the Polish Brothers. The Unitarian writings about tolerance are really a common achievement of the Polish intellectual community of this period and they were part of the general intellectual climate in the Polish-Lithuanian republic at that time.

Secular and scriptural arguments were used to defend tolerance. From the philosophical point of view the distinction between them was only formal. The quotations from the Bible were indeed introduced for humanistic purposes, but since their presentation was logical the conclusions arrived at also were logical. It is important from the historical, political, and even ideological point of view to distinguish between these two forms.

One of the basic arguments raised by the defenders of freedom of conscience and religion was that Christianity should be regarded not as a set of dogmas which should be uncritically believed but as a way of life, as a set of key guidelines for conduct: what is moral or immoral, just or unjust, proper or improper. It is more important to act according to the recommendations of the Holy Scriptures than to believe in theological and philosophical dogmas. It is not necessary, argued the Polish advocates of tolerance, to know or understand the details of theological doctrine; it is sufficient to read the Holy Scriptures and act according to them. This line of argumentation was acceptable neither to the Catholic Church nor to the majority of the Protestants.

For Polish democracy in this period, for Polish concepts of tolerance, both the Roman Catholic and Protestant points of view were unacceptable. The Poles favored tolerance for its own sake; they opposed the use of force against heretics because they did not believe that government could properly intervene in such matters. The idea was not only secular, but it defied the political, theological, and juridical views of the Roman Catholic Church and of many other reformers of the time.

Even ideas and beliefs which seem to be absurd—argued the Unitarians—should be tolerated by the Church, provided that their adherents live according to God's Commandments. Untrue *dogmas* will be condemned by God in the end and their followers will perish in the fires of Hell. However, *decent people* will be saved in any event, and they will enter the Kingdom of Heaven. The Unitarian conclusion was that we should not hate or persecute those who might be acceptable to God and whom we might meet once more in the Kingdom of Heaven. In other words, there is salvation outside of the Church.

We ought not to fear heretical ideas. If we do not know the truth, then wrong ideas are no danger to us. If we know the truth, then the heretics pose no danger either, because our truth can neither be conquered by words, nor by the sword, nor even by reason.

When an atmosphere of brotherly love and tolerance is finally instituted by God in the Church, then false beliefs will be crushed in the same way that a clay pot bursts when struck by a silver one. "If we fear such a mutual and friendly confrontation so much, then we must not have a high opinion about the righteousness of our own cause."[5]

People should be regarded as reasonable creatures—the Unitarians argued—who are able to use their reason even concerning questions of religion. It is not true that God and his Son tried to eliminate reason from religious belief. Some of the Unitarians, especially Andrzej Wiszowaty, used to argue that the Bible even appealed to experience and the senses in order to persuade those who had any doubts. For example, after the Resurrection, when one apostle still could not believe that he was in the presence of Jesus, He said to him: "Why are ye troubled? and why do thoughts arise in your hearts? Behold my hands and my feet, that it is I myself: handle me, and see; for a spirit has not flesh and bones as ye see me have. And when he had thus spoken, he showed them his hands and his feet." (Luke XXIV: 38, 39, 40). This is an obvious demonstration that God accepts the possibility of doubt and intends that people should use their senses and reason in order to persuade themselves of the truth.

A further continuation of this line of reasoning was the argument that the nature of man was not absolutely corrupted after the first sin and the expulsion from Paradise, that the Fall should not be taken for more than it was. It is, after all, a matter of fact that at different times after the expulsion, God revealed to the people many new truths and dogmas, including the Ten Commandments. God naturally wanted mankind to understand and obey them. If he had really believed that men's nature and reason had become wholly degenerate, then it would have been illogical to reveal truths to them or make these Commandments.

In this context, the sixteenth-century Polish philosophers held that the argument of many theologians that the mysteries of faith are so lofty that ordinary people are unable to comprehend them should also be rejected. These theologians, argued the Poles, are not good Christians nor are they good disciples of Christ and the apostles. After all, if this argument were correct, Christ and His apostles also would have known that their truths were too elevated; nevertheless, they told the people that they should study and strive to understand their teachings. Christ's attitude, according to the Polish authors, on this point should be regarded as an important argument that in the sphere of faith and religion, reason rather than blind belief is to be encouraged.

Once religion is based on reason, experience, and the senses, reasonable persuasion should be the only method employed in religious disputes and in criticizing so-called heretics.

Moreover, one who uses physical force in order to persuade or to exterminate his adversary, damages his cause. People who are exposed to cruelty learn to have compassion for the persecuted and hatred for the persecutors. With compassion comes sympathy for their beliefs as well.

People who suffer because of religious or other beliefs arouse confidence in those who know them while their persecutors generate the suspicion that they are lying, that they are hypocritical, and that they lack human feelings. One chooses his religion taking into account the moral values of its adherents. ("By their fruits shall ye know them.") If heretics acquire the reputation of being decent persons single-mindedly searching for the truth and are known to be prepared to suffer for their beliefs, their personal example and witness cannot fail to appeal to others. Even the strongest intellectual or theological argument for or against a belief has incomparably less appeal and persuasive force than the personal example of the believer. The adherents of the persecuted religion become even more convinced of the truth of their beliefs because they know that even their foes realize that arguments cannot undermine these beliefs. So, contrary to its intended effect, persecution rather strengthens those beliefs and generates even more ardent attachment to them.

Religious persecution is also pernicious from the moral point of view. Force can only compel people to express themselves contrary to their true convictions. Persecution and the use of force can only produce cynicism and hypocrisy. Simulation and dissimulation are harmful to people and to the Church, and God must hold hypocrites in abomination. Hypocrites are for the Church as vipers held in its own bosom. They are hidden foes of the Church, but worst of all is the fact that they are produced by the Church itself. The hypocrisy is extremely harmful to the hypocrites themselves because the salvation of their souls is endangered; it is stated in Holy Scripture that the lot of hypocrites will be "weeping and gnashing of teeth." (Matthew XXIV: 51). Hypocrites will be denied the Kingdom of Heaven, and their persecutors and the Church will be held responsible for their downfall. Furthermore, the sin of those who induce others to commit a mortal sin will be considered worse than that of those they forced.

One should also remember that the persecution of heretics can cause internal struggles and even civil war. Often, after the suppression of heresy, disputes and wars start among various factions in the victorious camp. Religious persecution does not contribute to peace but rather to war. This state of affairs cannot be blessed by God because, as is stated in Holy Scripture: "Blessed are the peacemakers; for they shall be called the children of God." (Matthew V: 9)

The followers of religious tolerance in Poland in the sixteenth and seventeenth centuries distinguish between discussion concerning religious dogmas and criticism of the Church and its clergy. The clergy tries to equate religion with what the clergy says, but it is neither necessary nor sensible to identify the two. That the servants are corrupt does not necessarily mean that their belief is unworthy. Religion and the Church as an institution should be carefully distinguished from the reputation of any individual clergyman be he ever so highly placed. One can use even more modern terminology in this respect: to slander the officeholder does not mean to slander the office or what it represents.

The other arguments in favor of tolerance which are predominantly scriptural are these:

1. Christ said to Peter: "And I say unto thee, That thou art Peter, and upon this rock I will build my Church, and the gates of Hell shall not prevail against it." (Matthew XVI: 18). If the Church is so firmly established then the obviously false ideas of some heretics cannot defeat it.

2. If the Church is based on truth, then the teachings of the

heretics who do not believe in the truth cannot undermine it, because truth cannot be weaker than falsehood.

3. Christ and His apostles were persecuted many times and violence was used against them, but they did not repay violence with violence, although the Son of God said he could call legions of angels to defend him against his persecutors if he chose. One should follow the example of the Saviour and His Apostles and not use force but only patience and persuasion.

4. There is the suspicion that those who use force in order to defend their religion are really using it not to defend the dogmas themselves but rather their own interpretation of them. The use of the secular sword instead of arguments is not a defense of the Holy Scriptures but only of some powerful person's interpretation of them. The first apostles and Christians did not ask the praetors and consuls to defend them against the arguments of other philosophers and the Jews; on the contrary, the first Christians were persecuted and died as martyrs (i.e., witnesses), but finally the truth triumphed.

5. And finally, the apostles regard as a heretic only one who knows the teachings of the Holy Scriptures and deliberately deviates from them. A person who truly believes that he correctly knows and understands the teachings of the Scriptures cannot be considered a heretic regardless of how objectively wrong he may be.

The Unitarians continued the traditional premedieval interpretation of the famous passage from the Letter of Paul to Titus about heretics: "But avoid foolish questions, and genealogies, and contentions, and strivings about the law; for they are unprofitable and vain. A man that is a heretic, after the first and second admonition, reject; Knowing that he as such is subverted, and sinneth, being condemned of himself. (Titus III: 9, 10, 11)

The proponents of the Inquisition interpreted that passage as justifying the use of physical force against heretics. The Unitarians, however, interpreted it in the following way: Sin should be condemned; one should eventually avoid all contact with a stubborn heretic, but one ought to do nothing more than discontinue social relations. There is no indication here that heretics should be tortured, killed, or burned at the stake.

After reviewing all these arguments one can see that they are the basic philosophical (and to a certain extent, theological) arguments in favor of tolerance and freedom of conscience, freedom of discussion, and freedom of publication.

The same arguments, although in another form, are also found in the writings of Spinoza, with whom the expelled Brothers were in close touch in the Netherlands. These arguments have become part of the spiritual heritage of all mankind.

The reaction against the Reformation in the seventeenth century was at the same time an assault against the Polish traditions of democracy and tolerance. This assault was the result of the decline of democracy and contributed to the downfall of the Polish republic of noblemen.

4. Enlightenment: Independence and Freedom

The development of progressive thought in Poland in the eighteenth century was based on the revival of Polish traditions of the fifteenth and sixteenth centuries, and on widespread contacts with Western artists and intellectuals. Three of the most eminent Polish philosophers, scientists, and politicians of the period studied in Italy (Hugo Kollataj, who received his doctorate of theology there), France (Stanislaw Staszic—College de France), and Germany (Jan Sniadecki—Goettingen, Utrecht). A fourth who should be mentioned was Tadeusz Kosciuszko, who studied in Paris; he then became a political thinker and statesman, an American general, a hero of the American Revolution (1776-1783), and leader of the Polish uprising in 1794.

The Enlightenment in Poland had some general features common to the Enlightenment in all European countries as well as some specifically Polish features, significant only for that country and nation. The general features are inseparable from the essential characteristics of the European Enlightenment. The peculiarly Polish features existed either as a variant of the general elements or as new ideas unknown in other European countries.

The common features of the Polish Enlightenment's political and social philosophy may be enumerated as follows:

1. Man is born rational; it is society that makes him irrational and corrupt.
2. Human beings have inalienable natural rights which must not be violated by any political or religious power. These rights include liberty and property.
3. To effect genuine changes in the social and political structure, one must educate people; hence education is essential to progress.
4. A government should be responsible to the people, but the people must not abuse their freedom; such abuse can change freedom into the worst sort of slavery.

The most significant causes of the specifically Polish features of the Enlightenment are, from the historical point of view, these: A nation that is threatened with the loss of its very existence is compelled to change more swiftly than other nations, or else it will fail to progress at all. The perpetual threat of the German, Austrian, and Russian superpowers was at the same time demoralizing to the Poles and a source of inspiration, a reservoir of political realism and romanticism alike, of Machiavellian cleverness, and, on the other hand, of demeaning irresponsibility.

The Poles were among the first, if not the first, to elaborate a sophisticated system of political philosophy in defense of national sovereignty against the usurpations of the Roman Pope and the German Emperor. These traditions of political, religious, and ideological tolerance were abruptly suppressed in the seventeenth century, during the counter-reformation and Catholic reaction. The "democracy of noblemen" became corrupt, it degenerated into the institutions of serfdom, despotism, clericalism, and obscurantism. The links between progressive Polish thinkers and artists and their Western and Southern European counterparts were cut, and replaced by the channels of communication between the Roman Curia and the Polish clergy, who controlled the mind of the nation.

In Poland the Enlightenment started in the middle of the eighteenth century. The first part of that century was indeed a continuation of the Catholic reaction of the seventeenth century and of the total decomposition of the "noblemen's republic." The Polish-Lithuanian state was not a truly united state under a central administration, but was rather a conglomerate of territories under the rule of the most powerful magnates, *Królewieta*, Petty Kings as the people called them.

In the first half of the eighteenth century the country was devastated by wars. The Polish economy had been ruined by the armies of Charles XII of Sweden. In the 1730's there was a civil war between the duly elected King Stanislaw Leszczynski and the pretender to the Polish throne—Frederic August of Saxony, who was supported by foreign armies from Austria and Russia. In the 1750's Poland was robbed by the Russian and Prussian armies campaigning on Polish territory during the Seven Years' War. The foreign armies destroyed the Polish economy with impunity because the Polish kings were too weak to protect their subjects.

The humiliating occupation and arrogation of Polish territory was an additional painful sign that the whole social and political structure of the Republic was sick and that reforms were urgently needed. In the middle of the century there were two main aristocratic political and cultural centers: the one associated with the Potocki family, defenders of the *ancien régime*; and the one associated with the Czartoryski family, which understood that some changes and reforms were necessary in order to strengthen the executive power and to preserve national independence.

At this time the Czartoryskis did not have any far-reaching plans; they wanted to carry out some reforms within the framework of the old feudal, social, economic and political order, they wanted to end the extreme abuses, which were endangering even their own aristocratic interests. But their moderate reforms and ideas prepared the path for the "revolution" at the end of the century.

Of course the general ideas of the Enlightenment and of the

rebirth of the Kingdom of Reason were bound up in Poland with the idea of the *rebirth of the nation*. The humiliation of the nation by Poland's neighbors deeply impressed all social strata including the enlightened aristocracy. One of the reasons commonly given for the fall of the nation was that the traditions of the Renaissance had been forgotten and disregarded. During the Golden Age of the Renaissance—it was argued—Poland was one of the most powerful nations in Europe and that was because of the free development of the arts, literature, and education. When all these proficiencies fell into disuse, argued the philosophers, the republic and the nation also started to deline. Therefore, the rebirth of rationalism must be accompanied by a national awakening, and the only way the nation can rise again is through the development of science, education, and national independence.

Another characteristic of the Polish Enlightenment was that just as in France, where the Encyclopedists became the center uniting the most progressive minds, so in Poland it was the movement to change the structure of government which united the progressive social elements with various philosophers and political thinkers who wanted reform. For some time it was the Czartoryskis' Court in Pulawy and the Commission of National Education, then the Four Years' Sejm, and afterwards the Constitution and the personality of Kosciuszko that became the visible centers of the Enlightenment. Just as the French Encyclopedists were not only the intellectual and philosophical center, but also a political focus, so in Poland the political center at the same time became an ideological, philosophical and educational core, inspiring and stimulating all kinds of studies and opening up new paths and new prospects.

The third specific Polish feature: In France, England, and the Netherlands, the most troublesome economic problem was the rights of the towns and the bourgeoisie. In Poland the towns were still in such a decline that for a variety of reasons the basic and most controversial economic subject was the state of the peasantry and the reform of property relations in agriculture, without which economic development and political change were impossible. And finally, without all these internal changes, it was impossible to reorganize the army and to oust the foreign invaders.

In a very short time it became clear to the philosophers of the Enlightenment that the national problem was fundamentally a social problem, without a patriotic peasantry it would be impossible to defend the independence and sovereignty of the country. The Polish philosophers were possibly the first Europeans to use the expression that Poland embraced "two nations"—the nation of noblemen and the nation of the people, the peasants and the city dwellers. Staszic even wrote that these "two nations" were completely separate, that the only link between them was the same as the link between a victim and his executioner. Very similar expressions were used, of course, during the French Revolution and during the Restoration, but the Poles either used them first or developed them independently.

The fourth specific Polish aspect of the Enlightenment: The concept of the "nation of the people" as distinct from the "nation of the noblemen" became the point of departure for the political and military strategy of Tadeusz Kosciuszko, who in 1794 became the head of the Polish state, commander-in-chief of the army, and the dictator of the uprising. During the uprising, Kosciuszko tried to form battalions of peasants who were promised that after their return home they would be freed from feudal duties and would regain personal and economic liberties for themselves and their families. The result was not very significant from the military point of view, but extremely important politically. Kosciuszko's first peasant battalions were armed with scythes and sickles.

After the last partition of Poland, Kosciuszko elaborated his idea in a special treatise, *"Will the Poles Be Able to Gain Independence?"* In this treatise he propounded, perhaps for the first time in modern history, the idea of the people's war as a peasants' partisan war. In order to mobilize the people to participate actively in such a war, one must give them an honest, rational, political purpose: their own liberation, the abolition of all forms of feudal servitude, the prospect that the people will govern in the future independent country. It was obvious that Kosciuszko sought to combine the American experience of the Revolutionary War against the British colonialists with the specific situation of the Polish people oppressed by Czarist, Prussian and Austrian invaders.

It is one of history's paradoxes that the first political and military theory of a peasants' partisan war for national and social liberation was developed by a Polish-American general who drew his logical and consistent conclusions from the ideas of the Enlightenment and the American revolution.

And the last, specific feature of the Polish Enlightenment is the Polish philosophy of international peace. This question is discussed in a separate chapter.

In their philosophy of man and of knowledge, the Polish philosophers deliberately carried forward the English and French traditions drawing on Bacon, Locke, Descartes, Condillac, Diderot and Hume. They very often quoted Aristotle—but as a philosopher of truth, not as the father of scholasticism. The Poles deliberately and consciously embraced the traditions of Bacon's empiricism and rejected the speculation concerning innate ideas or innate moral rules. The Polish philosophers of the Enlightenment especially stressed the need for expressing their ideas clearly and distinctly, according to the Cartesian model. For this reason German philosophy was regarded by the Poles in this period as unscientific and unclear.

One of the first objects of Polish criticism was Kant's philosophy of "pure reason." The Polish philosopher Jan Sniadecki relentlessly criticized the Kantian idea of the "thing in itself" as separated completely from our knowledge of it: if there is an unbridgeable chasm—Sniadecki argued—between the world and our thinking about it, then the only result of the examination of the chasm could be dementia, not knowledge. German philosophy, he wrote, loves to find new terminology; the Germans love divisions, subdivisions, and subdivisions of subdivisions; and in the end we usually have new words but we have not moved ahead in our examination of nature. If Kant wants to investigate reason aside from the practical use of reason, he is like a man after a good dinner who starts to consider how beautiful life would be without any need to eat. It is easy to see that this argument of Sniadecki was similar to the famous argument of Hegel: Kant is like the "sophist" who wanted to learn swimming without entering the water. The upshot of Sniadecki's considerations is that German idealistic philosophers are like an association of crippled people seeking to persuade the world that the best method of walking is on crutches. Murky German philosophy is hampering all efforts at enlightenment and is transforming philosophy and science into Eleusinian mysteries, Sniadecki concluded.

Jan Sniadecki quotes these words while criticizing the idealism of Mallebranche, and makes the following comments:

> Let us Poles be. . . more modest in our ventures and let us stick to reason. Let us listen to Locke in philosophy, let us follow the recommendations of Aristotle and Horace in literature, let us follow the rules of Bacon in observation and experience.[6]

And then:

> Let us try to write and to think so as never to be afraid of the tribunal of truth.[7]

These words should by no means be interpreted in the sense that the Poles were to follow foreign examples blindly. On the contrary, some thinkers deliberately sought to be unfashionable:

> Let us not compete with other nations (in the field of fashion- M.M.) . . . let us seek glory and importance at home only in the good of our countrymen, because the influence a nation enjoys among foreign nations derives from its internal strength.[8]

The struggle against muddled philosophy that violated common sense was also expressed in Polish literature and art. Ignacy Krasicki, known as the "prince of poets," wrote in one of his satires: "The arrogance of ignorance—that is what makes a philosopher."

Hugo Kollataj is the author of the term "gentle *(lagodna)*

revolution." According to him gentleness was characteristic of the Polish "revolution" in the eighteenth century which culminated in the Constitution of May 3rd, in the peaceful changes in the government, the acquisition of new rights by the cities and the improvement of the position of the peasants. The term "gentle" meant a "non-French" revolution, non-violent, bloodless; it meant a revolution which was for almost everybody and was not against anybody; for the people and for the nation and not against the magnates and the church hierarchy, provided they were reasonable and patriotic. It was, finally, a revolution of common sense and of liberty against ignorance, prejudice, license, and tyranny; a gentle revolution against undeserved privilege, for true justice, equity, law, and order.

In short, the progressives, including the most radical elements, tried to make it appear that the "gentle revolution was not a revolution at all, but just a "rebirth," a "resurrection" *(wskrzeszenie)*, an "organization of the new Poland." The famous concept of 1980, called "renewal" *(odnowa)*, referred to this tradition.

To a certain extent this terminology reflected social and political reality, but it also garnished it, if indeed it did not camouflage it.

The term "gentle" expressed the fact that the Polish radicals (including the group of "Jacobins") were not so "radical," so demanding, so far-reaching as their French counterparts. The Polish revolutionaries did not have the same social support as the Frenchmen; the Warsaw bourgeoisie was weaker, less numerous, less self-conscious than the Paris bourgeoisie, while the bourgeoisie in other Polish towns was still so weak that it had not yet emerged as a significant social force. The Parisian proletarians, including manual workers and sans-culottes, were a conscious social and political force; they had no counterparts in Warsaw or in any other Polish town.

The social basis of the Polish radicals was weaker, their social support and appeal to the public was more limited—therefore they were less "revolutionary," less "extreme," "softer," "gentler," and reformist. The Polish patriots, radicals, and progressives could never forget that the Russian bears and Prussian eagles were watching them and recording all their sins and all their heresies.

Accordingly, the Polish revolutionaries had to adopt a typically heretical tactic: they alleged that they wanted improvement only within the framework of the "cardinal laws" and within the "traditional order" of "golden Polish freedom," although they were undermining the basic pillars of this order.

On the other hand, the Polish progressives really feared a bloody peasant revolution such as the uprising of the Russian and Ukrainian peasants under Stepan Razin. Kollataj knew exactly to whom he was appealing when he asked, "Is is not safer to have a revolution of the noblemen than of the mob?"[9]

The implied answer was simple and logical: Change and reform are unfortunately inevitable, therefore, let us make them in a reasonable, peaceful, "gentle" way, because otherwise the "mob" will take matters into their own hands, and then woe to culture, fortunes, religion, property and prosperity. Let us be prudent, the most radical thinkers and politicians suggested. Let us, the nobility, bring about what is inevitable anyway.

The argument that an uprising or revolution by the mob was inevitable and inescapable unless reforms were instituted promptly, was used to soften the conservative hardliners, and even the Tsarist government who officially assumed the role of the the guarantor of the "golden freedoms."

Kollataj and other reformers believed that the "titles" of the magnates were doubtful, that the great fortunes had their source in the expropriation of the relatively poor gentry and the peasants. Therefore they insisted that steps be taken to return the land to the "successors of the brave Polish knights," to the noblemen whose ancestors had fought for the independence, freedom, and greatness of the Republic.

Neither Kollataj nor Jezierski regarded the magnates' fortunes as property legally and justly acquired. On the contrary, they regarded those fortunes and the feudal system as a whole as being what the philosophers of Western Europe used to call: *le brigandage systematique.*

The peasants, of course, were unimpressed by the legal arguments of the aristocrats. In Poland they had had a long tradition—unknown in the West—of avoiding bondage and unlimited exploitation. For centuries they had escaped to the "wild fields" of the Ukraine and joined the Cossack *stanitsas.*

In the second half of the eighteenth century many peasant revolts took place in Poland, especially in the years 1768-69 and 1788-89 (the period of the Four-Year Sejm). The revolts were especially violent in the Eastern provinces of Poland, where the greatest *latifundia* were and where the majority of the population was not Polish, but Ukrainian and Byelorussian— and Orthodox rather than Catholic. The peasants were an important element in the uprisings in the Eastern provinces of Poland not only for social and economic reasons, but also as a result of religious and national oppression.

The fear of the peasants' rebellions was one of the reasons why some aristocrats from the Eastern provinces made reforms on their estates and supported the progressive party during the preparations for the May 3rd Constitution.

But the secular and clerical conservatives among the aristocrats did not understand those problems; they enjoyed the status quo and felt that all the reformers, progressives, and insurgents should be crushed—if necessary with Russia's help, in order to bring about "normalization."

The counter-arguments of the magnates opposing the reforms were rather primitive. In a contemporary pamphlet one reads:

> . . . It is not good policy for a free nation to destroy and to ruin the best families. They should necessarily be preserved . . . one should not hate them, because hatred violates order and decency and does not provide what one should get according to divine and human laws. Let us not envy, let us give up opposition to the law, and let us drop attempts to interfere with the established order, let each cherish the privileges to which he is entitled.[10]

This aristocratic "trickle down" philosophy was accompanied by a peculiar theory of foreign policy. The supporters of the *ancien règime* in Poland presented their ideas in the following way:

—The weakness of Poland is the source of its strength; no one will be afraid of her and therefore nobody will try to harm her.

—The rivalry between Russia, Austria, Prussia, and Sweden resulted in a certain kind of European balance. A weak Poland is a part of the general equilibrium, and therefore everybody is interested in her survival and existence.

It was a historical paradox that the absolute monarchies, especially Russia, actively supported the principles of "Golden Polish Freedom." They understood that this Polish "freedom" in its final corrupted form was indeed slavery for the majority of the people (the peasants and the bourgeoisie); it was connected with the corruption of the lower and middle strata of the nobility, and it guaranteed unrestricted license for the aristocratic oligarchy.

History can scarcely show a better example of how "freedom" may be a mask for oligarchical license.

There were two basic political institutions characteristic of the republic of the noblemen: *free elections* and *liberum veto* (free veto).

Among the noblemen it was generally understood that *"free elections"* are a legal and institutional guarantee against the *absolutum dominium* of the king. The noblemen thought that with *"free elections"* the king would be obliged to act as a public servant rather than an absolute ruler.[11]

In the seventeenth and eighteenth centuries it became obvious that these ideological and political presumptions were unfounded. First, the *"free elections"* were not as free as the noblemen had hoped and as the founding fathers of this institution had intended because of the dominant role of the aristocracy. Second, every free election during the period of the political and moral decline of the country created an arena for internal factional struggles, giving foreign powers an excuse to intervene. When some of the European powers were too busy with their own troubles, as was France with her revolutionary ferment, or busy with other political purposes, as England was with its overseas colonies, that was the time for the European powers interested in Polish affairs to exercise pressure. When the Western powers lost interest in Polish affairs, it was Russia, Austria and Prussia that replaced them. Poland's *"free elections"* thereby became an institution which was especially important for Poland's closest neighbors.

The authors of the May 3rd Constitution decided to abolish *"free elections"* because, they claimed, they were terrified by the "disasters of the interregnum;" they wanted to "block evil foreign influences" and to prevent the powerful Polish magnates from nominating themselves as kings.

The second institution of the "golden freedoms" was *liberum veto.* The old idea that truly "democratic" decisions are unanimous found its expression in Poland. If a single deputy announced his *liberum veto* all decisions of the Sejm made during a given session were invalidated.

Since the seventeenth and eighteenth centuries the majority of those who used *liberum veto* were agents either of the Russians, or of the powerful magnates. Poland as a free state was paralyzed. The Russian tsars announced that they themselves were the defenders of this freedom.

In Poland there were other freedoms as well: of the press, of assembly, and of the theater. These true freedoms were not approved of by the Russian ambassadors and they used their influence to compel the Polish authorities to suppress them.

5. Liberation and Progress

During the first part of the nineteenth century the course of democratic thought in Poland ran parallel to that of the Western European countries. Polish democratic thought opposed feudalism, absolutism, despotism, and all kinds of "old regimes," while favoring democratic liberties and national sovereignty. The fact that Poland was partitioned and had ceased to exist as an independent state resulted in no basic changes in its democratic ideology, as compared to that of Western Europe.

The most characteristic feature of Polish democratic thought was the close connection between the ideas of national liberation and democracy. New concepts of democracy in Poland had been evolving since its loss of independence and the Napoleonic Wars. The participation of Polish legions on the side of the French was a deliberate decision that linked the fight against the "old regimes" with the struggle for national independence.

I will leave aside the question of whether and to what extent Napoleon really promoted progressive changes in Europe, and truly wanted to abolish the remaining feudal and absolutist remnants all over Europe and especially in Poland, for this is not central to our presentation. As for the Poles, their alliance with Napoleon was based on their support of and desire for social and political transformation as well as for national and social liberation.

The abortive November uprising of 1830 and the defeat of the Polish patriots helped the development of specific political and ideological concepts within the country and also within the so-called "Great Emigration" which settled predominantly in France and, to a lesser extent, in Belgium, England, and Switzerland.

The strength of any political idea ought not to be evaluated by the number of its domestic or foreign supporters. The most important factor in evaluating political ideas is their ideological and historical impact. This holds true even if the impact of the ideas is delayed for decades or even centuries.

The ideas which were set forth by Polish patriots and democrats in the first part of the nineteenth century obviously had no impact compared with those of the liberal parties in France and England, or even those in Germany and Italy.

But the liberal, tolerant, and democratic beliefs prevalent among the enlightened elements of Polish society established a deeply rooted tradition which influenced the attitudes of the nation at the end of the nineteenth century and throughout the twentieth.

I do not intend to present here a strict historical evaluation of all the trends which existed in Poland and among Polish emigrés during this period. However, roughly speaking, three trends or parties should be singled out for the purpose of this analysis. The first was represented by the followers of Czartoryski who were quartered at the Hotel Lambert in Paris. The Towarzystwo Demokratyczne Polskie (TDP), or the Polish Democratic Society, was the second influential group. And the third tended toward the ideas advocated by the European utopian and democratic socialists.

The ideology of the party represented by the Hotel Lambert group can be described as an enlightened aristocratic concept that had played a progressive role in the eighteenth century; however, as a result of the logic of historical events, it was anachronistic in the nineteenth.

The Hotel Lambert party made it a practice to call attention to the historical significance of the Constitution of May 3rd and of the Kosciuszko uprisings and manifestoes; but they were unable to understand that their progressivism was always limited, and in the nineteenth century fell short of what was needed for the political and social liberation of the nation. Even their opposition to feudalism and support for land reform and the peasants' liberation were very limited. Nevertheless, the general democratic phraseology of the followers of Czartoryski represented a sign of the times and had its historical impact.

Of greatest importance from the historical perspective, though, was the activity of the TDP. While this group was never unified ideologically or organizationally, its adherents managed to issue various documents and generally accepted statements which fairly represented the main European liberal, democratic, rationalistic outlook. But the TDP was not simply a mirror of European liberalism.

In all TDP documents one senses a limitless belief in the power of human reason together with a boundless faith in the progressive and humanistic evolution of mankind.

The rationalism of the TDP is seen in all their political and social pronouncements and declarations, even though they made no purely philosophical statements. "Our society," as W. Heltman used to stress, "is not a school of philosophy. It is a political body working to recover a democratic Poland. We are not going to engage in philosophical research, but we want to create a new social order."[12]

Heltman, along with other members of the society, did not represent an anti-philosophical attitude that could be interpreted as being opposed to theory. Rather, he wanted to avoid sterile speculation which could lead nowhere, and could only deflect the attention and energy of the members of the society away from the real social and political problems that were facing Poland.

In framing their declarations, the TDP employed such expressions as the "tribunal of reason," "universal conscience," and the "power of reason," or the "belief only in what we understand." And at the same time they condemned everything mystical, prophetic, or unsupported by reason and evidence.

Regardless of the concrete elements of their political program, one thing is certain: The TDP connected the fight for national and social liberation with the struggle for education and against darkness, backwardness, and the dead past.

The TDP's hatred for all forms of prejudice was acquired from the works of the European, and especially the Polish, Enlightenment, and in particular from the writings of Staszic and Kollataj. This rationalism was naturally strengthened in the minds of the emigrés in France when they studied the French tradition of rationalism and also the writings of Babeuf and Saint-Simon.

Using the concept of the "tribunal of reason," the TDP condemned the obsolete institutions of the old regime, attacking the monarchy, oppression, serfdom, and the absence of democratic liberties.

They were critical of the concept of monarchy advocated by the party of the Hotel Lambert. They wrote that whoever sincerely has the welfare of the country at heart should do battle

under the banner of democracy. That is—according to them—
an authentic, original, Polish political concept and not an imported
one.

They were critical of the concept of monarchy advocated by
the party of the Hotel Lambert. "The thought of Czartoryski
was never really Polish; it is foreign. He dreams about royalism
and thinks that next to the King's house there should be a house
of aristocrats. . . ."[13]

It is most interesting to note that the concept of democracy
was considered by the Poles to be a *national* Polish concept,
whereas the idea of *monarchy* was thought to be alien to the
Polish spirit.[14]

The TDP also elaborated a program of democratic government and liberty. In his "Short Political Catechism" the Polish
author Janowski posed this question, "What is democratic
government?" He gave the following answer: "It is the government in which everyone can do whatever he wants, provided
that he does not violate the rights of others. It is the government
of the power of the people, which is the accomplishment and
organ of the entire nation and the executor of its will. There is no
master in the government other than the laws which are to represent the will of not one person or of a privileged minority but the
will of all, or at least of a majority of the citizens . . . Good
government should be a simple apparatus established to execute
the will of the omnipotent people, and the officials ought to function only as the springs in this machine."[15]

The will of the people should be expressed by the deputies
who represent the people and are elected by them. They ought to
be paid out of the public treasury so as to assure their independence. The officials should be subject to recall at any time if
their activity so warrants or if by their actions they fail to maintain the confidence of the people.

The TDP agreed with the sixteenth and seventeenth century
Polish democrats, the Unitarians and their ally Benedict Spinoza, that freedom of speech, being the foundation of all democratic liberties, cannot exist without other liberties; similarly,

without freedom of speech and publication, all other liberties would become extinct.

"Freedom of publication serves as the shield of all freedoms in a free nation and therefore must be unlimited."[16] and further:

"Freedom without liberty of publishing is a sterile phantom. Where freedom of the press exists the reign of despotism, monarchy, and aristocracy cannot last for long. Prejudice must give way to truth, privilege to equality, and the state of oppression must be replaced by the state of general happiness."[17]

But the TDP also realized that in the transition period during the revolution for national independence and social liberation it might be necessary to limit this right in order to prevent its abuse by the enemies of freedom. Here they repeat the well-known concept of "no freedom for the enemies of freedom," expressed by Saint-Just. They especially emphasized that freedom of association should not be granted to the enemies of freedom. We realize today how this principle can be perverted, but the TDP did not have sufficient historical experience to recognize this.

The TDP stressed that during the fight for freedom the army is most important. All their writings concerning the army were inspired by Kosciuszko's famous pamphlet based upon the French and the American revolutions. They felt that the new army should be very different from former mindless and despotic armies. They wanted the new army to be composed of free citizens who understood the political issues and who were aware that they were fighting for the interests and freedom of the people, and not for the interests of despots.

Thus they developed the idea—as they themselves put it—of the "citizen-soldier," that is, a soldier who is not a ruthless and mindless instrument of his superiors but a conscious *citoyen* of his fatherland.

This new army will be strong as a result of the moral attitude of the soldiers and not because of its superior armaments and military drill. The commanders of the army should be made up of those dedicated to democracy who are also brave, reasonable, and trained in the military arts. They added that the military leader of this democratic army should be a conscious citizen and not merely a trained professional officer.

The TDP was likewise aware that the fight for freedom never ends, and that even when freedom is achieved it is still threatened by those seeking to destroy it. At times they interpreted the idea of democratic liberties not only as an end result of some activity but also as a means to achieve it. Making use of one of the recommendations of the French revolutionary, Danton, the TDP stressed that one should be prepared to sacrifice "the form in order to preserve the essence," and also that one should be prepared temporarily to subject himself to "the despotism of freedom in order to fight the despotism of tyranny."

But against whom should this "despotism of freedom" be employed? And whose interests ought to be defended by it?

One of the ideologues of the TDP wrote that the Polish revolution must simultaneously be both political and social and that it must fight against two enemies—the internal as well as the external. Especially dangerous, though, is the resistance put up by internal foes because they resort to all sorts of secret schemes and traps.

Every revolution knows treason and intrigue. The people too are weak and are particularly susceptible to flattery and appeals to their vanity. Every revolution experiences these dangers, there is no reason whatsoever to believe that the Polish aristocracy and noblemen would somehow be better than others like them.

As we have seen, within the program of the TDP were expressed all the basic Western concepts of freedom, representative government, unlimited political liberties, as well as the idea of a fighting, active, militant democracy, not of a democracy satisfied with forms while neglecting the essence. They developed an idea of democracy in a country surrounded by foreign despots.

In Poland during the 1820's, '30's and '40's, a very strange development in philosophy took place. This was a period when philosophy came increasingly to reflect the conscience and the spirit of the nation. Philosophy and literature came to be the necessary means for preserving the enslaved nation. It was also during this time that they became an indispensable instrument of progressive change.

The Polish philosophers were well trained in history and European philosophy, and they were able to distinguish among various trends in the development of English, Franch, and German philosophy. But they never enjoyed the advantage of the Western philosophers who could devote themselves entirely to highly theoretical problems. The Polish philosophers were hard pressed by current issues and felt obliged by circumstances, if not by their milieu, to deal with real, current problems.

In the clearest possible way this state of affairs was reflected in the works of Henryk Michal Kamienski. Until now, wrote Kamienski, the greatest deficiency of philosophy has been its impracticality; philosophy remained closed within its own sphere and so was unable to solve the real problems of life.

There are two trends in Western European philosophy, according to Kamienski, and both of them are limited. On the one hand there is a theoretical secular German philosophy whose latest phase is Hegelianism, or the "philosophy of the Absolute." On the other hand, there is the French philosophy which is fighting for progress, studying empirical facts, and creating theories of social change, such as the philosophy of Saint-Simon, Fourier, and others.

Unfortunately, however, there is a chasm between these two schools of philosophy. German philosophy underestimates facts, empirical experience, the true science of life, and the programs of social progress. The French school underrates the importance of theory which, in their view, is regarded as sheer speculation and pure mental gymnastics. However one should attempt to bridge this chasm and create a new synthesis, resulting in a higher phase that will promote the advantages of both schools while rejecting the disadvantages. And, in the process, this synthesis ought to transcend the one-sidedness of both schools.

This philosophy, Kamienski believed, would simultanously be both a truly *universal* philosophy and a *genuinely Polish* philosophy. Such a synthesis would indeed be original, it would be patriotic, populist, and many-sided. Such a philosophy, while being Polish and directed toward solving Polish problems, would at the same time be a universal theory of progressive mankind. Philosophy, wrote Kamienski, being the product of the universal human mind, must be rational since it has to reject all irrational ways of acquiring knowledge. Faith and feeling cannot be a way to make scientific discoveries, according to Kamienski; they may be instrumental as a preconscious hypothesis, but nothing more.

In this way Kamienski rejected all phraseology concerning the soul or the spirit of a nation, although he did write about the nation and national independence, national traditions and a national way of life. He did not give these terms a narrow nationalistic connotation but regarded them as part of a universalistic human interpretation of the past and present.

Philosophical knowledge, he stressed, should make clear to the people what the national principles are that determine human knowledge and self-consciousness. Philosophy ought to be knowledge of the Absolute as well as knowledge of every part and phase of human life. Philosophy should be an abstract reflection of real life.

In order to realize this ideal of Absolute knowledge that combines theory with practice and ideas with reality, philosophy has to overcome the Cartesian principles (developed, as Kamienski asserted, by Hegel): *Cogito ergo sum*. The *cogito* is the result of human activity and of man's more or less conscious struggle against blind physical forces. The point of departure of true philosophy should not be the *cogito*, but *creation* and the *transformation* of nature and the environment. Moreover, the starting point should not be that of a thinker but of a human being who is acting and creating. In this way, philosophy will become a true "teacher of life" instead of only theoretical principles.

We ought to have as the maxim of our behavior—this is Kamienski's main philosophical assertion—*Creo ergo sum,* or "I create therefore I am." Philosophy based on this foundation will be both practical and theoretical. It will not only be a philosophy that explains, but it will also give advice on how to act and create.

It is only the past and the present which can be explained; the future must be created. Therefore a philosophy of action and creation should be regarded as a philosophy of the future, or as a philosophy that is oriented toward progress and not toward effete, impractical speculations about the past.

In the works of Kamienski the mere concept of life is interpreted as a permanent progression. "To live means to create . . . To create means to progress. Progress is life."[18]

There are two elements within this philosophy which are closely connected with progressive philosophical and scientific developments in the West during this period. The first element is the belief that progress is solely the fruit of human activity. This optimistic view has never taken into consideration the fact that mankind has had to pay a horrible price for its every step forward.

Kamienski saw and understood not only the misery of serfdom and of the feudal way of life, but also the evils of liberal capitalism. Nevertheless he remained true to his belief that all undesirable elements were only accidental and did not change the essence, which was progress.

The second element is the combining of the European traditions of empiricism and rationalism which were not developing separately, as has often been suggested by historians of philosophy; instead, according to him they were actually impinging upon one another and stimulating one another.

In his writings about the past and the future, Kamienski repeated the famous prediction of the Saint-Simonists that the so-called "Golden Age" of mankind is not a thing of the past but is yet ahead of us and it is even to a certain extent now among us since it is called into being by our day to day activity and creativity. Progress as an Absolute is therefore not a future, faraway stage of man's development; it is a process which has already begun and is constantly proceeding.

Kamienski has associated universal progress, as in Hegel's philosophy, with the progress of the ideas of freedom, democratic liberties, and individual identity. Hence his "tribunal of reason" is both a source and a result of the development of freedom. Therefore it is clear that for Kamienski progress meant not only the overcoming of material poverty and political oppression, but also the full development of free human creativity. This individual creativity depends upon unrestricted political freedom; political freedom becomes, in this interpretation, the end and the means of the individual's creativity; and creativity is the essence and the body of genuine human freedom.

6. The Stormy Years 1980-81: Victory Against Oppression

a. Historical Antecedents

We have discussed various concepts of democratic thought in Poland during the periods of early and late feudalism, at the end of the First Republic, and during the first part of the nineteenth century. Now we will focus on more recent developments, and concentrate on those democratic trends that have evolved in Poland under the communist regime.

From the beginning of the communist ideology and later under communist systems, a variety of trends have developed under the names of socialism and communism. At the end of the nineteenth century and the beginning of the twentieth, it became quite obvious that the European socialist movement was divided into at least two different parts. One was known as the social-democratic or socialist movement, and it was denounced by the radicals as being "right-wing" socialism; the other was radical and revolutionary, and it was this trend that gave birth to the communist parties all over the world. It is most frequently connected with the Leninist interpretation of Marxism and communism; Leninism itself soon became divided.

The Poles took an active part in the formation of European social-democracy. One of the leaders of the Polish socialists in *Galizia* (the part of Poland which then belonged to Austria),

Ignacy Daszynski, was also one of the well-known leaders of European social-democracy.

From the outset Polish socialism represented national, patriotic and, at the same time, progressive socialist ideas. The Polish Socialist Party (PPS) was characterized by more or less the same ideology as all the other Western socialist parties which were seeking to combine the ideas of progress, independence, patriotism, socialism, and democracy. Between the wars, the PPS was simultaneously both anti-fascist and anti-Leninist. The party exhibited all the good points, as well as all the shortcomings, of European social-democracy.

However, one thing is certain: the PPS tried from its inception to unite the concept of socialism with the ideas of progress, rationalism, democracy, and anti-clericalism. It represented a typically liberal attitude.

It is not our intention here to analyze the ideology and traditions of the PPS; literature is available on this subject. Instead, we mean to concentrate on one democratic and patriotic trend within Polish communism.

Within every leading powerful trend in history, even if it be defined as anti-democratic, there can be found ideologues and politicians who represent more liberal and more rational positions and who disagree with the official expression of the given ideology and its institutions. It happened so during the period which lasted for more than 1,000 years when the Church dominated affairs in Europe. The same thing was true in absolutist France, Germany, and Russia, and there are even examples of it in the Oriental countries.

No scholarly analysis of communism, which seized power for the first time more than sixty years ago, and is regarded today as the dominant and official ideology of approximately one-third of the world's population, could possibly conclude that there is any monolithic communist bloc or ideology. We are aware that from the political point of view one can distinguish at least three groups of communist countries—the Chinese, the Soviet, and a group of relatively independent communist countries, particularly Yugoslavia. The differences between these countries and blocs are not only political but ideological and philosophical as well. One should also take into consideration the existence of various Western communist parties or Western representatives of communism that either represent the dominant tendencies in the communist blocs or else are trying to make their independent way based on their own perception of Marxist philosophy and Western democratic traditions.

The contribution made by Poles to the development of democratic trends in communism was very substantial. The events of October, 1956, were the real practical beginning of democratic communism; we have not yet seen the end of this process, which is still evolving.

Differences between the official Leninist interpretation of communism and its democratic interpretation arose immediately after the Russian Revolution. In this regard the writings of Rosa Luxemburg, the famous European revolutionary of Polish origin, are especially noteworthy. From the very beginning, she accused Lenin and the Bolsheviks of violating the democratic principles of Marxism and of revolutionary socialism. In particular, she declared that the revolutionary struggle cannot excuse the elimination of basic democratic liberties and guarantees. She felt that freedom for one party only is really no freedom at all. In her arguments for freedom, Rosa Luxemburg repeated the well-known principle of both Polish and liberal European thought: freedom should not be granted exclusively to the leaders and followers of the ruling party, but should be extended to the members of the opposition.

During the same period, Justice Holmes argued that the First Amendment to the Constitution of the United States gives guarantees for freedom of expression that are rather more important for those whose ideas we detest, than for others.

This was a historic meeting of minds, that of a Polish-German-Jewish woman revolutionary and one of the most distinguished representatives of the American judiciary. Both were explaining the fundamentals of freedom to their respective establishments.

Thus we have approached the latest state of the *Polish road to freedom.*

* * *

Although at the moment of this writing the 1980-1981 up-heaval in Poland has not yet spun itself out, it has already had great historical impact in communist as well as Western countries. The movement toward democratization was arrested by outside pressures and internal military intervention, but the significance of the Polish example for the world will still be enormous.

In August and September 1980, the Polish workers shattered the bureaucratic system and dogmatic ideology that has prevailed in their country for thirty-five years. The constitutional system was not changed officially, but within the framework of existing political institutions the spirit of tolerance and democracy began to spread. In 1980-1981, the Poles accomplished what they had twice tried to do—in 1956 and 1970—without success. The Poles proved that it is possible to compel a communist government to introduce fundamental political, social, and even administrative changes. The concessions were won peacefully, without bloodshed, thanks to the unified national will.

The first effort at liberalization started after Stalin's death in 1953. Stalinism caused a deep political and economic crisis, to say nothing of an ideological one, which affected the governing Communist Party in its entirety.

The 1955-1956 crisis in Poland was in every sense revolutionary. Polish society did not want to be ruled by the old, discredited, autocratic methods, and the government found itself unable to go on ruling and preserve those methods unchanged. As an oppressed people grows more and more self-confident, the established authority is more and more paralyzed. The bloody suppression of the workers in Poznan in June, 1956, demonstrated the inability of the government to have its dictates respected with the use of force. Consequently, a factional struggle emerged in the government and in the Central Committee of the Communist Party. It became obvious that substantial reforms must be introduced or else the direct and permanent intervention of Soviet troops would be necessary to preserve the existing system of the Communist bureaucracy. In the summer and fall of 1956, and especially during the Polish October, social pressure led to many changes of personnel in the Party and the government. The new ideas were the forerunners of a whole new way of thinking.

Even conservative members of the Party had to reflect on what was happening. Many things occurred against their will. Censorship was relaxed, political prisoners were released, Cardinal Wyszynski was allowed to leave his place of detention and resume his duties. The Catholic Church regained elementary freedom of activity, the people ceased to fear to express their thoughts openly. Worker's councils were established in government enterprises. Interesting books were published, a whole Pleiad of gifted poets made their debuts. Social sciences and universities gained substantial independence. Youth organizations of the Soviet Komsomol type ceased to exist. But the most important elements of the Party apparatus, the security organization, the administration, the government-controlled trade unions, remained basically untouched. Any liberalization in such circumstances was predestined to be ephemeral.

Gomulka and his friends who were then elected to the Politburo had previously been jailed. Almost overnight the victims of Stalinism became Poland's new leaders. No wonder they were pronounced national heroes, and their assurances that socialism would become humane were taken seriously. In those days, for the first time the Party began to cooperate with the Roman Catholic Church. The Primate of Poland, Stefan Cardinal Wyszynski, actively urged his countrymen to remain calm. Neither the Polish Politbureau nor the Catholic clergy wanted a repetition of the Hungarian tragedy. They preferred, each for its own reasons, to avoid Soviet tanks and direct Soviet occupation. Wyszynski demonstrated in that way his intellectual and political superiority over Cardinal Mindszenty of Hungary.

But the new governors of Poland were unable to seize their historic opportunity and use it to best advantage. They were intellectually weak and ideologically limited; they had no experience in working within a democratic framework. Almost immediately they began to revert to the traditional bureaucratic methods and to proclaim the old, worn-out ideology. They could not, of course, entirely reconstitute the *ancien régime*. With the collectivization of agriculture dead, the Party divided, and the police demoralized, they were unable to revive the old Bolshevik *élan*. In the following period, they sought, step by step, to restrict creative, democratic, liberal thought, but the Poles never fell to the level of servility prevalent in the Soviet Union or other communist countries. The new chiefs never were able completely to expel the ghost of freedom which had entered even the Party, the government and the trade unions.

A return to the discredited Stalinist methods could not resolve Poland's social problems. Around 1967, the country entered a new period of acute economic crisis and social disruption. In order to overcome this crisis, the ruling group in the Party and the government decided to arouse friction between the workers and the intellectuals. They accused Polish intellectuals, especially students, of being "revisionists," "counterrevolutionaries," and of course, Zionists. On March 8, 1968, the government used an old familiar pattern of provocation: members of the security police disguised as workers began to beat up students—at first on the campus of Warsaw University, and later throughout the country. Using anti-Zionist slogans, the government began to persecute everyone suspected of intellectual independence. And the government gained the upper hand, though only for a short time. Nevertheless, Polish intellectuals had been isolated from the factory workers and the peasants.

The economic and political crisis continued and deepened. The result was a second uprising of the Polish workers, this time in the seaports, in December, 1970. Wladyslaw Gomulka, who had returned to power as a result of the 1956 uprising in Poznan, used methods which he himself had condemned at that time—he ordered strikers to be shot. His popularity which was unprecedented in Polish and Communist history, evaporated, and he left the scene in disgrace.

The leaders of the new team were the first secretary, Edward Gierek, and the minister of security, Mieczyslaw Moczar.

There were new promises of a "thaw" and "renewal," there

were new assurances that the government and the party would remain in close touch with the working people. They even managed to raise the standard of living for a short time. The basic structure of the government, its political and economic methods, however, were not changed.

The new ruling group became even more demoralized than the previous one. Stalinism used to assure special privileges to a relatively narrow group of super-bosses. The rest of the party had to live, at least ostensibly, in keeping with the principles of communist austerity. The pressures and terror were so strong that even those who were better off pretended to observe the standards of Franciscan poverty. The downfall of Stalinist terror, without the disappearance of the Stalinist system and organization, was accompanied by limitless corruption and disorganization. The new rulers built their own socialist palaces. They even followed the tradition of the French elite: they had their own "*ballet rouge*," and adopted the old principle, *enrichez vous*, for themselves.

Stalinist terror had helped to prop up and preserve some discipline and certain responsibilities. With the end of unlimited terror, the regime lost its most important governing tool. The attempt to maintain totalitarian rule without an efficient terror system resulted in total disorganization. The principles of hierarchy formulated by Erasmus of Rotterdam once more prevailed; stupidity and hypocrisy were valued, intellect became an obstacle to a career. Labor productivity declined, economic plans remained unfilled, the gross national product did not increase. The Polish party and government had to acknowledge the existence of unemployment, whose absence had always constituted the chief boast of communism over capitalism. Newspapers became even duller. Poland's hard-currency debt became the highest in the communist bloc, reaching 27 billion in 1980. The economic crisis grew even more severe. There was an unusual shortage of industrial commodities, and the meat, butter, and milk shortage became chronic.

In the middle of 1980, everyone was dissatisfied. The situation once more became revolutionary. That the outbreak did not happen earlier was due to the looming shadow of Soviet tanks. Perhaps even more important was the fact that the rapproachement which began in 1956 between the Party and the hierarchy of the Roman Catholic Church had led to a continuous collaboration between them. A policy of appeasement had become habitual; the existence of Gierek's regime depended on the benevolence of the Bishops, the Cardinal-Primate of Poland, and finally, the Pope.

In 1980 the government "overdid it," as Gomulka said in 1956 when he justified the Poznan uprising. In this situation strikes erupted in the Polish ports. In a short time they spread all over the country, especially in the densely populated industrial centers.

The government was compelled to sign special agreements with the representatives of the striking workers and finally had to legalize "*Solidarity*," the new independent autonomous trade-unions of the working people in the urban and rural areas.

b. Results of the August Victory

The visible result of the strikes, and the agreements signed between the government and the various committees of the strikers, may be summed up as follows:

For the first time in the history of communist regimes, the government negotiated and compromised with groups of its own population represented by freely elected delegates.

The communist government had to admit officially that the working masses in a socialist country needed an organization to protect their interest against their socialist employers.

The communist government legalized new freely organized trade unions which began to embrace nearly all the working population in the country. It pushed aside its own bureaucratic trade unions, but did not dissolve them.

Six months later (1981) the communist regime had to legalize "*Rural Solidarity*," a body representing private landowners and farmers.

Under social pressure, the government was obliged to repeal

existing labor laws and promise new ones more appropriate to the new political balance.

The government had to amend its censorship law in order to assure freedom for trade-union journals. Furthermore, it had to agree to assure freedom, albeit limited, to the mass media to publicize the view of the trade unions, the Catholic Church, and other nonconformists.

The courts began to be used both by the trade unions and the government in order to interpret the Constitution and the laws and apply them in a more equitable fashion. The courts even intervened to supervise administrative procedures.

The government legalized the right to strike, since prohibited, which had afforded socialism the chance to enter a more civilized era as it had capitalism during the 19th century.

Poland had become a new type of democracy, with its own limited but authentic system of the rule of law.

Perhaps the most important changes were in the attitudes of the people. Traditional revolutionaries, especially socialists, always considered that once the situation was ripe to attack the old regime and to establish new institutions, the passive masses would awaken and join the vanguard party. That is precisely what happened in Poland. Apathy, skepticism, spinelessness, and lack of vision gradually disappeared, and were replaced by new energy and vision. What were at first sporadic acts of resistance became an avalanche which overwhelmed the government. New leaders suddenly appeared as if to confirm the old Hegelian observation that whenever history creates a new opportunity, it also produces the appropriate personalities. The new leaders of *Urban* and *Rural Solidarity*, who had been unknown workers and peasants, suddenly turned into astute politicians, gifted strategists, persuasive speakers; they also learned instantly how to wheel and deal behind the scenes.

History has not known such an outburst of political creativity since the period of the English, American, French, and Russian revolutions. But history once more confirmed another truth: the new leaders had received their education in the old schools only to apply it creatively in new circumstances against their own teachers.

Lech Walesa and his friends were taught a thousand times that a revolution can win only if it is based upon an alliance of the workers, the peasants, and the intellectuals. This is precisely what they achieved. For the first time in the history of a communist state, a real, not a bureaucratic, political alliance arose between the townspeople and the peasants. Even more, resurrecting the old socialist principles, they found that the workers who were concentrated in large industries were their most effective agents. Those workers possess and represent greater power because of their sheer number, their concentration, and their direct influence over the economic nerves of a modern state. Workers' councils had first been organized in modern Poland in 1956-1957. They emerged as spontaneously as the Russian workers' councils (soviets) did during the revolution of 1905. History repeated itself—once again at a "higher level." From their inception the Polish workers' councils both in 1956, and again in 1980, were independent of the Party. They were regarded by their organizers and new theorists as a new germ of true socialist democracy even in 1956. Therefore the Russian, East German, and Czechoslovak bureaucrats concentrated their criticism of the *"Polish road to Socialism"* on the workers' councils, although in 1956 they still were in their infancy. After his seizure of power, Wladyslaw Gomulka with his neo-Stalinist entourage immediately began to restrict them. They later emasculated the workers' councils to such an extent that they ceased to exist. The experience and theory behind these councils however, did not vanish. The new revolutionary upheaval of 1980 started with the revival of the form which had arisen in 1956: independent councils of employees in the most important industrial plants.

These new councils reflected a new social development in Poland. Polish workers of the 1980's are highly skilled and have a good general and professional education. Many have earned university degrees and most of them have had secondary education. The average intellectual level of the delegates was higher than that of the party and administrative bosses. They knew that they were capable of running their factories without party and union hacks. A cultural and educational revolution really did take place during the thirty-five years of Communist rule. The results, however, were not anticipated by the party bosses.

The Marxian prediction that an obsolete social system trains its own gravediggers came true under bureaucratic communism. This type of communism really proved to be a "prison of the productive forces" (a phrase from *The Communist Manifesto*), but before it could disappear from history, it had trained new cadres in its own schools, universities, factories, and laboratories. These cadres are better equipped to run a modern industrial society than the ossified *politruks*, the faceless bureaucrats without initiative.

The bureaucrats used to argue that socialism is a higher type of humanism and freedom, and that in a socialist society no discrepancy should exist between theory and practice. The discrepancy between slogan and reality actually had been increasing and the people decided to put an end to that. They wanted the freedom referred to in the books and speeches to become *freedom for them*. The triumph of the Polish movement was the triumph of freedom. The Poles pushed history ahead, and history is—as Hegel wrote—always a history of the development of the idea of freedom. In the course of the struggle for freedom, everyone changed. Even the dogmatic leaders of the party started to use language and express ideas for which they would have been jailed by Poland's eastern and western neighbors. Nothing is more intoxicating than freedom. There have been irreversible changes in the psychology, perceptions, and attitudes of all Poles. Freedom and tolerance were newly reborn, and almost every member of the society has been transformed by it. Therefore it was impossible to bring previous terror to bear except by employing brute military force. Such a military resolution is indeed always possible, but that is always an admission of political and moral defeat. The grave prepared for totalitarian authority became deeper, the potential gravediggers multiplied.

c. *Cooperation Between Church and State*

One of the consequences of ideological totalitarianism in

communist Poland was truly paradoxical: the government out-
lawed all political theories and ideologies with the sole exception of Catholic moral and social teaching. All forms of liberal,
secular humanistic, personalist, existentialist philosophies
were prohibited. But the government's grip failed to subordinate
the Catholic religion and its social philosophies. Totalitarian
despotism caused the entire opposition to concentrate around
and within the Roman Catholic Church. The Church became a
vociferous and "official" spokesman for all the oppressed, the
deprived and the persecuted, the only lawful redoubt for creative intellectuals. In that way at least one of Stalin's ominous
philosophical and political premises was realized: those who are
closest to us are the most dangerous and should be eliminated
first. A layman, not trained in official dialectics, might have presumed that socialist, liberal, humanist philosophies would be
regarded as kin by the communists and therefore as more or less
friendly. That is not so according to classic Stalinism, which
revived certain premises of the Inquisition.

The Polish communists defeated their "heretics" in the 50's
and 60's, but were unable to overcome their "pagans," the
Catholic Church. However, in a very short time they found that
there were many advantages in having only one center of dissension. They discovered that religious dogmatism is less dangerous than non-dogmatic pluralism and rationalism.

The Church, for its part, also was satisfied that criticism of
its traditional dogmas was now restricted to less respectable
neo-dogmatists. Dogmatism thereby became the philosophical
basis for antagonism as well as cooperation between Party
and Church.

The position of the Catholic Church was strengthened by
two additional factors: the internally weak Polish communist
régime needed the Church to support its rule without Soviet
tanks, while the Church needed the Polish communists lest their
country be subjected to the bloody terror imposed in the Baltic
countries, Byelorussia and the Ukraine.

This symbiotic relationship between the Party and the
Church hierarchies was complicated by the emergence of new

trade unions and the resurgence of the Polish independent, liberal, secular intellectuals.

Poland has been becoming more and more a pluralistic society and even the members of the Central Committee had to admit that.

Pluralism means the simultaneous undermining of two ideological monopolies; that of the Party and that of the Church. Both must compete with powerful rivals: common sense and a mass movement.[19]

* * *

The victory of Polish political rationalism in 1980-81 presents a challenge not only to dogmatic communism, but also to the ideological stagnation which has become so characteristic not only of the Eastern but of Western countries during recent decades, as well. This is an especially important, although little noted, element of the Polish challenge to the world.

What has happened in Poland proves that it was possible to make a communist regime more humane, and to do so without foreign intervention. Such changes cannot be called anti-socialist because the people do not want to change the basic principles on which their socialist system operates.[20] Among the Polish trade unionists and intellectuals no call has been heard to return public property to private hands. The overwhelming majority wanted to find a new way of managing a socialist nation and its productive forces. They believed that public property should truly benefit the public. They have not decided how this should be accomplished, but they knew that the fundamental faults of bureaucracy could not be cured by more bureaucracy, that political despotism was the principle cause of economic inefficiency, and that democracy, freedom, and tolerance will not only be powerful politically but also economically.

Already in 1956 some Polish thinkers propounded the idea that "nationalization" or "socialization" of the means of production should not be identified with the "*verstaatlichung*," i.e., with primitive forms of governmental ownership. The Soviet ideologues and their vassals denounced those concepts as anarcho-syndicalist heresy. Indeed, as long as the bureaucracy is the sole agent of the legal property-owner ("the state"), the workers are as expropriated and alienated as under capitalism. To the extent that the workers wield real influence, bureaucratic privilege will be undermined.

Recently Polish workers received powerful support: the encyclical of John Paul II, *Laborem Exercens*. The Pope insists that production should be organized in a way that recognizes the creative human nature of the workers, giving them outlets for their initiative. The Pope declares that these demands can and must be fulfilled under any system of property ownership. In this way, he challenges both communism and capitalism.

The Polish people have embarked on this road. This fact was manifested during the famous consultations by the Party-Government, Church hierarchy, and Solidarity triumvirate.

That is the deep significance of the Polish challenge to Eastern and Western economic and social systems: the Poles started to construct an alternative to bureaucratic despotism without returning to capitalism. Such experiments may be subversive to the Soviet empire and to simplistic Western economists, but they are refreshing to the rest of the world.

The historical significance of the Polish experiments, even though their successes were limited in time and space, cannot be overstated. A new avenue has been opened, it is so far-reaching that no temporary success of a martial law and neo-Stalinist terror regime could close it for good. The discovery of new forms of freedom and new roads to its achievement cannot now be undone.

FREEDOM AND RESPONSIBILITY
IN OUR TIME

1. Is Freedom a Burden?

After our long, philosophical journey through the ages we have arrived at the fundamental problem of freedom and tolerance in our time: Do people really want to be free? Should the partisans of freedom not be alarmed because there are so many defectors from their cause? Is the phenomenon that Erich Fromm termed the "Escape from Freedom" a deeply rooted danger or a passing mood?

Throughout this book we have argued that the ideas of freedom and tolerance emerge, develop, and crest in every epoch. The enemies of these ideas invariably succeed in restricting them, if not annihilating them from time to time. We have analyzed many of the sources promoting freedom and tolerance and the forces opposing them. In order to complete our reflections, two additional points should be analyzed to facilitate our grasp of the latest developments in this sphere of philosophy and life:

— Erich Fromm's idea that in our time there is a mass tendency to "escape from freedom."

— Jean-Paul Sartre's idea that freedom is not a joy in itself but a burden which we are condemned to carry.

As we consider the widespread submission to oppressive political and religious movements, we cannot help but repeat the question posed in various ways by such authors as Jean-Paul Sartre, B.F. Skinner, or Erich Fromm: is the desire for freedom inherent in human nature or is this desire a result of passing, short-lived, social, cultural, and historical circumstances? Is freedom a good in itself, is it possible for freedom to be a source of pleasure and happiness? Or, must it be a burden which at times becomes so heavy that many attempt to escape from it in pursuit of their own peace of mind and contentment? Is it inevitable that for some, freedom is a goal, a dream, and a hope, while for others it is a threat?

As Dewey and Fromm emphasized, the threat to democracy and freedom is not only external, it exists within ourselves and our institutions, within our own personal attitudes and social conditions which can provide a victory for external authority, uniformity and "dependence upon the Leader in foreign countries."*

Emancipation from the feudal system led to "negative freedom" as Fromm called it. People were liberated from the old bonds and ties, and from their fixed place in society. They were even freed from various forms and obligations of family life. They acquired freedom, but in a negative sense only. The essence of "negative freedom" can be narrowed down to the following: an individual stands alone without legal restrictions, but he is powerless and unable to achieve what is meaningful for him.

The destruction of medieval bonds and ties has gone on for several hundred years and is still incomplete in many parts of the world. Some who have not yet been freed from ancient bondage are already exposed to the chains of a new dependence characteristic of the twentieth century.

The emergence of "negative freedom" is a prerequisite for the evolution of a positive, affirmative, freedom. A person may be truly free when he acts according to his own will. The problem in a modern democracy is that he does not know exactly what he wants, what his authentic thoughts and feelings are, or what his genuine interests are. He is influenced by mass media and inundated with information, contradictory opinions, the forms of art to which he is exposed, and the endless flow of propaganda from countless sources, official and unofficial, open and

---

*Erich Fromm, *Escape from Freedom* (New York: Holt, Rinehart and Winston, 1976), p. 5. Dewey argued in the same vein in 1939 in his *Freedom and Culture*.

covert. The average man tends to get lost in the profusion of pros and cons, of appeals and threats, of suggestions and contradictions. No wonder then that his thoughts are not his original thoughts and his feelings not his own, since they do not originate entirely from him, but are submitted and suggested and then are uncritically selected and absorbed. If a free act is one performed according to one's own wishes and persuasion, it is evident that once an individual is conditioned by his social situation with all the popular ideas inherent in it, then real choices are almost illusory.

Every person must adjust to society in order to survive. Adaptation and assimilation mean that one submits to the requirements of public opinion and social demands. Are they known to each individual? In a very vague and broad manner only. The old feudal masters have been replaced by an anonymous power. It is unknown and unpredictable. It creates a situation that is unbearable for many. They feel alone, alienated, powerless, and insecure. They therefore become anxious, angry, and defensive, seeking some type of security. In order to achieve it they are prepared to give up their own ambitions, searches, the right to choose, and many other attributes which comprise the network of negative freedom and the precondition of positive freedom. In brief, they are prepared to abandon—more or less consciously—the basic freedoms assured by modern society. We have argued that a person becomes free not through an act of thinking, but through a process of working, through participation in social endeavours, thereby realizing one's intellectual, emotional, and physical potentials. Every individual is endowed with them and their diversity can enrich humanity as a whole as well as each single individual. In other words, positive freedom as expressed by Erich Fromm consists of "the spontaneous activity of the total, integrated personality."[1]

Spontaneous activity can be described as activity based on one's own will. Such endeavour must be an act of creation, a giving birth to something new. Spontaneity and creativity are incompatible with the ways of a human automaton. They disrupt and destroy old prejudices and conventions, customs and obsolete convictions.

An individual who is creative in a modern society must have the foundation of a good education and enjoy a certain amount of financial security. One might argue that creativity is possible without good material conditions, but such an assertion is merely another version of the old myth that the free spirit *flat ubi vult* (flies where it chooses). Privation is not a source of inspiration. One should not apply to freedom the method described by Axel del Munthe in his *Book from San Michele:* the natives who wanted the birds to sing more beautifully blinded them.

An axiom of the day is that society must assure a minimum of education and economic security. These political requirements are popularly known as the ideals of a welfare state. If certain libertarian or conservative ideologues and politicians resent these ideas, they may follow the advice of George Will and create a "conservatism with a kindly face."[2]

One should always remember that a lack of economic security forms the basis of instability, consequently of authoritarianism, in industrial democracies. Many specialists in the psychology of politics argue that social "material" conditions are never sufficient to cause powerful public movements or trends which might lead to a change of power and the institution of a new form of government. They argue that these are the feelings, desires, and ideas of the people who exert pressure to initiate and accomplish transformations. Freudians, in particular, and various other thinkers inspired to a certain extent by Freud, are unanimous in the belief that authoritarianism is a result of sado-masochistic tendencies that characterize authoritarian leaders and the powerless, anxious masses. Analyses of events in Germany, the seizure of power by the Nazis, the behavior and attitude of the German people provide, they say, classic examples of their theories.

Sadism, in its socio-political aspects, is, according to these scholars, a drive for unrestricted power over others combined with a tendency to be destructive.

Masochism, according to the same theory, is a tendency to

dissolve one's self in a strong power so as to participate in its glory.

The underlying social and psychological causes of both sadism and masochism are the same. Individuals are incapable of standing alone; they are fearful, feel isolated, consequently need social relationships in order to overcome their alienation and terror of loneliness.

Even if one disagrees with these theories, one has to admit that many of the phenomena described in them are well illustrated by the rise of Hitler and his Party. The National Socialist Movement created an illusion of cameraderie, of mutual assistance, care, and mutual well-being. After Germany's defeat in World War I, in the midst of economic crises and unemployment, hunger and devaluation of its currency, the vast majority of the people felt humiliated and perceived themselves to be insignificant, powerless, and helpless. The Nazis integrated them into their various organizations and in this way created an illusion of their participating in a great historical venture.

In fact, the Nazis did not solve the people's problems; theirs was a bogus solution. The price which the people had to pay was horrendous: they had to give up their own thoughts, feelings, and emotions and uncritically submit to the leaders and organized masses. Abandonment of one's own conscience was the price required for participation in the ladder of power.

The example of Germany is of enormous historical significance.

It shows that in a society of great industrial enterprises, of large unions and expanding governmental bureaucracy, people are like cogs in a machine. And against simplistic expectations they are not an innocent, formless crowd. In periods of economic and social crises these masses might form the social basis for a party and be exploited by persons with totalitarian ambitions, be they of the right or left. What happened in Germany in the 1930s can be repeated, one way or another, in any industrial democracy when hopelessness and powerlessness prevail. Lack of real information and political education can only enhance the likelihood.

It is also true that although there is no censorship in industrial democracies and the people are exposed to a powerful stream of all kinds of information, they do not usually discern tendencies or general trends. They see the trees but miss the forest, hence they fail to assemble the messages of ostensibly unimportant events into a pattern which could be frightening. When a thousand bits of information are presented as equally important, all appear unimportant. Relativism is inherent in democracy, and as we have already pointed out, it can become a philosophical basis for disbelief in all moral values or political principles. When everything is relative, the authoritarians are afforded the opportunity to impose their values and principles.

Freedom, by the logic of its existence, creates and fosters its own adversaries and life-threatening tendencies.

Authoritarian personalities all over the world have many characteristics in common with the Nazis: they admire and respect the powerful and conversely despise the powerless. The Nazi attitude toward the Weimar Republic is an example. When the republican government tried to appease the Nazis by treating them leniently, the Nazis lost respect for it; leniency aroused contempt because of its lack of firmness and power. Hitler hated the Weimar Republic because it was weak; he admired the industrialists, bankers, and the generals because they had power and demonstrated their willingness and ability to use it. Hitler admired Great Britain as long as he perceived it as being powerful, but after the Munich conference he despised the Empire; his contempt for Prime Minister Neville Chamberlain was overwhelming.

The following conclusions ensue: whenever free countries try to "appease" authoritarian and dictatorial governments or movements, they lose the respect of the half-barbarian tyrants or would-be tyrants. Democracies perceived as weak or lacking the will to impose their demands on others are despised, thereby making compromise and cooperation impossible.

Free democratic governments, by their very nature, are inclined to seek compromise and peace; they are therefore at a certain disadvantage in dealing with the brutal force of "sadomasochists" of whom an authoritarian movement is made up.

In the eternal struggle between freedom and tolerance on the one hand and oppression and tyranny on the other, the latter have a basic initial advantage: the powers exercising oppression and tyranny are resolute in the use of force and consistently follow the precepts of their hatred and contempt, whereas the partisans of freedom contemplate and hesitate. The cause of freedom and tolerance may get the upper hand in the long run, but it requires vigilance, will power, and the determination to use force if needed. Freedom, not perceived as powerful and determined to defend itself, is in mortal danger.

* * *

The "escape from freedom" is the ground on which the existentialist philosophy of man, his dignity, and responsibility was built. Every day's experience adds additional dimensions to Sartre's famous assertion that the essence of man is his past, *Wesen ist, was gewesen ist.* [3] The very act of living is at the same time an act of leaving the past and of creating and expanding one's present and one's own essence with it. Individuality and consciousness are like the river of Heraclitus, they are never the same, never at rest. The Cartesian *cogito* must be extended and also regarded as a process, because otherwise it becomes meaningless. To assume consciousness, Sartre concluded, never implies the existence of "a consciousness of the instant," for the instant is only one view and one moment of the mind and even if its existence could be isolated, such consciousness that "would apprehend itself in the instant would no longer apprehend *anything*" [Sartre's emphasis.] [4]

A man is always full of projects and every project is an outline of a solution of the problem of one's being, [5] it becomes a part of our personality, of our intended or projected future. Therefore a human being is not only the past but also his vision of the future. We make it exist by our own commitment, we are present to ourselves, but we are never "completed", never "accomplished" like a marble statue. The amalgam of the past and future is the substance of human freedom. The fundamental act of freedom always reveals itself in "a choice of myself," in the world; by the same token it is "a discovery of the world."[6]

Man is constantly *creating* himself and is responsible for his own creation. The only limitation on his free creativity is the fact that he cannot cease to be free, he cannot be saved or spared from freedom. Freedom is the foundation of all human and individual *essentiality*; man acts and in that way he modifies the shape of the world and of himself. The world exists objectively, but human perceptions and activity are changing it and it gets a specific subjective human meaning inseparable from the existence of mankind.

In a world of constant human re-creation man is free to contemplate and to choose between given alternatives. He is aware of certain causes (not all) that inspire his actions and in the moment of this awareness he transcends objects of his own consciousness and then the causes—as Sartre (under Hegel's influence) wrote—are already "*outside.*" We are permanently forming our past and our existence.

"I am condemned to exist forever beyond my essence, beyond the causes and motives of my act. *I am condemned to be free.* This means that no limits to my freedom can be found except freedom itself or, if you prefer, that we are not free to cease being free."[7]

It would appear that Sartre has given another basic answer to the question of how freedom can become a burden and why anyone might wish to escape from it: the free individual is left alone with his conscience and must make decisions for which he alone, he himself, is responsible. An individual who renounces his responsibilities and transfers them onto a priest, minister, the secretary of the party, the *Gruppenleiter*, and ultimately the *Fuehrer* or the *Duce*, feels relieved from the burden of choice. He believes himself to be free from the responsibility of making decisions; he feels unburdened. It is an illusion because indeed we always are morally responsible for doing and not doing, for *facere* and *non-facere*; there is no escape from accountability.

And it is no consolation for us when one argues that because of the fact that we are free there must be certain elements of unpredictability in our behavior. Human beings can never be entirely predictable for themselves or for others. In view of this fact one must conclude that certain forms of philosophical positivism and determinism are one-sided: According to them there may be acts that impose themselves *a priori*, as unconditionally necessary. This means that the individual becomes a social agent only, one who is contingent but strictly conditioned. He is "the point of intersection of a series of external causes."[8]

If all of the causes were known the behavior of an individual could be predicted—this well known concept of eighteenth-century mechanical materialism does not take into account that no human being is absolutely "conditioned" by prevailing material circumstances and even in a period of the most intensive terror there will be those who will be willing to *sperare contra spem*, to hope against hope, to feel morally obligated to act in a way which opportunists would decry as "unreasonable" and "impractical."

* * *

2. Pluralistic Ways To Freedom

We live in a period when the traditional philosophies of materialism, atheism, and rationalism, diametrically opposed to fideism and religion, have become more diversified than ever. Materialistic philosophy and atheism have never had a monopoly on representing progress and enlightenment as has been claimed by many authors, especially in the Soviet Union, who passionately defend this thesis. Many forms of materialism and atheism which now prevail have become part of the ideology of bureaucratic communist establishments. They are used against freedom and reason. One can argue that their kind of philosophy is not a "true" but a "distorted" materialism. It can be countered, nevertheless, that there never has been a "pure" or "true" materialism or idealism, empiricism, or positivism, nor has there ever been a "true" or "unique" Christianity or Judaism. All these intellectual or religious systems as they have existed in various historical epochs assume concrete forms and constantly develop. It is typical for our age, however, that certain forms of materialism, including so-called dialectical and historical materialism have become closely connected with the Communist regimes and bureaucratic dogmatism; they represent intolerance and denial of freedom.

There are of course forms of materialism, secularism, rationalism, and atheism that have preserved their traditional qualities; they are critical, open minded, instrumental in the endless struggle for human freedom, tolerance, and individual happiness.

The same could be said about Judaism, Catholicism, Protestantism, and many other religions, sects and cults. They exist in many forms and urge people not only to be moral and decent, but also to participate in social and political endeavors to promote freedom and tolerance, to further democratic reform and promote human relief projects such as housing and feeding the needy and employing the jobless.

Whatever the points of departure of those humanitarian, philosophical, political and ethical trends may be, they all contribute to the evolution of the spirit of humanitarianism, freedom, and tolerance; they help to transform them into reality, they are instrumental in removing obstacles that could impede progress.

Marx wrote that religion is the spirit of a spiritless world. Religion, however, is not the only spirit of a heartless world; there are other social theories which also provide consolation for humanity. The point is to transform the world and this is where various forms of religion and secular philosophies will be valuable.

Every criticism and protest against spiritual dogmatism and political slavery adds to the treasure chest of ideas encompassing freedom and tolerance. Every type of despotism and oppression has unique and peculiar features of its own; the ideas of freedom which confront them must therefore be equally unique and unusual, if not newly created or re-created when applied against new forms of oppression.

Communist totalitarianism, like every preceding despotism, has been challenged by its own offspring. Many who have matured within that system and have been nurtured by its politics and ideologies, have been the ones to create a "liberal" or "humanistic" version of communism. They have in fact re-interpreted the principles of dialectical and historical material-ism in a manner contrary to its official version sponsored by the politbureaus and their ideologues. Consequently, the "liberal" communists or socialists represent heresies. Heresy is a dra-matic, painful, but fruitful critique of the powers that be. It is criticism that stems from the depth, from the "womb" of the tyranny. Despots are able to deal with external enemies. They do not fear them because they are well acquainted with the weapons employed by their external adversaries. Generally speaking, the adversaries on both sides of the fence know each other and after some time will need each other to such an extent that they will be able to co-exist without inflicting painful wounds on one another. Nearly everything is predictable that tran-spires between two "blocs" or two great "adversaries;" there can be no surprises. The situation may even develop into a com-fortable one and comfort undermines antagonism.

The internal "enemy," however, the true "heretic" is more dangerous than the avowed enemy or apostate. A heretic trans-substantiates the basics of the official ideas. He must be better educated, more devoted to his cause, more original and creative than his antagonists. He attacks the deeply hidden life-lines of the establishment, he strikes at the vital nerve centers of ossification.

Most of today's innovative thinkers are therefore "defec-tors" from the communist or capitalist, Catholic or Protestant camps. A heretic and defector may be any one who knows the status quo from personal experience and challenges it. Such a defector need not emigrate; he may maintain his old address and telephone number, retain the same university chair. But he has departed from the official way of thinking, be it ideological or administrative. The confessions of those who have broken with the Eastern or the Western establishments, the Party sec-

retariates or presidential offices are more illuminating (sometimes simplistic) than meticulously prepared treatises, with
hundreds of references. Witnesses to inhumane activities serve
the cause of freedom far better than extensive essays by
gifted philosophers.

Without the nourishment provided by anonymous observers, obscure whistle-blowers, and decent outraged citizens,
humanity would not possess the most powerful weapon against
tyranny known: confirmation of facts, the objective truth that is
indispensable for every generalization and conclusion in philosophy.

Although every philosophy or religion can be viciously perverted, it might still contribute to the edification and maturation
of individuals in the spirit of decency, responsibility, charity,
and compassion. These humane qualities are inimical to the
meanness of spirit of every despotism, especially to the low
ésprit de corps of bureaucracy, the cancer of our century.

All paths, all contributors to a successful campaign against
that moral and political plague are today indispensable. The
traditional disputes between believers and non-believers, atheists
and fideists, and Christians, Muslims, Jews, Protestants and Catholics should be regarded as obsolete in the face of a common danger: totalitarianism   and   the   danger   of   nuclear
annihilation. There are new divisions within every ideological,
religious or philosophical camp. These antagonisms frequently
are more important and substantial from the viewpoint of freedom, tolerance, welfare, and survival than the traditional disputes. More and more paths lead to freedom. Some headed
nowhere if not actually in the opposite direction not so long ago,
but the situation changed. All those who hold a very broad view
of freedom, tolerance, and democracy must take the new facts
into consideration with their impact on the human condition. An
antitotalitarian alliance of those who favor reason and the freedom and survival of humanity must converge on the most important single item on the human agenda.

Today, more than ever in the past, the Judeo-Christian

traditions and religions can powerfully oppose new forms of oppression, totalitarianism, and the imminent danger of nuclear destruction.

Such a possibility for Judeo-Christian and secular cooperation has never before existed.

* * *

A great, perhaps fundamental, attainment of the Judeo-Christian theology is the conviction that God himself has given people the power to do good or evil and that the road to sin has not been closed entirely by the Creator.

This theological approach concerning free will coincides with secular philosophy. This concept of free will, regarded as a source and foundation for moral responsibility, is meaningful and of prime importance to the entire structure of the philosophy of freedom. However, should the same concept be interpreted in an exaggerated way so that it is identified with freedom itself, then both the notions of free will and freedom are rendered meaningless.

From the political and social points of view, once God himself gave his children the right to be mature, to make good or bad decisions, the people were granted the freedom to err, to sin, to prefer untruth to moral awareness and the light.

One of the conclusions to be drawn from a broadly interpreted concept of free will is: individuals should endeavor to create an environment that will be conducive to living according to the principles of morality, not contrary to them. In this way the problem of free will becomes social.

* * *

Judaism as a religion and theology received its basic shape with the elaboration of the Talmud.

The Torah (Pentateuch) occupies the most important place among the basic Jewish books; it is the main source of belief and knowledge. All the later scriptures are officially commentaries only. However, any attempt to understand Judaism solely on the basis of the Torah would be as fruitless as an attempt to study the Civil Code of Napoleon or the US Constitution divorced from the commentaries and judicature worked out during the last two centuries.

The Talmud is not written in a dogmatic, catechetic form. Almost every question is analyzed in an argumentative and sophistic way, from various points of view and by many scholars. Hardly any opinion is regarded as definitive and representing the ultimate truth. On the contrary, its forms and contents invite further research and fresh opinions.

Louis Finkelstein, for many years president and chancellor of the Jewish Theological Seminary, observed:

> ... the synagogue was from the beginning an institution of democracy. Anyone could lead in the prayers; anyone could read the prescribed sections of the law; anyone could become the head of the synagogue.[9]

Not everybody would be eager to accept the assertion that the synagogue has always been an institution of democracy, but this is beside the point. Important, rather, is the existing democratic potential and the existing potential of tolerance inherent in the fact that controversial discussions in the Jewish communities have always been welcomed and spiritual contributions appreciated. Of course, the past and present examples of intolerance on the part of Jewish orthodoxy (including the infamous political campaigns in Israel concerning conversions, archeological excavations, and autopsy) show that religious narrowness can infiltrate even the most tolerant and open minded teaching. But the abuses and phobias of certain representatives of any particular theology or philosophy should not be regarded as a decisive basis upon which to pass judgment concerning the given school of thought.

Rabbi Ben-Zion Bokser commented: Throughout Talmudic times,

> the Jews lived under the domination of foreign imperialisms ...
> Whether a Jewish commonwealth would have developed a democratic representative government, we do not know. But within the framework of the limited autonomy which the Jews enjoyed, they did develop certain democratic institutions. The

most important instrument of Jewish autonomy was Jewish civil and religious law, and the Talmud developed the theory that the ultimate sanction of all law is the consent of the people who are to be governed by it. . . (But) man is endowed with free will, and his unrestrained conscience must give its assent to every legal institution that is to have moral claims over him . . . Indeed, the Talmud even traced the authority of the Bible itself not so much to its divine source as to the consent of the people who fully agreed to live by it.[10]

This observation of Rabbi Ben-Zion Bokser is most important for our further considerations. If a theological doctrine does not rely on divine authority only, but also on the power of persuasion and finally on the consent of the believers, then such a set of beliefs is in itself rationalistic and democratic, although not all the members of such a community may be democratically minded or inclined to play according to the democratic rules.

Elements of such an attitude must have penetrated and are ingrained in one of the continuations of Judaism—Christianity.

Certain notions of freedom elaborated on the basis of Judaic tradition are truly universalistic. Abraham J. Kook, chief Rabbi of Palestine (prior to the establishment of the State of Israel) wrote:

"We must never forget that in every conflict of opinions, after the furor passes, critics find that there is light and shadow on each side . . ." (Letter 314). "There is no reason to be confused when confronting great contradictions . . . The masters of clear thinking reach out with their thought into various and broad horizons, and they embrace the treasure of the good in all places and unite all in the togetherness of a comprehensive whole."[11]

The approach of Abraham J. Kook is truly dialectical and argumentative, in the best meaning of the word. The author leaves no room for philosophical dogmatism or intolerance. It is a matter of fact, nevertheless, that not all representatives of Judaism think along the same lines. Ben-Zion Bokser continues in Kook's spirit: "Freedom is the goal of human life . . . man comes into the world as an unfinished product . . . Each person is an original creation, embodying distinctive excellencies . . . Freedom is the capacity of self-realization.''[12]

In this way we approach a synthesis between the Judaic and Renaissance concepts of freedom as creation and development.

***

Many aspects of the evolution of Christianity have been analyzed in this book. The trends supporting freedom and tolerance and those opposed to them have abounded in Christian thought and practice in every century.

The most important development as far as the Catholic Church is concerned took place during the last three decades. The Second Vatican Council acknowledged that freedom and tolerance are values in themselves and should be practiced. The moral and intellectual values of other religions also were confirmed and pronounced a common heritage of humanity which should be protected, studied, assimilated, and developed. In one way or another, pluralism as a source of moral strength and creativity, was recognized. The number of axioms has been reduced.

From the viewpoint of freedom in the social and economic arena, the greatest contribution was made by John XXIII and continued by John Paul II: the recognition that workers, apart from decent and sufficient earnings, should occupy a place in the process of production that would enable them to develop their personality and creativity; that they should not merely be cogs in the bureaucratic machines of the state or giant corporations; and that the formation of autonomous, independent, trade unions is an inherent, inalienable right of employees.

The pastoral letter issued by the American National Conference of Catholic Bishops: *The Challenge of Peace: God' s Promise and Our Response* (Chicago: May, 1983), has achieved a very special place in the evolution of the Catholic social and political doctrine.

This document has not been officially approved by the Holy See, nor has it been disapproved. In such a centralized and hierarchical organization as the Catholic Church, this means a great deal. Even more important is the fact that the first drafts of the letter had been distributed nearly two years ago, consequently, the Pope would have had ample time to rebuke the chairman of the bishops' ad hoc committee on war and peace, Archbishop Joseph Bernardin, had he found that appropriate. On the contrary, Msgr. J. Bernardin has been promoted to higher offices twice during the past two years. He was appointed to one of the most important American dioceses in Chicago and in 1983 he was the only American raised to the rank of Cardinal. The Pope could not have signalled his approval of the Chairman's work and ideas in a clearer way.

The letter updates Catholic teaching on just wars and deterrence in the era of nuclear weapons. The conclusions reached by the American bishops go beyond those of any Vatican documents:

—The arms race is one of the greatest curses to afflict the human race;

—Under no circumstances may nuclear weapons or other mass-destruction instruments be used for the purpose of wiping out population centers and other predominently civilian targets;

—Under no circumstances can the initiation of nuclear war be morally justified;

—The concept of a limited nuclear war should be treated with the greatest scepticism; leaders should resist the notion that "nuclear conflict can be limited, contained, or won, in any other traditional sense;"

—The Bishops support immediate, bilateral, verifiable agreements to halt the testing, production, and deployment of nuclear systems; negotiations must be pursued in every reasonable way possible.

The letter is addressed to Catholics and non-Catholics, to Americans and to the nations of the world. It contains every humane principle including the principle that the reply to aggression should be limited, being directed against unjust aggressors, not against the innocent caught up in a war.

The bishops also considered the question of how to translate a *"no"* to nuclear war into personal and public choices which would move humanity into a new direction. They see "with increasing clarity the political folly of a system which threatens mutual suicide" and they decided to speak as pastors, and not as politicians, teachers, or technicians. In this capacity they regret that billions are readily being spent for destructive instruments while "pitched battles are waged daily in our legislatures over much smaller amounts for the homeless, the hungry, and the helpless here and abroad."

When discussing the current policy and social philosophy of the Catholic Church, one must remember that the Church is a diversified institution and that its centralization often is illusory. There can be a discrepancy between theory and practice, and between attitudes in various countries and continents. The hierarchy and the apparatus of the Church moves slowly; they are conservative but the social demands (apart from the problems of abortion and schools) connected with the domestic and the international situation accord with humanistic, secular, and multidenominational proposals to save mankind from destruction, hunger, and disease.

In our troubled era, this contribution of the Roman Catholic Church to freedom and tolerance is of great value.

***

Martin Luther stated that human beings need no intermediary in their relationship with God. In this way he undermined suggestions that intermediaries are needed to attain freedom and liberation. Even if people should require no intermediaries in their pursuits, as a social being they need associates. According to Luther, a person needs no one to light the way, to carry the lantern before him.

Let us remember the favored parallel of the Encyclopedists: man can take the torch and carry it himself.

Once the Protestant idea of man's being self-sufficient in earthly matters became an official credo, powerful spiritual forces of intellectual liberation were set in motion. Those who have once been told to seek, will continue to search, and will try to overcome all impediments on their road to happiness and freedom. Whatever limits on freedom of conscience and thought may have been imposed by Protestant theologians, they become irrelevant when viewed from long-term historical perspectives. Luther's teaching in this respect is omnipresent. It cannot be obliterated.

The Protestant Reformation contributed to many fundamental political and social reforms in the Western development of modern democracy.

The modern concept of individual responsibility led toward two motifs, as observed by Roger L. Shinn: the criticism of all political structures and an impulse to enter social and political life fully.[13]

***

After a long and complex history, a tendency among American Protestants has developed to equate the Christian ethic with democracy.

Protestant ethics more than any other system of ethics connected with religious beliefs learns from historical experience and from other moral and political philosophies including the secular. Various Protestants have discovered the democratic ideas "latent" in the Bible and in the churches.

At the beginning Protestantism could not accept as a general principle that the majority was right. The biblical heritage points toward dogmas and absolute truths.

"But its faith recognized also the sin of pride and the peril of concentration of power in the hands of a few. So it quickly came to see the values of representative government which makes decisions by majority votes, subject to checks and balances which prevent centralized power . . . "[14] "Christians, Jews, agnostics, and atheists as well as the impersonal political and economic forces of history, have produced modern democracy."[15]

The point of view presented by Roger L. Shinn, and shared

in one or another way by the most representative Protestant authors and many students of political philosophy,[16] is an illustration and a confirmation of the general thesis which this book tries to substantiate: pluralistic efforts of all the basic moral and political, religious and secular philosophies of freedom, tolerance, and democracy are necessary to preserve sanity and even the existence of humanity today.

Protestantism at long last contributed to the modern understanding of the principle that no "coerced acceptance of the truth can redeem the soul"[17] and on the other hand: tolerance should not take an "irresponsible attitude towards ultimate issues,"[18] because unmitigated scepticism can become a forerunner of cynicism with all its disastrous political consequences.[19]

The great Protestant contribution to the problem of tolerance is a coalescence of this notion with the concept of freedom, duty of search for truth, and personal responsibility.

Kathleen Kennedy Townsend writes in the same spirit[20] when she reminds us that William Penn advocated religious tolerance because of his religious belief, not in spite of it. The Abolitionists in the 19th century and many of the civil rights advocates of the 20th century fought for freedom and equality of the black people and other minorities, quoting biblical arguments; Louis D. Brandeis, defending the Ladies Garment Worker's Union, drew on biblical traditions; Dorothy Day was a socialist because of, not in spite of, her Catholicism. Today, as Kathleen K. Townsend argues, one should dispute the morality of the budget which penalizes "the poor and the meek." One should criticize the foreign policy which does not aim to "beat the swords into plowshares." Fighting for the change of the present policy one should speak in "Biblical language."

"For if we—the true moral majority—do not organize and remain unwilling to speak to the millions of Bible readers in this country, then the religious traditions of an entire nation shall be surrendered to a misnamed faction."[21]

Any humanistic trend, including the secular one, should today be responsive to believers' desires to defend freedom and tolerance by using "biblical language." Once the "right-wingers" decide to use "biblical language" for their political purposes, the opposition must reply. Political weapons of a certain type invite the use of similar weapons by those who are attacked. This basic logic of warfare holds in every social and political struggle.

***

We live in a period where the fact that we are free compels us to make decisions which surpass normal human mental capacity. The basic problem today is an inescapable one: the survival of mankind in an era of nuclear weapons which can destroy our planet and its inhabitants with their civilization, or at least, the style of life to which they have become accustomed. More and more voters must decide whether to elect or oust a belligerent administration or political party that pledges only to enhance defense. However, such is the logic of active and efficient deterrence—they prepare the means which could get out of control and forever bury the aggressor and the innocent, the attackers and the defenders. Are we responsible for the existence of the world? For the existence of our own nation? For the continents? For the life of our neighbors who may die as an unintentional side-effect of our decision to participate actively in deterrence or attack?

The choices in a "strictly" private life also are becoming more complicated and further-reaching, more meaningful and important: the choice of profession, the acceptance of certain jobs in certain governmental and private agencies, keeping secret immoral or illegal activity of corporations, or willingness to take a humiliating lie detector test. All these create a nostalgic longing for a situation in which someone else would make the choices for us, or would direct us. Never has the burden of freedom been such a curse as it is in modern society.

Our civilization and the inevitable process of bureaucratization, the polarization in the world and in every nation, constitute as a last resort the social ground on which the responsibility for the choices of affirmation or omission is increasing. The effects of our actions (or non-actions) weigh more and more heavily. In such a situation an increasing number of people seem to be unable to bear their responsibility and they abandon it; they prefer not to choose, not to vote, to give up their burdensome freedom. The sheer burden of certain decisions is so heavy that it exceeds normal human capacity.

The same mechanism which has enabled people to expand the sphere of their freedom has pushed it to limits which surpass their moral and intellectual, actual and potential ability to learn, absorb, analyze and make an enlightened decision.

One may argue that in the society of today every individual has to make more and more decisions for *doing* or *not doing* than ever before. One is so integrated in the social fabric that one is compelled to do more and more of moral consequence; actions pertain to the well-being and even the existence of many, of the known and the unknown; it happens more and more frequently that one prefers not to consider moral responsibilities; one deliberately tries to restrict one's own freedom, pretending that one is simply executing an impersonal law and acting on a decision made by a higher authority.

The modern feudal ladder restricting freedom does not automatically dispose of one's functional and moral responsibilities. The remnants of freedom (nevertheless forming the basis of responsibility) are a source of burden rather than of joy. We face a paradox: every individual in the bureaucratic government, corporation, and trade union tries to acquire as much power as possible and at the same time be liberated from the responsibility of freedom and moral accountability. People long for a dispensation which they do not deserve and cannot be granted.

Autocracy and totalitarianism create illusions of stability and security. Proponents of those ideologies argue that democracy is too risky; that by its very nature (elections and political struggles) the hazards of chance prevail over clarity and predictability. However, authoritarian stability and totalitarian "order" (including the Nazi *Neue Ordnung)*, are illusory. No one is secure under the regimes of general terror, fear, and arbitrariness.

We should always remember that people in fascist, communist, and other authoritarian countries relinquished their freedom not only as a result of so called objective social and political conditions, but also for "purely human," exclusively "subjective" reasons: "the longing for submission" and "paternalistic protection."[22]

The new, ominous threats to freedom and tolerance emerge and increase every day. They can be countered successfully only with the most powerful weapon: more freedom and tolerance, more awareness of their necessity for our survival, more passion and art employed in their creation, development, and defense.

Notes

CHAPTER I
Introduction: The Popular Yet Detested Theme

[1]Erich Fromm, *The Sane Society* (Greenwich, Conn: Fawcett Publications, 1955), p. xi.

CHAPTER II
Evolution of the Philosophy of Freedom
1. Philosophical Foundations of Freedom
a. Pico Della Mirandola—A Saga on Creative Man

[1]Pico Della Mirandola, *On The Dignity of Man* (New York: The Bobbs-Merrill Co., Inc., 1965), p. 4.

[2]*Ibid.,* pp. 4–5.

[3]*Ibid.,* p. 5.

[4]*Ibid.,* p. 7.

[5]*Ibid.,* p. 7. Mirandola quotes Propertius: "... in great things it is enough to have willed." (*Ibid.,* p. 21).

[6]*Ibid.,* p. 10.

[7]*Ibid.,* p. 11.

[8]*Ibid.,* p. 23.

[9]*Ibid.*

[10]*Ibid.,* pp. 23–24.

[11]*Ibid.,* p. 29. "I have dug up from the ancient mysteries of the Hebrews and have brought forward in order to confirm the holy and Catholic faith."

[12]*Ibid.,* p. 24.

[13]*Ibid.,* p. 25.

[14]*Ibid.*

[15]*Ibid.,* p. 34.

c. Thomas Hobbes

[1]Thomas Hobbes, *Leviathan,* edited by C. B. Macpherson (Penguin Books, Penguin Classics, 1974). Introduction by C. B. Macpherson, p. 81.

[2]*Ibid.,* p. 227. Chapter 17.

[3]*Ibid.,* introduction by C. B. Macpherson. "He had absorbed the implications of Galileo's law of inertia. . . . In the old prevailing view, rest was the natural state of things—nothing moved until something else moved it. Galileo postulated that motion was the natural state—things moved unless something else stopped them."

[4]*Ibid.,* p. 161, Chapter XI.

[5]*Ibid.,* p. 183, Chapter XIII

[6]*Ibid.*

[7]*Ibid.,* p. 184.

[8]*Ibid.,* p. 185.

[9]*Ibid.*

[10]*Ibid.,* p. 186, Chapter XIII.

[11]*Ibid.,* p. 227.

[12]*Ibid.,* p. 385, Chapter XXX

[13]*Ibid.,* p. 261, Chapter XXI.

[14]*Ibid.,* p. 189.

[15]*Ibid.,* p. 267.

[16]*Ibid.,* p. 262.

[17]*Ibid.,* p. 150, Chapter X.

[18]*Ibid.*

[19]*Ibid.*

[20]*Ibid.*

[21]*Ibid.,* p. 151, Chapter X

[22]*Ibid.,* p. 152.

[23]*Ibid.,* p. 153.

[24]*Ibid.*

[25]*Ibid.,* p. 155, Chapter X.

[26]*Ibid.,* p. 263, Chapter XXI.

[27]*Ibid.*

[28]*Ibid.,* p. 185, Chapter XII.

[29]*Ibid.,* p. 190, Chapter XIV.

[30]*Ibid.*

[31]*Ibid.,* p. 199, Chapter XVI.

[32]*Ibid.,* pp. 201–203, Chapter XV.

[33]*Ibid.,* p. 209.

[34]*Ibid.,* p. 209.

[35]*Ibid.,* p. 210.

[36]*Ibid.,* pp. 215–217.

[37]*Ibid.,* p. 85, Chapter I.

[38]*Ibid.,* p. 160, Chapter XI.

[39]*Ibid.*

[40]*Ibid.,* p. 161, Chapter XI.

[41]*Ibid.,* p. 18. Crawford B. Macpherson observed: "How soon Hobbes made the connexion in his own mind between the certainty of the method of geometry and the uncertainty of current moral and political theory we cannot be sure. He had clearly made it by 1640 when he had composed *Elements of Law, Natural and Politic*"

[42]*Ibid.,* p. 295, Chapter XXIV.

[43]Karl Marx openly admitted that the construction of his *Capital* is an elaboration of these concepts, as substantiated by Smith and Ricardo, and also regarded Hobbes as his predecessor in this respect. The road first laid down by Hobbes led to classic bourgeois economics and "scientific socialism."

Benjamin Franklin wrote that the value "of all things" is "most justly measured by labour" and trade is nothing more than "the exchange of labour for labour." *The Works of Benjamin Franklin*, ed., Sparks. (Boston; 1836), p. 207, vol. II.

[44]*Leviathan*, p. 53.

2.The Essence of Freedom

[1]George Tapley Whitney and David F. Bowers, eds., *The Heritage of Kant* (New York: Russell & Russell, Inc., 1962), p.257.

[2]*Ibid.*, p. 257.

[3]*Ibid.*, p. 253.

[4]Nathan Rotenstreich, *From Substance to Subject* (The Hague: Martinus Nijhoff, 1974), p. 34

[5]Immanuel Kant, *Critique of Practical Reason,*trans. by Lewis White Beck (Indianapolis, New York: The Bobbs-Merrill Co., Inc., 1956), p. 4.

According to Kant's philosophy we can think the ideas of God and the world *a priori,* but we can know neither God nor the world. Why not? Because they are on the other side. But the idea of freedom is "susceptible in itself of no presentation in intuition, and consequently of no theoretical proof of its possibility." (Kant, *Critique of Judgment,*Gulik, p. 383). This concept of freedom is obviously connected with the concept of man as a noumenon which, according to Kant, logically presupposes the existence of freedom as well as the fact that reason influences free decisions.

[6]Erwin De Haar, ed., *Im Zeichen der Hoffnung* (Muenchen: Max Hueber Verlag. 1962), pp. 333-34. Trans. and abridged "Kurt Huber, Schlusswort vor dem 'Volksgerichtshof' "by I.E. Previti (manuscript).

[7]Immanuel Kant, *Critique of Pure Reason,* trans. by Norman Kemp Smith (New York: St. Martin's Press, 1965), p.312.

[8]*Ibid.*, p. 312.

[9]Shlomo Avineri, *Hegel's Theory of the Modern State* (Cambridge: Cambridge University Press, 1972), p. 239.

[10]Hegel, *Philosophy of Right,*trans. by T.M. Knox (Chicago: Encyclopaedia Britannica, Inc., 1952), p. 16.

[11]Georg Wilhelm Friedrich Hegel, *The Philosophy of History,* trans. by J. Sibree (New York: Dover Publications, Inc., 1956), p. 19.

[12]*Ibid.*, p. 23.

[13]*Ibid.*, p. 21.

[14]Shlomo Avineri, *Hegel's Theory of the Modern State* (Cambridge: Cambridge University Press, 1972), p. 132.

[15]*Ibid.*, p. 99.

[16]*Ibid.*, p. 229.

[17]Georg Wilhelm Friedrich Hegel, *Philosophie der Weltgeschichte,* VI. The quote is my own translation from the original German text which reads:

"Aeussere Uebermacht vermag nichts auf die Dauer: Napoleon hat Spanien so wenig zur Freiheit, als Philip II Holland zur Knechtschaft zwingen koennen." Band "Die Deutsche Welt" (Leipzig: Felix Meiner Verlag, 1944), p. 932.

[18]Cf. Shlomo Avineri, *Hegel's Theory of the Modern State.* A correct translation of this sentence would have to read "It is the way of God in the world, that there should be (literally: is) the state." What Hegel meant to say was not that the state is the "March of God" on earth or anything of this nature, but that the very existence of the state is part of a divine strategy, not a merely human arbitrary artifact (pp. 176-77).

[19]Karl Marx, *On Freedom of the Press and Censorship*, trans. and ed. by Saul K. Padover (New York: McGraw-Hill Book Company, 1974), p. 142.

[20]*Ibid.,* p. 144.

[21]Marx & Engels, *Basic Writings on Politics & Philosophy,*ed. by Lewis S. Feuer (New York: Doubleday & Company, Inc., Anchor Books, 1959), p. 360.

[22]*Ibid.,* p. 361.

[23]Frederick Engels, *Anti-Duehring,* C.P. Dutt, ed., trans. by Emile Burns (New York: International Publishers Co., Inc., 1970), pp. 125-26.

[24]*Ibid.,* pp. 309-10.

[25]Karl Marx, *Selected Writings in Sociology & Social Philosophy,* eds., Bottomore and Maximilian Rubel (New York: McGraw-Hill Book Co., 1964), p. 95.

[26]John Dewey, "Philosophies of Freedom," in *Philosophy and Civilization* (New York, N.Y.: Milton, Balch & Co., 1931), pp. 274-275.

[27]*Ibid.,* p. 276.

[28]*Ibid.,* p. 277.

[29]*Ibid.*

[30]*Ibid.,* p. 280.

[31]Cf. Benito Mussolini: *The Doctrine of Fascism,* and J. Stalin, *Anarchism and Socialism.*

[32]John Dewey, "Philosophies of Freedom," *op. cit.,* p. 281.

[33]*Ibid.,* p. 282.

[34]*Ibid.,* p. 278.

[35]*Ibid.,* p. 286.

[36]*Ibid.,* p. 291.

[37]John Dewey, *Individualism, Old and New* (New York: Capricorn Books, 1962), p. 36.

[38]*Ibid.,* p. 38.

[39]*Ibid.*

[40]*Ibid.*

[41]John Dewey, *The Public and Its Problems* (The Swallow Press, Chicago, 1957), pp. 56-58.

[42]See John Dewey, *Democracy and Education* (New York: The Free Press, 1966), pp. 307-309; 341-345.

[43]John Dewey, *Freedom and Culture* (New York: Capricorn Books, 1963), pp. 175-176.

[44]Compare Benjamin Constant's interpretation of the difference between modern and ancient conceptions of freedom: in ancient Greece and Rome the people were permitted to do what was allowed by law; in a modern republic

they have the right to do anything except what is prohibited by law.

[45]Thucydides, *The Peloponnesian War* (Baltimore: Penguin Books, 1965), p. 117.

[46]*Ibid.*

[47]Samuel D. Warren and Louis D. Brandeis, "The Right of Privacy" *Harvard Law Review*, Vol. 4 (1890), pp. 193-195 (emphasis added).

[48]Thomas E. Emerson, *The System of Freedom of Expression* (New York: Random House, 1971), p.545.

[49]*Ibid.*, p. 546-547.

[50]*Ibid.*, p. 549.

[51]*State v. Woodward,* 58 Idaho 385, 74P2d 92, 114 ALR 627; quoted from 6 *Am Jur,* 2d, para 71, pp. 65-66.

[52]*Ibid.*

[53]*State v. Anderson,* 230 NC 54, 51 SE 2d 895; 6 *Am Jur,* 2d, para 70, p. 66.

[54]*People v. Sonier,* 113 Cal App 2d 277, 2486 2d, 155.

[55]*State v. McLeon,* 82 Ohio App 155; 37 Ohio Op 5 522; 50 Ohio L. Abs 475; 80 NE 2d 699; 6 *Am Jur* 2d, para 71, pp 66-67.

[56]Cf. *State v. Hickam,* 95 Mo 322; 8 SW 525; cf. 6 *Am Jur* 2d, para 72, p. 67.

[57]Cf. *State v. Scott,* 142 NC 582; 55 SE 69; *Shields v. State,* 187 Wis 448; 204 NW 486, 40 *ALR 945; 6 Am Jr* 2d, *ibid.*

[58]Cf. *State v. Anderson, Ibid; Floyd v. State* 36 Ga 91; *State v. Cessna 170 Iowa 726, 153 NEW 194.*

[59]This was especially stressed in *Floyd v. State,* 36 Ga 91; e.g. when the victim is in ill health, the relative physical superiority of the attacker would be greater, allowing the person attacked to use means which in other circumstances would be regarded as excessive.

[60]*State v. Gloldberg,* 12 NJ Super 293, 79 A 2d 702.

[61]Cf. *Rowe v. U.S.,* 164 US 546, 41 Led 547, 17 S Ct 172; *State v. Mier,* 74 SD 515, 55 NW 2d 74; *Gafford v. State,* 37 Ala App 377, 68 So 2d 858; 6 *Am Jur* 2d, para 75, pp 68-70.

CHAPTER III

The Evolution of Tolerance
1. The First Battles: Religious Tolerance

[1]St. Augustine, *Letters,* LXXXVII, in, *The Political Writings of St. Augustine* (Chicago: Henry Regnery Company, a Gateway Edition, 1962), p. 192.

[2]*Ibid.*, p. 196.

[3]*Ibid.*, p. 197. XCIII.

[4]*Ibid.*, p. 400.

[5]*Ibid.*, pp. 216–217.

[6]St. Thomas Aquinas: *De Regimine Principum,* trans. J. G. Dawson,(Oxford: Basil Blackwell, 1954), p. 77.

2. Spinoza's Classic Arguments for Tolerance, Freedom and Peace

[1]Hegel, *The History of Philosophy,* (New York: The Humanities Press, Vol. Three, 1974). pp. 252–290.

Bertrand Russel, *A History of Western Philosophy* (New York: Simon and Schuster, Eighteenth Paperback Printing), pp. 569-580.

Will Durant, *The Story of Philosophy* (New York: Simon and Schuster, 1953), pp. 113-151.

[2]Leszek Kolakowski, "Individual and Infinity," in *Jednostka Nieskonczonosc* (Warszawa: Panstwowe Wydawnictwo Naukowe, 1958), p. 529.

[3]Cf. Thomas Hobbes, *Leviathan*, Part II, ch. xxi: "A Free Man, is he, that in those things, which by his strength and will he is able to do, is not hindered to do what he has a will to do." (England, Australia: Penguin Books, 1974), p. 262.

[4]Concerning this contradiction see Leszek Kolakowski: "Individual and Infinity," *op cit.*, p. 524.

[5]Benedict De Spinoza, *"Ethics"* in *The Chief Works of Benedict De Spinoza*, On the Improvement of the Understanding. The Ethics. Correspondence, trans. R. H. M. Elwes (New York: Dover Publications, Inc., 1955) p.209.

[6]*Ibid.*, Cf. "A Political Treatise," ch. 11, pp. 20-22.

[7]*Ibid.*, p. 298.

[8]Mieczyslaw Maneli, "Three notions of Freedom," *Interpretations*, No. 1, 1978. Also analyzed in a paper submitted to the Conference on Political Science, Graduate Center, CUNY, N.Y., December, 1977.

[9]Benedict De Spinoza, *A Theologico-Political Treatise. A Political Treatise*, trans. R. H. M. Elwes (New York: Dover Publications, Inc., 1951), ch. VII, sec. 27.

[10]*Ibid.*

[11]*Ibid.*, p. 372.

[12]*Ibid.*, pp. 327-328.

[13]*Ibid.*, p. 292.

[14]*Ibid.*, p. 292.

[15]*Ibid.*, p. 294.

[16]*Ibid.*, p. 294.

[17]*Ibid.*, pp. 295-296.

[18]Benedict De Spinoza, "Ethics" in *The Chief Works of Benedict De Spinoza. On The Improvement of the Understanding. The Ethics Correspondence.* (New York: Dover Publications Inc., 1955) p. 194.

[19]Benedict De Spinoza, *A Theologico-Political Treatise. A Political Treatise*, trans. R. H. M. Elwes (New York: Dover Publications, 1951), p. 289.

[20]*Ibid.*, p. 372.

[21]*Ibid.*, p. 205.

[22]*Ibid.*, p. 205.

[23]*Ibid.*

[24]*Ibid.*, p. 206.

[25]*Ibid.*, p. 341.

[26]Spinoza's criticism of war policy was not only general and philosophical, it was topical as well. Practical political criticism of war and the praise of peaceful coexistence of peoples was a criticism of the militaristic tendencies of the Party connected with the House of Orange. Immanuel Kant argued in a similar way in his essay, "Zum Ewigen Frieden."

[27]Benedict De Spinoza, *A Theologico-Political Treatise. A Political Treatise*, p. 317.

[28]*Ibid.*, p. 308.

[29]Cf. Verdross "Das Voelkerrecht im Systeme von Spinoza," in *Zeitschrift fuer Oeffentliches Recht*, Bd. VII, p. 100, and Adolf Menzel, *Beitraege zur Geschichte der Staatslehre* in Akademie der Wissenschaften, Wien, Sitzungsberichte, 210. Abhandlung (Wien und Leipzig: Kommissions-Verleger der Akademie der Wissenschaften in Wien, 1929).

[30]Benedict De Spinoza, *A Theologico-Political Treatise. A Political Treatise.* pp. 302–303.

[31]H. Lauterpacht believes that Spinoza denies the binding force of international contracts. H. Lauterpacht, "Spinoza and International Law," in the *British Yearbook of International Law*, 1927, p. 89. For a citique of Lauterpacht's ideas, see Menzel, *op., cit.,* pp. 410–419.

[32]Menzel, Verdross, *op., cit.*

[33]*Ibid.*

[34]*Ibid.*

[35]It is the contention of Lewis S. Feuer that "The Amsterdam Jewish Community was dominated by a small commercial oligarchy which could impose its will in matters of politics and theology. Economic interest, political ideology and philosophical convictions were enmeshed in the conflict which led to Spinoza's excommunication" (p. 5). "The oligarchy of the Amsterdam Jewish community did not hesitate to use the weapon of excommunication when they felt their power threatened. Excommunication for them was not primarily a device for the control of theological speculation; it was first and foremost a means by which the unity of the community as conceived by its affluent leaders was to be preserved." (p. 11). Lewis Samuel Feuer, *Spinoza and the Rise of Liberalism* (Boston: Beacon Press, 1966), pp. 5–10.

[36]Benedict De Spinoza, *A Theologico-Political Treatise. A Political Treatise*, p. 46.

[37]Benedict De Spinoza, *The Chief Works of Benedict De Spinoza*, trans. R. H. M. Elwes (New York: Dover Publications, Inc. 1955), p. 368, "Letter to Isaac Orobio."

[38]*Ibid.*

[39]See Robert J. McShea, *The Political Philosophy of Spinoza*, (New York and London: Columbia University Press, 1968), p. 71. Also note George Washington's observation concerning the distinction between liberty and tolerance: In his speech to the Jewish Congregation in Newport, R.I., August 1770, Washington said: "All possess alike liberty of conscience and immunities of citizenship. It is now no more that toleration is spoken of as if it was by the indulgence of one class of people that another enjoyed the exercise of inherent natural rights." These well-known words by Washington reflect Spinoza's philosophy of freedom.

[40]Benedict De Spinoza, *A Political Treatise, op cit.*, p. 381.

[41]*Ibid.*

[42]Spinoza made the following recommendation for an aristocratic regime. It would be vain to establish laws covering sumptuousness. It is not the way to

avoid the evils of ostentation and luxury. Such laws can be broken without injury and they can even stimulate the drive for luxury because, as Ovid already wrote in his *Amores*, we are eager for forbidden fruit and a desire for what is denied.

The "vices" should rather be denied indirectly. For instance, if a rich patrician should lose his fortune, then he should be deposed from the ranks of patricians. Every state should develop means agreeable to each nature and the spirit of the population. "That the subjects may do their duty rather spontaneously, than under the pressure of law," Spinoza, *A Political Treatise*, op. cit., p. 382.

***

3. Tolerance and Freedom—A Necessity of Human Nature.
a. The Encyclopedists' Understanding of Tolerance

[1]Voltaire. A Philosophical Dictionary, in *The Works of Voltaire*, vol. 5, (New York: E. R. DuMont, 1901), p. 5., trans. and ed. William F. Fleming.

[2]*Ibid.,* p. 15.
[3]*Ibid.,* p. 17.
[4]*Ibid.,* p. 19.
[5]*Ibid.,* p. 18.
[6]*Ibid.,* p. 20.
[7]*Ibid.,* p. 26.
[8]*Ibid.,* p. 19.
[9]*Ibid.,* p. 25.
[10]*Ibid.,* p. 128.

***

b. Diderot: Tolerance and Happiness

[1]Denis Diderot, "Observations on the Drawing up of Laws," in *Diderot's Selected Writings* (New York — London: The Macmillan Company, 1966), p. 304.

[2]*Ibid.*
[3]*Ibid.*
[4]*Ibid.,* p. 305.
[5]Denis Diderot "Philosophic Thoughts," in *Diderot's Early Philosophical Works*, (Chicago — London: The Open Court Publishing Co., 1916), par. I, p. 27.

[6]*Ibid.,* par. III, p. 28.
[7]*Ibid.,* par. V, p. 29.
[8]*Ibid.,* p. 306.
[9]*Ibid.,* p. 300.
[10]*Ibid.,* p. 301.
[11]*Ibid.,* p. 301.
[12]*Ibid.,* pp. 29-30.
[13]*Ibid.,* para. XII, p. 31.
[14]*Ibid.*
[15]*Ibid.,* para. XII, p. 32.

[16]*Ibid.,* para. XXIX, p. 45.

[17]*Ibid.,* para. XXXI, p. 45.

[18]*Ibid.,* para. XXXII, p. 46.

[19]*Ibid.,* para. XVI, p. 34.

[20]*Ibid.,* para., L, p. 59.

[21]*Ibid.* Incidentally, Diderot interprets the concept of soul in a typically rationalistic way. Once we admit, he writes, that the world is infinite, the soul should be understood as "an infinite system of perceptions."

[22]Denis Diderot, "Philosophic Thoughts," in *Diderot's Early Philosophical Works.* (Chicago — London: The Open Court Publishing Co., 1916), pp. 47–48.

[23]*Ibid.*

[24]Denis Diderot, "On the Interpretation of Nature," par. XV, in *Diderot's Selected Writings* (New York — London: The Macmillan Company, 1966) p. 73.

[25]Denis Diderot, "The Life and Character of Dr. Nicholas Saunderson," in *Diderot's Early Philosophical Works,* trans. and ed. Margaret Yowrdain (Chicago and London: The Open Court Publishing Company, 1916), pp. 10–11.

[26]*Ibid.,* para. LVIII, p. 87.

***

4. J. J. Rousseau: Freedom and the General Will

[1]Jean-Jacques Rousseau. *The Social Contract.* trans. Maurice Cranston (Harmondsworth: Penguin, 1971) Book I, ch. 1, p. 49.

[2]*Ibid.,* p. 55.

[3]*Ibid.,* p. 65.

[4]*Ibid.,* p. 72.

[5]*Ibid.,* p. 84.

[6]*Ibid.,* p. 84

[7]*Ibid.,* p. 85.

[8]*Ibid.*

[9]*Ibid.,* p. 60.

[10]*Ibid.,* p. 60.

[11]*Ibid.,* p. 61

[12]*Ibid.,* p. 64

[13]*Ibid.,* p. 114.

[14]*Ibid.,* p. 114.

CHAPTER IV

Tolerance

[1]Walter Brugger, Kenneth Baker, *Philosophical Dictionary* (Spokane, Washington: Gonzaga University Press, 1972), p. 421. This article was signed by W. Brugger.

[2]Walter Brugger, *Ibid.*

[3]Stephen S. Fenichel, "Humanist Heritage," *The New Republic*, September 9, 1981, No. 3, 478, p. 4.

[4]*Ibid.*

[5]*Ibid.*

[6]Reinhold Niebuhr, "Tolerance." *Colliers Encyclopedia*, Vol. 22. (New York. The Crowell Collier Pub. Co., Inc.), p. 351.

[7]*Ibid.*

[8]George Seldes, *The Great Quotations* (New York: Pocketbooks, Simon & Schuster, Inc., 1971), p. 580.

[9]Morris R. Cohen, *The Faith of a Liberal* (Freeport, N.Y.: Books for the Libraries Press, 1970), pp. 198–210.

[10]*Ibid.*, p. 207 (emphasis added).

[11]*Ibid.*, pp. 199–200.

[12]Walter Bagehot, "The Metaphysical Basis of Toleration," in *The Heritage of Freedom. Essays on the Rights of Free Men.* Edited by Wilfred S. Dowden and T. N. Marsh (New York:. Harper and Brothers, Publishers, 1962), p. 125.

[13]This expression was used by Jeanne Kirkpatrick, "Dictatorship and Double Standards" in *Commentary* No. 5, vol. 68, Nov. 1979, p. 35.

[14]Editorial in *The New York Times*, December 7, 1980, p. 22E (emphasis added).

[15]Terence Des Pres., Introduction to the book: Jean-Francois Steiner, *Treblinka* (New York: Mentor Books, New American Library, 1979) p. xii.

[16]The type of "profits" or "gratifications" which are used in a totalitarian system could be incomprehensible to one who has never lived under such a regime. In the communist states in which shortages are permanent, the access to special shops in which one can buy daily necessities without queuing is a privilege requiring collaboration. In the Soviet Union many people were denounced by their neighbors who wanted their apartments or just one or even a part of a common room—the author of this book received first hand information of such facts while he lived in Lwow in 1940. In those years he found that the life of a person was worth 9–18 square feet of "living space."

[17]In 1944 the local SS ordered a group of Auschwitz prisoners to steal certain expensive raw materials, not available on the market, from the I. G. Farbenindustrie, Buna-Werke. The local SS needed these materials for their own comfort and for their own hospital. In this connection one of my friends, an experienced German politician (imprisoned since 1934) and a leader of the underground organization, made a memorable observation: "The Third Reich exists thanks to the SS, and the SS is the greatest and most dangerous saboteur in this state." One can apply this remark to any onmipotent police or military organization in any contemporary authoritarian state.

[18]The United States Supreme Court recognized a "close nexus" between the freedoms of speech and assembly, particularly in *DeJonge v. Oregon*, 299 U.S. 353, 364; *Thomas v. Collins*, 323 U.S. 516, 530; *N.A.A.P. v. Alabama ex. rel. Patterson*, 357 U.S. 499, 460–461.

[19]*N.A.A.C.P. v. Alabama ex. rel. Patterson*, 357 U.S. 499, 460–461 (1958).

[20]*Cox v. Louisiana* 379 U.S., 559-564 (1965).

[21]*Amalgamated Food Employees Union v. Logan Valley Plaza, Inc.*, 391 U.S. 308–326 (1968).cf. Thomas T. Emerson, *op. cit.*, p. 295–297.

[22]*Ibid.*

[23]Leonard Swidler, *Küng in Conflict* (Garden City, N.Y.: Doubleday & Co., Inc., 1981).

CHAPTER VI
The State as Leviathan: Endangering and Protecting Freedom

[1]Ralf Dahrendorf, *Class and Class Conflict in Industrial Society* (Stanford: Stanford University Press, 1959), p. 254.

[2]*Ibid.*

[3]An analysis of the book by Earl Shorris, *The Oppressed Middle, Politics of Middle Management* (Garden City, N.Y.: Anchor Press, Doubleday, 1981) is presented in section 5 of this chapter.

[4]*U.S. News and World Report.* March 30, 1981, vol. XC. No. 12, p. 39.

[5]*Cf., The Wall Street Journal,* December 8, 1981, p. 34.

[6]Dahrendorf, p. 242.

[7]*Ibid.,* p. 290.

[8]*Ibid.,* pp. 239–49.

[9]*U.S. News and World Report,* July 19, 1982, p. 10.

[10]Nozick, *Anarchy, State and Utopia,* 1974, p. 26.

[11]*The Houston Chronicle,* May 21, 1982, sec 2, p. 11.

[12]*Ibid.,* May 21, 1982, sec. 2., p. 9.

[13]Quoted from the article by Edwin Guthman: "Probes require safeguards" (Knight-Ridder Newspapers, August 26, 1982). See also *The Houston Post,* August 27, 1982, p. 2B.

[14]*Ibid.*

[15]*Time,* Vol. 116, No. 24, Dec. 15, 1980, p. 55.

[16]*Ibid.*

[17]*Ibid.*

[18]Karl Jaspers, *The Future of Mankind* (Chicago, London: The University of Chicago Press, 1961), p. 98.

[19]Margaret Canovan, *The Political Thought of Hannah Arendt* (London: Methuen and Co., Ltd, 1974), p. 25. She refers to Arendt's, *The Origins of Totalitarianism,* 1966, p. 475.

[20]Ralf Dahrendorf, *Class and Class Conflict in Industrial Society* (Stanford: Stanford University Press, 1959), p. 243.

[21]Earl Shorris, *The Oppressed Middle, Politics of Middle Management, Scenes from Corporate Life* (Garden City, New York: Anchor Press, Doubleday, 1981), pp. 3–10.

CHAPTER VII
Tolerance and Truth

[1]Aristotle, *Metaphysics,* trans. Hippocrates G. Apostle (Bloomington-London: Indiana University Press, 1966), 1011a 19–21, p. 69. "not every appearance would be true; for an appearance is an appearance to someone, so he who states that all appearances are true makes things relative."

[2]*Ibid.*, 1028, 20–29, p. 158.

[3]*Ibid.*, 1051b, 3–5, 6–8, p. 158.

[4]*Ibid.*, 1011b, 25–20, p. 70.

[5]*The New York Times*, September 1, 1981. Quoted in a letter by Ely E. Pilchik.

[6]Chaim Perelman, *The New Rhetoric and the Humanities. Essays on Rhetoric and its Applications*. Trans. William Kluback (Dordrecht, Boston, London: D. Reidel Publishing Co., 1979), p. 8.

[7]Chaim Perelman, Eugene Dupreel, "L'homme et L'oeuvre," trans. William Kluback, in *Revue Internationale de Philosophie* (Bruxelles: Editions de l'Institut de Sociologie, 1968), p. 230. See also, Chaim Perelman, *The New Rhetoric and the Humanities*, pp. 62–63.

[8]*Ibid.*, p. 231.

[9]Chaim Perelman, *The New Rhetoric and the Humanities. Essays on Rhetoric and its Applications*. Trans. William Kluback (Dordrecht, Boston, London: D. Reidel Publishing Co., 1979), pp. 111–116.

[10]*Ibid.*, p. 30.

[11]*Ibid.*

[12]*Ibid.*, p. 117.

[13]*Ibid.*, p. 118.

[14]*Ibid.*, p. 123. There is a link between the dialectic of the reasonable and the dialectic of justice and equity.

[15]There are conservatisms which officially are based on irrational ideas, but the modern Western and Eastern conservatisms present themselves as rationalistic social movements.

[16]C. Wright Mills, *Power Politics and People*, ed. Irving Louis Horowitz (New York: Oxford University Press, 1974), pp. 603–610.

[17]Chaim Perelman, "Legal Reasoning" in *Justice, Law and Argument* (Dordrecht: D. Reidel Publishing Co., 1980), p. 135.

[18]Aristotle, *Metaphysics*, trans. Hippocrates Apostle (Bloomington, London: Indiana University Press, 1966), p. 69.

[19]Hans Kelsen, *Von Wert und Wesen der Demokratie* (Tuebingen: 1929).

[20]Preston King, *Toleration* (New York: St. Martin's Press, 1976), p. 22.

[21]*Ibid.*, p. 67. According to Preston King tolerance and intolerance are value-neutral: ". . . tolerance and its chief contrary, intolerance (taken in terms of the logical formulae to which they may be reduced), are, strictly speaking, *value-neutral* (emphasis added), in themselves."

[22]Kenneth L. Woodward and David Gates, "Giving the Devil His Due," in *Newsweek*, August 30, 1980, pp. 72–74. Referring to a revival in the belief in Satan the authors wrote: "In the '70s, demonology invaded American popular culture in the form of hit movies. . . . By 1980, the devil was a major concern of two increasingly influential groups: the new religious right, which sees Satan's hand in everything from rock music to the World Council of Churches, and the fast growing charismatic movement, which has revived the ancient practice of casting out demons."

Why did the Devil make such a triumphant come-back in America, and, let us add, all over the world? "In times of great social unrest and political instability, observes Northwestern University historian Josef Barton, the individual's feeling of impotence tends to elicit a sense of overwhelming evil at work."

[23]These problems were discussed by me in two essays, "Peace and Freedom" in, *International Problems* (Tel Aviv: The Israeli Institute for the Study of International Affairs, 1982), and, "Peace and Freedom" in, *The Changing International Community. Some Problems of its Laws, Structures, Peace Research and the Middle East Conflict* (The Hague-Paris: Mouton & Co., 1973), pp. 261–265. No important purpose would be served by repeating them here.

[24]The question of legality was theoretically outlined in my previous book: *Juridical Positivism and Human Rights (1981)*. My present conclusions are drawn from those previous considerations.

[25]Alkmeon was ordered by his father to kill his mother under the threat that he, Alkmeon, would be cursed and never have children. Alkmeon obeyed his father's order. Aristotle commented that no threats or tortures could justify such a crime. There are deeds so heinous as to exclude in advance the possibility of excuse (Aristotle, *Nichomachean Ethics*, 1110a-b)

[26]Erich Fromm, *Escape from Freedom* (New York: Avon Books, 1965), pp. 273–274.

[27]*Ibid.*, p. 274.

[28]Robert Faurisson, *Mémoire en Défense*. Contre ceux qui m'accusent de falsifier l'Histoire. La question des chambres a gas. Preface de Noam Chomsky (Paris-La Vieille Taupe, 1980).

[29]Erich Fromm, *Escape From Freedom* (New York: Avon Books, 1965), pp. 274–275.

[30]Absolute skepticism is an absurdity in itself: if everything is doubtful, then this statement must also be doubted. Leon Ploszowski, a hero of the novel *Without Dogma* by Polish Nobel Prize winner, Henry Sienkiewicz, used to describe himself as a "square skeptic"—he was skeptical in regard to his own skepticism. But he added that he could afford this kind of skepticism, because he was so rich that he did not have to work and not even have to administer his estate. Ploszowski was intellectully more honest than Chomsky: he was so skeptical that he refrained from praising or condemning anybody, whereas Chomsky is a relativist who dares to advise others how they should behave.

CHAPTER VIII
New Dangers: The New Right and the New Left

[1]Peter Steinfels, "Apple-Pie Authoritarianism" in, *The New Republic*, September 6, 1982, p. 28. The books under review are: *The New Right Papers*, ed. Robert W. Whitaker (New York: St. Martin's Press, 1982), p. 236, and Kevin P. Phillips, *Post-Conservative America* (New York: Random House, 1982).

[2]Daniel C. Maguire, *The New Subversives. Anti-Americanism of the Religious Right* (New York: Continuum Publishing Company, 1982), pp. 1–2, describes the "New Rightism (as) a powerful, ongoing, and well-financed movement of many intersecting interests that poses a distinct threat to the American way. . . . These radical rightists, with a flag in one hand and a Bible in

the other, have plans for our future, and we ignore them at our peril.

Who are the New Right? . . . They are a motley group of ultraconservative, self-defined "Christian fundamentalists," the Moral Majority . . . the Religious Roundtable, Christian Voice, the Library Court, the National Conservative Political Action Committee, the Committee for the Survival of a Free Congress, the Heritage Foundation, and others."

[3]Thomas Fleming "Old Rights and the New Right," in *The New Right Papers* (New York: St. Martin's Press, 1982), pp. 190–191.

[4]*Ibid.*, p. 199.

[5]*Ibid.*, p. 199.

[6]*Ibid.*, p. 189.

[7]Kevin P. Phillips, *Post-Conservative America* (New York: Random House, 1982), p. 208.

[8]*Ibid.*, p. 209.

[9]*Ibid.*, p. 210.

[10]*Ibid.*, p. 214.

[11]*Ibid.*, p. 214.

[12]*Ibid.*, p. 212.

[13]*Ibid.*, p. 73.

[14]*Ibid.*, p. 218.

[15]*Ibid.*, p. 218.

[16]*Ibid.*, p. 217.

[17]*Ibid.*, p. 218.

[18]Peter Steinfels, *The Neoconservatives, The Men Who are Changing America's Politics* (New York: Simon and Schuster, A Touchstone Book, 1979), pp. 2–3.

[19]Fred Wertheimer, "Fixing Election Law" in *The New York Times*, September 3, 1981, p. A19.

[20]*Ibid.*

[21]A half-truth, let us remark once more, is not just a half-lie, but a full lie. Any analogy with a bottle that is half full or half empty is unimportant. In politics and philosophy it can be essential.

[22]Dean Norman K. Wessells of Leland Sanford Jr. University School of Humanities and Sciences: Address to a Phi Beta Kappa convocation. Excerpts published in *Parade*, August 23, 1981, p. 12.

[23]*Ibid.*

[24]*Ibid.* Dean Wessels further remarked: "And remember, that there is no crime against man, however hideous, that has not been morally justifiable to some perpetrators, including theologians. . . ."

[25]Professor A. Bartlett Giamatti, President of Yale University. Address was distributed and the excerpts published in *The New York Times*, September 1, 1981, p. A 1.

[26]*Ibid.*, p. B 6.

[27]*The New York Times*, September 6, 1981, p. 18E. "Several volunteers at the Natchitoches Parish Hospital in Louisiana surprised the hospital administration last year by resigning in protest against the hiring of a philosopher from Northwestern State University as 'humanist-in-residence.' At the same time in Maine, the federally funded State Humanities Council was fending off attacks on its activities by *The Maine Paper*, a conservative weekly tabloid. Somewhat

earlier, in Virginia, Professor Robert S. Alley resigned the chairmanship of the Religion Department of the University of Richmond at the urging of the administration; Mr. Alley had come under fire from the local Baptist community, which condemned his biblical scholarship as heretical.

Such incidents are part of an increasingly visible campaign, conducted by the new Christian right and spearheaded by the Moral Majority against a force they label 'secular humanism.' "

[28]James M. Perry "The New Right Campaign for Its Social Issues," *The Wall Street Journal*, September 11, 1981, p. 30.

[29]Pericles. Funeral Oration, in Thucydides, *Peloponnesian War*.

[30]Three months after Buchwald's column was published, Bill Moyers mentioned (CBS Evening News, August 19, 1982) an example how a young boy was persecuted because he did not want to pray with the rest of the class. The boy was following the will and recommendation of his parents. The teacher who tried to influence him, behaved more or less the way the teacher in the Buchwald column did.

[31]All the quotations are from the article: "Showdown in Texas," *Time*, August 23, 1982, Volume 120, No. 8, p. 47.

[32]A representative of another organization which is against censorship, People for the American Way (PFAW) commented in this connection: "The United States was founded on protests. We find it ironic that people who make a living protesting would object to protests by others." *Ibid.*

[33]*Ibid.*

[34]*Ibid.*

[35]Kevin P. Phillips, *The Emerging Republican Majority* (New York: Arlington House, 1963).

[36]Kevin P. Phillips, "Apple-Pie Authoritarianism," *Post-Conservative America. People, Politics and Ideology in a Time of Crisis* (New York: Random House, 1982).

[37]Peter Steinfels, *The Neoconservatives. The Men Who are Changing America's Politics* (New York: A Touchstone Book, Simon and Schuster, 1979), pp. 274-275. See also Godfrey Hodgson, *America in our Time* (New York: Doubleday, 1976). pp. 73-90.

[38]Samuel T. Francis, "Of The New Right" in *The New Right Papers*, ed. Robert W. Whitaker (New York: St. Martin's Press, 1982), pp. 64-83.

[39]*Ibid.*

[40]*Ibid.*

[41]*Ibid.*

[42]*Ibid.*

[43]*Ibid.*

[44]*Ibid.*

[45]William A. Rusher, "The New Right: Past and Prospects" in *The New Right Papers*, ed. Robert W. Whitaker (New York: St. Martin's Press, 1982) pp. 23-24.

[46]Thomas Fleming, "Old Rights and the New Right" in *The New Right Papers* (New York: St. Martin's Press, 1982), p. 186.

[47]Professor Phillip Green, "Apple-Pie Authoritarians." *Post-Conservative America* by Kevin Phillips, in *The Nation*, July 3, 1982, pp. 20-22.

[48]*The New York Times*, May 13, 1971, op-Ed., p. 45.

[49] *Ramparts* (reprinted in the *Morning Freiheit* English ed.), September 12, 1971.

[50] Stein, "A Critical Spirit," *Essays in Honor of Herbert Marcuse* (Boston: Beacon Press, 1967), p. 369.

[51] Herbert Marcuse, *Counter-Revolution and Revolt* (Boston: Beacon Press, 1972), p. 5.

[52] *Ibid.* Emphasis added.

[53] *Ibid.,* p. 24.

[54] *Ibid.*

[55] Herbert Marcuse, "Re-examination of the Concept of Revolution" in, *The New Left Review*, July-August 1969, No. 56, pp. 27-34.

[56] Herbert Marcuse, *An Essay on Liberation* (Boston: Beacon Press, 1969).

[57] Herbert Marcuse, "Re-Examination of the Concept of Revolution" *Ibid.*

[58] *Ibid.*

[59] *Ibid.,* p. 28.

[60] *Ibid.,* p. 29.

[61] *Ibid.,* pp.29–30.

[62] *Ibid.,* p. 29.

[63] *Ibid.,* pp. 32–33.

[64] *Ibid.,* p. 32.

[65] "These contradictions assert themselves in the sustained resistance against new-colonial domination; in the emrgence of new powerful efforts to construct a qualitatively different society in Cuba, in China's cultural revolution; and, last, but not least, in the more or less 'peaceful' coexistence with the Soviet Union." *ibid.,* p. 33.

[66] *Ibid.,* p. 32.

[67] *Ibid.,* p. 32.

[68] *Ibid.,* pp. 32–33.

[69] *Ibid.,* p. 33.

[70] Herbert Marcuse, "Represessive Tolerance" in *A Critique of Pure Tolerance*, (Boston: Beacon Press, 1969), p. 81.

[71] *Ibid.,* pp. 83–84.

[72] Mao Tse-tung, *Four Essays on Philosophy* (Peking: 1968), p. 114.

[73] *Ibid.,* p. 117. (Emphasis added).

[74] *Ibid.,* p. 120.

[75] *Ibid.,* p. 117.

[76] *Ibid.,* pp. 119–120.

[77] Quoted from Mao Tse-tung and Lin Piao, *Post Revolutionary Writings*, ed. by K. Fan, Anchor Books, 1972, p. 515.

CHAPTER IX
The Vatican on Freedom and Tolerance in the Twentieth Century

[1] Mieczyslaw Maneli, *Juridical Positivism and Human Rights* (New York: Hippocrene Books, 1981). The term "creeping totalitarianism" is the author's original phrase.

[2] *The Church Speaks to the Modern World. The Social Teachings of Leo XIII.* ed. Etienne Gilson (Garden City: Image Books, Doubleday & Co., 1954), p. 50.

[3]*Ibid.*, pp. 50–51.

[4]*Ibid.*, pp. 206–207; 224–226; 238.

[5]*Ibid.*, Encyclical "*Libertas Praestantissimum*," pp. 57–85.

[6]*Ibid.*, Eccles. 15:14.

[7]*Ibid.*, p. 57.

[8]*Ibid.*, p. 81.

[9]*Ibid.*, p. 66.

[10]*Ibid.*, p. 789.

[11]*Ibid.*, intro. Etienne Gilson, p. 17.

[12]*Ibid.*, intro., p. 14.

[13]*Ibid.*, p. 72.

[14]*Ibid.*

[15]*Ibid.*, pp. 72–73.

[16]*Ibid.*, p. 72.

[17]*Ibid.*

[18]*Ibid.*, p. 65.

[19]*Ibid.*

[19a]Pope John XXIII, *Mater et Magistra* (Glen Rock: Paulist Press, 1962, p. 16.

[19b]*Ibid.*, para. 59–60, pp. 25–26.

[19c]*Ibid.*, para. 62. p. 26

[19d]*Ibid.*, para. 82–93, p. 32.

[19e]*Ibid.*, para. 103, p. 37.

[19f]*Ibid.*, para. 157.

[19g]*Ibid.*, para. 12.

[19h]*Ibid.*, para. 73.

[19i]*Ibid.*, para. 143.

[19j]*Ibid.*, para. 75.

[19k]*Ibid.*, para. 106.

[19l]*Ibid.*, para. 12–13.

[19m]*Ibid.*, para. 113.

[19n]*Ibid.*, para. 118.

[19o]*Ibid.*, para. 127.

[19p]*Ibid.*, para. 158.

[20]*Ibid.*, p. 64.

[20a]*The Documents of Vatican II*, Walter M. Abbot, S.J. and the Very Reverend Monsignor Joseph Gallagher, eds. (Baltimore: The American Press, 1966), pp. 672–673.

[21]*Ibid.*, p. 673. "In all honesty it must be admitted that the Church is late in acknowledging the validity of the principle of freedom." John Courtney Murray.

[22]*Ibid.*, pp. 678–679.

[23]*Ibid.*, para. 2, p. 679.

[24]*Ibid.*, para. 9, p. 688.

[25]*Ibid.*, para. 9, p. 688.

[26]*Ibid.*, para. 4, p. 683.

[27]*Ibid.*, p. 683.

[28]*Ibid.*, p. 698.

[29]*Ibid.*, para. 1, p. 677.

[30]*Ibid.*, p. 662.

[31] *Ibid.*, p. 664.

[32] *Ibid.*, p. 664.

[33] *Ibid.*, p. 665.

[34] *Ibid.*, pp. 665–667.

[35] The most famous words in the Bible which have been used against the Jews are: "His blood be upon us and upon our children." (Matt. 27:25). This cry is attributed to the Jews in Jerusalem. Cardinal Bea commented that this crowd did not have the right to speak "for the whole Jewish people." The severity of Christ's judgment on Jerusalem (Matt. 23:37 ff., et.) "does not presuppose or prove collective culpability of the Jewish people for the crucifixion: that judgment caps a long history of Jerusalem's disobedience to God, crimes against the prophets, etc., and is a 'type' of the universal, final judgment." *Ibid.*, p. 666.

[36] *Ibid.*, *Decree on Ecumenism*, para. 4, p. 347.

[37] *Ibid.*, pp. 349–350.

[38] *Ibid.*, p. 354.

[39] *Ibid.*, p. 212.

[40] *Ibid.*, p. 280.

[41] *Ibid.*, p. 281.

[42] *Ibid.*

[43] *Ibid.*, p. 281.

[44] *Ibid.*, p. 224.

[45] *Ibid.*, para. 62, p. 268.

[46] *Ibid.*, p. 269.

[47] *Ibid.*, pp. 269–270.

[48] There are Catholic theologians, like Monsignor Victor J. Pospishil, who question the validity of the official Vatican doctrine concerning divorce and abortion. Msgr. Pospishil bases his theory on the interpretation of the Scripture and Christian theologians who lived prior to St. Thomas Aquinas.

[49] The story of the struggles around the Reverend Hans Küng's "heresy" is best told by Leonard Swidler in his monumental work, *Küng in Conflict* (Garden City: Doubleday and Company, Inc. 1981). The importance of Swidler's analysis far exceeds the Benedictine presentation of the historical facts.

[50] John Paul II, *On Human Work, Laborem Exercens* (Washington: Office of Publishing Services, U.S. Catholic Conference, 1981), p. 26–27.

[51] *Ibid.*, pp. 32–33.

[52] *Ibid.*, p. 33.

[53] *Ibid.*, p. 34.

CHAPTER X
The Polish Road to Freedom and Tolerance

[1] Boguslaw Lesnodorski: *Kuznica Kollatajowska*, Ossolineum, p. ix.

[2] Andrzej Frycz-Modrzewski: *Dziela wszystkie*, (Warszawa, 1954), t.l, pp. 376–77; cf. also *Filozofia polska*, (Warszawa; 1956), p. 181.

[3] cf. Waldemar Voise, *Frycza Modrzewskiego nauka o panstwie i prawie (Warszawa: 1956), p. 181.*

[4] *Ibid.*

[5] Samuel Przypkowski: "De pace et concordia Ecclesia," in: Zbigniew Ogonowski, *Socynia nizm Polski*, (Warszawa: 1960), p. 179.

[6]Jan Sniadecki: *Selected Works*, (Warszawa: 1954), p. 131.

[7]*Ibid.*

[8]*Ibid.*, pp. 132.-33.

[9]Boguslaw Lesnodorski: *Dzielo Sejmu Czteroletniego (The Accomplishment of the Four Year Diet)*, *op. cit.*, p. 49.

[10]*Ibid.*, pp. 36.-37.

[11]Stanislaw Staszic: *Warnings to Poland*, (Warszawa: 1956).

[12]Bronislaw Baczko: *Poglady spoleczno-polityczne i filozoficzne Towarzystwa Demokratycznego Polskiego*, (Warszawa, 1955), p. 362; cf. chaps. I and III.

[13]*Ibid.*, p. 58.

[14]Let us observe that some radical English thinkers of the seventeenth century, (e.g. Gerard Winstanley) also used to argue that the idea of monarchy was not English people, but was brought to England by William the Conqueror.

[15]*Ibid.*, p. 364.

[16]*Ibid.*, p. 365.

[17]*Ibid.*, p. 369.

[18]*Filozofia Polska*, *op. cit.*, p. 420.

[19]The Western press, especially the American newspapers, presented the reforms in Poland as if they were the result of the providential leadership of the Polish masses by the Catholic hierarchy. The Catholic hierarchy's contribution was undeniable, but it is nevertheless a matter of fact that they felt uneasy over the spontaneous upheaval which could not be controlled by any of the anointed leaders. On May 1981, *The Wall Street Journal* published an article, perhaps unique in the U.S., which sought to overcome the simplification which reduced the existing controversy in Poland to a struggle between the government and the Church. Although there is some truth in this alternative, it is "the truth . . . twisted by the knaves to make a trap for fools." (Rudyard Kipling, the poem "IF—.") Through such oversimplifications the democratic essence of the Polish upheaval was tarnished.

[20]The polls taken in Poland and published in Poland and in the USA show that only a small minority favors the restoration of private capital.

CHAPTER XI
Freedom and Responsibility in Out Time

[1]Erich Fromm, *Escape from Freedom* (New York: Holt, Rinehart and Winston, 1976), p. 258.

[2]George Will, "In Defense of the Welfare State," in *The New Republic*, May 9, 1983, pp. 20-24.

[3]Sartre, *Being and Nothingness*, p. 439.

[4]*Ibid.*, p. 462.

[5]*Ibid.*, p. 463.

[6]*Ibid.*, p. 461.

[7]*Ibid.*, p. 439. Emphasis added.

[8]Jean-Paul Sartre, *Selected Prose*, p. 242.

[9]Louis Finkelstein, "Foundations of Democracy in the Scriptures and

Talmud," in *Judaism and Human Rights*, ed. Milton R. Knovitz (New York: W. W. Norton and Co., Inc., 1972), p. 142.

[10]Ben Zion Bokser, "Democratic Aspirations in Talmudic Judaism," in *Judaism and Human Rights* (New York: W. W. Norton and Co., 1972), p. 147.

[11]The English text of Abraham J. Kook's writings was kindly made available to me by the translator and commentator of his works, Ben Zion Bokser. I gratefully acknowledge his courtesy.

[12]Ben Zion Bokser, "Freedom and Authority," in *Judaism and Modern Man* (New York: Philosophical Library, 1957), pp. 118-120.

[13]Roger L. Shinn, "Responses of Protestant Ethics to Political Challenges" in *The Ethic of Power: The Interplay of Religion, Philosophy and Politics*, eds. Harold D. Lasswell and Harlan Cleveland (New York: Harper Brothers, 1962), p. 146.

[14]*Ibid.*, p. 152.

[15]*Ibid.*, pp. 152-154.

[16]For examples see James Hastings Nichols, *Democracy and the Churches*. James Bryce, *The American Commonwealth*. Reinhold Niebuhr, *The Nature and Destiny of Man*.

[17]Reinhold Niebuhr, *The Nature and Destiny of Man. A Christian Interpretation* (New York: Charles Scribner's Sons, 1949), volume II, p. 234.

[18]*Ibid.*, p. 238.

[19]*Ibid.*, p. 239.

[20]Kathleen Kennedy Townsend, "The Bible and the Left" in *The New York Times*, August 9, 1981, p. 21.

[21]*Ibid.*

[22]Erich Fromm, *Escape from Freedom*, o.c. p. 6.

Index